Client-Server Software Testing on the Desktop and the Web

ISBN 0-13-183880-6

90000

9 780131 838802

Client-Server Software Testing on the Desktop and the Web

Daniel J. Mosley

Client-Server Software Testing (CSST) Technologies
10431 Savannah Ave.
Frontenac, MO 63131

Prentice Hall PTR
Upper Saddle River, NJ 07458
http://www.phptr.com

Library of Congress Cataloging-in-Publication Data

Mosley, Daniel J.
    Client-server software testing on the desktop and
    the web / Daniel J. Mosley.
      p. cm.
    Includes bibliographical references and index.
    ISBN 0-13-183880-6 (hardcover)
      1. Computer software—testing. 2. Client/server computing.
    I. Title.
    QA76.76.T48M67 2000
    005.2'76—dc21   99-26488
                                 CIP

Editorial/production supervision: *BooksCraft, Inc., Indianapolis, IN*
Acquisitions editor: *Jeffrey Pepper*
Editorial assistant: *Linda Ramagnano*
Marketing manager: *Dan Rush*
Manufacturing manager: *Alexis R. Heydt*
Cover design director: *Jerry Votta*
Cover designer: *Anthony Gemmellaro*
Project coordinator: *Anne Trowbridge*

Prentice Hall books are widely used by corporations and government agencies for training, marketing, and resale.

The publisher offers discounts on this book when ordered in bulk quantities. For more information, contact:

Corporate Sales Department
Prentice Hall PTR
One Lake Street
Upper Saddle River, NJ 07458
Phone: 800-382-3419   Fax: 201-236-7141
E-mail: corpsales@prenhall.com.

Printed in the United States of America

10 9 8 7 6 5 4 3 2 1

ISBN: 0-13-183880-6

Prentice-Hall International (UK) Limited, *London*
Prentice-Hall of Australia Pty. Limited, *Sydney*
Prentice-Hall Canada Inc., *Toronto*
Prentice-Hall Hispanoamericana, S.A., *Mexico*
Prentice-Hall of India Private Limited, *New Delhi*
Prentice-Hall of Japan, Inc., *Tokyo*
Prentice-Hall (Singapore) Pte., *Singapore*
Editora Prentice-Hall do Brasil, Ltda., *Rio de Janeiro*

For my father-in-law, the late
Edward Gheen Ricker II

Contents

Preface

Client-server system development is the preferred method of constructing cost-effective department- and enterprise-level strategic corporate information systems. Client-server development allows the rapid deployment of information systems in end-user environments. Client-server development is ad hoc in nature, using, in many instances, new software development platforms. Client-server development workbenches can be used both by IS professionals (programmers, analysts) and by nontechnical knowledge workers in functional business areas. Because implementation of client-server tools do not require technical education or experience they present an additional set of software development problems to system development.

The client-server computing model has also been extended to include the Internet, bringing another new and unique set of computing problems. The Forrester Report describes this new computing model as "Internet Computing." The report defines Internet Computing as, "Remote servers and clients cooperating over the Internet to do work," and says that Internet Computing extends and improves the client-server model.

The report differentiates between what is currently happening on the World Wide Web and Internet Computing. In the latter, users do not go to a site and request a file or run a Java script through their browser, but they request a "session" and receive a client code from the remote server. With the code loaded on the client computer, the two can begin to communicate and exchange data. The report describes this as a "conversation."

Internet Computing will be truly interactive. It will feature computing sessions that are global and on a massive scale as opposed to client-server computing, which is localized and limited to a small group of users.

Software testing for client-server systems (Desktop or Webtop) presents a new set of testing problems, but it also includes the more traditional problems testers have always faced in the mainframe world. Client-server software testers must test client software applications, server software applications, middleware, and network software applications. Even so, the tester must assess client-server applications, regardless of application level, with respect to the software's system (external) quality, and its functional/ technical (internal) quality.

The client's Graphical User Interface (GUI) applications are much more complex than the traditional Character User Interface (CUI) applications found on mainframes. GUIs present a "fluid" interface that can be changed at the whim of the user. This causes software testers to acquire a new testing perspective and places a larger burden on them. The complexity of testing the GUI drives the tester to automate the GUI testing process.

GUIs have some unique characteristics that lend themselves both to testing in general and automated testing in particular. They are object-oriented in nature, which simplifies testing because classes of Windows objects have precisely defined sets of behaviors. Object orientation lends itself to automation. The majority of commercially available software tools to aid GUI testing have taken an object-oriented approach. This approach has been dubbed "Structured Capture/Replay."

Applications at the server level can involve replicated processes and data. The tester must be able to test an application's ability to deal with these types of redundancies in a client-server system. These applications must also be performance tested.

Network software applications must be load tested for and monitored in terms of the volume of network traffic. This kind of testing is only doable using automated testing tools such as IBM's TPNS, Mercury's LoadRunner, or SQA's LoadTest PC. Also, network nodes must be tested with respect to their ability to stand alone when other nodes are down. Web-enabled client-server applications involve further complexities.

Finally, several influences shaped my thoughts in this book. First, my background in software testing theory has forced me to cling to Black Box and White Box concepts and their associated test-case design strategies. A second influence is my leaning toward MIS and business computing systems. Third, my experiences as a software developer and as a tester and test manager have slanted my views towards the practical. Fourth, my experience testing client-server applications for the past five years has opened my eyes to the intricacies of desktop systems. Fifth, my recent encounters with Web-enabled client-server software applications have convinced me that the testing complexities of these systems are limitless.

One other factor has had a strong influence on this book's content—SQA TeamTest. I have become intimately familiar with it after having used it on every client-server project I have tested to date. I have completed almost all of my client-server testing on systems developed to run in Windows 3.1.1, Windows 95, Windows NT 3.51, and NT 4.0. SQA TeamTest was the choice of all of the companies where I consulted. Thus, many of the practical tips and advice offered in this book are slanted toward test automation and, in particular, toward SQA TeamTest.

Acknowledgments

I want to thank all of the software testing professionals who have provided information on the client-server testing that I have referenced in this book. Without those individuals, much of the practical knowledge that is contained in it would not have been available. In particular, I want to thank Bob Binder for several of his ideas, which were important in the formulation of this book. I also want to express my gratitude to Jerry Durrant for the enlightening conversations on testing tools we had at the STAR conference.

My thanks go out to Richard Bell at Deutsche Financial Services, who started me down the road to data-driven testing; to SQA TeamTest scripting guru and business partner Bruce Posey for all of the script-writing tips and tricks he has taught me, some of which are included in this book; to Dave Magditch, who has kept me gainfully employed as a software testing consultant over the years; to Don Kaag, for keeping me entertained while I was executing my testing responsibilities; to VB programmer Richard Pandorf, for all the practical jokes he played on me; to Jerry Schwartz, for providing the WinRunner script example I used; to all of the other testers and programmers I have worked with while consulting in software testing; and to all of the individuals who have attended our advanced test scripting seminar.

My love and thanks go to my wife and daughter for their patience with me while I was writing this book.

About the Author

Daniel J. Mosley completed his undergraduate work at the University of Missouri—Columbia, where he graduated Phi Beta Kappa, with honors in Psychology, in 1973. He received an MS (Research) in Psychology from Saint Louis University in 1977 and completed the requirements for his doctorate degree, with the exception of the dissertation. He is currently the President of CSST Technologies. He was formerly an information systems professional in the publishing, broadcasting, financial, brewing, and construction industries. He has extensive experience developing, testing, and maintaining commercial software applications.

He held a joint appointment as a Senior Technical Associate in the Center for the Study of Data Processing and as a faculty member of the School of Technology and Information Management in the School of Engineering and Applied Sciences at Washington University in St. Louis from 1985 to 1992. He led MIS professional development seminars for the Center and taught in both the undergraduate and graduate academic programs, and he directed the Information Engineering area of concentration in the Master of Information Management degree program.

His expertise includes software and system engineering life-cycle methods, techniques, and tools; continuous software process improvement, statistical software quality engineering; software metrics; software testing methods, techniques, and tools. He is the author of the TEST-Rx (Test Prescription) methodology.

He is a past chairperson and current board member of the St. Louis federation chapter of the Quality Assurance Institute. He has contributed to industry publications such as *American Programmer*, *Chief Information Officer Journal*, and *IEEE Software Magazine*. He is a frequent presenter at national and international industry conferences.

He is the author of the *Handbook of MIS Application Software Testing: Methods, Techniques, and Tools for Assuring Quality Through Testing*, Yourdon Computing Series, Prentice Hall, 1993.

Client-Server Software Testing
on the Desktop and the Web

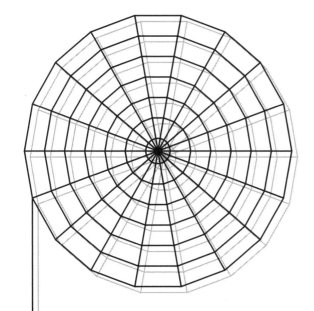

Client-Server Development Methods, Techniques, and Tools

1.1 INTRODUCTION

The MIS and PC cultures are being brought together to a new middle ground—the server level of software, which presents challenges to both.

—John Desmond, *Software Magazine* [4]

Andersen Consulting [1] attributes the current trend to client-server (C-S) architecture to several factors. First, there is the exponentially increasing power of desktop workstations. At the current rate of increase in available MIPS with each new generation of PC, we are now able to run mission critical applications on desktop machines.

Second, these machines have become increasingly more affordable. The cost-per-MIPS gap between mainframes and workstations is continuously widening. Andersen Consulting estimates that by the turn of the century workstation MIPS will be 2000 times less expensive than comparable mainframe MIPS. This means that client-server is a very cost-effective approach to information system implementation.

Third, the trend is toward placing computing processes on machines of appropriate size. They term this trend "right-sizing." It is most apparent at the level of department and personal productivity computing. The increased reliability of Local Area Networks (LANs) has fortified this as a viable approach.

Fourth, the workstation's Graphical User Interface (GUI) is more intuitive than the Character User Interface (CUI) of the mainframe. CUIs tend to be very rigid and require cryptic commands that are far from intuitive. GUIs have a lower learning curve than CUIs so they require less user training. In fact, users at one major Fortune 500 company are already asking for information systems that do not have user manuals and require no training at all.

Fifth, organizations want to extend their information-processing capabilities. These organizations are relying on a combination of centralized and distributed data and processes as this approach is probably the most cost-effective in the long term.

1.2 ADVANTAGES AND DISADVANTAGES OF CLIENT-SERVER COMPUTING

Berson [2] sees the benefits of client-server architecture as the ability to "leverage" the current desktop computing technology trend, the ability to keep processing close to the data, the facilitation of the GUI, and the encouragement of "open systems." Berson also sees two distinct disadvantages to C-S computing architecture. The server can become a major processing bottleneck if the application logic is not properly distributed between the client and the server. Distributed systems are also more complex to design, build, and maintain than nondistributed systems. They are also much more complicated to test.

1.3 DEFINING CLIENT-SERVER COMPUTING

What is client-server computing? What are client-server architectures? What are enterprise servers, midrange servers, and clients? What are the major differences between the client-server computing environment and the traditional mainframe computing environment? How does client-server development differ from mainframe-based Information Engineering/CASE development? What are the important project management issues in client-server development? What is the role of Data Base Management Systems (DBMSs) in client-server environments? What kinds of software tools are available to facilitate client-server computing? These are important questions, and they will be answered in this and subsequent chapters.

A survey conducted by *Software Magazine* in conjunction with Sentry Market Research was sent to 500 PC buyers, 500 midrange buyers, and 500 mainframe buyers. "The survey proposed to clarify what users mean by the term "client-server." While there were some differences in how the sample populations defined the terms, the overall results were consistent:

- ☞ Client-server computing is seen as a subset of cooperative processing
- ☞ LANs are not seen as needed to enable client-server computing
- ☞ Any hardware platform can act as the server
- ☞ The server's role is seen as administration
- ☞ Applications and user interface are entrusted to the client

This study resulted in a second multiclient study of the client-server market again conducted by Sentry Market Research [9]. This study focused on client-server migration—spending and perceptions.

The second survey instrument was similar to the original questionnaire but contained some enhancements. A stratified random sample of 2000 software professionals was selected. The sampling procedure ensured that each participant was involved in recommending, evaluating, purchasing, or implementing client-server software (databases, applications, or tools).

The respondents typically included senior-level software managers: 37% of the respondents described their job function as software development management/staff. Additionally 12% were classified as end users. The remainder included members of database management, network management, data center staff, and operations. Most respondents were from manufacturing firms (17%), finance and banking (16%), and federal/state/local government (11%).

The great majority (93%) indicated that they were involved in client-server product evaluation. Eighty-nine percent indicated that they were involved in recommending C-S products, and 83% said they also used the products. *What is more significant for readers of this book is that 66% indicated that they use client-server to develop systems.* Sixty-one percent indicated they used client-server for system integration purposes, and 40% used C-S to rearchitect systems.

An interesting finding is that central MIS controlled the budgets for the majority of C-S products and services. The tightest control was in system administration/management tools; development tools; networking software; DBMS software; server hardware; and in-house development. Nearly half of the staffing, consulting, training, client hardware, and applications packages were controlled by an independent business unit or the end-user department. The budgeted moneys were primarily for server hardware ($443,510) and client hardware ($475,607); DBMS software ($172,444); development tools ($109,804); networking software ($80,645); training ($77,783); and system administration/management tools ($60,509). C-S implementation consulting also grabbed a rather large chunk ($4,155,909).

Based on a Likert-type attitudinal scale (1 through 6, with 6 being very significant and 1 not a significant benefit) the majority of the respondents saw seamless access to corporate data as the most significant benefit (5.05) of C-S. This was closely followed by ability to add capacity modularity (4.94), ease of use (4.82), and price/performance improvements (4.72). Of interest is the fact that increased user involvement in development (4.09) and standards enforcement (4.01) are seen as reasonably significant, but are still at the bottom of the list (less significant than all the other benefits). Because these are areas considered very important in traditional software development organizations, this finding indicates that C-S and traditional MIS development differ strongly in these domains.

1.3.1 More Formal Definitions

Francett [5] describes client-server as a "multi-protocol, heterogeneous" environment possibly spanning multiple operating systems and executing multiple copies of software. The kinds of networking and change management issues client-server systems must address dramatically increase their complexity. A major issue confronting client-server developers is the melding of mainframe project management with the unique requirements of client-server.

Hurwitz [6] sees client-server as a moving away from "host-based monolithic" systems which run on a single platform to "distributed" systems which span multiple platforms. She defines "distributed computing" as the distribution of *display*, *function*, and *data*. The most commonly distributed system element is the display. The advent of the desktop PC environment has resulted in a GUI that is common across all desktop applications. Even DOS applications can be, and are, retrofitted to operate in this graphical environment. Examples of this type of system interfaces are Windows from Microsoft Corp. and OS/2 from IBM, both of which run on IBM PCs and compatibles, and MIT's X window systems which run on Unix-based machines such as Sun Sparc Stations.

Hurwitz used the term "function" synonymously with the term "application." Thus distributed functions refer to application systems that are distributed. Distributed applications can run on a client workstation or on the server or on both. Furthermore, applications can be distributed across several servers. This "splitting" of functions across machines forces a reliance on a strong telecommunications (networking) technology as interprocess communication and coordination are necessary.

Distributed data can consist of replicated data across computers or servers. Distributed data is a necessary evil that has evolved in order to reduce the communications strain from the sheer volume of requests which users can generate in a distributed computing environment.

1.4 CLIENT-SERVER COMPUTING REQUIREMENTS

Berson [2] describes the architectural requirement for client-server computing. In his view, C-S computing requires "robust" client-to-server and server-to-client communications as the foundation for the system. The client initiates client-server cooperative interactions. The processing logic is distributed between the client and the server. There is "server-enforced control" of services and data, which the client can request, and the server arbitrates conflicting client requests.

1.5 CLIENT-SERVER ARCHITECTURES

In *Understanding Client-Server Models*, Hurwitz [6] describes four client-server computing models. She sees these models as starting points for formulating migration strategies to distributed computing. She describes the current computing infrastructure strategies of organizations as being either host-centric infrastructure or LAN-centric. This, and her other reports, are available for purchase from Hurwitz Consulting Group, Inc. Hurwitz's client-server reference models are described below.

1.5.1 Host-Centric Models

1.5.1.1 Front Ending Front-ending client-server systems are characterized by distributing the display on client workstations while distributing data and application logic on the host. In this environment, host applications continue to execute on the mainframe, with access to these applications through workstation-based GUIs. These are typically graphically based terminal emulation software products (X Window Systems is an example of a graphic front end to a Unix host). The key here is that the user, working in a desktop environment, can access several mainframe application system screens at once.

Hurwitz describes the benefits of this client-server model as providing the ability to

1. Change the interface to mainframe applications without changing the applications themselves
2. Combine workstation applications with host applications
3. Concurrently operate multiple host-based applications on one desktop
4. Add value to the host-based application by extending its logic

An obvious benefit that she did not note is the ability to extend the life of the host-based application through its client-server GUI wrapper. Hurwitz describes these disadvantages of this model:

1. Modifications to mainframe systems might disrupt the integrity of the front-ending applications.
2. A lack of documentation describing the mainframe application screen layouts and sequences.
3. A lack of flexibility the other more distributed models have.

Hurwitz views this model as transitional, representing the first step in moving from centralized legacy systems to one of the other LAN-centric distributed models. Vendors have clearly seen their opportunities here and have rushed to expand their products to include tools that can create GUI wrappers for mainframe systems. As examples, Hurwitz cites Enterprise Workbench, Knowledgeware's Flashpoint, System Strategies' EXPRESS, and Mozart.

1.5.1.2 Data Staging Data staging refers to presenting the data in an understandable format to end users. The majority of mainframe applications are COBOL, transaction-based applications. Data-staging applications make the data more accessible by locating them on high-performance servers, by further massaging the data, and by denormalizing the data for presentation to the end users.

Hurwitz described the most important data-staging technologies as

1. A database engine for storing and delivering data in an appropriate format
2. A data manipulation language or other suitable tool for accessing the data
3. "Job control language" for automating the data extracts
4. Methods for converting transaction data into an end-user accessible form

Hurwitz lists several tools for data staging. They include Red Brick Systems' Red Brick Warehouse, Prism's Warehouse Manager, Trinzic InfoPump, and Information Resources' Express.

1.5.2 LAN-Centric Models

1.5.2.1 Resource-Centric   Resource-centric describes the model in which specialized networked system resources are delivered to the desktop workstation. The fundamental design concept is resource sharing among multiple clients. Such resources include back-end data, file servers, and print servers.

Hurwitz cites the primary advantage of this approach as end-user access to data and other resources. She describes the primary disadvantage as the lack of control over how the resources are used. Because of the potential for users overloading the system, she recommends using this model only for departmental or smaller applications.

Hurwitz cites as key technologies for resource-centric computing

1. Strong networking capabilities
2. Ability to send requests to the provider and return resources to the client
3. Servers that support multiple users

Hurwitz lists a number of tools that are "heavily focused on providing graphical intuitive access to SQL relational database servers" for resource-centric computing support: Knowledgeware's ObjectView, Powersoft's PowerBuilder, Gupta's SQL Windows, IBM's Visual Age, Uniface, and Progress Software's Version 7.

1.5.2.2 Distributed Logic   In the distributed logic model, application logic is proportioned among networked computers. An application runs on more than one machine and communication services are used to synchronize the distributed processes. Hurwitz see this approach as a "highly scaleable and sophisticated model" requiring a level of organizational commitment not unlike that needed to build traditional mainframe systems. She recommends this model for doing transaction processing in a distributed environment.

Hurwitz argues that although distributed logic systems can be constructed with client-side development tools (as described in the section above on resource-centric computing), more powerful tools are required. Supporting this model requires tools that provide design and implementation of partitioned application logic and client- and server-level code generation.

To support distributed logic, Hurwitz also lists several tools: Seer HPS, Dynasty Development Environment, Texas Instruments' Information Engineering Facility, Andersen's Foundation for Cooperative Processing, IBM's Highpoint and NextStep.

1.6 TYPES OF CLIENT-SERVER APPLICATIONS

According to Binder [3], there are three basic types of client-server applications: environment configuration, technology upgrade, and new application systems.

1. *Environment configuration* applications occur when "system software is configured and integrated to manage a pool of resources for a group of users." In this type of application, utility software (file servers, print servers) is configured for broad classes of applications as opposed to particular applications.

2. *Technology upgrade* represents the enclosure of a text (command based) interface with a GUI wrapper. In this type of C-S application there is minimal functional change with the mainframe DBMS becoming the server. This is an implementation of Hurwitz's front-ending model.

3. *New application systems* occur when a new or replacement system is developed solely in a client-server milieu. System functions are apportioned between "resource clients" and "resource servers" via a LAN. The functionality is in the form of such general-purpose application software as spread sheets, query-based languages, workstation-level language compilers, and test environments. These can be developed using software tools such as Microsoft's Visual Basic.

Binder divides the system's requirements into two processes: a proactive front end (the client) and a reactive back end (the server). He assigns the following functionality to the client:

☞ Implements user interface with basic input validation

☞ Formats queries for server processing

☞ Communicates with server

☞ Accepts and formats server response

He assigns the remaining functions to the server:

☞ Accepts client requests

☞ Presents a high-level interface to client

☞ Makes implementation transparent to client

☞ Performs resource-intensive processing

1.7 CLIENT-SERVER VERSUS MAINFRAME

The difference is one of perspective. As Robert Sheirer says, "Mainframe people are used to looking at what the whole group is doing, the whole organization." [8]

Mainframe-oriented MIS professionals have been conditioned to work with the whole and not the parts. On the other hand, client-server developers have grown up viewing the parts and ignoring the whole. In many ways, this accounts for the high percentage of failed client-server projects. C-S projects developed for department-level computing tasks are not capable of supporting enterprise-level tasks, and the result is failure when departmental C-S systems are implemented enterprise-wide.

This difference in perspective has implemented itself in the form of a completely new set of IS skills. Scheier sees today's hottest IS (client-server) skills as those found in the following areas.

1. *Front-end development tools* including PowerBuilder, Visual Basic, C++, and Gupta SQL Windows

2. *Databases* including SQL server, Oracle, Ingres, Informix, and DB/2

3. *Networking* including NetWare and TCP/IP

4. *Operating systems* including DOS/Windows (for PC desktop) and Unix (for servers)

5. *General skills* including GUI design, database administration, soft skills (communication and negotiation), and ability to use technology to solve business problems

In addition to these C-S related skills, Scheier has found that some traditional mainframe-related skills are becoming prized in the C-S arena. Some examples are project management, change control, documentation control, and quality control. Furthermore, the operating disciplines of security, backup, disaster recovery, and data integrity are establishing themselves in the C-S world.

The question companies must address is whether to hire recent college graduates with four or more years of hands-on experience with Windows and Unix programming tools, but lack business knowledge, or should they invest in retraining displaced mainframers who have business knowledge, but lack the tools experience.

1.8 THE LAYERS OF CLIENT-SERVER SYSTEMS

Client-server systems have several layers which can be visualized in either a conceptual or a physical manner. Viewed conceptually, the layers are presentation, process, and database. Viewed physically, the layers are server, client, middleware, and network.

1.9 C-S 2-TIER AND 3-TIER ARCHITECTURES

The simplest client-server architecture is the 2-tier model [10]. It is also known as the client-centric model which implements a "fat" client. All of the processing happens on the client, and the client accesses the database directly rather than through middleware. In the 2-tier architecture, all of the presentation logic and all of the business logic are implemented as processes on the client.

For software testing, this model has several advantages. It is simple to implement and, thus, relatively simple to test. It is also the most stable form of client-server software implementation, making most of the errors that testers find independent of the implementation. Direct access to the database makes it much simpler to verify test results.

This model is limited in scalability and can only accommodate a limited number of users. It does not partition the application logic very well (presentation and business logic are mixed). It becomes a maintenance nightmare because changes require reinstallation of the software on all of the client desktops. Because of these limitations, most client-server systems have been developed as modified 2-tier or 3-tier applications. Web-based client-server applications have been dubbed N-tier because of the additional layers that the Internet adds to the architecture.

Modified 2-tier architecture moves the business logic to the database. The logic is implemented as stored procedures or triggers. This approach is more complicated to test because of the relationship that can exist among stored procedures and between stored procedures and triggers. It is much more difficult to create a direct test of the business logic, and special tools are required to implement and verify the tests. It is possible to test the business logic from the GUI, but there is no way to determine the number of procedures and/or triggers that fire and create intermediate results before the end product is achieved.

Another complication is dynamic database queries. They are constructed by the application and exist only while the program needs them. It is very difficult to be sure that a test generates the query "correctly," or as expected, and special utilities that show what is running in memory must be used during the tests.

In 3-tier client-server architectures, the application is divided into a presentation tier, a middle tier, and a data tier. The middle tier is composed of one or more application servers distributed across one or more physical machines. This middle layer can consist of several types of software collectively called middleware. Business and database objects are created and stored in the middleware. This architecture is also termed the "thin client-fat server" approach.

Typically, transaction processing monitor or object request broker software intercepts requests from the client and invokes instances of business and database objects that are required to fill the client's request. These applications use either the Distributed Common Object Model (DCOM) or the Common Object Request Broker Architecture (CORBA) as object standards for their implementation. For example, Microsoft Transaction Server, a transaction monitor package running on Windows NT, is based on the DCOM standard.

This greatly complicates testing because the business and/or data objects can be invoked from many clients and the objects can be partitioned across many servers. Adding the middle tier doubles the points of communication [10]. The matter is further complicated in that the structure of the database is hidden from the client and many database changes can be made transparently. To test for these changes is very difficult.

In summary, the characteristics of the 3-tier architecture that make it desirable as a development and implementation framework at the same time make testing more complicated and tricky.

1.10 CONCLUSION

Distributed cooperative processing under the guise of client-server computing is a current reality for professional system developers and for sophisticated departmental computer system users. It is leveraging the power of networked desktop PCs, or their equivalent, to service the computing needs of the individual and the department (functional business area).

1.11 REFERENCES

1. Andersen Consulting. *Evaluation Criteria for Client-Server Cooperative Processing.* A white paper available from Andersen Consulting, Suite 2010, 69 West Washington St., Chicago, IL 60602.

2. Berson, Alex. *Client-Server Architecture.* McGraw-Hill Series on Computer Communications, McGraw-Hill, Inc., New York, 1992.

3. Binder, Robert. "A CASE-Based Systems Engineering Approach to Client-Server Development." *CASE Trends*, 1992.

4. Desmond, John. "Introduction: The Advance of Client-Server." *Software Magazine, Client Server Computing supplement*, September 1991, p. 2.

5. Francett, Barbara. "Introduction: Kinks in Systems Management Order Are Likely: Complexity Barometer Rising in Struggle for Systems Control; Travelers

Invents Own Solution." *Software Magazine, Client Server Computing supplement,* September 1991, pp. 12–15.

6. Hurwitz, Judith. *Understanding Client-Server Models.* Technology Assessment Report, Hurwitz Consulting Group, Inc., Watertown, MA 02172, 1994, 25 pp.

7. Kampwerth, Judy. "Society Membership Interest Survey: The Results Are In." *The St. Louis IE / CASE Society Newsletter,* Vol. 2, No. 4, April/May 1993.

8. Scheier, Robert L. "IS Veterans Retool Talents for the '90s." *PCWEEK,* March 1994, pp. 1, 12.

9. Sentry Market Research. *1992–93 Client-Server Study Summary and Highlights.* Sentry Market Research, Westborough, MA 01581.

10. Woodger Computing, Inc. Multi-Tier Architectures, http://www3.sympatico.ca/jwoodger/archmult.htm.

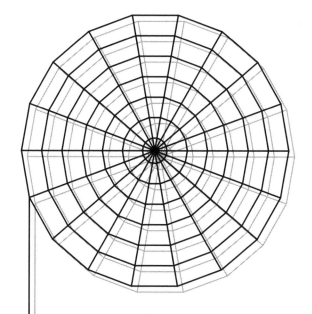

Establishing Controls in a Client-Server Development Project

2.1 INTRODUCTION

Just because Client-Server applications run on PCs, they can't be taken casually. They need to be thought out, designed and analyzed.

—David Litwack

Client-server requires the same kinds of rigor and controls as the more traditional software development frameworks. Managing software development in client-server environments is a "sticky wicket" compared to the centralized development of the past. In traditional centralized MIS software, development is controlled via project management frameworks such as the System Development Life Cycle (SDLC), a monolithic waterfall model. Over the years, this monolithic ideal has evolved into a more useful iterative (e.g., Boehm's Spiral Model [2]) framework. The SDLC is employed to control the complexity of the system development process, dividing it into manageable work tasks.

Within the bounds of the SDLC the disciplines of structured programming, structured design, and structured analysis evolved to control the complexity of the software itself. It has been demonstrated that software components exhibiting a high structural complexity are error prone and, thus, are very difficult to maintain.

Client-server is the essence of "ad hoc" development. We have traditionally used this term to describe an unstructured approach, but that is not its true meaning. Ad hoc means an approach directed to a specific end or result. It also means that every time the result changes so does the approach. In this sense, all software development is ad hoc. The problem is that an ability to change the approach before the result is achieved is an absolute requirement, but one that has been very difficult to achieve when developing large systems using a traditional SDLC-based methodology.

Client-server development attacks this issue directly, but in turn brings its own unique brand of problems. For instance, if client-server development is allowed to proliferate in an uncontrolled manner, the result is incompatible small islands of automation using different languages, development platforms, and database server software. This defeats the most important (and most frequently stated by C-S proponents) benefit of C-S—that of improving system integration.

Some, but not all, proponents of client-server development advocate the abandonment of the kinds of controls that are present when the SDLC and the structured methods are applied. It is understandable given the miserable record associated with their use (or "misuse," because most professionals are substantially undertrained in their implementation). These controls have appeared to neither improve the productivity of development nor increase the quality of the resulting system. They have substantially increased the overhead of system development in terms of the cost per system and the time to install. Probably the worst side effect is the inflexibility that the controls have placed on the development and production support processes. In today's business world, software systems must be developed quickly and must be extremely malleable. This is not the case when large projects are developed using traditional methods, tools, and techniques. So, it is easy to understand why the skeptics are skeptics.

The SDLC was not designed to control small software development projects. To use it in a project of less than six person months' duration is to waste resources [6]. It can be scaled down, but it is still too cumbersome for small development projects. Perhaps client-server is the alternative to the SDLC at this level. If so, it must have a measure of control built into its development process—not enough control to rob the process of the dynamism necessary to respond to changing client requirements on the fly, but enough to give the software some maintainability and the corporate database some security.

2.2 CLIENT-SERVER VERSUS TRADITIONAL APPLICATION DEVELOPMENT

Hanna [4] argues that C-S programmers must face many new areas of problem, requiring them to master many utilitarian functions that were previously handled by the mainframe development infrastructure. The new areas include even-driven programming, network architecture, network protocols, Application Programming Interfaces (APIs), Open Data Base Connectivity (ODBC), etc. Mastering these new technical areas can result in reduced developer productivity.

In mainframe development environments, programmers benefit from a standardized environment, which includes an operating system, a database manager, a transaction processor and associated utilities, and integrated auto-mated development tools.

The standardized development platform has provided developers with luxuries such as configuration management and version control. The net result is that a single point of entry to production systems is maintained. Change control and concurrency are provided through the production support manager, the database administrator, or the quality-assurance group. Config-uration management is important because mainframe application develop-ment is completed via development teams and the development environment is a multiuser environment. Configuration management and change control add the needed restrictions that prevent redundancy in work products and loss of work products.

The client-server development environment is a more complex multiuser environment. Hanna says that the software modules are greater in number and more easily accessed by team members than in the mainframe develop-ment environment. The level of control provided by configuration manage-ment and change management are blatantly absent, and multiple entry points to production software modules are a reality. This means that one developer can update a module with respect to a particular aspect of its function but have those changes wiped out because another developer had the same mod-ule checked out at the same time but for different modifications. The second developer will overwrite the first developer's work because his or her version of the module does not reflect those changes. Thus, a key issue is how to con-trol which modules are running in the client-server system.

2.3 CLIENT-SERVER SYSTEMS MANAGEMENT

Hurwitz Consulting Group, Inc. has provided a framework [5] for managing cli-ent-server systems that identifies eight primary systems management issues.

1. Performance management
2. Problem management
3. Software distribution management
4. Configuration and administration management
5. Data and storage management
6. Operations management
7. Security management
8. License management

The framework is available from HCG in report form. The report, titled *Client-Server Systems Management: Technology Assessment and Directions*, covers these client-server systems management issues in detail, lists commercially available systems management products, provides a competitive analysis of the vendors, and provides a functional tools characteristics matrix which managers can use to make informed decisions about client-server systems management tools.

2.4 CLIENT-SERVER DEVELOPMENT FRAMEWORKS

The remainder of this chapter is devoted to two distinctly different client-server methodologies for guiding and controlling client-server system development. The first approach, the Client-Server Iterative Rapid Development (CSIRD), is most applicable to client-server development at the department level, but it is also used at the enterprise level. The second approach, Client-Server Systems Engineering (CSSE), is most applicable to enterprise-level distributed development.

The first methodology, dubbed CSIRD (pronounced "scissored"), was proposed by James Louderback [7]. The primary characteristics of CSIRD are phased functionality, an overall design phase, built-in feedback loops, and platform/tool selection. CSIRD is a team-driven process directed by a "system architect."

One advantage of CSIRD is that it is not dominated by the limitations of the existing hardware platform. Another advantage is that the methodology does not require the developer to attempt to "visualize" the entire system prior to construction.

This second advantage is definitely the more significant because the traditional SDLC approach is contrary to the way human beings tend to do work. It requires that developers complete all of the analysis and design (thinking) up front before constructing (doing work) any of the system. This is the primary reason that the SDLC ideal has never been successful in practice. Humans tend to work a little, then think a little, then work a little more, and then think a little more. This is an iterative or cyclic process.

Work is completed in cycles because we frequently do not have a clear idea of what we want to accomplish when we begin. As we do the tasks of work, the results of our effort begin to become clearer, and this enhances our understanding of what we are trying to achieve.

So, humans need to view a partially completed product in order to understand fully what the completed product will be. This explains why end users never seem to know what they want during the requirements-gathering phase of large system development, and why the requirements change once the users have seen a partial system product. When this happens, it slows down development and adds to costs.

CSIRD is a good fit in client-server development because it addresses this problem, yet still allows a measure of project management control of the project. CSIRD is a methodology designed to handle the complexity of making software programs work in tandem across LANs, of separating the processes and the data (client vs. server), and of integrating disparate hardware platforms.

2.5 CSIRD

2.5.1 CSIRD Development Team

The development team is a small group consisting of the project sponsor, several experienced analysts/programmers, and at least one end user.

The sponsor is a critical member of the team and must participate in every aspect of CSIRD because she or he has the authority to make sure the project is completed and must remain visible because that authority cannot be delegated [2]. So, no one else can push the project to completion except the sponsor. The sponsor must drive the vision of the system and must have an unchallenged mandate to allocate the resources to develop the system. Louderback suggests that the manager of the department requesting the system should fill the sponsor's role.

The analysts/programmers must be versatile, personable, and have excellent verbal and written communications skills. A good generalist with these qualifications is to be preferred over a technical expert (a specialist) who does not have them.

For complex C-S projects, Louderback suggests that the analysts/programmers be split into two subteams, each having two or three developers. The responsibilities of one team should include working with the database server to define the database tables, rules, and security. The other team defines the client-related processing including screens and reports and the processes supporting them.

Subteam members can also be divided into performing front-end or back-end tasks. Front-end (gathering requirements, etc.) activities should be allocated to the individuals with good communications skills and business savvy (generalists) and the back-end (construction and testing) work, to the more technically oriented individuals (specialists).

2.5.2 CSIRD Phases

CSIRD includes five more or less parallel phases: initial systems conceptualization, bounded discrete development, parallel design and implementation, continual tool and platform evaluation, and platform selection and installation.

These elements are not necessarily sequentially ordered occurrences (as implied by the word *phase*); they can overlap substantially in the development of a real client-server system.

2.5.2.1 Initial Systems Conceptualization Implemented as a "SWAT" team approach, this is really a Rapid Application Development (RAD) or a Joint Application Design (JAD) approach. The development team engages in a concentrated three- to five-day session that results in a high-level functional design comprising problem definition, functional decomposition, first module identification and bounding, an overall development plan, and wish-listing. An

additional consequence of the SWAT session is the sponsor's internalization of the system vision.

2.5.2.2 Bounded Discrete Development
By the end of the session the first phase of the system is completed down to the detailed design level ready for first module development. This development should take no more than two months at the most. The first module should not be too large or complex and should be chosen based on a combination of need for the function it implements and on how it will affect the development of later system functions. During this time, the first development subteam completes the module's detailed design while the second subteam works on the data model and begins bounding the second module.

2.5.2.3 Parallel Design and Implementation
The key tenet of this C-S methodology is that one module is being developed while the next is being designed so that pieces of the system can be in place and addressing the user's business needs very rapidly. The secret of success is that one group is given complete responsibility for each module. This goes a long way to assure the completeness, correctness, and consistency of the module and the information it delivers.

2.5.2.4 Tool and Platform Review
Subsequent to implementation, the front-end tools and the platform are reviewed. First is a test of fit between the module and the development tools. If the front-end tool(s) used are too slow or do not create the desired functionality it may be necessary to redo the module at a later date with a better choice of tool(s). Second is a test of fit between the module and the platform. If the database server becomes a bottleneck, decisions must be made about upgrading the software or hardware or both. If the network is too slow it must be analyzed and the problem component(s) replaced.

2.5.2.5 Platform Selection and Installation
In C-S development it is not assumed that the system will use a preexisting platform; thus platform selection is an important consideration. Even if the platform exists, it will probably require enhancement. The only component locked in at the beginning is the database server. The client tools may be chosen as the first module nears implementation.

With respect to hardware, the database machine should be acquired according to system needs. It should be fast enough to do system development, but cheap enough to replace if it cannot support the finished system. The client machines should be expandable through DOS to Windows, OS/2, and Unix, as the client software requires.

2.5.3 A CASE-Based Client-Server Systems Engineering Methodology

In a recent *CASE Trends* article [1], Robert Binder described a CASE-based C-S development methodology. He describes CSSE as a comprehensive approach for mission-critical systems whose cost is justifiable on a cost-quality basis. Binder's approach views a complete client-server system specification as consisting of requirements, architectural, and detail design models. The completed specification is the result of a three-phased process of defining concept, setting model system requirements, and preparing the design.

2.5.3.1 Requirements Model

Binder defines the requirements model as a description "of the functions and data necessary to solve the user's problem." The requirements model consists of these subtypes: the environmental model, the essential model, and the interface model. The environmental model is produced during concept definition. The essential model and the interface model are completed during the model system requirements phase.

Environmental Model The environmental model is used to analyze user requirements and consists of a data model and an events list. The data model maps out real-world entities that are involved in the user's system development enigma. The data model can be constructed using any of the traditional requirements-gathering techniques, but a JAD session is probably most efficient given the time constraints on client-server development projects. Binder notes that the data model can be developed in parallel with the creation of a corresponding process model.

Binder defines an event as "something that happens in the environment which requires a system response." Events are defined from the user's (an external) perspective. Hence events are physical occurrences that drive system responses. Binder believes that events can be used to build either a structured or object-oriented requirements model. Events affect the system through the GUI in a client-server system and the system's responses are in turn affected through the GUI.

Essential Model The essential model describes the "solution system" that is defined from the user's viewpoint. It is used to develop the general system design. The essential model describes:

1. The response of a system to events in its physical environment
2. The required data storage for each response
3. Data structures, flows, and stores
4. Data structure transformations

The essential model is a logical depiction of the system's responses to physical (external) events. It is devoid of implementation details.

Interface Model On the other hand, the interface model is an implementation-dependent model. It is driven by technical requirements involved in creating the human-computer interface and the interfaces to external systems and to system administration. The interface model extends the essential model to cover technical requirements which, according to Binder, produces "a constant, well-integrated model that meets both functional and non-functional system requirements."

GUI design and prototyping are major activities at this stage of development. Binder recommends using either a GUI generator product or one of the middle-level programming languages such as Visual Basic.

2.5.3.2 Architectural Model The architectural model is the implementation-dependent specification. It includes the specifications for computers, networks, programs, and databases required to build the system. Bender dubs the result the "system architecture," which he characterizes as being technology-independent, represented by the architectural model which is subdivided into a processor model and a task model and developed by implementation trade-off analysis.

The steps involved in constructing the architectural model are:

1. Partition: identifying collections of processes that are suitable for a particular processor
2. Allocation: within that partition, identifying collections of processes that can be equated to a specific task
3. Evaluation: reviewing each partition and allocation within a framework of implementation objectives and environmental constraints
4. Global Evaluation: reviewing the overall partitioning with respect to constraints and implementation objectives
5. Revision: altering partitions and allocations as needed

Processor Model The processor model illustrates which system functions are assigned to target processor components. It defines the hardware and technology interfaces among the components. This model is a direct translation of the essential requirements into an implementation model. For multiprocessor environments, it includes interprocessor communications specifications.

Task Model Binder defines a task as a "unit of work in the target environment—a program or a process." It illustrates how functional and technical requirements have been assigned different tasks on a given processor. Binder says the important considerations in task development are task allocation within a processor and task communication interfaces.

Binder suggests that an appropriate strategy is to allocate

1. Database access requirements from an event-response path to a single server task
2. Requirements for a single user interface to a client task
3. Requirements accessing a critical resource to a single task
4. Restart, recovery, or data integrity requirements under a common failure model

2.6 THE IMPACT ON TESTING

The immediate effect of client-server development on testing is that it exaggerates the traditional problems of software testing. Client-server development is very much date-driven and thus client-server testing is date-driven. The fact that testing is date-driven is not new, but the accelerated pace (RAD nature) of C-S development aggravates the problem. Testing has always been the activity that is shorted when it comes to allocated time. There has never been enough time to adequately test systems, but now that timeframe has become even shorter.

Another impact of C-S development is that testing tends to be more build-driven than in mainframe development projects. I know that Microsoft claims to create a build a day when developing software, but they have an automated testing approach which allows such luxury. On the C-S projects I have tested we averaged two builds a week, which was usually one build too many.

The builds were driven by several factors. First were "showstoppers": When we encountered an error so severe that further testing would have been either impossible or a waste of time, a new build was cut. Second, it was management's policy that we would produce a new build every Monday. Third, when the beta test sites required updates to catch up to the build number that was on the machines in the test lab a new build was made.

Even automated test cases require maintenance so it is difficult to update automated test scripts for every new build. It's hard enough to keep up with testing each build in an automated test environment, but manual testing is even more difficult. At one organization, we did not have automated test scripts, and we found our test process being driven by problem reports (PRs). For every new build we retested PRs that were pending validation. In retesting them, we frequently discovered new errors that were missed earlier, and we also discovered new errors that were caused by the fixes. The only reason we were able to test even halfway effectively was because we used SQA TeamTest's Manager product to track defects.

This problem becomes much worse at the level of the executable file (in Windows this is the .exe file). We found that the developers were so eager to fix problems that they would come into the lab between builds and copy executable files onto our test machines. After a while we had no idea what version of the software we were testing. This occurred because there was no management policy for software configuration and change control. After many arguments, and bad days in general, the test team finally convinced management to implement software configuration management (SCM) via Microsoft SourceSafe. After that things began to settle down and the number of errors introduced by the developers' fixes dropped.

Another impact of the RAD nature of C-S development is that system testing is reduced to an overstated integration test. Because there are few project management controls and because there is not a formal development process, the system requirements of C-S systems are frequently not documented. A system test (see chapter 10) is based on an "external" (user's) view of the system's functionality. Without a requirements statement it is very difficult to create system test cases (scenarios) that accurately reflect how the users will employ the system.

Thus, what we termed a system test was either a set of function tests or an integration test. There are, however, a couple of methods for reducing the guesswork and for creating a form of system test. The first is Business System Risk Analysis. Discussed fully in chapter 4, risk analysis identifies the areas of the system that would cause the most dire consequences if they failed and gives a weighted risk score that can be used to decide what to include in a system test. The second method is Binder's Scenario-Based Client-Server Testing Approach (discussed in chapter 10).

The RAD nature of C-S development precludes formal unit testing. Developers are very sensitive to the shortened cycle time and the first thing they omit is testing. In general, software developers have never really done unit testing as it should be. If they tested, it was informal at best. Now they have an even better excuse to avoid formal unit testing.

Finally, the cross-platform nature of C-S systems requires construction of a test laboratory that models the target software and hardware production environment. It is not enough to test the application software on isolated test machines. A complete network of test workstations is required. Furthermore, a standard desktop configuration is required for each machine in the lab. Consequently, tests run on developers' machines and on testers' machines are not valid for integrating system and acceptance testing because they do not represent a legitimate model of a typical user desktop.

2.7 CONCLUSION

Some sort of management of the client-server system development process is an absolute necessity if the systems are to be tested. Recent criticisms of client-server systems have centered on their ineffectiveness and lack of reliability when the user demands grow beyond 30 or 40 users. This problem is a direct result of not applying a management framework to the C-S development process, which in turn makes testing extremely ineffective. If C-S systems are to be as successful as their proponents have argued, they must be planned, controlled, and implemented for long-term enterprise-level use.

If the proper controls are applied, testing becomes a straightforward process that can be implemented in the C-S development environment as effectively as in the traditional MIS mainframe world.

Thus, major C-S development projects should use a RAD methodology to assure the effectiveness of the information the system will deliver to its users. The two approaches discussed above are intended to initiate critical thinking about what constitutes a C-S development methodology, how much control is necessary, and what level of development process implementation is required.

They are also viable approaches in themselves and should be seriously considered for use in your C-S projects.

If the developer does not apply a level of control and structure to the development process, the tester cannot adequately test the resulting software system. That is why CSIRD and CSSE methodologies are briefly described above. I strongly urge you to read the original Louderback article.

Even if no formal project management controls are placed on the C-S development process, some level of informal control—even if only SCM—is necessary for both automated and manual testing of C-S systems. When the testing process is out of control, which happens very quickly in a C-S environment where developers are free to update the test environment when the whim hits them, the process quickly loses its effectiveness.

2.8 REFERENCES

1. Binder, Robert. "A CASE-Based Systems Engineering Approach to Client-Server Development." *CASE Trends*, 1992.

2. Boehm, Barry, and Standish, Thomas. "Software Technology in the 1990's: Using an Evolutionary Paradigm." *IEEE Computer*, Vol. 16, No. 11, November 1983; pp. 30–7.

3. Bouldin, Barbara. *Agents of Change: Managing the Introduction of Automated Tools*. Prentice Hall, Upper Saddle River, NJ, 1989.

4. Hanna, Mary. "Teams of Developers Seek Benefits of C-S Platform." *Software Magazine*, February 1994, pp. 37–9, 44.

5. Hurwitz Consulting Group, Inc., *Client-Server Systems Management: Technology Assessment and Directions*. Hurwitz Consulting Group, Inc., Watertown, MA.

6. King, David. *Current Practices in Software Development*. Yourdon Press, New York, 1984.

7. Louderback, James. "The CSIRD Methodology." *DBMS*, June 1991.

8. Perry, William E. *A Standard for Testing Application Software 1992*. Auerbach Publishers, Boston, 1992.

9. Sentry Publishing. "Systems Management: Administration Challenge." *Software Magazine, Client-Server Computing supplement,* September 1991, p. 15.

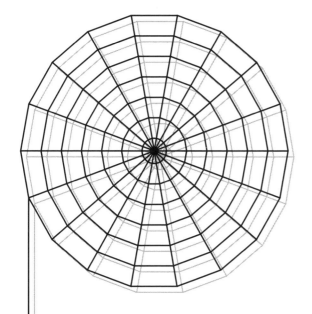

Software Testing in the Client-Server Milieu

3.1 INTRODUCTION

According to Glenford Myers [9], traditional testing approaches for large mainframe-oriented information systems assume a team of MIS development professionals, a "top-down" functional decomposition approach to analysis and design and a concurrent "top-down" testing and implementation of the design in a CUI environment. These assumptions are no longer valid when it comes to developing distributed or C-S information processing systems.

Some form of project management and process control must exist if C-S developers are to construct integrated information systems. Furthermore, some measure of control must exist if the systems are to be testable. It is a fundamental testing tenet that software systems must have some level of identifiable structure and organization or they cannot be tested. The level of control must be applied conservatively in the C-S development process, though, or the ability to deliver systems quickly and cheaply and the ability to modify the systems to meet dynamic business needs will be impaired.

The trade-off is one of testability. Those C-S proponents who advocate no project management or methodological control of the development process will be building systems that are very difficult to test, which means they will sacrifice quality (effectiveness) for productivity (efficiency). On the other hand, those C-S developers who apply a modicum of control to their development process will experience systems that are both effective in information delivery and efficient to develop.

Shaku Atre argues that the fast timetables associated with C-S development make testing impractical [1]; thus many groups either will not test at all or will skimp on the testing process. Developers underestimating the importance of testing risk producing C-S systems with little reliability and damaging data, among other potential problems. Such systems can have increased development costs and schedule overruns because of fixes to problems uncovered late in the development process and increased maintenance costs because of the large number of problems discovered after implementation. The most significant effect, however, may be the loss of confidence in client-server development technology and a loss of credibility by the group applying the technology.

The saving grace may be an iterative C-S development methodology (discussed in chapter 2) proposed by Louderback [8]. His CSIRD approach adds the necessary process controls to C-S development, but allows quick and cost-effective system construction. CSIRD is a phased fundamental design approach with built-in feedback loops and independent C-S tool and platform selection and reevaluation. The secret CSIRD ingredient is "parallel design and development."

Parallel design and development holds down the time-to-product (product = information delivery to customer) and the costs. The project management aspects of CSIRD make the system testable. However, the parallel design and construction and the platform selection aspects do affect how the system will be tested.

3.2 THE QAI SOFTWARE TESTING PRACTICES SURVEY

The Quality Assurance Institute (QAI) software testing survey [11] was conducted during the institute's annual testing conference in Orlando, FL, November 1994. The respondents were the conference attendees, representing a cross-section of companies, with most from organizations with more than a hundred employees. The industries represented included financial (13%), insurance (10%), telecommunications (11%), software (6%), aerospace (15%), consulting (10%), government (13%), and other (22%). All geographical areas of the U.S. were represented and nine attendees were from Canada.

Twenty-five percent of the survey respondents indicated that the most needed test-related improvement in their organizations is consistent testing methodologies/processes. Fifty percent said their organizations trained testers but their further comments revealed a specific need for hands-on training with testing techniques. They also indicated that the most effective training testers can receive is training in their organization's testing methods, techniques, and tools.

Sixty percent said their companies have testing standards in place, but a portion of the responses indicated that they were not followed and should be updated. Sixty-eight percent indicated that they created planning, execution, and analysis products such as test plans, test cases, test data, test environments, etc., but only 21% indicated that they maintain reuse test products.

Only three respondents indicated that they do regression testing! Less than 10% indicated that this is a testing area most in need in their organization.

Approximately 50% of the respondents indicated they perform project reviews and structured walkthroughs as part of manual testing. More than 33% also indicated they use customer reviews. Almost 66% indicated that they perform unit, system, and, in particular, performance testing (volume/stress) testing as automated testing. Approximately 50% also perform either acceptance testing or pilot testing.

Sixty-five percent indicated that their testing process is date-driven, 50% stated that users decide when to release the software, another 50% stated that the software is released when planned testing is completed, and approximately 30% indicated that the test team has some say in the matter.

Only 29% of the respondents indicated that the organizations measured testing effectiveness. Among them, defect counts, problem tickets, and other forms of posttest assessment were mentioned. Some mentioned statistical process control, defect management, and defect tracking. The majority of the respondents mentioning the latter indicated that they tracked defects by classification, severity, date detected, and status. Other respondents indicated they supplement the information above with project information, product information, and rework hours.

Approximately 25% of the respondents indicated that they plan 45% of the total project time for testing. They also indicated they allocate one-fourth of the project development budget to testing. The average time devoted to testing was 27%, and the average budget was 24%.

QAI survey respondents indicated that they spend as much time testing client-server systems as they do testing mainframe systems. They indicated that mainframe-testing approaches must be updated and improved for use in distributed environments. Furthermore, they indicated that client-server environments place more stress on testers because the testing of a single system program can require the testing of multiple system components. They felt that client-server testing must address such integrated processing system components as Workstations, servers, LANs, and WANs.

Although the respondents indicated that there are few tools available for testing distributed systems, this shows they lack information, as many new and old testing tools are available. They did, however, list Autotester, MSTest, and WinRunner/XRunner as automated tools used in their organizations. It is interesting that SQA's TeamTest was not mentioned because this product has a 70% share of the Windows testing market. Just over 20% indicated that automated testing tools are one of the areas most in need in their companies.

Respondents said that process improvement, test tool acquisition, and testing metrics were in their plans for improving testing. They indicated that key issues for enabling software testing in their organizations were management commitment and skilled testing professionals and that the greatest obstacles to effective testing were time constraints, a lack of management support, and the need for testing automation.

Subsequent surveys in 1995 and 1996 yielded similar results. The issues were the same but their rankings based on importance-urgency changed. In 1995, the conditions that positively impact testing were seen as

1. Management support and commitment
2. Adherence to process/methodology
3. Success and enthusiasm of the test team

In 1996, the positive factors were

1. Management support and buy-in
2. Competent and dedicated staff
3. Established testing methodology
4. Automated testing tools

In 1995, the major inhibitors to testing were

1. Schedule and time constraints
2. Lack of management understanding, support, and commitment
3. Cost budget and funding

In 1996, they were

1. Time constraints
2. Inadequate testing resources
3. Management support, commitment, and understanding

In 1995, the testing functions that were in the most need of improvement were

1. Formal methodology and standards
2. Automated testing
3. Test planning
4. Test tools

In 1996, these areas were

1. Use of a methodology and standards
2. Test planning
3. Automated testing
4. Measurement and defect tracking

These results might seem a bit out of date now, but that is not the case. Many testing organizations still do not have standards in place, many have not implemented a formal testing process, and many either do not have automated test tools or have failed at implementing automated software testing.

One benefit of the Year 2000 problem is that it has increased the awareness of the role software testing must play if we are to deliver quality software to the marketplace. Many companies are scurrying to establish testing standards, implement testing processes, and acquire testing tools as a result of concern about the millennium bug.

3.3 PROBLEMS WITH TESTING PRACTICE

A survey by The Software Testing Institute found that the principal reason (cited by 30% of the respondents) for an increase in the number of defects was faster application development. This result was published in the Fall/Winter, 1995–96, issue of the *Software Testing Newsletter*.

Because of its RAD approach, client-server development often results in software components that have not been "engineered for testability." Koltun [7] sees a whole group of common problems related to testing such products. Testing these products under tight development schedules can be a real hassle if no time, or not enough time, has been allocated to testing. Furthermore, he says that we frequently have an inadequate understanding of what testing these products involves.

He describes what he considers to be the shortcomings of industry software testing practice and these shortcomings tend to be exaggerated by the client-server development approach. First, he feels that "planned" testing many times lacks focus, because an "explicit" test strategy has not been formulated. He also cautions us not to place too much emphasis on "demonstrating compliance with requirements," and to put more emphasis on demonstrating software robustness and freedom from defects. He also feels that testing frequently does not center on mission-critical system components (in chapter 4 I discuss business risk analysis for software systems). He does not think testing sufficiently stresses system capacity and functionality.

Second, Koltun says that testing preparation is most times inadequate because the testers do not distinguish between the test plan and the test procedure. The test plan should cover the scope, objectives, and resources for testing while the test procedure should address the input, execution, and output products of testing. The key to successfully bridging the gap between planning and process is in establishing clear testing objectives (refer to chapter 4 for a thorough discussion of testing objectives). Frequently, test planning lacks clear objectives, and thus disciplined procedures both for testing and for analyzing test results are not developed or implemented.

Third, he argues that testing resources are always inadequate. Too little time is allocated for testing. Not enough CPU cycles are allocated and not enough test cases are designed, constructed, and executed. Testing does not utilize commercially available automated testing tools often enough. It cannot be overstated that it is the tester's obligation and responsibility to automate the testing process.

Fourth, he declares the test function is not properly staffed. Testers are not brought into the project early enough and thus lack a good understanding of the system under test, and independent test teams are not used often enough. He overlooked the fact that testers are frequently undertrained in software testing methods, techniques, and tools. Software testers must understand and use state-of-the-practice methods and must be aware of what automated tools are available to support those practices.

Fifth, he says test result analysis is rarely adequate. Test results are not submitted to statistical analysis to determine whether to continue testing or how adequate test case coverage has been. A good risk analysis prior to testing and simple statistical analysis of defect trends (Shewardt Charting) can be used to determine how much testing is enough for each system component.

Last, Koltun feels that regression testing does not follow standard industry practices and is not used to make "rational" decisions about subsequent product releases.

Having had the pleasure of hands-on testing a number of client-server systems I have seen the inadequacies Koltun described. On all of those C-S projects there was no test plan until well into the later phases of testing. The testing process was ad hoc and driven by retesting of problem reports. The testing objectives were never clear and they were constantly changing. The hardware, software, and personnel resources were dreadful. We tested using help desk "hotline" personnel and we could not test on all of the target implementation platforms because they were not available. And no analysis of the test process other than weekly status reports was completed for any of the projects.

3.4 SOFTWARE TESTING IN THE DISTRIBUTED PROCESSING DOMAIN

3.4.1 Client-Server Testing Effort

Eckerson [6] says that client-server testing easily accounts for 30–50% of all C-S software development costs and uses up more than half of the allocated development time. Furthermore, the person power required is tremendous. Most of the C-S testers who have reported opinions on the tester/developer ratio think that a two-to-one tester-to-developer ratio is required to test C-S systems. Reality, however, usually provides no testers. Eckerson says, "For most companies, software testing is an afterthought to the development process, not an integral part of it." In organizations trying to test properly, the ratio varies, but my experience is that one tester is assigned per project and the test team is composed of that person, one or two users, and one or two of the developers.

Atre [1] describes the special requirements of testing client-server applications. She argues that it is necessary to test:

1. The client's user interface
2. The client's interface with the server
3. The server's functionality
4. The network

It is necessary to test all the permutations and combinations of GUI objects in the client/user interface: to test the transactions between the client and the server, the transaction results for efficiency and reliability, and the reliability and performance of the network.

3.4.2 The Object-Oriented Perspective

Since C-S is a form of distributed processing [3] it is necessary to consider its testing implications from that point of view. The term "distributed" implies that data and processes are dispersed across various and miscellaneous platforms. This means that data and processes will be replicated on different platforms.

Thus, from a software testing point of view, we must pay attention to these unique aspects of C-S system design. Binder [2] states that the issues will vary from one C-S environment to another, but are summarized as:

1. Client GUI considerations

2. Target environment and platform diversity considerations

3. Distributed database considerations (including replicated data)

4. Distributed processing considerations (including replicated processes)

5. Nonrobust target environment

6. Nonlinear performance relationships

These issues suggest an object-oriented approach to analysis, design. and testing [3,12] (which can be implemented through the CSIRD methodology [8]). Even if the system is not object-oriented in nature, treating it as object-oriented makes good testing sense because the replicated data and processes can be organized into classes of objects that share the same set of properties. Any object in the same class, or any object from a subclass of that class, should behave identically. All replicated instances of the same object (objects can contain both process logic and data structures) should respond in exactly the same way to the same set of test data that was created for objects from that particular class.

The parallel design and construction nature of the CSIRD methodology directly impacts integration testing. Traditional testing views module/subsystem/system integration and testing as top-down or bottom-up or some variation of the two [8]. Module integration in C-S development may have some top-down or bottom-up aspects, but integration in C-S projects tends more toward parallel development and integration of modules across all design levels and across multiple C-S layers [8]. Thus, integration testing in C-S projects leans toward an incremental not a "big bang" approach.

Siegel [13] has proposed a Parallel Design & Collaborative Testing Strategy (PD/CTS) for use in an object-oriented environment. Siegel's PD/CTS approach is based on the "spiral" model for system development developed by Boehm [4]. It involves several small development teams that work closely with the future system users. It also involves creating a series of miniprototypes

(Siegel terms these "design experiments") as the team "spirals" through analysis, design, coding, and testing.

As with the CSIRD approach, each PD/CTS team is responsible for a system component (a module or a subsystem, etc.). In addition, as with CSIRD, Siegel's method requires formal project planning, but he warns that *too much* planning is the same trap in which traditional development approaches have been caught. Siegel advocates two-person development teams where each member is responsible for writing 50% of the code and for testing the 50% the other team member creates.

PD/CTS can be combined with the CSIRD approach to create an overall client-server development and testing methodology. What PD/CTS brings into the picture is the object-oriented testing approach that can be applied to GUI testing and to object-oriented application code.

3.4.3 Cross-Platform Aspects

The fact that the system is not being built to use preexisting hardware and software impacts system testing. The networked cross-platform nature of C-S systems requires that we pay a lot more attention to configuration testing and compatibility testing.

Configuration testing doctrine forces testing of the system in all of the known hardware and software environments in which it will operate. Compatibility testing assures a functionally consistent interface across hardware and software platforms. For example, the Windows-type interface may be visually different but the same basic user behaviors should produce the same results regardless of whether the client interface is Multiview's Mascot, Desktop, or X, or ADDS' X Window Systems, or IBM's OS/2 Presentation Manager, or Microsoft's Windows. These products are all examples of GUIs that have evolved over the past 20 years.

The fact that GUIs are rapidly replacing the CUIs means that GUI testing is a very important aspect of testing in C-S environments. In a conference presentation in 1993, the GartnerGroup described a client-server test plan that is designed to cover the specific issues of C-S testing as completely as possible. A modified C-S test plan outline based on the GartnerGroup's work is discussed in chapter 4.

3.4.4 Cross-Windows Aspects

The current proliferation of Microsoft Windows environments—Windows 3.1, Windows 3.11 for Work Groups (3.11 WFW), Windows 95, and Windows NT—has created a number of problems for C-S developers. C-S software targeted for MS Windows frequently must run on all of these specific OS versions. The problem is that Windows 3.1 and WFW 3.11 are 16-bit environments and Windows 95 and Windows NT are 32-bit environments.

This creates a number of situations that can cause C-S systems to fail. One system I tested that was intended to run in all of the different Windows environments was forced to use the 16-bit version of MS Mail because the system was partially written in Visual Basic (VB) 3.0 (16-bit) and partially in Visual Basic 4.0 (32-bit). The 32-bit version of Mail caused the 16-bit VB code to blow up.

Mixing and matching 16- and 32-bit code/16- and 32-bit systems and products causes major problems, but it is, and will remain, a factor in Windows environments for the near future. Thus, testing in these situations must be adaptable to each environment. The phrase "cross-Windows testing" has become commonplace.

Until recently, the inhibitor to cross-Windows testing has been the lack of an automated test tool that can generate both 16-bit and 32-bit test scripts. SQA, Inc. released its cross-Windows testing tool, TeamTest Suite 6.1. SQA has since been acquired by Rational Software, Inc. The latest version of this product is Rational Test 7.1.

3.5 A CLIENT-SERVER TESTING METHODOLOGY

A formal client-server testing methodology is really an ad hoc test methodology because each testing situation is unique. A methodological framework that is malleable can be an aid to establishing an effective testing process. SQA developed a testing methodology [5] (RAD QA) that can be used in support of its Windows-based client-server software testing tool SQA TeamTest suite. SQA's approach specifically addresses the problems of client-server testing. It outlines the particulars of client-server testing and addresses the shortened iterative development cycles of client-server projects. Rational has replaced the SQA process with its Unified Testing process.

Chapter 4 discusses TestRx, a software testing methodology/process, and its supporting elements. The steps and tasks in TestRx can be easily adapted to client-server testing.

3.6 CONCLUSION

Because client-server is rapidly becoming the preferred software development approach in many varied types of companies, software testers must reevaluate traditional testing frameworks. They must modify the testing process based on the C-S design issues identified by Binder [3] and supplement the traditional with new techniques and processes aimed specifically at testing C-S systems.

If you think software testing is growing more complex and difficult because of distributed computing, just imagine the difficulties of testing the virtual reality interfaces of future information systems. As Pimental and Teixeira [10] observe, "Now, with virtual reality, the window of the GUI that has kept us outside the screen looking in has dissolved, and we can step through the looking glass—replacing the desktop metaphor with a complete environment."

Virtual reality is the ultimate future client-server environment. Can Lawnmower Man really be that far away?

3.7 REFERENCES

1. Atre, Shaku. *Client-Server Application Development Testing.* A special report by Atre Associates, Inc., 222 Grace Church Street, Port Chester, NY 10573-5155.

2. Binder, Robert A. "A CASE-Based System Engineering Approach to Client-Server Development." *CASE Trends,* 1992.

3. Binder, Robert A. *Test Case Design for Object-Oriented Programming: The FREE Approach.* Robert Binder Systems Consulting, Inc., Chicago, 1992.

4. Boehm, Barry. "A Spiral Model of Software Development and Enhancement." *Software Engineering Notes,* Vol. 11, No. 4, August 1986, p. 22.

5. Bourne, Kelly. "SQA Process." *DBMS,* Vol. 8, No. 12, November 1995, p. 34(3).

6. Eckerson, Wayne W. "Client-Server Test Tools: Client-Server Computing Has Created a Need for Robust New Test Tools and Test Methodologies." *Open Information Systems,* Vol. 9, No. 11, November 1994, pp. 3–21. The Patricia Seybold Group, Boston, MA.

7. Koltun, Phil. "Testing...Testing...." *ShowCASE Newsletter,* Harris Corporation, May 1993.

8. Louderback, James. "The CSIRD Methodology." *DBMS,* June 1991.

9. Myers, Glenford. *The Art of Software Testing.* Wiley-Interscience, New York, 1979.

10. Pimental, Ken, and Teixeira, Kevin. *Virtual Reality: Through the New Looking Glass.* Intel/Windcrest/McGraw-Hill, Inc., New York, 1992.

11. The Quality Assurance Institute. *The 1994 Survey Results on Software Testing.* QAI, Orlando FL, 1994.

12. Quin, Stephen R., Ware, John C., and Spragens, John. "Tireless Testers: Automated Tools Can Help Iron Out the Kinks in Your Custom GUI Applications." *INFO-WORLD,* September 1993, pp. 78–9, 82–3, 85.

13. Siegel, Shel M. *Strategies for Testing Object-Oriented Software.* CompuServe CASE Forum Library, September 1992.

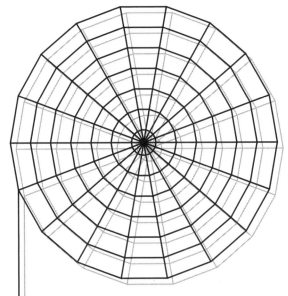

CHAPTER 4

A Prescription for Planning, Executing, and Controlling the Testing Process

4.1 TESTING APPROACH

I wrote this testing approach with SQA TeamTest Suite as the primary software testing tool. It can be adapted for use with other commercially available software testing tool suites.

4.2 TESTING PROCESS

This standardized software testing process can be used with any client-server software development project. The process is based on the proprietary TEST-Rx software testing methodology offered by CSST Technologies.

Software evaluation and testing is not an isolated function. It occurs in conjunction with other software development activities and within the context of the software development life cycle. Achieving the Test proposed capability maturity mode (CMM) key process area (KPA) [1] goals, commitment levels, abilities, and activities involves improving not only those activities that are specifically under evaluation or testing, but also those tasks that support the evaluation and testing process. Refer to chapter 14 for a discussion of software testing process improvement based on the CMM KPAs. A method for making operational the steps of the evaluation and testing process and its supporting elements is required. TEST-Rx outlines a set of process steps and supporting elements that will achieve the Test KPA goals by establishing the proper commitment levels, providing the required abilities, and defining the necessary evaluation and test activities.

TEST-Rx is a standardized software testing process that includes supporting elements for use with any software development testing project. The purpose of the process is to provide a baseline for software testing activities pertaining to the project. A standard testing process is required because it improves the effectiveness and efficiency of testing for the project. It:

1. Defines the testing process (satisfies CMM Level 3)
2. Makes the testing process repeatable (satisfies CMM level 2)
3. Makes sure that high-risk components of the system are tested
4. Avoids problems of omission (inadequately testing parts of the system)
5. Avoids problems of commission (testing parts of the system that are not important or that result in redundant testing)
6. Lessens the effects of individual differences (tester background and skill set)
7. Adds "intelligence" to testing
8. Provides metrics for managing and controlling testing
9. Provides metrics for assessing and improving testing
10. Provides a basis for test automation
11. Produces specific testing deliverables

4.3 OVERVIEW

The process consists of a series of steps. Each step consists of a set of tasks. Completion of the first step results in a set of *deliverables*. In some instances, deliverables, or partial deliverables, can be ascertained from individual tasks, or a series of tasks within a particular step. Elemental processes such as configuration management, defect tracking, peer reviews, test metrics, and test automation support the steps. Table 4.1 illustrates the TEST-Rx process.

The software testing process steps are described within the context of the SDLC approach. See Table 4.2. The life cycle deliverables required as inputs to several of the testing process steps will be produced within the methodological framework. Previous steps in the testing process itself will produce other deliverables. In addition, all testing process deliverables are produced by specific tasks with specific steps.

Conceptually, the process should be considered a spiral model. Its steps are not mutually exclusive; tasks from different steps can be completed in parallel. It is also cyclic in the sense that it is OK to return to a previous step and update the deliverables as testing progresses and more information becomes available about what to test.

All test projects should be set up in a repository via an automated test tool suite such as SQA TeamTest or Mercury Interactive Test Director. The test repository manages test assets and test deliverables at the level of the project. Each project should have associated test assets, test requirements, links to external test documents, software structure descriptions, test procedure scripts, and test cases described in full in the repository. In addition, automated test logs, defects, defect tracking reports, test result analysis, and test results reports should be produced and stored within the repository.

The test repository should be located on a network server accessible to all of the testers, developers, and managers involved in the project.

Table 4.1 CSST Technologies Recommended Testing Process and Supporting Mechanisms (TEST-Rx)

The Testing Process	Configuration Management	Defect Tracking and Reporting	Test Automation	Peer Reviews	Test Metrics
Assemble Test Team	Not Required	Not Required	Not Required	Required	Not Required
Perform Risk Analysis	Optional	Not Required	Optional	Required	Required
Define Test Objectives/ Requirements	Optional	Not Required	Required	Required	Required
Develop Test Plan	Optional	Not Required	Required	Required	Required
Design Test Cases	Optional	Not Required	Required	Required	Not Required
Execute Unit and Integration Tests	Required	Required	Required	Required	Required
Execute System Test	Required	Required	Required	Required	Required
Analyze and Report Test Results	Required	Not Required	Optional	Required	Required
Execute Regression Testing	Required	Required	Required	Required	Required
Analyze and Report Regression Test Results	Required	Required	Required	Required	Required

Table 4.2 TEST-Rx Testing Process Steps

Process Steps	Life Cycle Stage	Personnel
1. Establish Test Team	Analysis	Project Manager, Test Manager
2. Perform Risk Analysis	Analysis	Project Manager, Test Manager
3. Establish Test Objectives	Analysis	Test Manager, Test Analysts
4. Construct Test Plans	Analysis/Design	Test Analysts
5. Design and Construct Test Cases	Analysis/Design	Test Analysts
6. Execute Unit and Integration Testing	Construction	Developers (unit), Test Team (integration)
7. Execute System Test	Testing	Test Team
8. Analyze and Report Test Results	Testing	Test Manager, Test Analysts
9. Execute Regression Test	Maintenance/ Production	Test Analysts
10. Analyze and Report Regression Test Results	Maintenance/ Production	Test Analysts

4.4 SOFTWARE TESTING SUPPORTING ELEMENTS

4.4.1 Software Configuration Management

Software configuration management (SCM) is essential to productive software testing. Build management should be implemented so that sets of tests are conducted on stable software executables and all associated runtime components. SCM procedures are described in the Deployment phase of the development methodology.

4.4.1.1 SCM Procedures   For any software system that encompasses client-server or mainframe processes, the components that implement those processes must be coded, tested, and moved to production in an effective, efficient, and timely manner. To this end SCM must control the components.

This section defines a set of procedures that should be followed when moving software components. It defines the SCM activities required for maintaining all software and related items being constructed, tested, and kept in the production environment.

The list of components can include, but is not limited to, requirements and design specifications, source files, executable files, ini files, DLLs, stored procedures, data from the test environment to the production environment, regression test data and test data generation procedures, maintenance documentation, and updated user documentation.

4.4.1.2 Change Control Board (CCB) This group tracks and controls all changes to production software. This is a semipermanent committee composed of management-level IS staff. The quality assurance manager should chair the group. Members can include department managers who use the various software systems, the IS director, the data services director, the network services director, the data center director, and IS project managers who must present proposed/completed changes.

The group should meet at least once a week but can meet more often if necessary. The meetings should be kept as short as possible (no more than one hour). This group should continue to be a forum for evaluating software, database, network, and operations changes that will impact other production systems.

One CCB can have authority over all levels of the software development process, or it can be a hierarchy of boards. For example, a project-level CCB is often necessary to cope with the rapid pace of the development process prior to implementation. This is an absolute requirement in RAD development environments.

The kinds of issues that the CCB considers are:

1. Schedules
2. Interim delivery dates
3. Requirements changes
4. Design changes
5. Source code changes
6. Executable code changes
7. Library changes
8. Documentation changes
9. Defects/Failures
10. Software-related problem resolution

4.4.1.3 SCM Responsibilities

Software Identification The SCM process manages all software entities and their related representations in documentation. SCM extends the management approaches from hardware control to software. The following examples are meant to illustrate the type of entities that are managed. Some organizations will not need to manage some of these items, whereas, other organizations will manage additional items not in this list.

1. Management plans (project plan, test plan, etc.)
2. Specifications (requirements, design, test case, etc.)
3. Customer documentation (implementation manuals, user manuals, operations manuals, on-line help files)
4. Source code (PL/1 FORTRAN, COBOL, Visual Basic, Visual C, etc.)

5. Executable code (machine readable object code, exe's, etc.)

6. Libraries (runtime procedures, %include files, APIs, DLLs, etc.)

7. Databases (data being processed, data a program requires, test data, regression test data, etc.)

8. Production documentation

Basically, SCM should manage all software-related components that are used during development, testing, and production.

Software Configuration Control   Software Configuration Control (SCC) is the practice of managing the change process and tracking the changes. Its purpose is to assure that the configuration of the software is known at any specific point in time. To establish an accurate SCC process, the baseline characteristics of each software entity must be recorded. All later changes are tracked against these baseline values. This is usually accomplished through version control.

For example, the date/time stamp of an executable file can be used to determine which release of the program is running. In addition, some languages (e.g., Visual Basic) allow the version to be inserted as a statement within the program source code. Commercially available products use SCM databases to create and maintain versions of source code, executable code, libraries, and documentation.

These commercial tools are very important in the management of the SCM process. An SCM administrator must be appointed. The administrator should be a technical person who has or will receive training in SCM and in the SCM managed products your organization uses.

Configuration Status Accounting   Configuration status accounting must provide a set of reports—static and dynamic—that provide information concerning the software entities under SCM controls. Some examples of the kinds of information required include the status of

1. Management plans

2. Specifications

3. Source code

4. Executable code

5. Proposed changes

6. Approved changes

Reports needed include:

1. Proposed changes

2. Approved changes

3. Product versions/releases

4. Problems

4.4.1.4 SCM Audits and Reviews

SCM Audits   SCM audits must include a change control audit which produces the log used during the release control review.

SCM Reviews

Release Authorization Review   Release authorization is a management process that immediately follows the change authorization process. The release authorization procedure should include a review of the completed SCM Statement of Work. This process should include representatives from the test and development groups and the data center/operations group. Customers can be included as well. The release authorization process shoulders the following responsibilities: verification of all changes to the software since the previous release and verification that all changes since the previous release have been unit, integration, and regression tested.

Release Control Review   Release control is the process that correlates the release changes with the output of the release authorization process. This process should use the output of a change control audit log and the results of the release authorization review as inputs. It should produce a document that describes all of the software changes between the current and pending releases.

4.4.1.5 Release Description Documentation

Release Description Document Contents   Project-level production software releases must be described so that the customers will understand what is being delivered. In some cases, these recipients will also need installation instructions. The release document should describe the following:

1. The release media
2. Installation instructions, if required
3. New functions that are implemented
4. SCRs that are satisfied with the release
5. Inventory of software components and other items contained in the release
6. Special user considerations for the release
7. Problems that will be addressed in future releases

4.4.1.6 Documentation Controls

Creation and Storage   The software components that are under SCM control can be created using a variety of methods. For example, source code can be created using any number of editors supplied with differing programming languages. User documents can be created with any of the commercially available word processing packages.

   The important thing is that, regardless of source of creation, the software-related entities must be stored in a database that is under SCM control. Strict policies must be developed that define who can update/move the entities in and out of the database and under what circumstances they can be moved or updated.

Signoffs Policies must be established designating who is responsible for approvals when entities are updated and moved into and out of the database. Additionally, approvals must be made when the entities are elevated in status from development to test, and from test to production. All approval must be in written or electronic signature form.

4.4.1.7 Release Exceptions

In certain circumstances it may be necessary to implement unplanned "emergency" changes to production software. Emergency changes must have written approval from the appropriate department head and must be communicated to all other department heads. The changes must be reviewed at the following CCB meeting.

4.4.1.8 Records Collection

Copies of released material should be maintained for backup and disaster recovery purposes. This includes released software, documentation for released software, support software, audit reports, review reports, status reports, benchmarks, distribution records, and change history.

The records should be stored either on- or off-line or both, and should be retained during the life cycle of the released software.

4.4.2 SCM During Software Development and Testing

SCM is not limited to software that is in its postrelease phase. SCM must be applied to the process of building software. During development, software components are released for integration with other software components. Each set of integrated components is termed a "build." Each build must be integration tested. Builds/components that fail integration testing must be repaired and reintegration tested. SCM is critical during this build-test-repair-retest cycle. Without adequate SCM controls, the process frequently becomes unmanageable.

At the project level, defect reports drive the repair and retest process. The information in problem reports is used to guide developers when repairing the defects. The testers use the same reports when retesting the defects. In addition to the information contained in the problem reports, there is other important information that must be made available if the build is to be tested adequately. Testers need to know:

- ☞ What defects were corrected?
- ☞ What levels of unit tests were applied?
- ☞ What software components were added, changed, or deleted?
- ☞ What software libraries were updated?
- ☞ What changes were made to middleware and databases?

Software builds in client-server development environments should be controlled via MS Visual SourceSafe (VSS) or a similar product. VSS offers a repository-based framework for controlling versions of project software and related products. VSS or a related product should also be used to control project-level production software releases. Mainframe SCM should be implemented via ChangeMan or a similar product.

4.4.3 Project-Level SCM Activities

The project-level change control process should include two preproduction levels and a production rollback process. First, the changes from development to test must be carefully controlled. Second, the release of software from test to production must be a flawless process. Finally, the capability to roll back the production changes must be in place in case of catastrophic system failure.

4.4.3.1 Project-Level CCB At the project level, a temporary CCB should be formed for development and testing. See Figures 4.1 and 4.2. It assesses defect reports and decides which problems will be repaired in which build. At this

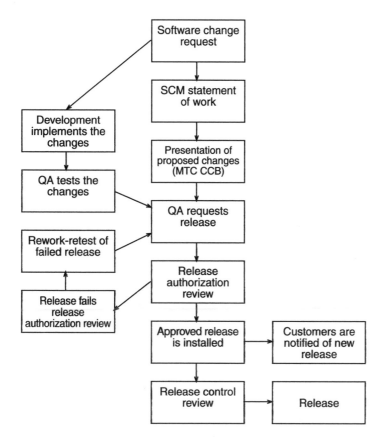

Fig. 4.1 Project-Level Software Change Control Process and Related Activities

System name: _____

Application name: _____

Date of release: _____

Person releasing the build: _____

Concurrent application releases (if applicable): _____

Type of machine(s): _____

Type of operating system(s): _____

Build release label name: _____

Source tag name: _____

Directory location of executable build: _____

Inventory list of source files in the build: _____

_____

Problem reports associated with this build: _____

_____

List new functions and enhancements added to this build:

1) _____

2) _____

3) _____

4) _____

List 3rd-party software and versions and libraries used in the build:

1) _____

2) _____

3) _____

4) _____

List any special installation instructions:

1) _____

2) _____

3) _____

4) _____

Special additional build comments: _____

Fig. 4.2 Version Description Document Template

level, the CCB prioritizes the defects according to severity and assigns repair priorities. The project-level CCB also serves as an arbitration board for disputes between developers and testers arising from defect reports.

4.4.3.2 Levels of Authority

Software components are promoted or demoted (these terms refer to a transition in the level of authority required to approve changes) as required during the process of engineering, constructing, and testing a software change. Access to each level must be restricted on the following bases:

☞ Developers can only promote software to test when it is ready.

☞ Testers can promote software to staging when it has passed all testing.

☞ At the staging level, only the project leader or a representative from the CCB or other reviewing body can move the software to production.

If the software is deemed unfit for release, the project manager can demote the software to the appropriate lower level for more work. The tester or test project leader can demote software from testing to development when it fails any level of testing.

Software remains at the development level while the developer is implementing and unit testing the requested changes. At this level, the developer can check software components in and out of the repository. When development is complete, the software is promoted to the test level. Here, it is integration, system, and regression tested. Testers are able to check software in and out as needed. When testing is complete, the software is promoted to the staging level. Now it is ready for final review and release to production. If the software does not pass testing it is demoted back to development for further work.

4.4.3.3 SCM Checklists

Checklists are invaluable for assuring that everyone remembers to complete any of the SCM activities for which they are responsible. These can include:

1. Developer's checklist
2. Tester's checklist
3. Project leader's checklist
4. Database administrator's checklist
5. Network administrator's checklist
6. Data center administrator's checklist
7. System administrator's check list

4.4.3.4 SCM Repository Structure

Directory Structure Reference   The top level consists of directories for each of the projects under development, and a utility and library directory contains the source code for the support developer libraries, the general use application systems, and the application systems that are used to develop or prepare installation packages.

Developers can compile the support library code and link these libraries with code that is stored in the subdirectories below the project directories. Therefore, the libraries in the library directory are those that are common to all of the applications systems.

☞ The top-level directories are the project directories.

☞ At least one or more build directories will reside under each of the project directories

☞ Below the build directory level are subdirectories for source and support files

Build Subdirectory Usage   The following is a list of suggested source and support file directory names.

☞ Source—source files

☞ Data—contains input and/or output data for application systems

☞ Documentation—contains .fm, .msg, .hlp, .doc, and other help files

☞ Testing—contains files used in testing

☞ Package—contains installation files

☞ Desktop publishing—contains word processor and desktop publishing documents

☞ Miscellaneous—contains files that do not fall in any of the categories above

Note: Miscellaneous files should not be any that are required for compiling. Also, the project manager is encouraged to create subdirectories within the source and support file directories to facilitate coherent organization of files.

At the top level, an SCM dictionary should include a description of the current approved directory structure and the recommended source and support file directory names. The dictionary should also list those application systems that deviate from these subdirectory naming conventions. This dictionary will be coordinated and maintained by the quality assurance staff.

A README file which gives an overview of how the application system or subsystem is constructed will accompany its respective make file and be stored in the same directory as the make file.

Build Management Process   Build management controls the creation of deliverable products in the software development Construction phase. Build management should be a defined process that is supported by an automated build utility software package. Build management should be a major component with an overall version control process.

Build management should be centralized around a person who controls the build process: the build administrator. The administrator should be familiar with software configuration management and version control principles and should be skilled with automated SCM tools. She or he should follow a standardized build process that is repeatable across builds for the same project and across builds for different projects.

Builds should occur on a separate server—not on the development server. The completed build should be operationally tested prior to release to testing. The build administrator can be charged with the testing, or a dedicated resource can be added. If the build is deemed operational, it is then copied to the test server.

The build process should either be checklist-driven or scripted for automation. The build components should be documented in a bill-of-materials (BOM) list. Figure 4.3 illustrates a BOM list as it might be used for PowerBuilder development. Where possible version-control headers should be manually or automatically inserted into build components. A build description document (a readme.doc file, *Pathname*) should be created and updated after each build. It should include descriptions of error fixes and new functionality.

Builds should occur often enough to satisfy construction phase deadlines, but must be limited to enough interim time as not to interfere with testing. Although automated test tools allow regression testing between builds, the time required depends on the number of software components under test. When there is enough time, one build per week is ideal.

4.4.3.5 Build Procedures

Development Procedures The following procedures should be completed when project development is ready to release a package build to SCM/QA Build Administrator:

1. All source and related files for this build are checked into the SCM repository.
2. All action is completed on problem reports (PRs) to be included in this build and a list of these PRs is generated.
3. All unit testing is completed.
4. All makefiles are updated to current standards.
5. All files are tagged with the correct revision level.
6. A build script is created or updated that checks out from the repository the correct revision-level tagged files and executes the build.
7. The build script creates the proper installable package.
8. A README and BOM file are created detailing the build contents and build environment (see Figure 4.4).
9. A unit testing certification form is completed and approved by the project manager and/or task leader (see Figure 4.4).
10. The unit testing certification form is submitted to SCM/QA (or build agent). SCM/QA (or build agent) is notified via e-mail of the release.

I. Application Component
    Target Platform
    DLLs
    EXEs
    INIs
    HLPs
    Destination Paths

II. PB Components
    Runtime
    DLLs
    EXEs
    INIs
    HLPs
    Destination Paths

III. ODBC Components
    CNT
    DLLs
    EXEs
    HLPs
    Destination Paths

IV. Database Components:
    Drivers
    DLLs
    Destination Paths

V. Reusable Components

VI. INI Settings
    Install
    ODBC
    Database
    Application

VII. Registry Entries

VIII. Install Information
    Configuration File
    Application Install Files
    Space Requirements
    Install Media
    Install Scripts
    Install Directions

Fig. 4.3 Software Build Management BOM for PowerBuilder

Date: _____

Project: _____

Author/Developer Name: _____

Software Unit Under Test: _____

Certification Checklist

Verified All Inputs Sources	Yes_____	No_____
Verified All Output Types	Yes_____	No_____
Verified Presence of All GUI Controls	Yes_____	No_____
Verified Initial States of All GUI Controls	Yes_____	No_____
Verified Keyboard Access to All Features	Yes_____	No_____
Verified Mouse Access to All Features	Yes_____	No_____
Verified All Client Functions	Yes_____	No_____
Verified All Server Functions	Yes_____	No_____
Verified All Database Procedures/Calls	Yes_____	No_____

Special Features Tested: *Passed*   *Failed*

1. _____   _____   _____

2. _____   _____   _____

3. _____   _____   _____

4. _____   _____   _____

5. _____   _____   _____

All dates Y2K Compliant   Yes_____   No_____

Known Unit Test Deficiencies:

1. _____

2. _____

3. _____

4. _____

5. _____

Defects Discovered in Integration Test Cycles:

1. _____

2. _____

3. _____

4. _____

5. _____

Comments: _____

Author/Developer Signature: _____

Project Leader Signature: _____

Fig. 4.4 Unit Test Certification Form

4.4.3.6 SCM/QA Build Administrator Procedures

1. The unit testing certification form is checked to determine project release version.
2. The submittal of a PR list is verified.
3. The files are checked out of the repository onto the build machine and the installable package is built, using the project's build script.
4. A log of the build script is recorded and checked for errors and proper libraries.
5. At the top-level directory, a list of version levels for each file is created.
6. A README and BOM file have been submitted and are complete.
7. The install package is copied to an archive and labeled with the proper release version. The package is available for testing.
8. The README and BOM are copied to the appropriate manifest directory repository.
9. Notification of the completed build is made via e-mail to all appropriate persons.

4.4.4 Post-Release SCM

4.4.4.1 Software Change Requests   After the initial post-beta release of the system, changes should be tracked via a manual or automated software change request (SCR). SCRs can be generated from a number of sources (e.g., a trouble report or a request for system enhancement). Problem reports are statements that the software as supplied to the customer does not conform to a system specification or is defective in some other manner. Customers, testers, and/or developers can generate problem reports. Enhancement requests are petitions to change the software as initially delivered. These petitions are generated for engineering changes (e.g., for performance improvements or extended functionality) or just cosmetic improvements.

SCM Statement of Work   A written statement of work must be generated which the Configuration Control Board or other body/person can use to determine the validity of an SCR and to assign responsibility to the appropriate developer or development team.

The process of change control assures all software changes are completed in accordance with the change authority and with the SCR statement of work.

The change control process should produce an audit log that can be used to verify the changes.

This is different from configuration control, which is the process of restricting changes to authorized changes only and assuring that production system changes occur only as a result of an approved change authority. Configuration control is implemented via central database repository framework that is partitioned into three software storage levels: development, test, and production.

4.4.4.2 Peer Reviews   Peer reviews should be conducted for all test products, including test requirements, test plans, test cases, test procedures, and test data. Peer reviews are described in the Requirements phase of the development methodology.

Peer Review Process   Although informal review sessions do not accomplish as much as formal review sessions, it is possible to bog down the review process by placing too much structure on it. This section describes a semiformal peer review process that can be used on IS projects to prevent defects and to improve the quality of the resulting products. The process accommodates the aggressive schedule and RAD nature of client-server software development projects.

The review process documented here can be used to conduct requirements document reviews (requirements walkthroughs), design document reviews (design walkthroughs), code listing reviews (code inspections), test plan reviews, test case specification reviews, and test results reviews.

The three-stage process described below is based on the work of King [6] and described in Mosley [8]. Each of the three stages has recommended schedules, timing, and activities based on the product under review.

Prereview Stage   The prereview stage begins when a review packet is given to all of the participants. The review packet contains all materials applicable to the product being reviewed; the guidelines for reviewing the product; rules that govern how the review will occur; and a quick description of who, what, when, and where involvements.

The guidelines for reviewing the product can be as simple as a checklist that is to be followed. The rules are a standard handout that explains the purpose of a review, the seriousness of a review, and the responsibilities of the attendees. The quick description names the attendees, the time, and the location of the review meeting proper.

The prereview stage is where the real work of the review is accomplished. Its purpose is to identify as many of the problems with the product before coming to the actual review session. The attendees should use the prereview time to examine the product in detail. While doing so, they should identify potential problem areas and create a written list which will be brought to the review meeting.

Review Stage   The purpose of the review stage is to bring designated attendees together as a group and discuss the problems that were identified during the prereview stage. Some new problems will be identified during the review, but the focus is on the problems the attendees have already identified. Some problems identified during the prereview stage will turn out to be insignificant when discussed in the review session.

A secondary objective of the review meeting will be to prioritize the problems based on importance. The prioritized problems will be entered into an action list, the written problem descriptions that the product's author will use to guide the rework cycle.

The review session lasts no longer than two hours. If more time is needed, the review will be divided into single two-hour sessions scheduled across several days.

Follow-up Stage   The follow-up stage is the period in which the product is changed and corrected. Another review might follow this stage. The rule-of-thumb is that any product that changes by 25% or more as a result of a review should be rereviewed. The authors must provide a written list of the changes and corrected problems to the project manager at the end of the follow-up stage.

Controls   The project manager will provide the QA analyst with a copy of the product under review. The QA analyst schedules a peer review for the specified product and prepares and distributes the prereview packet. The QA analyst also attends the review meeting and monitors the follow-up stage. If necessary, the QA analyst schedules a second review for the same product.

Review Timing Guidelines   Table 4.3 contains estimates of the time required for each review stage based on the product under review. The estimates are intended as guidelines to be modified based on the time available, the complexity of the product under review, and so forth. Each project and each project-specific product have unique characteristics that affect the timing considerations.

4.4.5 Defect Tracking and Problem Reporting

Administering software testing is one of the more labor-intensive tasks. It is particularly so during the later phases of testing (during the execution of test cases, the locating and repairing of errors, and the retesting cycles). Defect tracking and problem reporting are crucial to this part of the testing process.

Table 4.3 Review Timing Guidelines

Product Stage	Requirements Definition	High-Level Design	Low-Level Design	Source Code	Test Plans	Test Cases	Test Results
Preview Stage	1–5 days	1–5 days	1–3 days	1–3 days	1–3 days	1 day	1 day
Review Stage	1–3 days	1–3 days	1–2 days	1–2 days	1 day	1 day	1 day
Follow–up Stage	7–10 days	3–5 days	3–5 days	3–5 days	3–5 days	2 days	2 days

Thus, developing a defined defect tracking reporting process and picking the right automated tool to support it can make or break your testing process.

With respect to defining the defect tracking/problem reporting process, one approach is to investigate the professional standards available in this area. For example, *IEEE Std-829 Standard for Software Test Documentation* [14] defines a Test Incident Report as having four sections:

1. Test-incident report identifier
2. Summary
3. Incident description
4. Impact

Section 1 is a unique identifier assigned to a specific test incident.

Section 2 summarizes the situation in which the incident occurred. It lists the test items involved and specifies the revision level. It includes references to the test procedure, the test case, and the test log.

Section 3 provides a description of the incident. It includes the following items:

☞ Inputs
☞ Expected results
☞ Actual results
☞ Anomalies
☞ Date and time
☞ Procedure step
☞ Environment
☞ Attempts to repeat
☞ Testers
☞ Observers

Section 4 attempts to predict the test incident's impact on the testing process and its products.

Bill Perry's *A Standard for Test Application Software 1992* [9] has a Problem Tracking Report format that includes the following items:

☞ Product name
☞ Identifier
☞ Severity
☞ Date
☞ Originator
☞ Originator phone number
☞ Test number
☞ Defect category

☞ Defect description

☞ Function tested

☞ Test case

☞ Expected results

☞ Actual results

☞ Attachments

☞ Recommendation

☞ Action taken

4.4.5.1 Defect Tracking/Problem Reporting Process Issues Perhaps the most fruitful approach to defining a problem tracking process is to look at the pertinent issues. A number of relevant process issues loom large before any group trying to design and implement a defect tracking/problem reporting process [5]. They are:

1. How do we manage defects and problems?
2. How do we track defect trends in development projects?
3. How do we manage and track workflow?

     communicate the changes that must be made to the developer(s) assigned

     communicate that the change is completed and what code was changed to QA

     control retest and rework cycles

4. How do we know when a problem has been resolved?
5. How do we know when the software is ready for retest?
6. How do we know if and when the system has been retested?
7. What data is required to support defect tracking and problem reporting?

     single database?

     multiple databases?

8. How do we integrate defect tracking/problem reporting data from multiple sources?

A process that addresses as many of these issues as possible is the basis of a good defect tracking/problem reporting system. In the real world, however, defining a process that fits all needs is not easy.

On one consulting project, I was charged with finding a defect tracking/ problem reporting process that would support three standalone reporting systems already in place and one SCM tool. SQA TeamTest was chosen as the new standard for automated testing in the organization. Previously, MS Access had been used to track defects and report problems. SupportMagic was used by the help desk to track support calls. Finally, PVCS was used for software configuration management. My challenge was to integrate these databases into a workable system.

After some legwork, I found that MS Access could attach to the Paradox tables in SQA (current versions of SQA and Rational test suites use either MS Access or SQL Server as the defect tracking database) and that Access could load the B-Trieve database of SupportMagic. Of course, this was not a perfect solution because it was a one-way stream from SQA to Access to Support-Magic. I also found out that integration to PVCS was not so simple. In fact, this requirement was much more easily fulfilled with PVCS Tracker, which was designed and constructed to work directly with PVCS itself.

The system would support a process that allowed a limited number of SQA users to enter defects into the test repository. It would also allow the developers and testers who did not have SQA TeamTest to enter defects via the Access database. It would allow help desk persons to view defects and their current status in production systems when they experience problems and require fixes. Finally, the link to PVCS would allow the direct tracking of software modules as they were repaired. In this example, the defect reporting history within the company and the available tools were the process definition drivers.

4.4.6 Defect Tracking/Problem Reporting Objectives

We can formulate a set of objectives for a defect tracking/problem reporting system that are based on the issues and the example discussed above. The system must:

1. Provide the ability to track defects/problems
2. Provide defect tracking database integration
3. Provide project-level data entry support
4. Provide defect tracking/problem reporting workflow management
5. Provide standardized and custom query/reporting capabilities
6. Provide integration to software version management (PVCS) system
7. Provide integration to help desk (SupportMagic) system
8. Provide integration to the MS Access defect tracking and problem reporting system
9. Provide management information (cost of quality) and operational information (support project-level testing process)
10. Facilitate communication among testers/developers, the help desk, and corporate management

4.4.7 Defect Tracking Process Requirements

Based on the objectives above, the defect tracking/problem reporting system we need should provide:

☞ A permanently integrated database for defect tracking/problem reporting

☞ A defect tracking workflow

☞ An audit trail

☞ Control linkages (e.g., defect→code; defect→requirement)

☞ At a minimum, standardized (*IEEE Std-829* [14]) defect/problem documentation

Inputs	Procedure step
Expected results	Environment
Actual results	Attempts to repeat
Anomalies	Testers
Date	Observers
Time	

☞ Minimum additional, non-IEEE, defect/problem reporting documentation

Defect ID	Date assigned
Priority	Estimated time to fix
Severity	Resolution
Test cycle	Resolution description
Test procedure	Fix load date
Test case	Fix load number
Occurrences	Repaired in build
Test requirement	Date closed
Person reporting	Contact person
Defect status	Attachments
Defect action	Rework cycles
Defect description	Owner
Defect symptom	Work around
Found in build	Person investigating
Software module	Emergence/scheduled
Module description	Programming time
Related modules	Process or product
Person assigned	

☞ Customized defect/problem reporting data fields

☞ ACD capability

☞ Predefined queries/reports

☞ Custom query/reporting

☞ Free text searching

☞ Cut and paste

☞ On-screen report display
☞ Printed reports
☞ Support all network types
☞ Provide record locking
☞ Provide data recovery
☞ Support for dial-in access
☞ Interface to the e-mail system
☞ Manual notification
☞ Automatic notification of team members
☞ Password protection of team members
☞ Limited access to functions based on user type

4.5 A DEFECT CLASSIFICATION FRAMEWORK

This section defines a defect severity scale framework for determining defect criticality and the associated defect priority levels to be assigned to errors found in software. *ANSI/IEEE Std 729-1983* Glossary of Software Engineering Terminology defines criticality as "a classification of a software error or fault based on an evaluation of the degree of impact that error or fault on the development or operation of a system (often used to determine whether or when a fault will be corrected)."

The severity framework for assigning defect criticality that has proven most useful in actual testing practice is a five-level scale. The criticality associated with each level is based on the answers to several questions.

First, it must be determined if the defect resulted in a system failure. *ANSI/IEEE Std 729-1983* defines a failure as "the termination of the ability of a functional unit to perform its required function."

Second, the probability of failure recovery must be determined. *ANSI/IEEE 729-1983* defines failure recovery as "the return of a system to a reliable operating state after failure."

Third, it must be determined if the system can do this on its own or if remedial measures must be implemented in order to return the system to reliable operation.

Fourth, it must be determined if the system can operate reliably with the defect present if it is not manifested as a failure.

Fifth, it must be determined if the defect should or should not be repaired.

The following five-level scale of defect criticality addresses these questions.

1. **Critical**—The defect results in the failure of the complete software system, a subsystem, or a software unit (program or module) within the system.

2. **Major**—The defect results in the failure of the complete software system, a subsystem, or a software unit (program or module) within the sys-

tem. There is no way to make the failed component(s) work; however, there are acceptable processing alternatives that will yield the desired result.

3. **Average**—The defect does not result in a failure, but causes the system to produce incorrect, incomplete, or inconsistent results, or the defect impairs the systems usability.

4. **Minor**—The defect does not cause a failure, does not impair usability, and the desired processing results are easily obtained by working around the defect.

5. **Quality exception**—The defect is the result of nonconformance to a standard, is related to the aesthetics of the system, or is a request for an enhancement. Defects at this level may be deferred or even ignored.

In addition to the defect severity level defined above, defect priority level can be used with severity categories to determine the immediacy of repair. A five-repair priority scale has also been commonly used. The levels are:

1. **Resolve immediately**—Further development and/or testing cannot occur until the defect has been repaired. The system cannot be used until the repair has been effected.

2. **Give high attention**—The defect must be resolved as soon as possible because it is impairing development/and or testing activities. System use will be severely affected until the defect is fixed.

3. **Normal queue**—The defect should be resolved in the normal course of development activities. It can wait until a new build or version is created.

4. **Low priority**—The defect is an irritant that should be repaired but repair can be deferred until after more serious defects have been fixed.

5. **Defer**—The defect repair can be put off indefinitely. It can be resolved in a future major system revision or not resolved at all.

The defect severity and defect priority classifications described above are the ones I have successfully used in conjunction with the defect tracking/reporting that is implemented in SQA TeamTest suite and are based on the default categories found in that product with my own modifications.

4.5.1 Defect Repair and Retest

The status-action-workflow is a power component in the arsenal of test management capability SQA TeamTest's Manager provides. It imposes the needed control over the test/repair/retest cycles that normally happen. The status-action-workflow is customizable through the Admin menu in SQA Manager. Many status and action combinations are possible because users can create their own statuses and actions and create rules from them. If you do modify or add new workflow rules, remember that you can box yourself into a resulting status with no way to return to the previous status, which might be necessary at a later point in the workflow. All status-action-workflow rules should be circular in nature to avoid ending in terminal status. A minimal set of statuses and actions for controlling workflow is illustrated in Table 4.4.

SQA comes with most of these already in its default set of statuses and actions. SQA has a default of New for recently entered defects. The *New* status is so similar to the *Open* status that you can delete the New status category and its related actions and set your default status for new defects to be Open.

It is also necessary to add an action of *Defer* and a resulting status of *On-Hold* for defects that are not going to be addressed until a later build or release of the application. Defects are normally assigned to an individual (a developer, a tester, or a manager) when they are in various stages of the repair and retest work. When a defect is postponed, however, it is not assigned until it is reactivated for repair or for retest.

When first opened, a defect can be unassigned or a default assignment can take effect. The default can be either the tester who identified the defect or the project manager (who can assign it to one of the developers). Assigning defects directly to developers can work—taking the load off the project leader—but it often results in developers working to repair defects that are minor when they should be fixing other, more important defects. The project manager frequently has a better perspective about which defects are critical and which should be repaired first.

Table 4.4 Controlling Workflow

Starting Status	Action	Resulting Status
Open	Close	Closed
Open	Defer	On-Hold
Open	Reassign	Open
Open	Repair	Pending Validation
On-Hold	Close	Closed
On-Hold	Reopen	Open
On-Hold	Repair	Pending Validation
Pending Validation	Close	Closed
Pending Validation	Defer	On-Hold
Pending Validation	Reassign	Pending Validation
Pending Validation	Reject	Open
Pending Validation	Validate	Closed
Closed	Reopen	Open

An issue is who can set status and action flows. The user privileges and privilege groups that are established and applied through SQA Manager will control who has what rights. Some rules-of-thumb are:

1. No one, including testers, should be able to delete a defect from the database.
2. Developers should never be able to close a defect—only the tester who originally opened it or the project manager, with the tester's approval, should be able to close a defect.
3. Only the testing or development manager should be able to defer defects.
4. Every user should be able to enter new defects and update existing defects.
5. Every user should be able to reassign defects.

4.5.2 Automated Defect Tracking Tools

In addition to defining a process, it is important to find automated tools to support the process. Rational and Mercury Interactive both offer products (Manager ClearQuest and Test Director, respectively) that automate the planning and control of the testing process. In addition, companies such as Intersolv, Inc., offer SCM products such as PVCS and PVCS Tracker (Tracker is the defect tracking and reporting product), which provide an integrated software development and testing management environment.

Comparable products on the market include Archimedes' BugBase 1.6, Soffont's Track 2.5, and UnderWare's Track Record 1.5. An excellent and comprehensive comparison of PVCS Tracker, BugBase, Track, and Track Record can be found in the June 1995 issue of *Data Based Advisor* [2]. The article found that these products all had built-in multiuser support. They also all allowed users to enter a defect title, a defect description, a defect severity level, a defect status indicator, and the name of the person who originates the defect. Beyond the entries, the products were proprietary in what additional defect data they allowed the user to maintain.

4.5.3 Test Metrics

In order to manage, control, and improve the testing process, we must measure it. Estimates of anticipated defects, along with actual defect counts and measures of structural complexity, test coverage, release readiness, etc., are essential to the testing process. Collecting testing metrics is not always easy, but is a necessary aspect of software testing. Unfortunately, it is also the most frequently omitted testing practice.

Chapter 9 is a complete discussion of software test metrics and includes metrics for test coverage, release readiness, and IEEE software maturity.

4.5.4 Test Automation

SQA TeamTest Suite 6.1 or a similar product should be adopted for use with test management, test execution, and test analysis activities. In addition, all defects should be tracked using the product's defect tracking capabilities.

MS Project or a similar tool should be used to develop Gantt charts and other test management documents that automated test tools cannot provide. The documents should be linked together through a test repository.

MS Word can be used to develop the test plan documents. The documents should be linked together through the test repository.

MS Excel can be used to describe test conditions and construct test data values.

4.6 SOME NOTES ON TEST PLANNING

In the mainframe world, the majority of MIS organizations has traditionally neglected planning across the majority of system development projects. When it is done, it is frequently done informally and the resources allocated for testing are sparse at best.

Test planning should begin before any project development activities. Test planning should be based on organizational testing standards. If your organization does not have test standards, a good place to start developing them is to look at the IEEE standards documents relating to quality assurance and to software testing (information on the IEEE testing standard documents can be found on the World Wide Web as follows: STD 829 Standard for Software Test Documentation, http://bbs.itsi.disa.mil:5580/E2689T2806, STD 1008 Standard for Unit Testing, http://bbs.itsi.disa.mil:5580/E2690T2806). These documents can provide enough information to start your test planning process.

Test planning is usually based on the idea of a formal testing life cycle. I believe, though, that test planning is better done when testing is a function that is integrated into a formal system development life cycle. Each testing technique and its allied activities are associated with a specific SDLC phase. Typically, test planning occurs during the analysis and design phases and test execution occurs during the coding, testing, and implementation phases. Figure 4.5 illustrates an SDLC with integrated testing activities.

This does not mean that test execution is limited to the second half of the SDLC. In fact, review processes (Walkthroughs and Inspections) can be completed for any and all of the analysis and design phase deliverables [8]. It is well known that test processes executed late in the SDLC are not very effective at discovering flaws in the design logic. So, reviewing analysis and design documents as soon as they are available can drastically reduce the number of logic errors in the finished system. Figure 4.6 illustrates the levels at which review processes can be applied in the SDLC.

SDLC Phase	Test Plan Produced	Test Plan Executed
Analysis	System	
Analysis	Regression	
System Design	Integration	
Detailed Design	Unit	
Construction		Unit
Construction		Integration
Test		System
Production/Maintenance		Regression

Fig. 4.5 Test Planning and Execution Integrated with the SDLC

SDLC Phase	Test Plan Produced	Test Plan Executed	Review Requested
Analysis	System		System Test Plan
Analysis	Regression		Regression Test Plan
System Design	Integration		Integration Test Plan
Detailed Design	Unit		Unit Test Plan and Test Case Specification
Construction		Unit	Unit Test Results
Construction		Integration	Integration Test Results
Test		System	System Test Results
Production/Maintenance		Regression	Regression Test Results

Fig. 4.6 Traditional SDLC with Integrated Review Processes

A formal approach to test planning requires a formal approach to software development if it is to be effective. Many client-server practitioners argue that a formal project management approach is not necessary for C-S development. So, how do we test client-server systems? In chapters 2 and 3 of this book I argue that some level of formality is required to construct useful C-S software systems. Furthermore, some level of formality is required, if we are to adequately test C-S systems. Test planning and test execution for C-S systems do require some changes in the way we traditionally think about testing software systems.

In its approach to automating client-server software testing, Segue [13] provides another perspective for partitioning C-S testing with the C-S development cycle. Segue's method is to divide C-S testing into three phases, each containing specific tests. Figure 4.7 illustrates Segue's phased approach to C-S testing.

In phase 1, the testers verify the basic operability of the system. They concentrate on verifying that all of the interface controls the users will need are present, that the controls conform to the design specifications, and that the controls give the users the correct choices and visual cues for operating the application. Testers also verify that the tab key correctly allows users to move through the controls in correct sequence. (In my experience this is something that programmers frequently mess up.)

Another extremely important area that phase 1 addresses is keyboard use. Not everyone is a mouse user. It is necessary to be sure that keyboard short cuts/hot keys are in place and, in particular, that shortcuts/hot keys are not duplicated in the same window (another common problem I have found). (Refer to Figure 5.5A for a list of common GUI errors found in windows, child windows, and dialog boxes.)

Finally, phase 1 deals with user interface (UI) conformance to corporate GUI standards. This is also a common problem with C-S software.

In phase 2, testers verify the "essential" functionality of the system through tests of client-based and server-based functionality between a single

Phase 1 Operability Tests	Phase 2 Functionality Tests	Phase 3 Distributed C-S Tests
Presence of UI Controls	Client-Based Processes	Concurrency Tests
Initial State of UI Controls	Calculations/Values Shown in UI Controls	Trigger Notification Tests
Tab Order	UI Control State Changes	Performance/Load Tests
Keyboard Access	Middleware	
Standards Conformity		
	Server-Based Processes	
	Batch Processes	
	Triggered Processes	
	Database Tests	
	Structure and State Changes	
	Stored Procedures	

Fig. 4.7 Segue Software's Client-Server Testing Life Cycle Approach

client and a single server. During this phase, the testers verify that the processing logic produces the correct values and that the values are correctly displayed by the UI, that interaction with the application processing produces the correct UI control states, that server processes are activated under the correct processing conditions, and that interactions with the database from a single client or server produce the correct responses.

With respect to middleware, this phase verifies that Dynamic Data Exchange (DDE) and Object Linking and Embedding (OLE) occur correctly.

Finally, phase 2 executes a stress test on a single remote client and an extended use test to assure that performance does not degrade over time.

In phase 3, the system is tested under multiuser conditions. This usually involves multiple clients interacting with a single server, but may also include multiple clients interacting with multiple servers.

The testing verifies that, during current use, data locking, data access, and data modification function as expected, that events that trigger other events function as expected, and that system performance under varying load conditions is acceptable.

4.6.1 Test Planning in the Real World

The ideal test plan is one that is based on the project specifications. In the real world project specifications are formulated by committee. Project managers meet and come to some consensus as to what the project "really" is. The specifications may or may not be written down and are almost always wrong. They end up being changed as the managers review the partially completed system components. So, where does this put the test plan?

First, it prevents the test plan from being created as early in the development process as it should be. Second, it makes the current version of the test plan out of date as soon as you begin to write it. Third, it causes the test plan to be created after a good portion of the code has already been written. So, why even write a test plan? I think that Saile [12] said it best: "Your test plan is a brainstorming and communications document. No matter what the actual specifications of the product are, there are still many details that you need to think through."

4.6.2 Test Planning for Client-Server Systems

In many instances, testing client-server software cannot be planned from the perspective of traditional integrated SDLC testing activities because this view either is not applicable at all or is too narrow and other dimensions must be considered.

First, C-S test planning must include consideration of the different hardware and software platforms on which the system will be used. Many C-S systems are implemented across several platforms and are expected to be executed equally well on all of them. Second, C-S test planning must also take into account network and database server performance issues with which mainframe systems did not have to deal. Third, C-S test planning has to consider the replication of data and processes across networked servers. C-S test planning cannot assume that a formal project management approach with defined development stages will exist for client-server projects.

In many cases, the RAD nature of client-server development (see the discussion of the CSSIRD approach above) calls for another approach to development and testing that is more practical. Because development tends to be cyclic or build-driven, the testers ultimately become responsible for testing the builds that come from each RAD cycle. The builds appear fast and furious, and there is little documentation to help with testing. The tester must complete each test of a build and be ready for another as quickly as possible. This is the time when test plans go out of the window. This type of build/test/build/test is depicted in Figure 4.8.

Thus, test planning should take into account the cyclic nature and the rapidity with which C-S development occurs. This does not mean that a formal test plan would not help. A written test plan with the testing partitioned in test-build cycles for different areas of the system would prove more useful.

Figure 4.9 represents a revised version of the phases of client-server software testing that were illustrated in Figure 4.7. The phased approach is now more detailed and has become cyclic to allow for the iterative nature of client-server software development. Figure 4.10 is a client-server application-level test plan that is based on the phases in Figure 4.9. Together they provide a realistic template for implementing client-server software testing at the build/integration level.

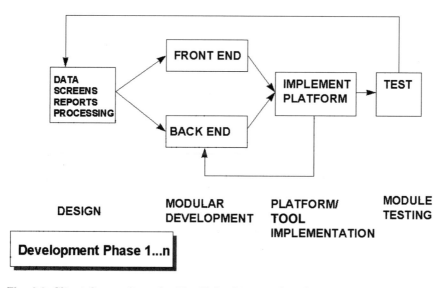

Fig. 4.8 Client-Server Iterative Rapid Application Development Cycle with Testing

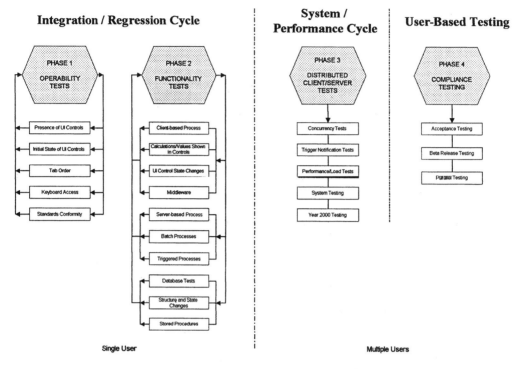

Fig. 4.9 The Phases of Client-Server Software Testing

Fig. 4.10 A Client-Server Software Test Plan Template

I. Introduction
    A. Overview
        Scope
            [General Testing Objectives]
            [Levels of Tests]
            [Types of Tests]
            [Areas Not Being Tested]
            [Risks]
            [Contingencies]
            [Supporting Documents]
        Methods
            [Test Case Design]
            [Test Case Construction]
        Standards
            [Naming Conventions]
            [Standards Reference Documents]

Fig. 4.10 A Client-Server Software Test Plan Template (Continued)

B. Test Environment Requirements
    Hardware (Add Info for All Target Platforms)
        [Network]
        [Workstation Type]
        [Workstation Configuration]
        [Quantity]
        [Required Installation Date]
    Software (Add Info for All Target Platforms)
        [Operating System]
        [OS Configuration]
        [Desktop Packages]
        [Application Software]
        [Runtime Libraries]
        [Utility Software]
        [Automated Test Tools]
    Personnel
        [Testers]
        [Developers]
        [Users]
        [Database]
        [Network]
        [Other]
C. Test Management and Procedure Controls
    Test Team
        [Leader]
        [Testers]
        [Other]
    Testing Schedule
        [Gantt Chart]
    Testing Inputs
        [Software Requirements Specification]
        [Software Design Specification]
        [Risk Analysis, if available]
        [Test Requirements Document]
    Testing Deliverables
        [Test Plans]
        [Test Conditions]
        [Test Cases]
        [Test Logs]
        [Test Reports]
        [Defect Reports]
        [Test Metrics]
        [Defect Metrics]

Fig. 4.10 A Client-Server Software Test Plan Template (Continued)

Test Analysis, Reporting, and Tracking Mechanisms
    [Test Repository]
    [Defect Repository]
    [Data Reduction Methods]
    [Data Reduction Tools]
    [Test Tracking and Control Metrics]
    [Defect Tracking and Control Metrics]
Testing Procedure Controls
    [Test Initiation Criteria]
    [Test Execution Criteria]
    [Test Failures Criteria]
    [Test Resumption Criteria]
    [Software Configuration Management/Build Control]
    [Test Configuration Management/Document Control]
    [Defect Specification Criteria]
    [Rework-Retest-Validation-Rejection Controls]
    [Test Completion Criteria]
Testing Management Tools
    [Automated Test Tools to Be Used]
    [Additional Software Control Tools to Be Used, e.g., MS Visual SourceSafe]

II. Operational Test Plan
  A. Graphical User Interface Tests
  GUI Description
    [Verbiage]
    [Screen Print]
  GUI Testing Objectives
    [Verify Presence of GUI Controls]
    [Verify Initial States of GUI Controls]
    [Verify Mouse Access]
    [Verify Keyboard Access]
    [Verify Conformance to GUI Standards]
  GUI Testing Methods
    [GUI Test Case Design]
    [GUI Test Data Creation]
    [GUI Verification Tests]
  GUI Objects to Be Tested
    [Object/Test Condition Matrix]
  GUI Events to Be Tested
    [Event/Test Condition Matrix]
  GUI Verification Testing
    [Manual Test Scripts/Test Cases to Be Executed]
    [Automated Test Scripts/Test Cases to Be Executed]
  GUI Testing Tools

Fig. 4.10 A Client-Server Software Test Plan Template (Continued)

[Automated Test Tools to Be Used]
[Additional Software Productivity Tools to Be Used, e.g., MS Excel or MS Word]
B. Functional Testing
    Functional Testing Objectives
        [Verify Client Application Logic]
        [Verify GUI Control State Changes]
        [Verify Server-Based Application Logic]
        [Verify On-Line Transaction Processing Logic]
        [Verify Batch Processing Logic]
        [Verify Middleware Processes]
        [Verify Application Process-Database Interactions]
        [Verify Database Structure/State Changes]
        [Verify Stored Procedures/Triggers]
        [Verify Single User Performance]
        [Verify Extended Single User Performance]
    Functional Testing Methods
        [Via GUI]
        [Via Drivers or Test Servers]
    Functions to Be Tested
        [Function/Test Condition Matrix]
    Functional Test Data Design
        [Function/Test Case Matrix]
    Functional Test Data Construction
        [Test Database Name]
        [Affected Master Tables]
        [Affected Data Tables]
        [Imported Data, e.g., from Production]
    Functional Verification Testing
        [Manual Test Scripts/Test Cases to Be Executed]
        [Automated Test Scripts/Test Cases to Be Executed]
    Functional Testing Tools
        [List All Automated Test Tools to Be Used, e.g., SQA]
        [List Database Utility Tools, e.g., RapidSQL]
        [Database Utilities to Be Used]

III. Regression (Build) Test Plan
    Regression Test Objectives
        [To Verify that Features that Worked in the Previous Build Still Work]
        [To Verify Any New Functionality in the Current Build]
    Regression Test Data
        [What Test Scripts/Cases Will Be Reused?]
    Regression Test Execution
        [Rerun of Previous Test Scripts/Test Cases]

Fig. 4.10 A Client-Server Software Test Plan Template (Continued)

[Execution of Additional Test Scripts/Cases for New Features]
Regression Test Tools
    [Automated Test Tools to Be Used]
    [Additional Software Productivity Tools to Be Used, e.g., MS Excel or MS Word]
    [Database Utilities to Be Used]

IV. Multi-User Performance Test Plan
Performance Testing Objectives
    [Verify Client Performance]
    [Verify Process Server Performance]
    [Verify Database Server Performance]
    [Verify Web Server Performance]
Performance Testing Methods
    Single User
        [Stress Testing]
        [Volume Testing]
    Multiple User
        [Stress Testing]
        [Volume Testing]
Performance Test Data Creation
Performance Verification Testing
Test Tools
    [Automated Test Tools to Be Used]
    [Additional Test Tools to Be Used, e.g., Network Sniffers]
    [Database Utilities to Be Used]

V. System Testing
System Testing Objectives
    [Business Scenarios to Be Tested]
System Test Case Design/Construction
    [Behavioral Analysis of Business Scenarios]
    [Business Scenario Test Script Creation]
System Testing Methods
    [Business Scenario Verification Testing]
    [Business Scenario Validation Testing]
System Testing Tools
    [Automated Test Tools to Be Used]
    [Additional Software Productivity Tools to Be Used, e.g., MS Excel or MS Word]
    [Database Utilities to Be Used]

VI. Acceptance Testing
Acceptance Testing Objectives
    [Business Scenarios to Be Tested]

Fig. 4.10 A Client-Server Software Test Plan Template (Continued)

Acceptance Test Case Design/Construction
   [Behavioral Analysis of Business Scenarios]
   [Business Scenario Test Script Creation]
Acceptance Testing Methods
   [Business Scenario Verification Testing]
   [Business Scenario Validation Testing]
Acceptance Testing Tools
   [Automated Test Tools to Be Used]
   [Additional Software Productivity Tools to Be Used, e.g., MS Excel or MS Word]
   [Database Utilities to Be Used]

4.6.3 The Test Team

Normally, a formal test team should consist of a manager, one or more analysts, and a body of other "interested individuals." Interested individuals can include the software's author(s), quality assurance analysts, end users, or computer operators. Anyone who must interact with the system is eligible. (A good psychiatrist would have helped on most of the projects in which I was involved.)

From a client-server perspective, the test team makes better sense if it is a test/development team consisting of one or more testers and one or more developers. In the RAD environment, testers do a better job when working directly with the developer(s).

4.7 THE CLIENT-SERVER TEST PLAN: AN OUTLINE AND EXAMPLES

The client-server test plan outline in Figure 4.10 is intended to be a guide to the areas of client-server testing that must at least be considered [3,8]. The sections of the test plan outline that are useful depend on the nature of the C-S system you are developing. The outline is also malleable as it can be changed to suit your C-S development needs and entire sections can be deleted if not needed. You may notice a similarity between the outline and the layout of topics in this book.

I worked on one C-S project in which it made more sense to organize the test plan around the structure of the software than to use the outline in Figure 4.9. In that instance, the functionality of the system was divided by whether specific functions belonged to the system infrastructure (communications) or whether they supported desktop data entry. The desktop involved a presentation, a process, and database layers. The infrastructure functions were hidden objects within the system and they tied all of the other layers together. The best approach was to use the test plan outline illustrated in Figure 4.11 and then assess the project along functional lines with the test plan phases.

Fig. 4.11 Revised Client-Server Test Plan Based on Application Functionality

Document ID
Document Locator

I. Introduction
  Scope
    General Testing Objectives
    Levels of Tests
    Types of Tests
    Areas Not Being Tested
    Supporting Documents
  Methods
    Test Case Design and Construction
  Standards

II. Environmental Requirements
  Hardware
  Software
  Personnel

III. Work Flow and Deliverables
  Testing Responsibilities
  Testing Milestones
  Testing Deliverables

IV. Test Management and Procedure Controls
  Testing Management
    Test Team
    Testing Schedule
    Required Resources
    Testing Deliverables
    Test Analysis, Reporting, and Tracking Mechanisms
      Defect Identification
      Defect Tracking
      Testing Quality Metrics
      Testing Process Improvement Metrics
  Testing Procedure Controls
    Test Initiation
    Test Execution
    Test Failures
    Configuration Management
    Document Control

V. Graphical User Interface Test Plan
  GUI Description
  GUI Testing Objectives
  GUI Testing Methods

Fig. 4.11 Revised Client-Server Test Plan Based on Application Functionality (Continued)

GUI Objects to Be Tested
GUI Test Case Design
GUI Test Data Creation
GUI Verification Tests
GUI Testing Tools

VI. Server Test Plan

Server Testing Objectives
Server Testing Methods
Server Functions to Be Tested
Stress Testing
Volume Testing
Server Test Data Creation
Server Verification Testing
Test Tools

VII. Network Test Plan

Network Testing Objectives
Network Testing Methods
Network Functions to Be Tested
Performance Testing
Stress Testing
Network Test Data Creation
Network Verification Testing
Network Testing Tools

VIII. Functional Testing

Functional Testing Objectives
Functional Testing Methods
Functions to Be Tested
Functional Test Data Creation
Black Box
Cause-Effect Graphing
Equivalence Partitioning
Boundary Analysis
Error Guessing
Gray Box
Decision Logic Tables
White Box
Basis Testing
Functional Verification Testing
Functional Testing Tools

IX. System Testing

System Testing Objectives
System Testing Methods

Fig. 4.11 Revised Client-Server Test Plan Based on Application Functionality (Continued)

> Business Scenarios to Be Tested
> Business Scenario Test Script Creation
> Business Scenario Verification Testing
> Business Scenario Validation Testing
> System Testing Tools
>
> **X. Regression Testing**
> Regression Testing Objectives
> Regression Testing Methods
> Regression Testing Tools

(Sources: The Gartner Group, Inc., Recommendations [3] and Mosley [7].)

I see this as a mistake that many C-S testers will be prone to make. The easiest part of the C-S system to develop is the GUI. Thus, the underlying functionality is usually coded after the GUI screens are completed. This can lead the tester astray because the GUI is tangible and it can be tested and what appears to be the system is only an empty shell. Also, developers frequently map out the GUI requirements in the formal requirements document but omit the functions that support the GUI screen. A client-server system is far more than just a GUI, and client-server testing is far more than just testing the GUI.

4.7.1 Test Plan Verification

Test plan verification is an extremely important activity [8]. It involves a peer review session with the testing manager, the test analyst, the developer(s), the development team leader, and, optionally, a user representative.

The review session should last no longer than two hours and should produce an "action list" which the test analyst can use to fortify the test plan. Excellent discussions of review procedures can be found in many texts [6, 8].

4.7.2 Some Notes on Regression Testing

Regression testing is one of the most profitable forms of testing you can implement. It has been shown that corrections to software during the maintenance cycle can introduce up to ten new errors for each error corrected. The errors are of two types: errors contained in the changed or enhanced code and errors that occur in related, but unchanged, code. Regression testing is extremely effective at identifying both kinds of error, but it is particularly useful in finding errors in functions related to the changed feature.

4.7.3 Regression Testing Objectives

The fundamental regression testing objective is to assure that all application system features remain functional after the introduction of corrections and enhancements to the production system. A second objective is to test any new, corrected, or enhanced system features. A third objective is to assure that the system documentation is kept current.

4.7.4 Regression Testing Procedures

Regression testing includes running previously conducted tests to ensure that unchanged system functions continue to function properly. It also requires reviewing user manuals to ensure that they are properly updated. It further includes reviewing system requirements and system design documents to ensure that they reflect the system's current functional architecture.

With the appearance of the recent generation of structured capture/ replay automated test tools, regression testing can be accomplished easier and more economically than before. The test scripts that were developed to test the system during integration/system testing can be recorded with tools such as SQA TeamTest Robot, Segue's QA Partner, Mercury Interactive's WinRunner, and Vermont Creative Software's Vermont High Test. Once recorded, the test scripts can be replayed to verify the system's interface, its database, and its functionality.

The initial recording is labor intensive and adds to development and testing costs, but the long-term savings can be substantial. Automated test scripts can be executed in an unattended batch environment, saving labor costs. One caveat is that automated test suites do require maintenance when certain software and hardware platform changes occur. These issues are discussed in depth in chapter 5.

4.8 TEST-RX METHODOLOGY: STEPS AND ACTIVITIES

4.8.1 Step 1.1: Staffing and Resources (Assemble the Test Team)

4.8.1.1 Purpose The test team performs verification and validation relating to implementation. For a specific project, the purpose of the test team is (1) to verify and validate the deliverables from development and deliver solutions during integration/build regression testing, system testing, acceptance testing, and application regression testing; and (2) to act as consultants to the development team during unit testing. The test team should be organized concurrently with the development team.

4.8.1.2 Timing Tasks 1.1.1–1.1.3 should be completed during the project planning phase of the application development methodology. Tasks 1.2.1 and

1.2.2 should be executed during the detailed design phase. For RAD C-S development, there should be a completed design anaylsys.

4.8.1.3 Tasks

Task 1.1.1: Identify Key Application Areas This task identifies the key application areas that must be involved in testing. It should also identify the testing group's responsibilities to those areas. For example, testing might be responsible to development for integration testing and system testing and to solution delivery for release testing.

Task 1.1.2: Identify Key Individuals This task identifies important individuals who will be involved, both directly and indirectly, in the testing process. The persons selected as members of the test team will be directly responsible for testing activities while others who act as sponsors will be indirectly involved.

Specific individuals involved in the test should include the following:

1. Quality assurance manager
2. Quality assurance analysts
3. Test manager
4. Test analysts
5. Project manager
6. Project team leader(s)
7. Analysts
8. Programmers
9. Database services personnel
10. Network services personnel
11. Data center (Operations) personnel
12. Customers

Task 1.1.3: Assign Individual Responsibilities The test team members will be responsible for:

1. Developing the test plan
2. Defining the required test resources
3. Designing test cases
4. Constructing test cases
5. Executing test cases in accordance with the test plan
6. Managing test resources
7. Analyzing test results
8. Issuing test reports
9. Recommending application improvements
10. Maintaining test statistics

Individual assignments must be made so that each area of responsibility is covered and someone can be held accountable. MS project can be used to accomplish this.

4.8.1.4 Outputs

Output 1.1: Statement of Application Areas When using an automated test tool, electronic copies of the documents should be linked and accessed via the test repository, as in SQA TeamTest Manager's **Test Plan** command on the **Test Assets** menu.

Output 1.2: Statement of Team Member Responsibilities This statement assigns specific responsibilities to the members of the test team. This should be the first step in the creation of the Test Work plan that is described in Task 1.3. The work plan should be developed in Microsoft Project or in the management component of an automated test tool.

The first action is to list the testing tasks to be completed. This should be followed by a review of the tasks by all of the test team members. When a consensus has been reached that the list is correct and complete, an individual team member must be assigned to each task. A final review based on each member's workload should be completed. MS Project makes this easy as it has several reports that will provide workload, as well as other statistics.

Output 1.3: Test Team Work Plan The work plan defines milestones and tentative completion dates for all assigned tasks. Microsoft Project can be used to create a Gantt Chart, which illustrates who is responsible for what and when.

The Gantt Chart should be appended to the test plan that is created in Step 4 below.

As above, electronic copies of the MS project files can be linked and accessed via the test repository.

4.8.1.5 Step 1.2: Approve the Test Environment/Resources: Tasks

Task 1.2.1: Approve Test Environment The purpose of this task is to verify that the required test environment (e.g., test lab networked clients machines) is in place before testing starts.

There are many types of test environments, ranging from very informal ones, where testing is completed at developer/tester workstations, to very formal test laboratories, where software is tested under conditions approximating the production milieu. The formality of the test climate is a function of available resources. Most test environments lie somewhere in between formal and informal.

What this means to the test team is that some resources will be scarce and some will not be available. Deficiencies in the test environment ultimately affect the implementation of the test plans. Some classes of tests may have to be omitted. It is important that the testing manager along with the test team members inform the development team and their management of any shortcomings that will affect testing. A formal statement of test environment/ resource deficiencies should be written and all responsible parties must sign off on the list.

Task 1.2.2: Approve Test Resources   The purpose of this task is to review and verify that all the required resources have been allocated and are available before testing begins. The resources can include people, funding, time, software tools, and the test environment.

The required test resources should be identified and put in a written statement that will be distributed to development management. Both the development manager and the testing manager should review the resources. The test team must further review any changes that are requested. When consensus has been achieved, all involved parties should sign off on the list of required resources.

It is important to identify all of the required testing resources before testing begins; however, that is not always possible. Any time identified test resources will be scarce or unavailable, it is the test team's responsibility to make the testing manager aware of the consequences. The testing manager must either find the resources or make development managers aware of the problem and its possible consequences.

Deficiencies in the test resources might affect the implementation of the test plans. Some classes of tests may have to be omitted. It is important that the testing manager along with the test team members inform the development team and their management of any missing resources that will affect testing. A formal statement of test resource deficiencies should be written and all responsible parties should sign off on the list.

4.8.2 Step 2: Perform Risk Analysis

4.8.2.1 Purpose   The purpose of business risk analysis during software testing is to identify high-risk application components that must be tested thoroughly and to identify error-prone components within specific applications that also must be tested rigorously. The results of the analysis can be used to determine the testing objectives (see Step 3) during test planning. The question that is being asked is "what parts of the system under test *absolutely must work?*"

The risk assessment should be performed as a separate task during the requirements gathering phase in the overall system development life cycle methodology. If this is not the case, the test team must perform its own risk assessment for each testing project.

When the assessment has already been performed, those data can be analyzed from a testing perspective. Additional data capture may be necessary, however, depending on how the project-level assessment was done. One way to avoid extra work is to include test team members in those risk assessment sessions. In addition, test-related questions should be included in the project-level risk assessment questionnaire.

When, and if, it is necessary for the test group to perform an assessment, the checklists illustrated below should be used. They can be modified as necessary.

The key to performing a successful risk analysis is to formalize the process. An informal approach to risk analysis methods leads to an ineffective analysis process.

Perry describes four risk analysis methods which testers can employ [9]. Each method applies a different level of formality to the risk assessment procedure. Automated risk assessment software packages are available that use the second and third approaches above; however, testers can create their own risk assessment questionnaires with MS Word and do the what-if-analysis with MS Excel. This is the approach we will use for C-S development projects.

Any of the suggested approaches could be used for testing projects; however, Identifying and Weighting Risk Factors is the most practical and applies a reasonable level of formality. It also produces the most accurate estimate of risk. This approach identifies and weights risk factors along three project dimensions: project structure, project size, and experience with technology. It is the method that is used here.

With respect to project structure, the more structured a project is the fewer the risks are. Thus, software development projects that employ some type of project management/development life cycle approach should be at less risk.

Project size is directly proportional to risk: The larger the project in terms of cost, staff, time, number of functional areas involved, etc., the greater the risk.

Technology experience is inversely proportional to project risk. The more experience the development team has with the hardware, the operation system, the database, the network, and the development language, the less the risk.

4.8.2.2 Timing The risk assessment should be performed during the Requirements phase of the methodology. It should be reviewed and updated during the General Design and Detailed Design phases. For C-S RAD development, the assessment should be performed during analysis.

From Requirements Phase

Risk assessment data (If performed by development team)

Context diagram

Data model

Process model

Control requirements

Performance requirements

4.8.2.3 Tasks

Task 2.1: Ascertaining the Risk Score   This involves conducting a risk assessment review with the development team. During the session a risk assessment questionnaire is used to structure the process. Each question is asked of the development team members in group session and a consensus is reached as to the perceived level of risk (an alternative approach would be to have individual developers each fill out the questionnaire and consolidate the responses). The questions are closed-end questions with the possible responses of Low, Medium, High, and Not Applicable. A numeric rating is assigned to the response. A final score is calculated using weighting by which the numeric rating is multiplied. The weighted scores are used to identify error-prone areas of the application and to compare the application with other applications.

The entire test team along with end-user representatives should be included in the session. Conduct the session early in the test process. It should last no more than two hours. It should be run formally by the test team manager who facilitates the session. The session should have two objectives. The first objective is to answer each question on the risk assessment questionnaire. The second is to brainstorm and let the participants voice their concerns about the system under development.

Task 2.2: Creating the Risk Profile   The weighted score reflects the importance of each area. Areas that are twice as important can be weighted with a value of 2 (e.g., an area with medium risk [2 points] could be considered twice as important as the other areas and have a final weighted score of $2 \times 2 = 4$ points [the weight multiplied by the risk points]). A total score is computed for the project, but the individual scores are used to develop the risk profile. Use the following approach (Perry's approach with some extensions) to construct the profile.

Once the risk data have been collected, create an MS Excel spreadsheet that computes the weighted scores. Sort the tabulated scores from the highest to the lowest (a pseudo-frequency distribution of sorts) and perform a Pareto Analysis (the 80/20 rule) [8] to determine what project areas fall into the upper 20% of the distribution. These are the areas that are most at risk and they are the areas that will need to be most tested. The results are rather obvious when charted using Kiviat Charts (radar charts), as shown in Figure 4.12. The high-risk areas stand out visually. (The charting should be done based on data sorted in ascending order by question number, not on data sorted in descending order by highest to lowest for the Pareto Analysis.)

Task 2.3: Modify the Risk Characteristics (this task is optional for testing)
Once the areas at risk have been identified, a proactive approach can reduce risk. Steps can be taken to change the development approach or the project

structure in order to reduce risk. When these alternatives are not feasible, the task of using the risk information to decide what areas to test becomes even more critical.

Task 2.4: Allocate the Resources Perry suggests allocating the most test resources to the high-risk areas, allocating less testing resources to medium-risk areas, and minimal testing resources to low-risk testing areas. A sound strategy is to assure that all, or as many as is possible, of the medium- to high-risk areas are tested. A possible split could be to commit 80% of the testing resources to medium- and high-risk areas, and commit the remaining 20% to low-risk areas. This is again applying the 80/20 rule.

Task 2.5: Compile a Risk Assessment Database A risk assessment database has two important functions. First, it can be used to improve the risk assessment process itself. Second, the data can be used to help management plan and structure development projects.

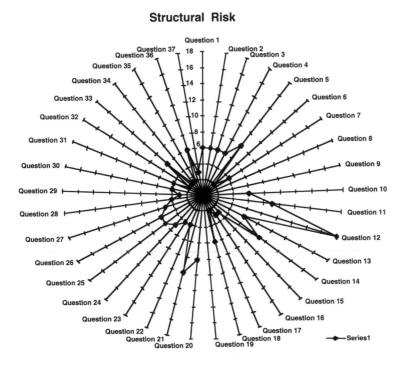

Fig. 4.12 Kiviat Charts of the RPS Project Risk Assessment Results

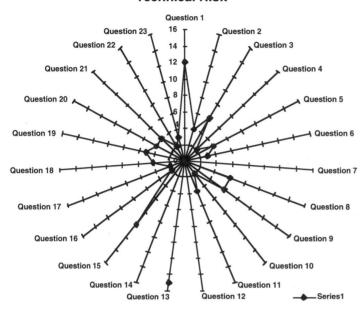

Fig. 4.12 Kiviat Charts of the RPS Project Risk Assessment Results (Continued)

4.8.2.4 Outputs

Output 2.1: Completed Assessment Questionnaires (Task 2.1) As the risk assessment review is completed, a preliminary score for each question should be recorded on the questionnaires. After the review session, the scores should be converted to weighted scores and entered into a spreadsheet for subsequent analysis. The original questionnaires should be filed for future reference. Electronic copies can be linked and accessed via the test repository in a tool such as SQA TeamTest Manager.

Output 2.2: Risk Score Analysis Results (Task 2.2) The results in the sample Kiviat Chart in Figure 4.12 were taken from the General Risk Assessment Questionnaire data. They are easy to interpret. The further out along the axis a risk factor is placed, the greater the risk. In the sample data it is obvious that the information of software development and the lack of documentation are major risk areas.

A second method for interpreting the results is to sort the data from highest to lowest risk. This creates a frequency distribution of risk factors also known as a Pareto distribution. The sample uses the same data as in the Kiviat Chart but is presented as a Pareto distribution.

Again, electronic copies can be linked and accessed via the test repository.

A Risk-Based Test Resource Allocation Plan (Task 2.4) A risk-based test resource allocation plan is a document containing recommendations for allocating test resources as based on the risk analysis results. It should list the risk areas from highest to lowest risk and should assign a percentage of the available testing resources to each risk sector.

Output 2.3: A Risk Database (Task 2.5) Maintain a risk database that contains the project name under test, the risk assessment results from the project on a question-by-question basis, the analysis of the results on a question-by-question basis, graphs/charts of the results, and the test resource allocation recommendations. The database can be either an MS Access database using Access forms or an MS Excel spreadsheet that is being used as a database.

4.8.3 Step 3: Establish Test Objectives

4.8.3.1 Purpose Establishing software-testing objectives is a critical part of planning the software testing process. Defining testing objectives is also one of the most difficult planning activities. It is difficult because humans frequently do not have a clear idea of what they want to do until they begin to do it. This means the best laid test plans change during test process execution. This is a problem without a solution, but there are some actions testers can take to improve test planning.

Establishing clear testing objectives goes a long way toward offsetting future execution problems. Before testers can do this they must understand what I mean by the word "objective."

An objective is a testing "goal." It is a statement of what the tester wants to accomplish when implementing a specific testing activity. Each testing activity may have several objectives and there are two levels of objective specification.

A test plan should contain both high-level general objectives in the overview section and specific low-level "provable" objectives for each particular type of testing being implemented. The latter are operational goals for specific testing tasks. A good set of operational objectives can make clear intuitively why we are executing a particular step in the testing process.

4.8.3.2 Timing   The test objectives should be developed during the General Design and Detailed Design phases of the development methodology. For C-S RAD development, objectives should be declared during analysis and revisited during construction.

4.8.3.3 Inputs

From Concept Origination phase
> Proof of concept prototype

From Project Planning phase
> Risk assessment data (performed by development team)

From Requirements phase
> Context diagram
>
> Data model
>
> Process model
>
> Control requirements
>
> Performance requirements

From General Design phase
> General systems design

From Detailed Design phase
> Functional components
>
> Report layouts
>
> Screen navigation flow
>
> Screens

Risk Score Analysis Results (Task 2.2)   Either from data obtained from the project-level risk assessment or from data obtained by a risk-assessment session implemented by the test team.

4.8.3.4 Tasks

Task 3.1: Identify Test Objectives   One approach is to hold a brainstorming session. The test team uses creative interaction to construct a list of test objectives. This is not a free-for-all process. It should be based on analysis products such as the diagrams/text of the requirements specification and the risk analysis results. High-level black box objectives should be specified first and then driven down to detailed white box objectives.

Black Box Objectives

The basis of this approach is to identify key system functions and specify test objectives for each function. Identify business transactions and base objectives on the transactions. This can be scenario-based as business cycles are used to drive the process.

White Box Objectives

GUI (client)

Identify test objectives related to GUI objects

Identify test objectives for GUI events

Identify test objectives for GUI-level data edits

Business (server)

Identify test objectives for business objects

Identify test objectives for their interactions with one another

Identify test objectives for their interactions with the database

Identify test objectives for business-level data edits

Database (server)

Identify test objectives for database objects

Identify test objectives for data transport objects

Identify test objectives for triggers and stored procedures

Performance

Identify test objectives for single-user performance

Identify test objectives for multiuser performance objectives

Identify test objectives for client performance

Identify test objectives for server performance

Identify test objectives for database performance

A test-requirements document template should be developed as a working document for developers to complete prior to entering test requirements into the test repository.

Task 3.2: Define Completion Criteria A completion criterion is the standard by which a test objective is measured. Completion criteria can be either quantitative or qualitative. The important point is that the test team somehow must be able to determine when a test objective has been satisfied. One or more completion criteria must be specified for each test objective.

Task 3.3: Prioritize Test Objectives   The test objectives should be prioritized based on the risk analysis findings. Priority should be assigned using this scale:

> High—Most important tests; must be executed
>
> Medium—Second-level objectives; should be executed only after high-priority tests
>
> Low—Least important; should be tested last and only if there is enough time

High and medium objectives should be assigned more resources than low-priority objectives.

Task 3.4. Make Test Objectives Operational

Manual   Test objectives should be implemented manually in the form of quality-review checklists, with one or more checklist items satisfying a specific objective. (Single checklist items can also satisfy more than one objective, as is the case for the date field objectives.)

Objectives are internally linked to testing activities because they drive the activities. The objectives can be worded in either positive or negative fashion. Manual test data and test procedures should be derived from the test objectives.

Automated   Test objectives can be entered into the test repository in tools such as SQA TeamTest or via Requisite Pro and imported into SQA. The result is a test requirements hierarchy that will drive automated testing. Automated test requirements will be used as the basis for constructing automated test scripts.

Note: Test requirements stored in an automated test repository can also be used as the basis for constructing manual test cases.

4.8.3.5 Outputs

Output 3.1: Statement of Test Objectives (Task 3.1)   The statement of the test objectives is really a statement of the test requirements. It can be created using any word-processing package or spread sheet. It can also be implemented as the test requirements hierarchy in SQA TeamTest. Each branch within the requirements hierarchy can have sub-branches, and sub-branches can also have sub-branches. The test requirements should be driven down to a sufficiently low level of detail. The final level will be dictated by the complexity of the system under test.

Output 3.2: Statement of Test Objective Completion Criteria (Task 3.2)   The important consideration is that each requirement and its validation be documented. Test requirements are completely useless unless they can be documented. Important test metrics that should be calculated and reported are the percentage of test requirements that have been covered by test cases and the percentage of test requirements that have been successfully validated.

The statement of objective completion criteria does not have to be a separate document. It can simply be an addendum to the statement of test objectives. Although not meant for such a use in SQA, the test requirement description field can be a statement of the requirement's validation rule(s). This field is limited to 256 characters.

If a separate document is written for the test object completion criteria, it should be linked and accessed via the **Test Assets** menu, **Test Plan** command.

Output 3.3: Prioritized Test Objectives (Task 3.3)   The test objectives should be prioritized according to the perceived risk and used to determine the nature of the test cases that will be constructed.

4.8.4 Step 4: Construct Test Plans

4.8.4.1 Purpose   The purpose of the test plan is to specify the who-does-what-when-why of the test design, test construction, test execution, and test analysis process steps. The test plan also describes the test environment and required test resources. It also provides measurable goals by which management can gauge testing success. Furthermore, it facilitates communications within the test team, between the test team and the development team, and between the test team and management.

The test plan is a planning and operations document that becomes the basis for testing. It describes test strategies and test cases. Although it is operational in nature, it has administrative aspects. Thus, it can be used for both new development and maintenance. It should also be considered an evolving document. Bill Perry says developing the test plan requires about a third of the entire testing effort [9]. The development should occur in the SDLC, as shown in Figure 4.5.

The test plan should be constructed from a standardized template. The template should follow an accepted test plan standard. There are several sources that contain test plan outlines: IEEE Standard 829 [14], Perry's *A Standard for Testing Application Software* [9], and Mosley's *The Handbook of MIS Application Software Testing* [8]. It is also acceptable to combine pieces of plans to construct a hybrid test plan standard. Test plans always should be designed with test automation in mind.

A standardized test client-server plan document template has been constructed from the sources quoted above and can be used for all test plans developed for C-S projects under test. Figure 4.10 illustrates the possible contents of this template file.

4.8.4.2 Timing   Test plan construction should begin during the Requirements phase and continue on through the General Design and Detailed Design phases of the development methodology. For RAD C-S development, it should be completed during analysis and updated during construction and testing.

4.8.4.3 Inputs

From Step 2: Perform Risk Analysis
>Risk score analysis results (Task 2.2)
>Risk-based test resource allocation plan (Task 2.4)

From Step 3: Establish Test Objectives
>Statement of test objectives (Task 3.1)
>Statement of test objective completion criteria (Task 3.2)
>Prioritized test objectives (Task 3.3)

From Requirements Phase
>Context diagram
>Data model
>Process model
>Control requirements
>Performance requirements

From the General Design Phase
>General systems design

From the Detailed Design
>Functional components
>Report layouts
>Screen navigation flow
>Screens

4.8.4.4 Tasks

Task 4.1: Construct the System Test Plan   Identify the business scenarios to be tested. The user will employ the application system to conduct business day in and day out and according to daily, weekly, monthly, and/or yearly business cycles. The task identifies the business processes and cycles that can be translated into scripted test scenarios.

A system test scenario is a set of test scripts which reflect user behaviors in a typical business situation. For example, the user logs on to the system, views some retail profile accounts, updates other retailer profiles, and deletes still other retailer profiles. The system test plan should be constructed according to **Section V** of the test plan template.

Task 4.2: Construct the User Acceptance Test Plan   The user acceptance test plan will be very similar to the system test plan. The major difference is direction. The user acceptance test is designed to demonstrate the major system features to the user as opposed to finding new errors. It should prove how well the system works. The acceptance test plan should be constructed according to **Section VI** of the test plan template.

Task 4.3: Construct the Operational Test Plan   The operational test plan involves two types of tests. It guides the single user testing of the graphical user interface and of the system functions. The plan should be constructed according to subsections A and B of **Section II** of the test plan template.

Task 4.4: Construct the Regression Test Plan   Regression testing occurs at two levels. In client-server development, regression testing happens between builds. Between system releases, regression testing also occurs postproduction. Each new build/release must be completely tested for three aspects:

1. To assure that previously functioning features still work correctly
2. To assure that previously reported errors have been repaired
3. To assure that new functionality works correctly

The regression test plan should be constructed according to **Section III** of the test plan in Figure 4.10.

Task 4.5: Construct the Multiuser Performance Test Plan   Multiuser performance testing must be performed to assure that the system will perform as expected under load. The multiuser performance test plan should be constructed from **Section IV** of the test plan template.

Task 4.6: Construct the Unit Test Plan   Unit test plans are not covered in the test plan template document. When implemented, the unit test plan should be constructed according to procedures described in "ANSI/IEEE Std 1008-1987, Software Unit Testing" and outlined below.

Unit Testing Phases
> Test planning
> General approach
> Resources
> Schedule
> Features to test
> Develop the test set
> Design the tests
> Implement the test plan
> Execute the tests
> Run test procedures
> Evaluate the test results

Unit Testing Activities
Plan the approach. The project plan and the software requirements specification should serve as inputs to unit test planning. The unit test plan should

include a description of the testing approach(es), criteria for test completeness, and test termination criteria.

Determine the features to be tested. This activity is based on the software design specification document (functional requirements). All functions to be tested have to be identified. Any additional test requirements (e.g., performance) should also be identified. All possible states of the software unit under test should be identified. All input and output data characteristics should be identified.

Refine the unit test plan. At this point, the test plan should be revisited and updated with any changed test requirements.

Design the tests. Design the test input data, write the test case specifications, and describe the test execution procedures.

The test data design should be completed using MS Excel or another suitable documentation medium. The test data should be designed in one spreadsheet using both Black Box and White Box techniques. The actual data values should be created in a second spreadsheet. When possible, the second sheet should be exported to a CSV text file for use as input to SQA test procedures.

Construct the tests. The test procedures should be either written manually or entered into a product such as SQA, where the test scripts are written in SQABasic using the SQABasic editor. Obviously, automated test procedures are preferred.

Evaluate the unit test effort. Review the test plan and requirements and note variances from the test cases/test procedures. Assess the comprehensiveness of unit testing. Report on the status of unit testing. Preserve the test data, test procedures, and the test results.

4.8.5 Step 5: Design and Construct Test Cases

4.8.5.1 Purpose   The purpose of this step is to apply test case design techniques to design and build a set of "intelligent" test data. The data must address the system as completely as possible, but it must also focus on high-risk areas, and system/data components where weaknesses are traditionally found (system boundaries, input value boundaries, output value boundaries, etc.).

The test data set will be a compromise of economics and need. It is not economically feasible to test every possible situation, so representative sampling of test conditions, etc., will be present in the test data.

4.8.5.2 Timing   Test case design and construction should occur during the general design and the detailed design phases of the development methodology. The user acceptance, system test, and multiuser performance test cases should be developed during the general design phase. The operational/regression test cases should be built during the detailed design. For RAD C-S development, test case design and construction should begin during analysis and continue throughout the development cycle.

4.8.5.3 Inputs

From Requirements Phase
>Control requirements
>Performance requirements

From the General Design Phase
>Data model
>Process model
>General systems design

From the Detailed Design
>Functional components
>Report layouts
>Screen navigation flow
>Screens

From Step 4: Construct the Test Plans
>System test plan (Task 4.1)
>Acceptance test plan (Task 4.2)
>Operational test plan (Task 4.3)
>Regression test plan (Task 4.4)
>Multiuser performance test plan (Task 4.5)
>Unit test plan (Task 4.6)

4.8.5.4 Tasks

Task 5.1. Specify the Test Case Design Strategies This task identifies which test case design approaches will be used at what levels of testing. Discussions of the available techniques can be found in Myers 1977, Mosley 1993, and in chapter 8. The following approaches should be used to design and build test data sets that will be read into the software under test by automated test procedures.

Black Box Techniques
>Cause/effect graphing
>Equivalence partitioning
>Boundary analysis
>Error guessing

Gray Box Techniques
>Decision logic tables

White Box Techniques
>Basis testing

Task 5.2: Design the Test Cases This task involves applying the test case design techniques in order to identify test data values that will be constructed. The developers will be responsible for designing unit testing trials. The test team will aid developers in use of the techniques. For integration, system, and regression testing, the test team members will apply the techniques themselves.

The test case description can be either documented manually or stored in the test repository of an automated testing tool suite. If the test cases are documented automatically, the format and content will be limited to what the input forms and test repository can accept. Each tool vendor will probably store a different set of descriptive elements.

Note: The test data must include a description of the expected behavior for each test case.

Task 5.3: Construct the Test Data   This task involves constructing the physical data sets that have been designed in Task 3. The medium in which the data are constructed will be determined at the time of construction.

Task 5.4: Do a Quality Review of the Test Data   This task assures that the test data are complete, correct, and consistent. It is a simple review process that follows the review format presented above. The output should be a list of corrections, modifications, and additions that are necessary to strengthen the test data.

4.8.6 Step 6: Execute Unit and Operational Tests

4.8.6.1 Purpose   The purpose of unit testing is to prove that the individual units of the software function as they were intended. The software developer who built the software unit under test should conduct the unit test. The testers should act as consultants to the developer during unit testing.

The purpose of integration testing is to prove that the software units work together properly. The test team should conduct the integration test.

4.8.6.2 Timing   This task occurs during the construction phase of the development methodology. Multiuser performance testing occurs during the testing phase of the methodology. This is also true for RAD C-S development.

4.8.6.3 Inputs

From Construction Phase
    Developer-constructed unit test data
    Development software

From Step 5: Design and Construct Test Data
    Operational/regression test data (Tasks 5.2, 5.3)
    Multiuser performance test data (Tasks 5.2, 5.3)
    System test scenarios (Tasks 5.2, 5.3)
    User acceptance test scenarios (Tasks 5.2, 5.3)

4.8.6.4 Tasks

Task 6.1: Construct Test Logs   Separate test logs should be constructed for the various tests: unit, operational, multiuser performance, system, user-acceptance, and all subsequent regression tests. For manual testing, this log can be created with a spreadsheet and printed prior to testing. For automated testing, test log is a by-product of test script execution, and it is automatically stored in the test repository at the finish of each test cycle. For example, SQA updates the test log each time the test script is executed.

Task 6.2: Execute Unit Tests   This task is the responsibility of each developer. The tests should be conducted so that the developer is able to certify that the software does what it is supposed to do. Test team members will act as consultants to developers during unit test execution if requested to do so.

Obtain any necessary special test resources. Execute the tests manually, or via test scripts. Capture the results in a test log. For manual tests, summarize the test results indicating the pass/fail status of each test, the resources used, and the defects uncovered. When executing automated test procedures, the test log is created as a by-product of test execution. Review the test log and generate defects from the log entries when necessary. SQA has a log test Quick Reports function to summarize the test results.

Task 6.3: Retest Problem Areas   This task is usually done informally by the software developer without a lot of supervision. It can be improved considerably if the developers can be influenced to use an automated defect-tracking tool. Using a tool such as the SQA TeamTest Test Manager helps management track and control unit testing, as well as track the types of problems that occur.

Getting developers to agree to use an automated defect-tracking tool is not an easy task, but it can be done. It requires support from the project team leader and from the project manager. It also requires reassurance that the defects entered will not be held against the programmers. When buy-in has been accomplished, the results are excellent. Developers ultimately see the value of the product and how it can help them organize their own work.

This task is cyclic in nature. Retesting continues until prespecified stopping criteria are met. For example, retesting could continue until all severity-1, -2, and -3 errors have been corrected. It could also be a function of the time allocated to retesting.

Retesting problems that were found during unit testing is the responsibility of the developer. The test team will aid developers during unit testing to retest executable files when necessary.

Task 6.4: Analyze and Approve Unit Test Results   The purpose of this task is to determine which test cases failed and which passed, to identify which failures should be entered into the defect database, and to provide weekly reports for defect tracking purposes.

A defect and a failure are two different things. Among the many definitions of the term "defect" is that it is a discrepancy of the observed from the expected. In software a defect is when the observed output differs from the expected output. This is an oversimplification, but it is enough for our purposes.

A failure results when the software does not perform. A defect may or may not cause a software failure; it may cause only some output to be incorrect while producing other, correct output.

It is the responsibility of the project-level configuration control board (CCB) to determine which problems are defects and which are failures. It is also the CCB's responsibility to assign a severity level to each defect and to set repair priorities.

Software will not be accepted for higher-level testing unless all features perform as described in the design specification document(s) and unless it installs correctly and is stable. The developer must provide a completed unit test log and unit test data files when available. As final proof of the software unit's quality, the developer must complete and sign a Unit Test Certification form (see Figure 4.4).

Task 6.5: Execute Build Installation and Checkout Tests   All integration and other high-order test builds should be held to the following process. The build should occur on a separate server, not on the development or test server. The completed build should be operationally tested prior to release to testing. The build administrator must be charged with the testing. If the build is deemed operational, it is then copied to the test server.

Installation and checkout (smoke) tests should verify that

- The install process is correct
- The system architecture is stable
- The data architecture is stable
- All middleware is processing as expected
- The GUI is usable
- The current business processing performs its intended functions
- New business functions perform as intended

Builds should occur often enough to satisfy construction phase deadlines, but must be limited to enough interim time so as not to interfere with testing. Although automated test tools allow regression testing between builds, the time required depends on the number of software components under test. When there is enough time, one build per week is ideal.

If the build fails during this task it should be repaired and it must then reenter this process step at Task 6.5.

Task 6.6: Execute Operational Tests   Operational testing should only begin after Task 6.5 has been performed and the verified build has been installed in the test environment. In addition, operational tests should not begin until completed Unit Test Certification Forms have been filed for all software components included in the build.

This task is the responsibility of the test team. Its focus is to prove that the integrated software units do what they should do and do not do what they should not do. For tests conducted in a formal manner, the testers use operational test cases that have predicted outputs and the test results are recorded in structured test logs. These structured test logs and test scripts drive the operational testing process.

Task 6.7: Regression Test This task is cyclic in nature. Regression testing continues until prespecified stopping criteria are met. For example, it could continue until all severity-1, -2, and -3 errors have been corrected. It could also be a function of the time allocated to retesting.

Problem reports drive a portion of the regression testing task. The test team will retest only CCB-approved and -corrected problems that are received in the form of installation- and checkout-tested software builds.

Task 6.8: Analyze and Approve Operational/Regression Test Results The purpose of this task is exactly the same as that stated in Task 6.4, and it should be executed in the same manner.

Task 6.9: Execute Multiuser Performance Tests Multiuser performance tests should be conducted to determine optimal system performance levels under light, normal, and heavy loads. System performance is generally assessed in terms of response times and throughput rates under differing processing and configuration conditions. If the tester can identify any business processing cycles (e.g., month-end, quarter-end, semiannual, and annual), the system performance should be tested under an emulation of each processing cycle.

This testing should cover performance under all hardware and software system configurations. In one particular C-S system, it was necessary to test performance under corporate and field environments (desktops vs. laptops, LAN vs. WAN) and to test the system in conjunction with a second system utilizing the same server and at times accessing the same database. These are circumstances that can severely impact performance in networked C-S systems.

There are three formal approaches to automated performance/load testing (see chapter 6). In all cases the test load is driven by automated test scripts. The first approach is a "single test per processor" configuration. In this model the tests are executed via test scripts that are recordings of actual user input with each user executing on a separate desktop machine. This is the most realistic scenario because it emulates a live production environment; however, it is largely an impractical method because of the problems amassing the resources for this type of test for even a medium-size C-S system.

The second approach is much more viable. It is the "multiple test per processor" model. This approach employs multiple simulated users on one or more test machines. With this technique hundreds of simulated users can be involved in a single test session. It is important to realize that this type of testing does not stress test the network while the approach discussed in the paragraph above does perform a network load test. To load test a network you must connect as many network cards as possible to the network. In simulated load there are multiple users going through a single network connection. This is not an effective test of network load capacity.

The third approach is a "hybrid" model. It is a combination of the two models discussed above, employing both single test per processor and multiple tests per processor models.

One or more of these approaches should be used to test system performance before it is released for general use.

4.8.6.5 Outputs

Output 6.1: Completed Unit Test Log (Task 6.2)   This form must be filled out and provided to the test manager when the software is presented for integration testing.

Output 6.2: Unit Test Incident Reports (Tasks 6.2, 6.3)   Unit test incidents can be entered into the defect tracking system by the software developer. With respect to SQA, they can be entered manually using SQA Manager or can be created from the test log using SQA Test Log Viewer.

Output 6.3: Unit Test Defect Data (Task 6.2)   Unit test defects should be permanently stored in the test repository. Individual defects should *never be deleted!* Old project defect information should be archived. The key word "Unit" should be assigned to each defect to identify it as an unit testing problem.

Output 6.4: Unit Test Defect Analysis Reports (Task 6.4)   Developers should track their unit test defects using SQA TeamTest Manager or a similar product. The defects should be entered and tracked exactly as they would be for the other phases of testing that follow unit tests.

The defect metrics described above in the "Software Testing Supporting Elements" section can be used to analyze the defects at any level that you want. The metrics should be presented to management in the form of charts, graphs, or tables that illustrate the general defect trends. The trends can indicate what should be done to correct or prevent defects of the classes found in the charted data.

Output 6.5: Unit Test Certification Form (Task 6.4)   The developer who authored the software that was unit tested should prepare this form. A complete form is required for entry into operational testing.

Output 6.6: Completed Operational Test Log (Task 6.6)   This log can be used when operational testing is manual. When at all possible, integration test procedures should be constructed and executed using a tool such as SQA Robot. In this case, the test log is a by-product of the automated test execution process.

Output 6.7: Operational Test Reports As defined in the development methodology input/deliverables list for the construction phase.

Output 6.8: Operational Test Summary Reports These are defined in the development methodology input/deliverables list for the construction phase.

Output 6.9: Operational/Regression Test Incident Reports (Tasks 6.6, 6.7) Operational test incidents either can be entered manually into the defect tracking process or entered from the SQA Test Log Viewer with the **Defect** tool bar button or via the **Defect** menu.

Output 6.10: Operational/Regression Test Defect Data (Tasks 6.6, 6.7) The operational test defect data should be stored in the SQA TeamTest Test or some other test repository along with the unit test defect data. The key word "Operational" should be assigned to each defect to identify it as an integration testing problem.

Output 6.11: Operational/Regression Test Defect Analysis Reports (Task 6.7) The defect metrics described in section 4.4 and in chapter 9 can be used to analyze the defects at any level that you want. The metrics should be presented to management in the form of charts, graphs, or tables that illustrate the general defect trends. The trends can indicate what should be done to correct or prevent defects of the classes found in the charted data.

Output 6.12: Completed Multiuser Performance Test Log (Task 6.8) This form can be used when executing performance testing manually. When at all possible, integration test procedures should be constructed and executed using a capture/playback tool. In this case, the test log is a by-product of the automated test execution process.

Output 6.13: Multiuser Performance Test Reports Define in the development methodology input/deliverables list for the construction phase.

Output 6.14: Multiuser Performance Test Summary Report Define in the development methodology input/deliverables list for the Construction phase.

Output 6.15: Multiuser Performance Test Incident Reports (Task 6.8) These incidents either can be entered manually into the SQA defect tracking process or from the SQA Test Log Viewer with the **Defect** tool bar button or via the **Defect** menu.

Output 6.16: Multiuser Performance Test Defect Data (Task 6.8) The performance test defect data can be stored in the SQA TeamTest Test Repository along with the unit test defect data. The key word "Performance" should be assigned to each defect to identify it as an integration testing problem.

Output 6.17: Multiuser Performance Test Defect Analysis Reports (Task 6.8) The defect metrics described in the "Software Testing Supporting Elements" section can be used to analyze the defects at any level that you want. The metrics should be presented to management in the form of charts, graphs, or tables that illustrate the general defect trends. The trends can indicate what should be done to correct or prevent defects of the classes found in the charted data.

4.8.7 Step 7: Execute System and Acceptance Tests

4.8.7.1 Purpose   The system test uses the system in a "controlled" test environment, but does so as the user would use it in the production environment. The system test should prove that the complete system will do what it is supposed to do and that it will not do anything that it is not supposed to do.

System testing activities are intended to prove that the system meets its objectives. Some experts argue that the purpose of system testing is to prove that the system meets its requirements. This is not entirely true unless you consider acceptance testing a type of system testing because the purpose of acceptance testing is to demonstrate that the system meets the user's requirements. Acceptance testing is a validation process. System testing, in the strictest sense, is a verification process. Regardless of whether it represents verification or validation, system testing represents an external view of the system.

This is true because the requirements represent the eventual system user's view from outside the system. Users do not understand nor do they care about how the system works as long as it is "usable." Their opinions of the system are formulated strictly from what their senses tell them when they use the system. They interact with the system via a user interface using a set of manual procedures designed to invoke specific responses from the system. If the interface is difficult to master or the system's responses are inappropriate, the system is not usable. System testing should be approached from this perspective.

If you are saying to yourself, "but objectives are specified internally by the design team," you would be correct. However, objectives are direct translations of requirements into design goals that must be achieved. Therefore, objectives are formulated from external considerations concerning the system. If this basic translation process results in objectives that do not reflect the requirements, a discrepancy exists that must be resolved in system testing.

The design objective should be translated into system test objectives. Refer to step 2 for a complete discussion of establishing software testing objectives/requirements.

4.8.7.2 Timing   System and acceptance testing occur during the formal testing phase of development methodology.

4.8.7.3 Inputs

From Construction Phase
Development software
Product configuration
Customer procedures

Operations procedures

Operations training manuals

Disaster recovery procedures

From Step 4: Construct Test Plans

System test plan

User acceptance test plan

From Step 5: Design and Construct Test Data

Multiuser performance test data (Tasks 5.2, 5.3)

System test scenarios (Tasks 5.2, 5.3)

User acceptance test scenarios (Tasks 5.2, 5.3)

4.8.7.4 Tasks

Task 7.1: Execute System Tests   This task is the responsibility of the test team. Its focus is to prove that the completed system does what it should do and does not do what it should not do. For tests conducted formally, the testers use scenario-based system test scripts that have predicted outputs. Test results are recorded in structured logs, which, with the test scripts, drive the process.

For mainframe projects, system testing is carried out during the formal testing phase of the SDLC. As far as testing is concerned, this stage consumes the largest chunk of testing resources. As we saw in chapter 2, that amounts to approximately 12.5% of allocated reserves. Our discussion of system testing will refer to the activities of this stage of development.

System testing in the client-server world should include the same kinds of tests as in the mainframe environment, but it must also address all of the different layers in a C-S software system. So, system testing for C-S must include test scripts that address the user interface, application, and data layers.

System testing activities are controlled by the system test plan developed in step 4, but not implemented until now.

Task 7.2: Build Regression Test   Build regression testing is not done frequently during system testing. A new build should only occur when requested by the system test team. A new build will be required only if the number of new errors uncovered is no longer at a productive level or there is a complete system failure and testing cannot continue. When the errors uncovered during system testing have been repaired and must be regression tested, a new build is required as well.

This task is cyclic in nature. Regression will continue until a specified stopping criterion (criteria) is (are) met. The criteria for release readiness are described fully under No. 5, Software Testing metrics, in the "Software Testing Supporting Elements" section.

As with operational testing, problem reports drive a major portion of the retesting task. The test team will retest only CCB-approved and -corrected problems that are received in the form of installation- and checkout-tested software builds.

Task 7.3: Analyze System Test Results   The purpose of this task is to determine which test cases failed and which passed, to identify which failures should be entered into the defect database, and to provide weekly reports for defect tracking purposes.

Task 7.4: Design Release Regression Test Suites   This task identifies how much, and what categories, of the test data should be saved for regression testing postproduction system releases. The decision should be based on the system requirements, the risk analysis results, and the problems encountered during the unit, operational, regression, multiuser performance, and system tests.

Task 7.5: Automate Regression Test Suites   Microsoft has determined that automated tests can reduce the testing effort by 50%. Regression testing is the one area where automated test scripts can produce a substantial return on investment for the project. SQA Robot or a similar tool should be used to record and play back system test scripts for regression testing.

The automated test scripts should be retained and updated each time a new regression test is executed.

Task 7.6: Execute Acceptance Tests   This task is the responsibility of the test team in conjunction with the users. It demonstrates to the users that the completed system does what it should do and does not do what it should not do. This test is conducted formally. The users are the testers, and they use scenario-based test scripts that have predicted outputs. The test results are recorded in structured logs, which, along with the test scripts, drive the acceptance testing process.

Acceptance testing in the client-server world should include the same kinds of tests as in the mainframe environment, but it must also address all of the different layers in a C-S software system. So, acceptance testing for C-S must include test scripts that demonstrate the user interface, application, and data layers.

Acceptance testing activities are controlled by the acceptance test plan that was developed in step 4, but not implemented until now.

4.8.7.5 Outputs

Output 7.1: Completed System Test Log (Task 7.3)   The test log should be either a manual test log kept during the system tests in the form of a system test diary or the SQA Test log created when automated test procedures are executed or a combination of both these categories.

Output 7.2: System Test Incident Reports (Tasks 7.3, 7.4)   System test incident reports should be entered into the test repository. The incidents should be tracked to closure within this assemblage.

Output 7.3: System Test Reports   These are defined in the development methodology input/deliverables list for the testing phase.

Output 7.4: System Test Summary Reports   These are defined in the development methodology input/deliverables list for the testing phase.

Output 7.5: Acceptance Test Log (Task 7.6) The acceptance test log should be the same as that described in the system test log section above.

Output 7.6: Acceptance Test Incident Reports (Task 7.6) Acceptance test incident reports should be entered into the test repository. The incidents should be tracked to closure within this assemblage.

Output 7.7: Acceptance Test Reports These are defined in the development methodology input/deliverables list for the testing phase.

Output 7.8: Acceptance Test Summary Report This is defined in the development methodology input/deliverables list for the testing phase.

4.8.8 Step 8: Analyze and Report Test Results

4.8.8.1 Purpose
The purpose of the test report is to indicate which system functions work and which do not. This report should describe the level to which the system meets the test objectives. The report should include recommendations based on the system's success or failure at meeting the objectives.

This report covers all of the testing activities that have been completed. Its audience is management (project sponsor, project manager, development manager, and user representative).

4.8.8.2 Timing
This report should be produced at the end of the testing phase for both mainframe and RAD C-S development.

4.8.8.3 Inputs

From Step 6: Execute Unit and Operational Tests
Operational test reports
Operational test summary reports
Multiuser performance test reports
Multiuser performance test summary report

From Step 7: Execute System and Acceptance Tests (as described in the testing phase of the development methodology)
System test reports
System test summary reports
Acceptance test reports
Acceptance test summary report

4.8.8.4 Tasks

Task 8.1: Test Data Analysis It consolidates data from all sources into a spreadsheet format that can be used to make conclusions about the testing process. MS Excel can be used to complete this task. Several spreadsheets (e.g., defect data, test objective completion percentages) can be captured in a single Excel workbook.

Task 8.2: Formulate Test Findings/Recommendations Report This task results in a report summarizing the test results and release recommendations. The report should also include a list of known problems in the software that could not be—or purposely were not—fixed.

The test team, development team, and users should review the recommendations before they are finalized.

Task 8.3: Construct Test Findings/Recommendations Report This task puts the information in a standardized report format.

Task 8.4: Review Test Findings/Recommendations Report This is a formal peer review of the completed test report. Its intent is to check the report for completeness, correctness, and consistency. The review should be no longer than two hours and should follow the standard Walkthrough technique.

The attendees should include the test manager, test analysts, developer representatives, and user representatives.

4.8.9 Step 9: Execute Release Regression Tests

4.8.9.1 Purpose The primary purpose of regression testing is to prove that system enhancements and routine tuning and maintenance do not affect the original system functionality. The secondary purpose is to prove that the changes do what they are intended to do and do not do anything they are not intended to do.

Regression testing is repeated every time the system changes. This means that the regression test cases should not be discarded after each test.

Regression testing is the form of testing most amenable to automation. In this step, a capture/playback tool should be used to design and build automated test scripts. The scripts then can be enhanced and replayed for each subsequent regression test.

4.8.9.2 Timing Release regression tests should be implemented each time a new major or minor system release is constructed. The tests should be executed during the testing phase of the maintenance life cycle process.

4.8.9.3 Inputs

From Steps 5 and 7
Regression test data (Tasks 5.3, 7.2)

4.8.9.4 Tasks

Task 9.1: Execute Release Regression Tests

Task 9.1.1: Execute Old Test Data The purpose of this task is to run the system with existing test cases that were retained from the system tests. The reasoning is that if the test data are held constant and something does not work, it must be due to the change(s) made to the system. This can show that all of the previous system functions still work.

Task 9.1.2: Execute New Test Data The purpose of this task is to execute the system with new test data that are designed to prove that the changed portion of the system does what it is supposed to do and that it does not do something it is not supposed to do.

Task 9.2: Retest Problem Areas This task is the same as Task 7.2. Retesting continues until a specified stopping criterion (criteria) is (are) met.

The test team will retest only CCB-approved and corrected problems that are received in the form of installation and checkout tested software builds.

Task 9.3: Analyze Release Regression Test Results The purpose of this task is to determine which test cases failed and which passed, to identify which failures should be entered into the defect database, and to provide weekly reports for defect tracking purposes.

The criteria for rerelease readiness are described under No. 5, software testing metrics, in the "Software Testing Supporting Elements" section.

4.8.9.5 Outputs

Output 9.1: Completed Release Regression Test Log (Task 9.3) The test log should be either a manual test log that is kept during the regression tests in the form of a regression test diary or the test log created when automated test procedures are executed or a combination of both these categories.

Output 9.2: Release Regression Test Incident Reports (Tasks 9.3, 9.4) Regression test incident reports should be entered into the test repository. The incidents should be tracked to closure within this assemblage.

4.8.10 Step 10: Analyze and Report Regression Test Results

4.8.10.1 Purpose The purpose of the regression test report is to indicate which system functions work and which do not. This report should describe the level at which the system meets the test objectives. The report should include recommendations based on the success or failure of the system to meet the objectives.

As regression testing is an iterative process that occurs every time the system is changed, this report should be archived and updated after each regression test.

4.8.10.2 Tasks

Task 10.1: Regression Test Data Analysis This task performs data reduction and consolidates data from all sources into a spreadsheet format that can be used to deduce conclusions about the regression testing results. MS Excel can be used to complete this task. Several spreadsheets (e.g., defect data, test objective completion percentages) can be captured in a single Excel workbook.

Task 10.2: Formulate Test Findings/Recommendations Report   This task result in a report summarizing the test results and release recommendations. The report should also include a list of known problems in the software that could not be—or purposely were not—fixed. The test team, development team, and users should review the release recommendations before they are finalized.

Task 10.3: Construct Regression Test Report   This task puts the information in a standardized report format.

Task 10.4: Review Regression Test Report Release   This is a formal peer review of the completed test report. The purpose of this review is to decide whether or not the software can be released. The review should be no longer than two hours.

4.9 RESOURCES FOR SOFTWARE TESTERS ON THE INTERNET

4.9.1 USENET News Groups

Testers who have access to the Internet will find several FAQs listed in the *comp.software.testing* USENET News Group archives. They contain information about software testing consulting firms; software testing training seminars; and software testing tools, including complete vendor information (these can also be found at Brian Marick's web site, http://www.stlabs.com/marick/root.htm). Other news groups that I have found to contain testing-related messages are *comp.software.eng*, *comp.client.server* and *comp.human.factors*.

4.9.2 World Wide Web Sites

My company, Client-Server Software Testing (CSST) Technologies has a World Wide Web home page, which is a free resource for all testers, that can be accessed at http://www.icon-stl.net/~djmosley/. Our site contains information about CSST Technologies, software testing technical articles and white papers, links to the news groups listed here, links to other testing-related home pages, and links to software testing tools vendor home pages. (A caveat: The Internet is a dynamic environment and home pages will come and go, so a URL that exits today may not be around six months from now. The URLs listed above are current at the time of this book's printing.)

4.10 CONCLUSION

Management and control of client-server software testing is probably more important than was management and control of mainframe software testing. It is more important because client-server systems are more complex than other systems, and client-server systems are built without the project management controls associated with mainframe system development. Thus, a necessary part of client-server test planning is deciding how to proceed if the essential documentation is not available.

For example, what if there is no requirements definition document or no design documents? A good portion of your test planning will be spent compiling and sorting out the information that would normally be present in these documents. Furthermore, attempting to plan the testing process (via such processes as risk analysis) will flush out the fact that the documents aren't available and help determine the impact on testing and, ultimately, on system quality.

Support your test planning with a test tool that can assist the creation of a test plan, document test requirements, document and link test requirements to specific software modules, track and report on defects and chart defect trends, link defects back to specific test cases/requirements/software modules, and control testing workflow [1,4]. The test manager tool you choose must also support a team environment via a networked test repository that all testers and developers can access.

4.11 REFERENCES

1. Bender, Richard. *SEI/CMM Proposed Software Evaluation and Test KPA*, Revision 4. Bender and Associates, Larkspur, CA, April 1996.

2. Duchesneau, Dave. "Mind Your Bugs: Here Are Four Bug Tracking Tools to Keep Your Software Development on Track." *Data Based Advisor*, Vol. 13, No. 5, June 1995, p. 42(7).

3. The Gartner Group, Inc., conference presentation. 1993.

4. Humphrey, Watts. *Managing the Software Process*. Addison-Wesley Longman Publishing, Reading, MA, 1989.

5. Intersolv. *Choosing a LAN-Based Problem and Change Request Management Tool*. A report from Intersolv, Rockville, MD.

6. King, David. *Current Practices in Software Development*. Prentice Hall Yourdon Press, Englewood Cliffs, NJ, 1984.

7. Koltun, Phil. "Testing...Testing..." *ShowCASE* newsletter, Harris Corporation, May 1993.

8. Mosley, Daniel J. *The Handbook of MIS Application Software Testing: Methods, Techniques, and Tools for Assuring Quality Through Testing*. Prentice Hall, Englewood Cliffs, NJ, 1993.

9. Perry, William E. *A Standard for Testing Application Software 1992*. Auerbach Publishers, Boston, 1992.

10. Quality Assurance Institute. *1995 Survey Results on Software Testing*. Quality Assurance Institute, Orlando, FL, 1995.

11. Quality Assurance Institute. *1996 Survey Results on Software Testing*. Quality Assurance Institute, Orlando, FL, 1996.

12. Saile, Bob. *Introduction to MS Test*. Microsoft Technet CD, Test Technical Notes, Vol. 4, Issue 2, February 1996.

13. Segue Software Incorporated. *Boosting Productivity with Automatic Testing*. A Segue Software, Inc., White Paper for QA and Development Professionals, Segue Software, Inc., Lincoln, MA 02421.

14. The Institute of Electrical and Electronics Engineers. *Software Engineering Standards*, 3rd edition, ANSI/IEEE STD-829 Standard for Software Test Documentation.

15. The Institute of Electrical and Electronics Engineers. *Standard for Software Unit Testing*. ANSI/IEEE Std 1008-1987.

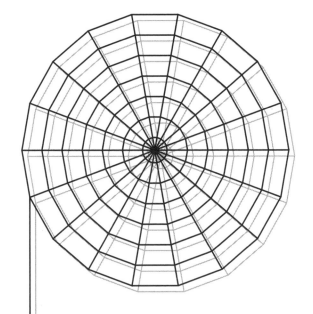

Testing Client Applications: Graphical User Interface Testing

5.1 INTRODUCTION

GUIs add a new dimension of complexity to software testing. Kepple [9], in *CASE Trends* magazine, goes so far as to suggest that traditional testing methods must be abandoned when testing GUIs. I disagree with this idea, but I see that some traditional approaches must be amended and some new approaches are necessary. Hayes [7] says, "You can have your cake and eat it too—all it takes is the right utensils." In this instance, the right utensils are automated GUI testing tools.

Farley [5], in a comparison of the DOS operating system (a CUI) and the Windows environment (a GUI), indicated that developers must be alert to such conditions as the application's input focus, its context in relation to other state information, and its relative desktop coordinates. Where the GUI departs from traditional system interfaces is in its cross-platform nature and in the increased number of logic paths due to the GUI's ability to produce a broad range of graphical objects. Testing is further complicated because the objects can be present or absent, they may exist for a length of time, and they can appear anywhere on the desktop.

Atre [1] suggests that GUI-based applications have increased testing requirements because they are in an event-driven environment where user actions are events that determine the application's behavior. Because the number of available user actions is very high, the number of logical paths in the supporting program code is also very high. The result is software modules that are extremely difficult to test because their structural complexity (as computed with McCabe's Cyclomatic Complexity metric [10]) is radically elevated.

The event-driven nature of GUI systems implies a need for synchronization in the application itself and in test scripts developed to test the application. In GUIs objects may appear unexpectedly or not at all, so applications must be able to handle unanticipated events and objects and must be able to compensate when expected events or objects do not materialize. Another problem is the positional nature of GUI objects (windows, dialog boxes, menu commands, etc.). The user is free to move these objects around the screen and, thus, objects may appear in a different location each time the application is run (e.g., child windows and dialog boxes). GUI objects may change position (e.g., menu commands) when the application is enhanced or modified, or a problem is corrected during normal maintenance. In some instances, the object's position is important and in other instances it is irrelevant.

The mouse, as an alternate method of input, also poses some problems. GUIs allow input from the mouse (single and double clicks of primary or secondary mouse buttons), from the keyboard (single keystrokes or keystroke combinations), or a combination of the two (key strokes and mouse clicks). It is necessary to assure that the application handles all of these forms of user input correctly regardless of timing or sequencing.

Further complicating GUI testing is the capture and comparison of bit-mapped images of GUI screens. Entire screens may be recorded and compared to subsequent occurrences of the same screen. Small differences that are undetected by human eyes can be detected this way. In some instances, areas of the GUI that can change from occurrence to occurrence (e.g., a text field displaying the current date or time) must be masked or an error is falsely indicated. A corollary to this is the need to test individual text entry boxes in windows and dialog boxes. The text must be captured and compared to subsequent entries in the same text box.

GUI testing also requires testing for the existence of files that provide supporting data/information for text objects. The application must be sensitive to the existence, or nonexistence, of these files. This is so because they have to be opened if they already are there, or if they are absent, they must be created.

Another complicating factor is the cross-platform nature of GUIs. The same GUI objects may be required to run transparently (provide a consistent interface across platforms, with the cross-platform nature unknown to the user) on different hardware and software platforms.

In a similar vein, GUI testing also involves the assurance that custom GUI objects function correctly. Many GUI development tools give the users the ability to define their own GUI objects. The ability to do this requires the underlying application to be able to recognize and process events related to these custom objects. Thus, the entire repertoire of custom objects or the entire set of characteristics used to define the objects must be tested.

What this means is that the traditional capture/playback approach to testing CUIs must be modified in order to handle the complexities of the GUI environment. A functional variation of the capture/playback paradigm has evolved for GUI testing known as "structured capture/playback" [5].

The basic difference between the two approaches is that capture/play-back occurs at an external level (recording physical events). It records input as keystrokes and output as screen images that are saved and compared against inputs and output images of subsequent tests.

Structured capture/playback is based on an internal (logical) view of external activities. The application program's interactions with the GUI are recorded as internal "events" that can be saved as "scripts" written in Microsoft's Visual Basic or in one of the C variants or in the vendor's proprietary language (refer to Figures 5.1, 5.2, and 5.3). With respect to MS Windows, Farley [5] says that a testing tool must create test suites that respond to all types of Windows input controls:

> ...in Windows you now have a number of input controls for the numerous means of manipulation....in Windows programming nothing changes as frequently as the user interface....Your test suite needs to treat all of these equally....This is an impossible job if you don't work at a high level instead of a simple RECORD EVENT level.

Fig. 5.1 Example of an Object-Level Visual Basic Test Script Created from SQA TeamTest Product

```
Sub Main ""''
    Dim Result As Integer

    'Initially Recorded: 02/15/95  23:38:25
  'Test Procedure Name: QBS Mortgage Prequalifier Account History

    InitPlay
    SetProcID "QBPRQ01"

    Window SetContext, "VBName=StartScreen;VisualText=QuarterByte Savings Bank", ""
    Window SetPosition, "", "Coords=118,92,425,381;Status=NORMAL"
    PushButton Click, "VBName=PrequalifyButton;VisualText=Prequalify"

    Window SetContext, "VBName=Main;VisualText=Mortgage Prequalifier", ""
    Window SetPosition, "", "Coords=60,95,506,362;Status=NORMAL"
    MenuSelect "File→Open Customer..."

    Window SetContext, "VBName=SelectCustomer;VisualText=Open Customer", ""
    Window SetPosition, "", "Coords=126,141,228,265;Status=NORMAL"
    ComboBox Click, "VBName=CustFilter", "Coords=172,9"
    ComboListBox Click, "ObjectIndex=1", "Text=Eastern Region"
    ListBox Click, "VBName=CustList", "Text=Aaron, Mark"
    PushButton Click, "VBName=SelectOK;VisualText=OK"

    Result = WindowTC (CompareMenu, "VBName=Main;VisualText=Mortgage Prequalifier",
        "CaseID=QBPRQ01A")

    Window SetContext, "VBName=Main;VisualText=Mortgage Prequalifier", ""
    Window SetPosition, "", "Coords=60,95,506,362;Status=NORMAL"
    PushButton Click, "VBName=HistoryButton;VisualText=Account History..."

    Window SetContext, "VBName=History;VisualText=Account History", ""
    Window MoveTo, "", "Coords=126,90"
    RadioButton Click, "VBName=Checking;VisualText=Checking Account"
    InputKeys "^+{F7}^+{F7}"

    Result = ListBoxTC (Compare, "VBName=HistoryList", "CaseID=QBPRQ01B")
```

Fig. 5.1 Example of an Object-Level Visual Basic Test Script Created from SQA TeamTest Product (Continued)

```
    Result = CheckBoxTC (CompareObjectState, "VBName=Overdraft;VisualText=Overdraft
        Protection", "CaseID=QBPRQ01C")

    PushButton Click, "VBName=HistoryOK;VisualText=OK"

    Window SetContext, "VBName=Main;VisualText=Mortgage Prequalifier", ""
    Window SetPosition, "", "Coords=60,95,506,362;Status=NORMAL"
    MenuSelect "File->Exit"
        EndPlay
End Sub
```

Fig. 5.2 Example of an Object-Level TSL (Test Script Language) Test Script Created from Mercury Interactive's WinRunner Product

```
# Multiple Authorizations/Rejected

set_window ("Show Totals");
button_press ("Authorize");

set_window ("Awaiting Authorization");

# sort in Requested Action descending to pick a non-updated record
colselect ("SummaryGrid", "Requested");
menu_select_item ("View;Sort_menu;Ascending");

rowselect ("SummaryGrid", "#1:3");                          # selects rows 1-3
button_press ("Reject");

set_window ("Block Rejects");
button_press ("OK");

set_window ("Reject Details");

for (row=1;row<11;row++) {
   tbl_get_cell_data ("NotifyGrid", "#"&row, "#1", state);
   # All rows
   if (state != ON)
      tbl_set_selected_cell ("NotifyGrid", "#"&row, "#1");
}
branchRow = getRow ("NotifyGrid", "Branch<Role>");
tbl_set_selected_cell ("NotifyGrid", branchRow , "#1");
gridlist ("NotifyGrid", "#1", branchRow , "#3");

set_window ("Reject Details");
button_press ("Apply All");

set_window ("Error");
if (obj_check_info ("error msg" "value" "You must select a Cancel Reason.") != E_OK)
   tl_step ("Multiple selection" FAIL, "Unexpected error message received");

button_press ("OK");

set_window ("Reject Details", 10);
button_press ("Cancel");

set_window ("Awaiting Authorization");
menu_select_item ("File;Exit");

set_window ("Show Totals");
```

Fig. 5.3 Example of an Analog (Low-Level) Visual Basic Test Script Created from SQA
TeamTest Product

```
SQA Robot-Windows Lowlevel Script File
02/20/95  02:23:58
File: C:\SQASAMPL\QSB\LLSCR\TEST1.001

        Message              X     Y            Cumul. Time
        =======================================================
        MOUSEMOVE           150   118               55
        MOUSEMOVE           150   120              550
        MOUSEMOVE           156   123              604
        MOUSEMOVE           165   128              659
        MOUSEMOVE           177   134              714
        MOUSEMOVE           184   140              714
        MOUSEMOVE           213   148              769
        MOUSEMOVE           263   149              824
        MOUSEMOVE           265   149              879
        MOUSEMOVE           263   156             1318
        MOUSEMOVE           249   176             1373
        MOUSEMOVE           238   223             1428
        MOUSEMOVE           238   244             1428
        MOUSEMOVE           244   272             1428
        MOUSEMOVE           273   312             1483
        MOUSEMOVE           280   320             1538
        MOUSEMOVE           290   330             1593
        MOUSEMOVE           293   333             1593
        MOUSEMOVE           294   334             1648
        MOUSEMOVE           294   335             1813
        MOUSEMOVE           296   376             1868
        MOUSEMOVE           306   417             1923
        MOUSEMOVE           313   424             1978
        MOUSEMOVE           318   425             2033
        MOUSEMOVE           318   421             2087
        MOUSEMOVE           317   421             2142
        MOUSEMOVE           317   420             2197
        MOUSEMOVE           317   419             2197
        MOUSEMOVE           317   416             2252
        MOUSEMOVE           316   414             2252
        MOUSEMOVE           316   412             2307
        MOUSEMOVE           315   411             2307
        MOUSEMOVE           315   407             2362
        MOUSEMOVE           313   403             2417
        MOUSEMOVE           313   399             2856
        LBUTTONDOWN         313   399             3131
        MOUSEMOVE           313   399             3351
        LBUTTONUP           313   399             3351
        MOUSEMOVE           313   399             5108
        MOUSEMOVE           310   397             5493
        MOUSEMOVE           306   392             5493
        MOUSEMOVE           302   389             5548
        MOUSEMOVE           299   387             5548
        MOUSEMOVE           297   385             5548
        MOUSEMOVE           295   383             5603
        MOUSEMOVE           293   379             5603
        MOUSEMOVE           291   374             5658
        MOUSEMOVE           287   369             5658
        MOUSEMOVE           284   363             5712
        MOUSEMOVE           282   352             5712
        MOUSEMOVE           282   331             5712
        MOUSEMOVE           282   311             5767
        MOUSEMOVE           283   290             5767
        MOUSEMOVE           287   264             5822
        MOUSEMOVE           290   230             5822
        MOUSEMOVE           289   229             6481
```

Fig. 5.3 Example of an Analog (Low-Level) Visual Basic Test Script Created from SQA TeamTest Product (Continued)

MOUSEMOVE	285	227	6536
MOUSEMOVE	282	226	6536
MOUSEMOVE	280	225	6591
MOUSEMOVE	277	224	6591
MOUSEMOVE	276	224	6591
MOUSEMOVE	275	223	6646
MOUSEMOVE	274	223	6646
MOUSEMOVE	274	222	6701
MOUSEMOVE	273	222	6756
MOUSEMOVE	269	222	6756
MOUSEMOVE	265	221	6756
MOUSEMOVE	261	221	6811
MOUSEMOVE	256	221	6811
MOUSEMOVE	253	221	6866
MOUSEMOVE	248	221	6866
MOUSEMOVE	244	221	6921
MOUSEMOVE	241	221	6921
MOUSEMOVE	238	221	6921
MOUSEMOVE	235	221	6976
MOUSEMOVE	233	221	6976
MOUSEMOVE	233	222	7141
MOUSEMOVE	233	225	7141
MOUSEMOVE	233	227	7141
MOUSEMOVE	233	229	7195
MOUSEMOVE	233	230	7195
MOUSEMOVE	233	229	7305
MOUSEMOVE	233	226	7360
MOUSEMOVE	229	223	7360
MOUSEMOVE	224	221	7360
MOUSEMOVE	217	219	7415
MOUSEMOVE	209	218	7415
MOUSEMOVE	203	217	7470
MOUSEMOVE	200	217	7470
MOUSEMOVE	199	217	7525
MOUSEMOVE	199	216	8404
MOUSEMOVE	199	212	8459
MOUSEMOVE	199	206	8459
MOUSEMOVE	195	201	8514
MOUSEMOVE	193	199	8514
MOUSEMOVE	190	197	8624
MOUSEMOVE	190	196	8624

5.2 THE ELEMENTS OF GUI TESTING

The first and most important element is a plan for testing the GUI. The complex nature of GUIs makes planning even more important than with CUIs. There are so many different facets of a GUI that must be tested that not planning the process insures that some will not be tested. The most important aspect of writing a plan is that the tester is forced to think about what she or he is going to do before doing it. The next most important aspect is that a written test plan makes the testing process repeatable and consistent across repetitions. Of course, the plan for testing the GUI should be only one component in an overall client-server test plan (refer back to the test plan outline

Fig. 5.4 GUI Prototype Test Plan

1. Set Test Objectives
2. Describe Modules and Associated GUIs to Be Tested
3. Generate Testing Schedules
4. Compose Test Team
5. Design Test Process/Create Test Case Design Specification
6. Define Test Cases
    a. Create scenarios for expected business uses (via scripting)
    b. Create test scripts for each business scenario (through automated testing tools)
7. Create Test Procedures Specification; Execute Test Cases
    a. Evaluate scripts (using walkthrough or inspection)
    b. Execute scripts (playback using test tool)
    c. Record test results (using test tool)
    d. Generate test incident reports (using test tool)
    e. Analyze results (using playback of tests)
    f. Generate management-level summary reports

described in Chapter 4). Figure 5.4 presents a rapid prototyping test plan for testing GUIs.

GUI testing is script-driven. Test scripts, which are based on expected and unexpected user interactions with the GUI, are designed, constructed, and executed in real-time situations. Furthermore, the scripts are frequently based on real user sessions at the workstation that reflect typical business processing work units (a day, a quarter, a year end, etc.). A set of scripts reflecting a business work unit is termed a test "scenario." The scripts in a scenario are either recorded or programmed using an automated test tool (see chapter 13). Testers who do not have previous programming experience can still develop scripts using a tool's recording capabilities, and testers with a programming background can write scripts from scratch using a built-in script editor.

Script-based GUI testing can be divided into *analog testing*, which involves low-level recording based on an object's position on the screen and the sequence of events that affect the object, and *context sensitive testing*, which involves object-level recording and is position independent.

Analog testing is based on the object's position on the GUI screen. Analog testing does not work for instances when the object's position changes in later tests because it falsely reports the situation as an error when that might not be the case. Another aspect of this approach is the complexity of the test scripts that must be programmed or that are recorded at the analog level. The scripts are difficult to read and therefore difficult to program or edit.

Context-sensitive testing involves object-level recording of GUI objects. Object-level recording has many advantages. The object is recorded independent of its physical description and location on the GUI screen. Location independence facilitates script-for-verification testing and script reuse for regression testing. Incorporating a "logical" rather than a "physical" description of an object in the script makes the scripts portable across hardware and software platforms. It also makes it easier to deal with custom GUI objects during verification testing. In general, object-level scripts are more flexible.

Both types of script recording require precise timing in certain situations. For instance, it is sometimes necessary for a script to suspend execution ("wait") until a certain event takes place (e.g., the appearance, or disappearance, of a dialog box). Thus, the script must be synchronized with the GUI itself. Scripts that run out of sync will appear to identify errors that are not actually there. Such wait states need to be open-ended in some circumstances and precisely timed finite intervals in other situations.

Timing is also important in the simple execution of menu commands. For example, a sequence of actions might include updating a data record. The record must first be displayed using an **Update** command in one of the applications menus. The displayed data record is changed and the changes are saved using a **Save** command under the **File** menu. When performing these actions manually, the process is slow because the user will wait until the record is displayed and modified before implementing the save. When executing, a prerecorded test script can read a test data file containing the keys that retrieve a record and the values that will be changed in milliseconds. The speed of execution will cause the script to fail, so delays must be inserted into the script before it will replay correctly.

5.3 AUTOMATED GUI TEST CASE CATEGORIES

An automated test case is a specific test that is embedded in a test script. Each embedded test case tests a single aspect of the application. For example, the kinds of test cases available in SQA Suite's Robot product have become increasingly more powerful since the first release of that product. The categories of automated test include the following:

Alphanumeric—tests for case-sensitive and case-insensitive text, an exact number, a number within a range, and a blank field; allows custom alphanumeric tests

Clipboard—captures and compares alphanumeric data that have been copied to the clipboard

DataWindow—captures and compares alphanumeric data from a Power-Builder DataWindow

File Comparison—compares the contents of two files

File Existence—checks for the existence of a specified file

List—captures and compares the alphanumeric contents of ListBoxes, ComboBoxes, and multiline edit controls

Menu—captures and compares the text, accelerator keys, and states of all the menus in the application for up to five levels of submenus

Module Existence—checks for a specified software module in memory

Object Data—captures and compares the data in objects

Object Properties—captures and compares the properties of objects

OCX/VBX Data—captures and compares the data in OCX/ActiveX and VBX controls

Region Image—captures a region of the screen

Table Window—captures and compares alphanumeric data from a Centura Table Window or SQLWindows Table Window

User-Defined DLL Call—calls an independently developed DLL test routine into the test procedure

User-Defined EXE Call—calls an independently developed EXE test routine into the test procedure

Window Existence—verifies that a specified window is displayed before continuing with playback

Window Image—captures a window for bitmap comparison during playback

These test cases can be used in both 16- and 32-bit test scripts across all the different Windows environments.

As of release 6.1 of SQA Suite many of the test cases have been collapsed into two types of test cases: Object Properties and Object Data. Together they effectively replace the List, Menu, OCX/VBX Data, DataWindow, and Table Window test cases from previous versions of SQA Robot.

The *Object Properties* test case provides specialized support for environment-specific objects such as PowerBuilder DataWindows, Delphi components, SQLWindows Table Windows, Centura Table Windows, Visual Basic controls, and OCX/ActiveX controls.

SQA 6.1 uses the *Object Data* to test

☞ PowerBuilder DataWindows, DropDownDataWindows, DropDownListBoxes, and DataStore controls

☞ VBX and OCX/ActiveX controls

☞ Visual Basic Data controls

☞ Delphi data-aware and DataSource components

☞ Centura Table Windows

☞ SQLWindows Table Windows

☞ Win 32 controls: list view, tree view, header, tab, and status bar

☞ Lists: list box, combo box, edit box

☞ Menus

An in-depth discussion of data-driven testing and of framework-based testing is found in chapter 8.

5.4 USABILITY

Usability is officially defined in ISO 9241 (Part 11, Guidance on Usability) as "the effectiveness, efficiency, and satisfaction with which users can achieve goals in particular environments."

The advent of the GUI has made the usability test a critical part of software testing. In C-S systems testing the client involves not only the correctness of GUI functions, but also the usability of the overall GUI design. GUIs are inherently easy to use; they are designed that way, but the improper use and placement of GUI objects, improper use of color, and the improper use of sound can result in a useless interface.

Johnson [8] stresses that increasing usability results in improved productivity, reduced expenditures for training and support, and longer retention of staff.

5.4.1 Usability Testing

Usability testing is a type of testing which began at IBM approximately 30 years ago and spread to other computer hardware companies. It has recently been advanced tremendously by Microsoft. Since the late 1980s Microsoft has stressed usability testing as a mechanism for improving its line of desktop software products. An important finding at Microsoft is that usability testing does not retard product development cycles. It has also found that for quality results, usability testing should be applied in conjunction with usability engineering to highly usable human-computer interfaces. Microsoft's goal is to create software that is so easy to use that it will be akin to driving an automobile. You just turn the key and drive away no matter which car you choose.

At Microsoft the information from product support calls has been used as feedback to product developers. This accomplishes two things. First, it provides important clues about user satisfaction and product feature usage patterns, and second, it places the information with the people who need it. There is an important distinction between user satisfaction as surveyed and user satisfaction as observed. Attitudes and behaviors are frequently discrepant. If users call for product support it means they are using that product feature, and it means that the usability of the feature must be improved. At Microsoft, the focus of usability testing is not on the user as a customer, but as a problem solver and a learner.

Usability testing can be approached in two ways. It can be completed manually, with human observers and human testers, or it can be carried out in semiautomated fashion using capture/replay tools. In both instances, video recordings of human computer interactions are critical. Perhaps the best framework is to use a hybrid approach that involves human observers, but at the same time records mouse movements and keystrokes with a capture playback tool. The playback and analysis of mouse movements and keystrokes can be used to validate the observers' findings.

5.5 DEVELOPING AND TESTING THE GUI PROTOTYPE

5.5.1 Discount Usability Engineering

Foody [6] cites usability testing as an overlooked but absolutely critical form of testing. He suggests that although even informal usability testing is OK, formal usability testing can accomplish a lot more. As Foody says, we cannot predict the manner in which users will accomplish a task. Users quite frequently develop shortcuts to make their work easier, and they adapt to the system (manual or automated) they are using. He summarizes by saying, "The bottom line here is that only through usability testing can developers learn how to support users in their real-world tasks."

Nielsen [14] has developed a user interface engineering approach dubbed "discount usability engineering." Nielsen's approach is perfect for developing GUIs for client-server applications because it is focused on rapid interface design at fractional costs using two-person development teams. Discount usability engineering methods are deliberately and necessarily semiformal. They rely mainly on the intuitive analytic and observational abilities of the engineers.

The methods result in high usability because the implemented GUI is based on the users' perceptions of how the system features should be organized in GUI. Commands that the users perceive as belonging together end up in the same menu, the menu names are meaningful because they were picked by the users, and so on.

The approach consists of a series of four studies conducted using a paper-and-pencil GUI prototype before construction of an electronic version. The results of each study are used to create a new and more complete iteration of the prototype. These studies are

1. Card-sorting categories
2. Icon intuitiveness test
3. Cards-to-icons distribution test
4. Home-page mockup walkthroughs

These studies can be conducted with small groups of three or four eventual interface users.

5.5.1.1 Card-Sorting Categories

The purpose of card sorting is to discover the user's mental model of the information space that will become the application's GUI. It can be used to generate menu structures. Nielsen [14] had user sort cards with command names with the intent that commands that end up together after the sort should probably be placed in the same menu.

The only drawback is that this approach requires a brainstorming session by the GUI designers before the sort in order to decide which commands to include in the sorting session. In fact, the one question Nielsen's group did not ask of the users is "What kind of information (command) is not available in the commands on the cards?" If the users had been queried in this manner at the end of each sorting session it would have fortified the process.

Nielsen's basic procedure is to write the name of each command on a 3-by-4 index card with a one-sentence explanation of the command. The cards are next scattered upon a desk in the usability lab. The engineers ask each user to sit at the desk and to place the cards into piles according to similarity. The users are cautioned not to try to produce large or small piles and not to aim for a specific number of cards in each pile. After the cards are sorted, the users are asked to group the piles into larger groups that appear to belong together. The users are also instructed to invent names for each larger group. The names are recorded on Post-it notes and placed by each larger group. The entire process can be complete in 30 to 40 minutes.

One engineer who produces a list of recommended groups of features for the GUI subjectively analyzes these data. The analysis requires about an hour to finish. The results are used to generate a group icon for each of the recommended groups.

5.5.1.2 Icon Intuitiveness Test

The group icons that are selected are then tested for intuitiveness. Each icon (displayed without a label) is shown to a user who is asked to tell the engineer what the icon represents. Icons that do not pass this ease-of-recognition test should be replaced or redesigned and retested.

Users may give more than one interpretation of the meaning of an icon. Thus, the decision of whether or not to redesign an icon is also a subjective one based in part on the user's response and on the engineer's judgment.

5.5.1.3 Cards-to-Icons Distribution Test

This test involves creating a mockup of the main GUI screen that includes color reproductions of the icons including the icon names or labels. The users are asked to place the command cards with the most relevant icon. Afterwards, the users are asked to comment on the aesthetics of each icon. Icons that are disliked or not intuitive enough as indicated by the card placement are replaced or redesigned and retested.

5.5.1.4 Home-Page Mockup Walkthroughs This test uses a paper model of the main GUI screen for the application (Nielsen's group used a magnified full color printed image). The users are asked to point to each icon and tell the engineers what information they think they can access through it. At the end of the session, the users are again asked to comment on icon aesthetics.

5.6 GUI REVIEWS

The GUI review is a powerful preventive technique. Even when implemented in a semiformal manner, reviewing the GUI can provide information about its design quality, its conformance to company standards, and its usability. Some of the problems uncovered during GUI reviews include:

☞ Absence of standard menu items (e.g., the **File** menu was missing in one GUI we reviewed)

☞ Nonstandard arrangement of menu items in the menu bar (e.g., the **File** menu should be the first menu on the left and the **Help** menu should always be the last menu on the right)

☞ Tool bar buttons that do not have corresponding menu commands

☞ Inconsistent use of Cancel and Close command buttons

☞ Inconsistent implementation of the Escape key to exit windows and dialog boxes

☞ Inappropriate Tab sequences within dialog boxes

☞ Improper default- and focus-setting for controls

☞ Improper placement of command buttons

☞ Overdependence on mouse actions as opposed to key sequences

☞ Improper grouping of controls

Figure 5.5A details common GUI errors Visual Basic developers make. The checklist in Figure 5.5B can be used to prepare for and conduct a GUI review for applications developed in Windows NT, Windows95, and Windows98 environments. The checklist can be customized to your company's GUI standards.

All of the problems cited in the list in Figure 5.5A are easily identifiable via the GUI review. The review doesn't have to be a major effort; it can be implemented as formally or as informally as your needs dictate. The requirements for review are:

☞ A set of standards for GUI design and implementation

☞ A checklist based on the standard that can be used to drive the review process

☞ A maximum of two hours for the review to take place (one hour is frequently enough time)

Fig. 5.5A Common GUI Errors Found in Windows, Child Windows, and Dialog Boxes—and How to Avoid Them

Among the actions you can take, make sure that

1. The startup icon for the application under consideration is unique from all other current applications.

2. A control menu is present in each window and dialog box.

3. The Multiple Document Interface (MDI) is correct for each window. Only the parent window should be modal (all child windows should be presented within the confines of the parent window).

4. All windows have a consistent look and feel.

5. All dialog boxes have a consistent look and feel.

6. The child widows can be cascaded or tiled within the parent window.

7. Icons representing minimized child windows can be arranged within the parent window.

8. There is a **File** menu.

9. There is a **Help** menu.

10. There is a **Window** menu.

11. Any other menus that are logically required by the application are properly located.

12. The proper commands and options are in each menu.

13. All buttons on all tool bars have corresponding menu commands.

14. Each menu command has an alternative key (hot-key) sequence that will invoke it where appropriate.

15. In "tabbed" dialog boxes, the tab names are not abbreviations.

16. In "tabbed" dialog boxes, the tabs can be accessed via appropriate hot-key combinations.

17. In "tabbed" dialog boxes, duplicate hot keys do not exist.

18. Tabs are placed horizontally across the top (avoid placing tabs vertically on the sides as this makes the names hard to read).

19. The **Escape** key (which is to roll back any changes that have been made) is used properly.

20. The **Cancel** button functions the same as the **Escape** key.

21. The **Cancel** button becomes a **Close** button when changes have been made that cannot be rolled back.

22. Only command buttons that are used by a particular window, or in a particular dialog box, are present.

23. When a command button is used only occasionally it is grayed out when it should not be used.

24. **OK** and **Cancel** buttons are grouped separately from other command buttons.

25. Command button names are not abbreviations.

26. Command button names are not technical labels, but rather are names meaningful to system users.

Fig. 5.5A Common GUI Errors Found in Windows, Child Windows, and Dialog Boxes—and How to Avoid Them (Continued)

27. Command buttons are all of similar size and shape.
28. Each command button can be accessed via a hot-key combination (except the **OK** and **CANCEL** buttons, which do not normally have hot keys).
29. Command buttons in the same window/dialog box do not have duplicate hot keys.
30. Each window/dialog box has a clearly marked default value (command button, or other object) that is invoked when the **Enter** key is pressed.
31. Focus is set to an object that makes sense according to the function of the window/dialog box.
32. Option button (AKA radio button) names are not abbreviations.
33. Option button names are not technical labels, but rather are names meaningful to system users.
34. If hot keys are used to access option buttons, duplicate hot keys do not exist in the same window/dialog box.
35. Option box names are not abbreviations.
36. Option box names are not technical labels, but rather are names meaningful to system users.
37. If hot keys are used to access option boxes, duplicate hot keys do not exist in the same window/dialog box.
38. Option boxes, option buttons, and command buttons are logically grouped together in clearly demarcated areas.
39. Each demarcated area has a meaningful name that is not an abbreviation.
40. The **Tab** key sequence that traverses the defined areas does so in a logical way.
41. The parent window has a status bar.
42. All user-related system messages are presented via the status bar.
43. Mouse actions are consistent across windows.
44. The color red is not used to highlight active GUI objects (many individuals are red-green color blind).
45. The user will have control of the desktop with respect to general color and highlighting (the application should not dictate the desktop background characteristics).
46. The GUI does not have a cluttered appearance (GUIs should not be designed to look like mainframe CUIs when replacing such data entry/retrieval screens).
47. All help screens are in place.
48. Both nonspecific and context-specific help are available.
49. All help hypertext jumps are correct.
50. Jump terms and Glossary terms are properly distinguished.
51. The help menu contains—at a minimum—**Contents**, **Index**, **Search**, and **About** commands.

Fig. 5.5A Common GUI Errors Found in Windows, Child Windows, and Dialog Boxes—and How to Avoid Them (Continued)

---

52. The help content is complete, correct, and consistent with the application's behaviors.

53. Each help topic is covered in sufficient detail.

54. Step-by-step instructions are included in help screens that describe complex tasks.

55. The **F1** key always invokes help no matter what the user is attempting to do.

56. **Alt-H** always invokes help no matter what the user is attempting to do.

57. Help can be invoked even when error-message dialog boxes have the focus.

This list is based on common errors found in GUIs. Consider it a starting point for organizing and implementing a GUI review. It is thorough, but by no means exhaustive. Suggestions for additions to this checklist are welcome and should be submitted to djmosley@csst-technologies.com.

Fig. 5.5B GUI Review Checklist

Item	Validation Rule	Results	Comments
MDI Frame (Parent Window)	Is the **System** menu (control box) present?		
	Is the Title Bar present?		
	Is the **Minimize** button present?		
	Is the **Maximize** button present?		
	Is the **Restore** button present?		
	Is the Menu Bar present?		
	Is there a Toolbar? (optional)		
System Menu (Control Box)	Is the **Restore** command present?		
	Is the **Move** command present?		
	Is the **Size** command present?		
	Is the **Minimize** command present?		
	Is the **Maximize** command present?		

Fig. 5.5B GUI Review Checklist (Continued)

Item	Validation Rule	Results	Comments
	Does each of the commands above have an appropriate short-cut (accelerator) key?		
	Is the **Close** command present?		
	Is the **Switch To** command present?		
	Is the **Switch To** command followed by three dots (ellipsis) to indicate that a dialog box will appear?		
	Does the Key Combination **Alt+F4** close the window?		
	Does the key combination **Ctrl+Esc** bring up the Task List dialog box?		
Title Bar	Does the application name appear in the Title Bar?		
	Is the form name of the child window appended to the application name in the Title Bar?		
Minimize, Maximize, and Restore Controls	No child window should appear visible when the MDI frame is minimized— is this so?		
	When a child window is minimized, does it appear as an icon within the MDI frame?		
Menus	Do the menus have standard names (**File**, **Edit**, **View**, **Help**)?		
	Do the menus appear in a standard order beginning with **File** and ending with **Help**?		
	Do the menu commands have standard names, such as **Open**, **Close**, **Save**, **Save As**, etc.?		

Fig. 5.5B GUI Review Checklist (Continued)

Item	Validation Rule	Results	Comments
	If required, is the **Window** menu present?		
	Is the **Help** (a **Help** menu is always required) menu present?		
Tool Bars *Note: Tool bars are optional*	Are the tool-bar buttons 3D?		
	Are the buttons initially raised?		
	Do the buttons require only a single mouse click to activate?		
	Are the button icons intuitive to the task the button performs?		
	For toggle buttons, do they appear depressed when on and raised when off?		
	Are all tool-bar buttons required initially placed and then activated/ deactivated when appropriate?		
	When tool-bar buttons are unavailable are they grayed out?		
	Is there an equivalent menu item for every tool bar button?		
	Are tool bar tips used?		
Dialog Boxes *Note: For each dialog box consider the following*	Is the dialog box modal?		
	Dialog boxes should not be sizable—is this so?		
	Can it be moved?		
	Does the dialog box have a Title Bar?		
	Does the dialog box have a **System** menu (control box)?		

Fig. 5.5B GUI Review Checklist (Continued)

Item	Validation Rule	Results	Comments
	Does the **System** menu have a **Move** command?		
	Does the **System** menu have a **Close** command?		
	The dialog box should not have **Maximize** and **Minimize** buttons—is this so?		
	Is the dialog box text stated in the affirmative?		
	Does the dialog box text state the problem clearly and concisely?		
	Is a context-sensitive **Help** button present in Warning/ Error-message dialog boxes?		
	For Error-message dialog boxes, is the severity of the error explained?		
	For Error-message dialog boxes, is the user directed to the appropriate source for help?		
	In general, is the message consistent with the messages across all dialog boxes?		
	Is the dialog box centered on the screen?		
	Do the command buttons in the dialog box make sense?		
	Is there a **Cancel** command button (for dialog boxes that involve lengthy actions)?		
	Is the format gray background, box centered on screen, no border, with microhelp?		

Fig. 5.5B GUI Review Checklist (Continued)

Item	Validation Rule	Results	Comments
Information-Message Dialog Boxes	Does the dialog box have only an **OK** command button?		
	Does the dialog box display the "i" icon to the left of the message?		
Warning-Message Dialog Boxes	Is there a positive response (**Yes** or **OK**) command button?		
	Is the positive response command button the default?		
	Is there a negative response (**No** and/or **Cancel**) command button?		
	Does the dialog box display the "!" icon to the left of the message?		
Critical-Message Dialog Box	Is there a positive response (**Yes** or **OK**) command button?		
	Is the positive response command button the default?		
	Is there a negative response (**No**) command button?		
	Is there a **Cancel** command button set with cancel properties?		
	Does the dialog box display the "STOP" icon to the left of the message?		
Controls			
General Considerations	Do all controls have a default value if applicable?		
	Are the most important controls in the upper left of the dialog boxes?		
	Are dependent controls grayed out until activated?		

Fig. 5.5B GUI Review Checklist (Continued)

Item	Validation Rule	Results	Comments
Check Boxes	Is there a minimum of 2 check boxes in each control group?		
	Control groups should not have more than 10 check boxes—is this so?		
	Can the users select more than 1 check box?		
	Do all check boxes have text labels?		
	Are the labels meaningful?		

The attendees should include one or more of the GUI designers, one or more end users, a representative of the standards group, and one quality assurance (QA) analyst. The designers are present to explain the GUI to the reviewers, the end users are there to assess usability, the standards group representative is present to assure conformance to the organization's visual interface standards, and the QA analyst is present to guide the review process.

The process we use provides access to the GUI via a prototype and to the printed checklist prior to the review. This allows the reviewers to formulate questions before the review that could be investigated during the review. This turns out to be a real time saver.

The following is excerpted from a write-up of an actual GUI review. The names have been changed to protect the guilty.

CASE STUDY

Introduction

The QA analyst subjects the prototype to a manual inspection process. The purpose of the review is to compare the GUI with the Corporate Visual Interface Standards, locate inconsistencies among GUI objects, identify missing GUI objects, and identify nonfunctioning GUI objects.

General Comments

The first nonconformity with the corporate guidelines is that there is not a **File** menu. The main application menu appears to be the **Proposal** menu. This menu contains commands for developing the various types of proposals, but also contains a **Print Setup** command and an **Exit** command, which are usually found in the **File** menu.

The status bar displays an informational message describing the menu when the left mouse button is pressed and held while the point is over the menu name. This is inconsistent across menus, as the descriptive information is not displayed for the **Volume** and the **Notification** menus.

There are no "dimmed" menu items. For example, the **Cascade** and **Tile** commands are still available when no windows are open.

There is no consistent usage of object focus and default object selection in the dialog boxes.

The **Escape** key does not consistently function as a **Cancel** command. Pressing the **Escape** key in any of the proposal dialog boxes results in another dialog box that asks users if they want to delete the proposal. Should it do that?

The command buttons are placed in line along the bottom of most dialog boxes; corporate guidelines recommend stacking the buttons except in message dialog boxes.

The tab sequence is not consistent across dialog boxes. In many dialog boxes the tab key does not cycle correctly. It requires many presses and the focus disappears for several presses before the cycle begins again.

The arrow keys work inconsistently when used to move from radio button to radio button. In some instances, the right or left arrow must be pressed to move up or down a sequence of radio buttons. In one specific instance, the up arrow key moved the option selection down. Radio buttons are not grouped as suggested by corporate guidelines.

Wizards

Wizards Menu

The procedure to review the wizards menu commands is to open the menu and select wizard commands one at a time. For each wizard, all of the dialog boxes are reviewed. The **Escape** key is pressed for each dialog box to verify that it functions the same as the **Cancel** command button. The focus and default settings are determined for each dialog box. The tab sequence from control to control is investigated.

New Summary Report Wizard

The **Escape** key does not work as a **Cancel** command in any of the dialog boxes.

There is no default control in the first-level dialog box. It should, however, be set to the **Next** command button. The default in subsequent boxes is the **Next** command button.

The tab key has to be pressed many times to complete a cycle of the controls. In the fifth-level box it takes 16 presses to cycle from the last command button to the package control. This type of situation exists for all of the dialog boxes.

In the final dialog box, there is no default setting or control focus. It should be the **Finish** command button.

New User Wizard

The **Escape** key does not act as a **Cancel** command.

In the first-level dialog box, the **Cancel** button has the focus and is the default.

In the second-level dialog box, **Next** has the focus and is the default.

The tab key does not function correctly and the focus never goes to the "Group" test box.

In the third-level dialog box, the **Next** button has the focus and is the default.

The tab key functions improperly and the focus never reaches the "Region" text box.

No focus or default exists in the final dialog box. It should be the **Finish** command button.

The Create Custom Groups Wizard

The **Escape** key does not function as a **Cancel** command.

The first-level dialog box has no focus.

The tab key does not work correctly.

The **Next** command button has the focus and is the default for the second-level dialog box.

There is no focus or default in the final-level dialog box. It should be the **Finish** command button.

Summary Report Detail Wizard

The escape key does not cancel the command.

In the first-level dialog box, the **Cancel** button has the focus and is the default. In the second-level dialog box, the **Next** button has the focus and is the default. The tab sequence (back→cancel→next) is different from that in the other wizards (cancel→back→next). The right/left arrow buttons must be used to move from radio button to radio button, but the buttons are stacked vertically.

In the third-level dialog box, **Next** has the focus and is the default. The tab sequence is different from the sequence in other wizards. The arrow keys all work to move from one radio button to another (up and left arrow move up the list of buttons, right and down move down the list of buttons).

In the final dialog box there is no focus and no default. **Finish** should have the focus and should be the default.

A manual GUI review may be too time consuming for some of the aggressive development schedules C-S testers face. When that is the case, an automated test script can replace the GUI review proper. Figure 5.6 is an SQA test script that was use to automate 90% of the review items in the checklist illustrated in Figure 5.5B. Individual testers reviewed the other 10% during integration test sessions. And a formal GUI review was not required.

Fig. 5.6 Script Automating Most Items from Figure 5.5B

```
Sub Main
    Dim Result As Integer

    'Initially Recorded: 10/07/97  09:44:42
    'Test Procedure Name: Generic menu / mode win test

Rem Check General menu properties and window plus child properties

    Result = WindowTC (CompareProperties, "Caption=xxxx", "CaseID=GEN_MNU1")

    Window SetTestContext, "Caption=xxxx", ""
    Result = WindowTC (CompareProperties, "Caption={*Neutral};ChildWindow",
        "CaseID=GEN_MNU2")
    Window ResetTestContext, "", ""
    'Result = WindowTC (CompareMenu, "Caption=xxxx", "CaseID=GEN_MNUQ")
    'Result = WindowTC (CompareMenu, "Caption=xxxx", "CaseID=GEN_MNUQ")

    Window SetContext, "Caption=xxxx", ""

Rem Check TC window modes    Neutral, Display, Add, Update and Delete using menu
        select
    Window SetTestContext, "Caption=xxxx", ""
    Result = WindowTC (Exists, "Caption={*Neutral};ChildWindow",
        "CaseID=GEN_MNUA;Status=NORMAL")
    Window ResetTestContext, "", ""

    Window SetContext, "Caption=xxxx", ""
    MenuSelect "Mode->Display"

    Window SetTestContext, "Caption=xxxx", ""
    Result = WindowTC (Exists, "Caption={*Display};ChildWindow",
        "CaseID=GEN_MNUB;Status=NORMAL")
    Window ResetTestContext, "", ""

    Window SetContext, "Caption=xxxx", ""
    MenuSelect "Mode->Display"

    Window SetTestContext, "Caption=xxxx", ""
    Result = WindowTC (Exists, "Caption={*Neutral};ChildWindow",
        "CaseID=GEN_MNUC;Status=NORMAL")
    Window ResetTestContext, "", ""

    MenuSelect "Mode->Add"

    Window SetTestContext, "Caption=xxxx", ""
    Result = WindowTC (Exists, "Caption={*Add};ChildWindow",
        "CaseID=GEN_MNUD;Status=NORMAL")
    Window ResetTestContext, "", ""

    MenuSelect "Mode->Add"

    Result = WindowTC (Exists, "Caption=Mode Exit?",
        "CaseID=GEN_MNUE;Status=NORMAL")

    Window SetContext, "Caption=Mode Exit?", ""
    PushButton Click, "Text=Yes"

    Window SetTestContext, "Caption=xxxx", ""
    Result = WindowTC (Exists, "Caption={*Neutral};ChildWindow",
        "CaseID=GEN_MNUF;Status=NORMAL")
    Window ResetTestContext, "", ""

    Window SetContext, "Caption=xxxx", ""
    MenuSelect "Mode->Display"

    Window SetTestContext, "Caption=xxxx", ""
    Result = WindowTC (Exists, "Caption={*Display};ChildWindow",
        "CaseID=GEN_MNUG;Status=NORMAL")
    Window ResetTestContext, "", ""

    Window SetContext, "Caption=xxxx", ""
```

Fig. 5.6 Script Automating Most Items from Figure 5.5B (Continued)

```
      MenuSelect "Mode->Display"

      Window SetTestContext, "Caption=xxxx", ""
      Result = WindowTC (Exists, "Caption={*Neutral};ChildWindow",
           "CaseID=GEN_MNUH;Status=NORMAL")
      Window ResetTestContext, "", ""

      MenuSelect "Mode->Update"

      Window SetTestContext, "Caption=xxxx", ""
      Result = WindowTC (Exists, "Caption={*Update};ChildWindow",
           "CaseID=GEN_MNUI;Status=NORMAL")
      Window ResetTestContext, "", ""

      MenuSelect "Mode->Update"

      Result = WindowTC (Exists, "Caption=Mode Exit?",
           "CaseID=GEN_MNUJ;Status=NORMAL")

      Window SetContext, "Caption=Mode Exit?", ""
      PushButton Click, "Text=Yes"

      Window SetTestContext, "Caption=xxxx", ""
      Result = WindowTC (Exists, "Caption={*Neutral};ChildWindow",
           "CaseID=GEN_MNUK;Status=NORMAL")
      Window ResetTestContext, "", ""

      Window SetContext, "Caption=xxxx", ""
      MenuSelect "Mode->Display"

      Window SetTestContext, "Caption=xxxx", ""
      Result = WindowTC (Exists, "Caption={*Display};ChildWindow",
           "CaseID=GEN_MNUL;Status=NORMAL")
      Window ResetTestContext, "", ""

      MenuSelect "Mode->Display"

      Window SetTestContext, "Caption=xxxx", ""
      Result = WindowTC (Exists, "Caption={*Neutral};ChildWindow",
           "CaseID=GEN_MNUM;Status=NORMAL")
      Window ResetTestContext, "", ""

      MenuSelect "Mode->Delete"

      Window SetTestContext, "Caption=xxxx", ""
      Result = WindowTC (Exists, "Caption={*Delete};ChildWindow",
           "CaseID=GEN_MNUN;Status=NORMAL")
      Window ResetTestContext, "", ""

      MenuSelect "Mode->Delete"

      Window SetTestContext, "Caption=xxxx", ""
      Result = WindowTC (Exists, "Caption={*Neutral};ChildWindow",
           "CaseID=GEN_MNUO;Status=NORMAL")
      Window ResetTestContext, "", ""
Rem Check TC window modes    Neutral, Display, Add, Update and Delete using
           ctl+i,u,d,y

      Window SetTestContext, "Caption=xxxx", ""
      Result = WindowTC (Exists, "Caption={*Neutral};ChildWindow",
           "CaseID=GEN_MNUA;Status=NORMAL")
      Window ResetTestContext, "", ""
      DelayFor 1000

      Window SetContext, "Caption=xxxx", ""
      InputKeys "^y" 'Display

      Window SetTestContext, "Caption=xxxx", ""
      Result = WindowTC (Exists, "Caption={*Display};ChildWindow",
           "CaseID=GEN_MNUB;Wait=4,90;Status=NORMAL")
      Window ResetTestContext, "", ""
```

Fig. 5.6 Script Automating Most Items from Figure 5.5B (Continued)

```
Window SetContext, "Caption=xxxx", ""
InputKeys "^y" 'Display

Window SetTestContext, "Caption=xxxx", ""
Result = WindowTC (Exists, "Caption={*Neutral};ChildWindow",
    "CaseID=GEN_MNUC;Status=NORMAL")
Window ResetTestContext, "", ""

InputKeys "^i" 'Add

Window SetTestContext, "Caption=xxxx", ""
Result = WindowTC (Exists, "Caption={*Add};ChildWindow",
    "CaseID=GEN_MNUD;Status=NORMAL")
Window ResetTestContext, "", ""

InputKeys "^i" 'Add

Result = WindowTC (Exists, "Caption=Mode Exit?",
    "CaseID=GEN_MNUE;Status=NORMAL")

Window SetContext, "Caption=Mode Exit?", ""
PushButton Click, "Text=Yes"

Window SetTestContext, "Caption=xxxx", ""
Result = WindowTC (Exists, "Caption={*Neutral};ChildWindow",
    "CaseID=GEN_MNUF;Status=NORMAL")
Window ResetTestContext, "", ""

Window SetContext, "Caption=xxxx", ""
InputKeys "^y" 'Display

Window SetTestContext, "Caption=xxxx", ""
Result = WindowTC (Exists, "Caption={*Display};ChildWindow",
    "CaseID=GEN_MNUG;Status=NORMAL")
Window ResetTestContext, "", ""

Window SetContext, "Caption=xxxx", ""
InputKeys "^y" 'Display

Window SetTestContext, "Caption=xxxx", ""
Result = WindowTC (Exists, "Caption={*Neutral};ChildWindow",
    "CaseID=GEN_MNUH;Status=NORMAL")
Window ResetTestContext, "", ""

InputKeys "^u" 'Update

Window SetTestContext, "Caption=xxxx", ""
Result = WindowTC (Exists, "Caption={*Update};ChildWindow",
    "CaseID=GEN_MNUI;Status=NORMAL")
Window ResetTestContext, "", ""

InputKeys "^u" 'Update

Result = WindowTC (Exists, "Caption=Mode Exit?",
    "CaseID=GEN_MNUJ;Status=NORMAL")

Window SetContext, "Caption=Mode Exit?", ""
PushButton Click, "Text=Yes"

Window SetTestContext, "Caption=xxxx", ""
Result = WindowTC (Exists, "Caption={*Neutral};ChildWindow",
    "CaseID=GEN_MNUK;Status=NORMAL")
Window ResetTestContext, "", ""

Window SetContext, "Caption=xxxx", ""
InputKeys "^y" 'Display

Window SetTestContext, "Caption=xxxx", ""
Result = WindowTC (Exists, "Caption={*Display};ChildWindow",
    "CaseID=GEN_MNUL;Status=NORMAL")
Window ResetTestContext, "", ""
```

Fig. 5.6 Script Automating Most Items from Figure 5.5B (Continued)

```
    InputKeys "^y" 'Display

    Window SetTestContext, "Caption=xxxx", ""
    Result = WindowTC (Exists, "Caption={*Neutral};ChildWindow",
        "CaseID=GEN_MNUM;Status=NORMAL")
    Window ResetTestContext, "", ""

    InputKeys "^d" 'Delete

    Window SetTestContext, "Caption=xxxx", ""
    Result = WindowTC (Exists, "Caption={*Delete};ChildWindow",
        "CaseID=GEN_MNUN;Status=NORMAL")
    Window ResetTestContext, "", ""

    InputKeys "^d" 'Delete

    Window SetTestContext, "Caption=xxxx", ""
    Result = WindowTC (Exists, "Caption={*Neutral};ChildWindow",
        "CaseID=GEN_MNUO;Status=NORMAL")
    Window ResetTestContext, "", ""
Rem check for help window
    'SQALogMessage sqaWarning, "Help not available at this time", "Replace with real
        test when help is available"

    Window SetContext, "Caption=xxxx", ""

    Window SetContext, "Caption={*Neutral};ChildWindow", ""
    InputKeys "{F1}"

    Result = WindowTC (Exists, "Caption=xxxx Help", "CaseID=GENHELP1;Status=NORMAL")

    Window SetContext, "Caption=xxxx Help", ""
    Window CloseWin, "", ""

    Window SetContext, "Caption=xxxx", ""
    Window Click, "", "Coords=222,-27"
    MenuSelect "Help->ABLE Help"

    Result = WindowTC (Exists, "Caption=xxxx Help", "CaseID=GENHELP2;Status=NORMAL")

    Window SetContext, "Caption=xxxx Help", ""
    Window CloseWin, "", ""

    Window SetContext, "Caption=xxxx", ""
    MenuSelect "Help->Index"

    Result = WindowTC (Exists, "Caption=Help Topics: xxxx Help",
        "CaseID=GENHELP3;Status=NORMAL")

    Window SetContext, "Caption=Help Topics: xxxx Help", ""
    PushButton Click, "Text=Cancel"

    Window SetContext, "Caption=xxxx", ""
    MenuSelect "Help->About ABLE"

    Result = WindowTC (Exists, "Caption=About xxxx",
        "CaseID=GENHELP4;Status=NORMAL")

    Window SetContext, "Caption=About xxxx", ""
    PushButton Click, "Text=OK"

    Window SetContext, "Caption=xxxx", ""
    MenuSelect "Help->Who Am I?"

    Result = WindowTC (Exists, "Caption=Who Am I?", "CaseID=GENHELP5;Status=NORMAL")

    Window SetContext, "Caption=Who Am I?", ""
    PushButton Click, "Text=OK"
Rem Generic Min max test
    Result = WindowTC (CompareProperties, "Caption=xxxx", "CaseID=BGENMNUA")

    Window SetContext, "Caption=xxxx", ""
```

Fig. 5.6 Script Automating Most Items from Figure 5.5B (Continued)

```
Window SetContext, "Caption={*Neutral};ChildWindow", ""
Window WMaximize, "", ""
Result = WindowTC (CompareProperties, "Caption={xxxx - * - Neutral]}",
    "CaseID=BGENMNUB")

Window SetContext, "Caption={xxxx - * - Neutral]}", ""

Window SetContext, "Caption={*Neutral};ChildWindow", ""
Window WMinimize, "", ""

Window SetTestContext, "Caption=xxxx", ""
Result = WindowTC (CompareProperties, "Caption={*Neutral};ChildWindow",
    "CaseID=BGENMNUC")
Window ResetTestContext, "", ""

Window OpenIcon, "", ""

Window SetContext, "Caption={xxxx - * - Neutral]}", ""

Window SetContext, "Caption={*Neutral};ChildWindow", ""
Window RestorePos, "", ""

Window SetTestContext, "Caption=xxxx", ""
Result = WindowTC (CompareProperties, "Caption={*Neutral};ChildWindow",
    "CaseID=BGENMNUD")
Window ResetTestContext, "", ""

Window SetTestContext, "Caption=xxxx", ""
Result = WindowTC (CompareProperties, "Caption=Main Menu;ChildWindow",
    "CaseID=BGENMNUE")
Window ResetTestContext, "", ""

Window SetContext, "Caption=xxxx", ""

Window SetContext, "Caption=Main Menu;ChildWindow", ""
Window OpenIcon, "", ""

Window SetTestContext, "Caption=xxxx", ""
Result = WindowTC (CompareProperties, "Caption=Main Menu;ChildWindow",
    "CaseID=BGENMNUF")
Window ResetTestContext, "", ""

Window WMinimize, "", ""

Window SetContext, "Caption=xxxx", ""
Window RestorePos, "", ""
Result = WindowTC (CompareProperties, "Caption=xxxx", "CaseID=BGENMNUG")

Window WMinimize, "", ""

Window SetContext, "Class=Shell_TrayWnd", ""
TabControl Click, "ObjectIndex=1;\;ItemIndex=0", ""
Result = WindowTC (CompareProperties, "Caption=xxxx", "CaseID=BGENMNUH")

Window SetContext, "Caption=xxxx", ""
Window WMaximize, "", ""

Window SetContext, "Caption={*Neutral};ChildWindow", ""

Window SetContext, "Caption=xxxx", ""
Window RestorePos, "", ""

Window SetContext, "Caption={*Neutral};ChildWindow", ""

Window SetContext, "Caption=xxxx", ""

Window SetContext, "Caption={*Neutral};ChildWindow", ""
Window WMinimize, "", ""

Window SetTestContext, "Caption=xxxx", ""
Result = WindowTC (CompareProperties, "Caption={*Neutral};ChildWindow",
    "CaseID=BGENMNUI")
Window ResetTestContext, "", ""
```

Fig. 5.6 Script Automating Most Items from Figure 5.5B (Continued)

```
    Window SetContext, "Caption=xxxx", ""

    Window SetContext, "Caption=Main Menu;ChildWindow", ""
    Window OpenIcon, "", ""

    Window SetTestContext, "Caption=xxxx", ""
    Result = WindowTC (CompareProperties, "Caption=Main Menu;ChildWindow",
        "CaseID=BGENMNUJ")
    Window ResetTestContext, "", ""

    Window SetContext, "Caption=xxxx", ""
    Window WMaximize, "", ""

    Window SetContext, "Caption=Main Menu;ChildWindow", ""
    Window WMinimize, "", ""

    Window SetContext, "Caption=xxxx", ""

    Window SetContext, "Caption={*Neutral};ChildWindow", ""
    Window OpenIcon, "", ""

    Window SetContext, "Caption=xxxx", ""

    Result = WindowTC (CompareProperties, "Caption={*Neutral};ChildWindow",
        "CaseID=BGENMNUK")
End Sub
```

5.7 GUI TESTING TOOLS

Fortunately, a number of companies have begun producing structured capture/playback testing tools that address the unique properties of GUIs (see chapter 13 for a complete discussion of C-S testing tools). Farley [5] describes effective GUI testing tools as ones providing reusable test components via a usable test suite programming language. Such tools have the ability to record test cases by running the test module through its available options. They are able to edit the recorded scripts to increase the test case's effectiveness. They support your particular approach to testing and provide ease of use and management of test cases, associated programs, screens, and test results.

The unfortunate side of these tools is they do not address traditional data-validation or the path-testing needs. Data validation can be handled at either the client or the server level, or split between the levels. GUI application software presents the logical place to include validation of input because it makes sense to validate and cross-check data items before using or storing them in files as GUI applications often do. The GUI should not allow the user to enter any data that is of the wrong type—outside the required range—or that is inconsistent with other data being entered.

Some of the most publicized and most serious errors in software systems have been the result of inadequate or missing input validation procedures. So, the importance of data validation cannot be overstated. Software testing already has powerful data validation procedures in the form of the Black Box techniques of Equivalence Partitioning, Boundary Analysis, and Error Guessing [11,12]. The Black Box approach looks at the system as an enclosed box with the only information available to the tester being a description of what goes into the system and what the expected output is for each unit of input. Test cases should be developed using these techniques and included in any test of GUI application software modules.

The software testing discipline also has procedures for functional testing that can be applied to C-S systems [3,4,11,12]. Binder [3] has provided us with "scenario testing," a system-level Black Box approach that also assumes good White Box logic-level coverage for C-S systems. These procedures are essential to the functional/code-level testing, and they can be applied to the various levels of interface server code that exists in C-S systems.

In addition, requirements-based testing has been thoroughly investigated and there are powerful tools for translating requirements into a test case specification [5,6]. The cause-effect graph can be used to map written requirements into a Booleanlike language that can be used to construct requirements-based test cases.

The decision logic table (DLT) represents an external (requirements-level) view of the functional specification that can be used to supplement Binder's scenario testing from a logic-coverage perspective [11]. DLTs provide an additional level of "comfort" because they include a check for completeness of the specification logic. In DLTs each logical condition in the specification becomes a control path in the finished system. Each rule in the table describes a specific instance of a pathway that must be implemented. It does not matter if a third-generation language or a client-server development tool is used, the same result should occur. So, test cases based on the rules in a DLT provide adequate coverage of the module's logic independent of its coded implementation.

Another important consideration is to assure that duplicated data and processes are in synchrony with update processes (Add, Change, or Delete) and affect all of the replicated data. Replicated processes should be uniformly maintained through good configuration management procedures. The DLT approach would be useful when designing test cases to assure that duplicated processes and data are properly updated during the maintenance cycle of the C-S system.

Finally, all automated C-S testing tools possess one major inherent deficiency: They are oriented toward postanalysis and design-defect identification and removal and do very little in the way of error prevention. Defect prevention is best achieved through the use of review techniques such as walkthroughs and inspections [11]. These human testing procedures have been found to be very effective in the prevention and early correction of errors.

It has been documented that two-thirds of all of the errors in finished information systems are the results of logic flaws rather than poor coding [13]. Preventive testing approaches can eliminate the majority of these analysis and design errors before they filter through to the production system. The trade-off is that these techniques are time consuming and are performed manually, substantially slowing the testing process. Still, I highly recommend their use when possible in C-S testing.

Even with their drawbacks, the GUI testing tools described above are extremely useful during design and prototyping activities. Their implementation should be carefully planned, however. Figure 5.4 suggests a GUI prototyping test procedure that could be used to manage and control the use of any of the commercially available GUI testing tools.

5.8 CONCLUSION

Siegel [15] has noted that the object-oriented nature of the GUI in client-server systems makes it a rich and complex interface. Thus, it is impossible to test all the meaningful paths or mouse actions; however, he sees the "saving grace" as the standardization of GUI objects in the various windowing environments. He sees the defining of higher-level GUI objects as a substantial saving of testing costs. This also makes automating GUI testing across C-S platforms feasible.

Properly engineering the GUI, however, is the most effective way to increase user interface quality. Techniques such as discount usability engineering will do more to produce an intuitive and usable GUI than any method for testing it can ever do. A set of company-wide GUI design guidelines is an absolute requirement and the details governed by company policy can reach as far down as individual screen icons.

5.9 REFERENCES

1. Atre, Shaku. *Client-Server Application Development Testing.* A special report by Atre Associates, Inc., 222 Grace Church Street, Port Chester, NY 10573-5155.

2. Binder, Robert. "Scenario-Based Testing for Client-Server Systems." *The Software Testing Forum*, Vol. 1, No. 2, November–December, 1993, pp. 12–17.

3. Elmendorf, William. *Cause-Effect Graphs in Functional Testing.* IBM System Development Division, TR-DD.2487, Poughkeepsie, NY, 1973.

4. Elmendorf, William. "Functional Analysis Using Cause-Effect Graphs." *Proceedings of Share XLI–II*, IBM, New York, 1974, pp. 577–87.

5. Farley, Kevin J. "Software Testing for Windows Developers." *Data-Based Advisor*, November 1993, pp. 45–6, 50–2.

6. Foody, Michael A. "When Is Software Ready for Release?" *Unix Review*, Vol. 13, No. 3, March 1995, p. 35(5).

7. Hayes, Linda G. "Automated Testing for Everyone." *OS/2 Professional*, November 1993, p. 51.

8. Johnson, Andrew W. "Usability Is Much More Than Mice and Menus." *PC User*, No. 245; October 19, 1994; p. 49.

9. Kepple, Lawrence. "GUI Testing Architecture Can Help Meet QA Challenge." *CASE Trends*, 1993.

10. McCabe, Thomas J. *Structured Testing, A Testing Methodology Using the McCabe Complexity Metric*. NBS Special Publication. Contract B82NAAR5518, 1983.

11. Mosley, Daniel J. *The Handbook of MIS Application Software Testing: Methods, Techniques, and Tools for Assuring Quality Through Testing*. Prentice-Hall Yourdon Press, Englewood Cliffs, NJ, 1993.

12. Myers, Glenford. *The Art of Software Testing*. Wiley-Interscience, New York, 1979.

13. Myers, Glenford. *Software Reliability*. John Wiley & Sons, New York, 1977.

14. Nielsen, Jakob. "Applying Discount Usability Engineering." Portions reprinted, with permission from *IEEE Software*, January 1995, pp. 98–100. © 1995 IEEE.

15. Siegel, Shel M. *Strategies for Testing Object-Oriented Software*. CompuServe CASE Forum Library, September 1992.

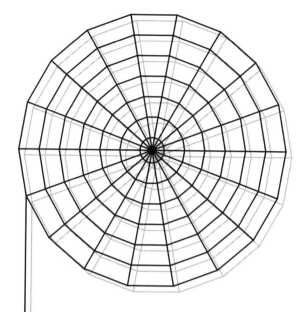

CHAPTER 6

Testing Server Applications

6.1 INTRODUCTION

There are several kinds of situations that scripts can be designed to invoke during server tests: load tests, volume tests, stress tests, performance tests, and data-recovery tests.

6.1.1 Client-Server Load Testing

Client-server systems must undergo two types of testing. First is single-user function-based testing. As I described earlier, this approach focuses on testing a single client against a single server. Reality tells us that C-S systems are rarely if ever single-user systems. The typical scenario is one in which several hundred users are simultaneously logged into the system. This makes the second type of client-server testing, multiuser load testing, essential.

Multiuser load testing is the best method to gauge client-server performance. Load testing involves testing in an environment that may consist of a variety of software applications and hardware platforms. Load testing is necessary in order to determine the suitability of application server, database server, and web server performance.

Multiuser load testing requires emulating a milieu where multiple clients access a single-server application. This type of testing is rarely possible without automation. There are several reasons why manual load testing is not usually a viable option. First, it is tremendously difficult to amass the physical resources that are required. Second, a large number of testers are required. Third, it is very difficult to coordinate and synchronize the testers and machines. Fourth, a significant level of organization is required to capture and organize the results. Fifth, manual tests are rarely repeatable.

139

There are many good products on the market that can assist your load-testing efforts. SQA TeamTest Suite offers Loadtest PC, as well as the newer Performance Studio Product, and Mercury Interactive has LoadRunner PC. But before purchasing a tool, you should consider your load-testing requirements. The first and most obvious is the computing environment, e.g., Windows 95, Windows NT, and Unix. You should analyze the system to be load tested, develop a set of load test requirements, then acquire a load-testing tool that meets your system's needs.

When you analyze the system you should catalog the hardware and software components, describe the system architecture, and develop an expected "typical" usage model that includes peak and heavy load periods. You must be able to broach educated guesses as to:

- How many clients will be connected
- What the production client workstation configuration will be
- What the server configuration will be
- How the clients and server(s) will communicate
- The C-S architecture (2-tier vs. 3-tier)
- How the servers will interact with one another
- The configuration of middleware
- What network components might affect response times
- What the throughput of the communication devices is
- The maximum number of users the devices can support

The next step is to define a set of common user tasks that can be grouped into load test scenarios. The tasks must be analyzed and a frequency distribution plotted that is based on frequency of occurrence for each task. Obviously, your test scenarios should reflect the distribution by running the more frequently used more often than the less frequently used tasks. If you are replacing a legacy system or automating a manual process, the frequency count should be based on interviews with task experts (end users) and on task usage statistics that the users may have compiled.

Next, develop a set of load test objectives. Some common objectives might include:

- Measuring the length of time to complete an entire task
- Discovering which hardware/software configuration provides optimal performance
- Tuning database queries for optimal response
- Capturing Mean-Time-To-Failure as a measure of reliability
- Measuring system capacity to handle loads without performance degradations
- Identifying performance bottlenecks

The load test objectives should be stated in clear terms. They should precisely specify which results are acceptable and which, unacceptable.

Based on the test objectives, a set of performance measurements should be described. Typical measurements include:

☞ End-to-end response time
☞ Network response times
☞ GUI response times
☞ Server response times
☞ Middleware response times

These measurements can then be analyzed and related back to the load test objectives. Decisions can be made as to what remedies, if any, are necessary in order to achieve the required system performance. Once the necessary steps have been implemented, the load test should be repeated and the results analyzed again. This cycle should be repeated until the system meets its performance criteria.

A significant question is when multiuser load testing should be done. Of course, it cannot be implemented until there is a working build of the client and server software components. If possible, load testing should begin during development and continue through integration of the system and user acceptance testing.

Performance measurements should continue to be made even after the system is in production. It is important to test the performance of system upgrades. Part of the regression testing strategy should be to include a suite of load tests.

6.1.2 Volume Testing

The purpose of volume testing is to find weaknesses in the system with respect to its handling of large amounts of data during extended time periods. For example, this kind of testing ensures that the system will process data across such physical and logical boundaries as servers and, on one server, disk partitions.

6.1.3 Stress Testing

The purpose of stress testing is to show that the system has the capacity to handle large numbers of transactions during peak periods. An example of a peak period is when everyone is logging back on-line after the system has been down. In a batch environment a similar situation would exist when numerous jobs are fired up after down time. As an example, a script might require users to login and proceed with their daily activities while, at the same time, requiring that a series of workstations emulating a large number of other systems are running recorded scripts that add, change, or delete from the database.

The scripts should include activities purposely designed to compete for server resources.

6.1.4 Performance Testing

Performance testing can be accomplished in parallel with volume and stress testing because you want to assess performance under all load conditions. System performance is generally assessed in terms of response times and throughput rates under differing processing and configuration conditions. If the tester can identify any business processing cycles (e.g., month-end, quarter-end, semiannual, and annual) the system performance should be tested under emulations of each processing cycle.

Performance testing should cover performance under all hardware and software system configurations. In one C-S system it was necessary to test performance under corporate and field environments (desktops vs. laptops, LAN vs. WAN) and to test the system in conjunction with a second system utilizing the same server and accessing the same database. These are circumstances that can severely impact performance in networked C-S systems.

Hamilton [5] says of C-S performance problems, "Here's another myth that bites the dust: Client/server performance problems can usually be fixed by simply plugging in a more powerful processor." He says this because the performance degradation may be related to other system components, rather than the processor, and when it is not the processor, adding a box with more horsepower does not solve the problem. He adds, "Your problem may be the network, the computer, the application logic itself. Whatever it is, you'll want to know it before it happens."

He also notes that in his experience the problem is usually not the LAN, except in the rarest cases. It is most often the result of the client or server being configured inappropriately. Look at cache settings, disk I/O, and network cards first, and then at the interaction between the application and the network.

Hamilton believes that the key to successful C-S performance is modeling. Modeling allows developers (and testers) to view simulated system components such as client and server applications, user queues, network flows, etc., before the system is in production.

Hamilton sees the primary problem as a "lack of any kind of established methodology for designing client-server performance controls." In view of this deficiency, he suggests attacking performance problems with an "interdisciplinary" team composed of experts in data center operations and networks, and the IS manager. I would also add a testing specialist to this group.

Hamilton suggests a three-step approach. First, have the team decide what is important in your configuration. Second, collect data for those parts of the system. Third, distill the data into usable information. He also says it is important to know the physical performance characteristics (for instance, NT servers have monitoring software which can be used to observe physical performance), and the traffic loads.

The kinds of questions to ask are how much application logic should be remotely executed, how much updating should be done to the server database over the network from the client workstation, and how much data should be sent to each in each transaction. Look at all of the processes running on the machine and all of the resources each process receives.

Rossheim [8] suggests a "client-centric" approach to client-server load management. He advocates putting as much of the processing on client machines as possible (90% or more). Of course, the workstations have to be powerful Pentium processors with plenty of memory.

The best strategy for improving client-server performance is a three-step process. First, execute controlled performance tests that collect the data points described in the paragraphs above. Second, analyze the data (MS Excel works very well for charting performance data). Third, examine and tune the database queries and, if necessary, provide temporary data storage on the client while the application is executing.

Taylor [13] describes three formal approaches to automated performance/load testing. In all cases the test load is driven by automated test scripts. The first is a "single test per processor" configuration. In this model the tests are executed via test scripts that are recordings of actual user input with each user executing on a separate desktop machine. This is the most realistic scenario because it emulates a live production environment, but it is largely impractical. It is impractical because of the problems amassing the resources for this type of test for even a medium-sized client-server system.

The second approach is much more practical. It is the "multiple test per processor" model. This approach employs multiple simulated users on one or more test machines. With this technique hundreds of simulated users can be involved in a single test session. It is important to realize that this type of testing does not stress test the network while the approach discussed in the paragraph above does perform a network load test. To load test a network you must connect to it as many network cards as possible. In the simulated load there are multiple users going through a single network connection. This is not an effective test of network load capacity.

The third approach is a "hybrid" model. This is a combination of the two models discussed above, employing both a single test per processor and multiple tests per processor. If you have the resources this approach provides optimal performance testing.

Finally, Taylor suggests that multiuser load testing is necessary in order to validate that your client-server computing architecture possesses the *scalability* to carry your organization into the twenty-first century; it is necessary for tuning the configuration of your client-server systems. Load testing is required after hardware and software system upgrades and after system revisions. From this, it is obvious that performance/load testing procedures and test scripts must be included in your regression testing suite.

If, after executing the tests, optimizing the application configuration and the database accesses, the performance is not satisfactory, two channels remain open. First, conduct network testing and optimization. Second, purchase more server horsepower. The latter is to be a last resort after exhausting all of the other possibilities.

If you do decide on more server horsepower, consider CPU speed. Van Name and Catchings [14] feel that for Windows-based client-server applications you must purchase the fastest CPU available because of the overhead that Windows puts on the file server. In addition, they recommend a file server that has multiple processor capabilities.

One final alternative for improving performance is to distribute the database across several file servers. This approach improves performance and it creates a fault-tolerant server environment (see the section below on Data-Recovery Testing).

Regardless of performance testing strategy, it is important to have the right tools when performance testing [3,4]. Mercury's LoadRunner PC, SQA's LoadTest PC, and Rational's Performance Studio can create multiuser tests. These products not only help create and execute tests, but also graphically display the results. If your budget does not allow purchase of these tools. SQL-EYE, SQL Inspector, and ODBC Inspector can be used during those manual performance tests to analyze database performance. These are examples of the kinds of tools that can expedite performance testing. They are discussed in the section on automated tools later in this chapter. A big question, however, is what you can do about performance if you don't have any automated tools.

I had the pleasure to work in such an environment. We were charged with testing the performance of two small (20–30 users) client-server systems that shared a server and some database tables (the configuration was an SQL server database running on an NT server with two processors). Performance was a nonissue until the first system was up and using the server. In fact, I was told by one of the project managers to remove the performance test section from my test plan because we would not have the time or resources to do it; when the response times were miserably slow, however, performance testing suddenly became a mandate.

The problem was that we had no tools and because we had to test the performance right away there was no time to acquire any tools. The approach we took was to write two Visual Basic driver programs, one for each of the systems. Each driver program randomly initiated one of ten SQL queries designed for its system. The queries ranged from simple to extremely complex.

We began the test with the driver program running on one workstation. Thirty minutes later we executed a second program from another workstation and then a third and a fourth were started. When we had four users running on the first system we started the first user running on the second system. Thirty minutes later a second user was initiated and so on until we had eight users running simultaneously, four on each system. We then began to logout the users from the first system, leaving the second system's workstations operative. We did this until there were only the four users from the second system hitting the server. Then we began logging these out at short intervals.

The driver programs also wrote the name of each query they ran to an MS Access database table along with the query compile time and the query move time. We imported the data into MS Excel and charted the data. This was sufficient to determine which queries were causing the slow performance. Later examination of the queries revealed that the queries that were degrading performance were poorly constructed because they were requesting a lot more data than was actually used.

In addition, we determined that table locking during updates under the SQL server caused a major performance problem. The solution was to update the table in batches. The queries were changed so that a small number of rows (250) was updated with each pass, and the query was set to loop until all of the updates were completed. This approach degrades performance a bit, but not anywhere close to the degradation created by locking the entire table. This is a good example of how the limitations of the database technology can affect performance. (Future plans call for porting the application to Oracle.)

There is one flaw in the approach we used. In client-server applications many queries are created dynamically. Thus, using a driver program does not always adequately simulate the user interactions via the GUI that would result in the creation of the dynamic queries. Of course, if you manage to identify the circumstances under which queries are created on the fly, you could use a driver program to emulate those situations. One approach is to use test tools which employ scripts that interact with the application via the GUI (SQA TeamTest or Mercury Interactive WinRunner, for example) and to execute the scripts on multiple workstations (SQA LoadTest PC or Mercury Interactive LoadRunner PC, for instance). Another approach is the use of "proxy" servers, which capture the database calls and replay them from test servers that simulate multiple users but bypass the GUI.

It was only after we finished our database performance testing that I read the February 1996 Microsoft TechNet CD and discovered performance testing using the ODBC Software Developer's Kit (SDK) that I could see a much easier way to do the tests we had done. The SDK has a program called ODBC Test (gator.exe) that can exercise the ODBC API and display or save the results (the time required to pass the request and return the results to the PC). The ODBC Test program can be driven from any record/playback tool via its own screens allowing unattended performance testing. If we had only known about this approach earlier, testing would have progressed much more smoothly. C'est la vie!

6.1.5 Data-Recovery Testing

Data-recovery testing is an extremely important type of server testing. Scripts that investigate data recovery and system restart capabilities can save a lot of money and time that could be lost when a production system fails. Recovery testing is even more important because data stored on networked servers can be configured in many ways. There are several different levels of redundant array of inexpensive disks (RAID) technology [12], which is a framework for spreading data across several databases or file servers. RAID is an approach aimed at assuring data recovery if one of the servers fails (RAID is often equated with fault tolerance, but Ruber [10] says this is an overstatement of the technology).

Schroeder [11] identified several situations in which data loss can occur. He says data loss can happen when hard disk subsystem failures occur or when system software fails, through accidental or malicious deletion, destructive viruses, natural disasters, or theft. Sharp [12] sees disks as one of the most likely points of failure on a system because they are partially mechanical. So, no matter which level of RAID is implemented, the recovery capabilities must be tested because they will be used sooner or later. He says that the recovery time associated with the RAID level you implement should be carefully considered. He also says that there will be performance degradation during the recovery period. So, you must consider what recovery options a RAID system supports. From a testing perspective, it is important to test all of the recovery options for your RAID system while monitoring system performance. The focus of this testing is not to test the hardware but how the disk hardware is configured.

With respect to system software, Meyer [7] has determined that the majority of Novell NetWare server crashes are due to ABENDs originated by NetWare. He identified the three most common ABENDs as GPPE errors, IOPE errors, and NMI errors. He also determined that a secondary cause is code that forces NetWare to enter its internal debugger (Break Points).

GPPE errors occur when an invalid processor operation is attempted. They are usually the result of a routine that is attempting to access memory that is out of range, e.g., a memory location that is larger than the installed memory. *IOPE* errors occur when the server encounters an invalid execution path, e.g., when an execution path points to a memory location that contains data rather than code. *NMI* errors are hardware-generated errors usually resulting from power fluctuations or RAM failures.

Break Points occur when the stack is corrupted, resulting in an invalid return point, or when a function pointer references an invalid code location.

Thus, server recovery testing should include testing recovery from the four types of errors described above because they are the most likely to occur during the life of a client-server system. In some instances, it will be tough to simulate these errors, but a little creative thinking can go a long way when devising ways to test software. Jerry Durrant (through personal communication) suggests that a simple method to test server crashes is to replace good hardware with hardware that is known to be bad. This suggestion could be implemented by replacing good RAM with corrupted RAM to test GPPE, IOPE, and, in particular, NMI errors.

6.2 ERROR TRAPPING

Error-trapping capabilities that allow an orderly shutdown of the application rather than allow operating system errors to be generated should complement data recovery and system restart procedures. Error-trapping logic can record the problem, bypass the corrupt data, and continue processing as an alternative to a system shutdown. It is the tester's duty to assure that the system can properly trap errors.

6.3 DATA BACKUP AND RESTORING TESTING

Data backup and restoring testing is another area of concern. All database and file servers should have defined backup procedures and defined restore procedures. These procedures should be tested as part of server testing. Schroeder [11] feels it is necessary to simulate failures from many different causes in order to test your backup and recovery procedures because you want to uncover as many of the vulnerable areas that could threaten data recovery as possible. He says that even with RAID, technology backups are necessary because theft or physical destruction could occur. Backup and recovery testing can also provide a benchmark for time and resources required when restoring databases.

A backup strategy plan is key to avoiding data loss. Schroeder outlines the issues that the plan must address.

1. How often should the backups be done?
2. What is the backup medium (cartridge, disk)?
3. When will the backups be done?
4. Will the backups be manual or automated?
5. How will it be verified that the backups occur without errors?
6. How long will backups be saved?
7. Where will the backups be saved?
8. How long will it take to restore the last backup?
9. Who is responsible for assuring that backups are done?
10. Who is responsible to do backups and restores if the primary person is not available?

These issues, along with other issues that may be specific to your environment, must be addressed by the backup and recovery plan. Backup and recovery testing should address as many of the issues as possible in order to find weaknesses in the strategy.

If warm backups are used, thorough testing is necessary to determine the procedures for dumping the database to the backup server, loading the transaction log to the backup server, and bringing the backup server on-line if the primary server goes down for an extended period.

6.4 Data Security Testing

Data security testing is extremely significant in client-server systems. According to Roti, misuse of the database is more of a concern than unauthorized access [9]. In C-S systems data entry and updating is accomplished in a controlled manner through the application interface. Application users have Add, Change, and Delete (ACD) privileges, depending on their assigned user group. The problems arise from third-party software that allows users to log into the database with ACD privileges outside of the controlled C-S application environment. A mechanism to control access to the database by third-party tools is necessary.

Roti suggests several solutions to the third-party tool problem. The first is to control access to third-party tools. This is a far from foolproof solution because even experienced responsible users with commonly distributed database products such as MS Access can attach to tables in production databases and accidentally update them outside of the application without realizing that they have changed the database contents.

The second approach Roti suggests is to hide the database driver. For a C-S application, set up a menu choice that loads the database driver, runs the application, and—when the user logs out of the application—unloads the database driver. Of course, sophisticated users can probably find and load the driver themselves so this solution is not perfect either.

A third approach, he suggests, is to use stored procedures to control access to specific database tables. All accesses to the database are then routed through a custom data-entry program that calls the stored procedures. When third-party tool users try to login and update the database they find that they do not have ACD privileges. The hole in this approach is that some third-party tools have the ability to run stored procedures.

The fourth method Roti suggests is to use encrypted passwords. When the user enters his or her password it is encrypted before being sent to the server. The user is unaware of this and sees only his or her login ID and the unencrypted password. Third-party software tools that do not have the encryption algorithm would not be able to access the database or could access it with read-only privileges.

The fifth solution, he suggests, is to use shadow user names. All users login with read-only access while their privileges are checked. If they are allowed both read and write access, they are reconnected with a shadow user name which they cannot see. This would allow the use of third-party software packages, but just with read-only access.

Regardless of the security mechanism, testing the security of C-S system databases is absolutely essential. Controlled tests with third-party tools should be conducted separately or as part of the system test. In addition, tools such as SQLEYE can be used to monitor and restrict database access with third-party tools [14].

6.5 TESTING REPLICATED DATA INTEGRITY

In the future many client-server systems will opt for data replication servers as opposed to distributed transactions because of the improved performance. There is a trade-off in data integrity. Distributed transactions virtually assure data integrity at a global level through the "Acid" test. Acid is an acronym for Atomicity, Consistency, Isolation, and Durability. Applying Acid conditions keeps data in sync because it achieves system-wide consensus before a change is made.

Atomicity means that all changes are committed or rolled back and implemented in the form of the two-phased commit. *Consistency* means the data are changed correctly. *Isolation* makes sure that transactions don't collide with one another through record-level locking. *Durability* assures that committed changes survive system failures.

Replication servers, on the other hand, apply Acid at a local level and resolve data conflicts after the fact rather than before the commit. The changes are committed locally and later replicated to the rest of the network. This is when reconciliation occurs.

If your system is going to use replication servers you must develop a test strategy to ensure that the inevitable conflicts will occur, and then you must examine the results closely for areas where the conflicts were not adequately resolved.

Such tests would be conducted from clients who are hitting the replicated copies of the data and that are updating the same data, but entering conflicting values. You must ask which values should have been propagated and which should not, and which values were actually propagated? If the results are not what you expected, devise more test cases and rerun the tests. If the results are the same, it is time for a fix or a chat with your vendor.

6.6 AUTOMATED SERVER TESTING TOOLS

The data layer of client-server systems can be difficult to test because its functionality is hidden from direct testing through the GUI. If automated tools are not available, stored procedures and database triggers are tested best using driver modules that directly access the database layer. Simple driver modules with their GUIs are reasonably simple to create and use. They can place calls directly to database function libraries and return the results to the driver's GUI. An alternative to using driver modules is to execute the test via proxy servers using tools that capture and replay calls to database objects.

Mercury Interactive offers LoadRunner/XL, an automated testing tool that tests the server side of multiuser client-server applications. It is Unix-based and can emulate large numbers of PC workstation users accessing a server application. This tool can be used for capacity planning and for identifying the best server configuration for database performance. In addition, Mercury offers LoadRunner/PC for load testing in Windows environments. Both tools implement the multiple users-per-processor approach described above.

LoadRunner uses Scenarios and *Vusers*, or virtual users. The load testing requirements/objectives are used to develop scenarios. Scenarios define events that happen during testing. A typical scenario defines the number of users, the actions the users perform, and the machines on which they execute.

Vusers emulate human users, but many Vusers can run on a single workstation that would only accommodate one human user. Vusers can be made to execute tasks simultaneously emulating peak usage periods. LoadRunner offers three types of Vusers.

DB Vusers can generate server loads directly by going through the GUI. They address server application through API functions. GUI Vusers operate the application through the client-side GUI. GUI Vuser actions are defined through GUI Vuser scripts. RTE Vusers operate character-based applications on a Unix platform.

WinRunner is required to execute Windows Vuser scripts and Xrunner and VXRunner are required for X Window systems. The Windows version allows only a single user per Windows-based host, while X server allows many Vuser scripts to execute on a single Unix host.

SQA also offers a load-testing product as a component in its TeamTest Suite Client-Server line: LoadTest PC. SQA's approach allows a single test per processer. Rational's new product, Performance Studio, allows for both approaches.

Hamilton [5] has found that for complex client-server environments it is necessary to "piece together" a performance management toolkit. The tools must

1. Perform end-to-end performance analysis
2. Operate from a single point of control
3. Collect performance data automatically
4. Monitor performance thresholds
5. Have an open interface for data analysis purposes

Mercury Interactive has acquired Blue Lagoon Software and offers tools for testing the link between the client and the server. The products are SQL Inspector and ODBC Inspector. SQL Inspector works with Sybase's DB-Library, Visual Basic VBSQL implementations, and Intersolv's QELIB. ODBC Inspector works with any database engine.

These products monitor the database interface pipeline and collect information about all database calls or a selected subset of them. The information includes execution time, calling application name, API call name, the SQL string and its parameters, and the return value. The database commands can be logged to a window or to a file for inspection.

For tuning database calls, Mercury offers SQL Profiler, which stores and displays statistics about SQL commands embedded in C-S applications. The

information captured by SQL Profiler can provide more efficient table indexing and more efficient client-to-database communication.

Microsoft's SQLEYE is an NT-based tool that can track the information
passed between SQL Server and its clients [12]. SQLEYE is a *pass-through*
gateway program: Client applications connect indirectly to SQL Server
through SQLEYE. The SQLEYE link is transparent to the client applications.
SQLEYE allows its users to view the queries sent to SQL Server, the returned
query results, row counts, messages, errors, and attentions. These items can
be viewed on the screen or logged to file for later inspection.

Williams [15] lists some typical uses of SQLEYE. He says it can be used to:

1. Confirm queries sent to SQL Server
2. Monitor the activity of third-party software
3. Collect server-wide statistical information
4. Provide a high-level view of server activity
5. Restrict new logins for select users

Ontrack Data Recovery, Inc., offers Ontrack Data Recovery for NetWare
4.01, which can recover data from dismounted volumes and test and repair
corrupted file system structures [1]. The NetFile4 module can read, salvage,
modify, and copy files on corrupted NetWare volumes; the NetScan4 software
can diagnose and repair corrupted file system structures; and the NetDisk4
program can read and edit data at the sector level across volumes, partitions,
or files.

6.7 CONCLUSION

Server testing is an important component of client-server development. It
becomes even more important as more of the application's processes are
placed on the server. The Forrester Group has predicted that the growth of the
Internet will result in a move toward "server-centric" computing. Server-centric computing will mean that the majority of the process layer of the C-S system will run on the server, along with the data layer, and the client will
execute the presentation layer.

6.8 REFERENCES.

1. Dixon, Cory. "Ontrack Saves Data from Corrupted Volumes." *LAN Times*, Vol. 11,
   No. 7, April 11, 1994, p. 74.
2. Durrant to Mosley, conversation at the STAR Conference, 1996.
3. Eckerson, Wayne W. "Client-Server Test Tools: Client-Server Computing Has Created a Need for Robust New Test Tools and Test Methodologies." *Open Information*

Systems, Vol. 9, No. 11, November 1994, pp. 3–21. The Patricia Seybold Group, Boston, MA.

4. Gryphon, Robert. "Debugging the Client-Server Link." *Data Based Advisor*, Vol. 12, No. 12, December 1994, p. 28.

5. Hamilton, Dennis. "Don't Let Client/Server Performance Gotchas Getcha." *Datamation*, Vol. 40; No. 21; November 1, 1994; p. 39.

6. Lipchus, Edward J. *Client / Server Performance Testing: A Different Use for MS Test*. Microsoft Technet CD, Test Technical Notes, Vol. 4, Issue 2, February 1996.

7. Meyer, Steve. "Debugging ABENDs: Knowing What Causes Them Is Key to Averting Server Crashes." *LAN Times*, Vol. 11; No. 16; August 22, 1994; p. 85 (2).

8. Rossheim, John. "Remember Client Power in Dividing Network Load: A Client-Centric Approach Paid Off for Kemper National Insurance." *PC Week*, Vol. 11; No. 33; August 22, 1994; p. 22.

9. Roti, Steve. "Client/Server Security: A Look at Client/Server Security Problems and Some Possible Solutions." *DBMS*, Vol. 7, No. 4, April 1994, p. 91.

10. Ruber, Peter. "How Redundant Is Your RAID?" *Datamation*, Vol. 40; No. 21; November 1, 1994; p. 54.

11. Schroeder, Gary. *Backup and Recovery Guidelines for Microsoft SQL Server*. Microsoft Development Library Technical Note, 1995.

12. Sharp, Bill. "RAID: Now You Can Take Your Pick." *Datamation*, Vol. 40; No. 22; November 15, 1994; p. 81.

13. Taylor, Sandra. "Load Testing: A Developer's Crystal Ball." *Application Development Trends*, Vol. 3, No. 10, October 1996.

14. Van Name, Mark L., and Catchings, Bill. "Your File Server May Need More Power." *PCWEEK*, Vol. 12; No. 40; October 9, 1995; p. N10(1).

15. Williams, Peter. *SQLEYE: A SQL Server Analysis Tool*. Microsoft Development Library Technical Note, 1995.

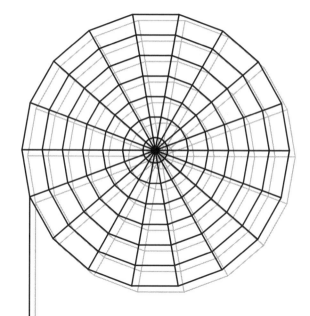

Testing Networked Applications

7.1 INTRODUCTION

If you haven't tested a network solution, it's hard to say if it works. It may "work." It may execute all commands, but it may be too slow for your needs.

—Robert Buchanan [1]

Testing networked client-server applications is a problem for several reasons. First, testing the network is beyond the scope of an individual project or development team as it may serve more than a single client-server project and testing it would involve looking at all of the C-S systems that will use it. Thus, testing falls into the domain of the network management group. Naturally, the two groups have different perspectives on network testing. For example, if you ask a software tester what tools are available to test the network that will support a C-S system, she or he would probably answer with Xrunner or Win-Runner from Mercury Interactive, WinRobot from Promark, or LoadTest from Rational. A network group member would probably mention LANMeter by Fluke or Compas and PentaScanner by Microtest. The choice of a network testing tool depends on what the person doing the testing wants to accomplish. I present a complete discussion of network management and testing tools later in this chapter.

Second, the issue of who owns the network and who should be allowed to "play" with it from a testing perspective is politically sensitive. The network management group does not want the C-S development team messing around on its turf. Plus, there may be different network domains controlled by individuals who must cooperate if the network is to be tested. So, in many

153

instances, network testing must be a coordinated effort involving several competing groups within an MIS organization.

Third, network testing tools can be very expensive and beyond the budget of a single C-S development effort.

Fourth, the logistics of network testing can be daunting. How and when can the network be tested? What levels of tests need to be executed? How many workstations will be involved? How many testers will be required? Will any special hardware or software be needed? Can the network be tested during normal business hours or must the test be conducted in off-hours?

7.2 COMMON SENSE NETWORK MANAGEMENT

Cornetti [2] says, "Network downtime remains the Achilles heel of U.S. corporations." He notes the increased number of network nodes resulting from the decentralization of computing required by independent business units. In turn, this is making network management more difficult. He views this as the biggest networking problem. He projects that the problem will only become worse as networks become mission critical to the corporation. This is exactly what is happening as companies begin to rely more and more on networked client-server systems.

Cornetti sees client-server and other new information technologies as already overburdening the network. He argues that client-server systems increase network load, and C-S security and backup processes slow network traffic. New client-server techniques such as the three-tier architecture and the two-phase database commit put new demands on the network.

Rossheim [9] offers some no-nonsense strategies, requiring no expensive tools, for measuring and reckoning network load:

1. Be proactive
2. Assess network-level performance issues
3. Consider the effect of applications on network load
4. Assess configuration of PCs

To be proactive means addressing key issues in advance. Decide on network uses and investigate the trade-offs for conflicting uses. Decide what you can live with and what you can't. Investigate what hardware and software technologies can support your objectives.

Assessing network-level performance issues includes completing a risk analysis for the application under development. The analysis may enable you to predict network bottlenecks and to determine the growth needs and the network's scalability.

To consider the application's effect on the network load, you need to define the data requirements and try to predict how users will query the system. Above all, be creative in your predicted uses because the users will be.

Consider application and data partitioning as a technique for managing network load. Recent technologies such as RAID provide a way of partitioning data for performance as well as data-recovery considerations.

Assess the configurations of the client PCs: Performance problems can benefit from use of scaled-up PCs. The client workstations should have a lot of memory, a powerful CPU, and a high-performance disk. With the current PC market, this is an inexpensive solution to performance problems.

7.3 MODELING THE ENTERPRISE NETWORK

Nemzow [7] blames the majority of network performance problems on insufficient network capacity. He sees capacity planning as crucial for networks supporting enterprise-level complex distributed client-server applications.

To determine the network's capacity, the LAN manager must measure the actual capacity or model the expected capacity. Nemzow warns us to be careful using network benchmarking tools because they are not characteristic of real network loads.

He views bandwidth (the size of the pipe) and latency (the time required to traverse the network) as the critical determinants of network speed and capacity. He also sees interactions among intermediate network nodes (switches, bridges, routers, and gateways) as adding to the problem.

Network capacity planning addresses these issues through a modeling approach. Modeling the network differs from measuring the network. Network measurement involves gathering performance and operational data on an existing network. Measurement can shed light on current problems but it is not as good at predicting future problems. This is where network performance modeling takes over the task. Nemzow has identified four types of modeling approaches that can be applied to networks: extrapolation, simulation, statistical, and emulation.

7.3.1 Extrapolation Modeling

Extrapolation modeling is based on linear extensions of existing information. Nemzow presents the following example. If a network currently has 60 users and the bandwidth is 60% and the response time is one second, the linearly extrapolated maximum is 40 more users. According to Nemzow, however, this model does not account for network overhead, network interprocesses, and timing effects. The resulting conclusion is that network loads and latencies are not linear and any extrapolation model must be nonlinear.

7.3.2 Simulation Modeling

Simulation modeling comes in two forms: a deterministic model and a stochastic model. In either model, baseline data are used to define network tasks, processes, devices, and interactions as "behavioral templates," which are used as objects in a model of the simulated network. The objects are logical representations of real-world network components.

The deterministic model is a discrete mathematical model that uses baseline data and produces bandwidth and latency predictions. The stochastic model is a state-change model based on a set of conditions and events that can alter bandwidth. The latter model cannot simulate latency because of the complexities involved. Nemzow calls this approach the "Monte Carlo" simulation. In either case, many hours of computer simulation must be run to bring the models into a state of equilibrium. Nemzow says, "Critical interactions and bottlenecks—particularly in a complex, multiple path enterprise network may be revealed only after many hours of simulated network activity have elapsed."

7.3.3 Statistical Modeling

Statistical modeling is a process in which network traffic flows and network processes are defined as mathematical distributions. The model solves simultaneous equations and produces latency and bandwidth predictions. This approach is nonlinear and is an excellent fit for modeling network dynamics.

7.3.4 Emulation Modeling

Emulation modeling involves constructing a physical network prototype in a laboratory or research facility, and using prerecorded test scripts that have captured keystrokes, mouse movements, etc. This approach is the basis for many of the proactive network testing tools on the market today. See the discussion on tools in section 7.7.

Nemzow says that the major problems with this approach are that scripts may not be executed with the same loads and overheads as the original run, and the load originates not from multiple points but from one point in the network. He argues that single-source test load generators are not going to compete for bandwidth, experience collisions, or experience latencies of the same magnitude as those generated from multiple points. He also notes that duplicated packets may be dropped by routers and bridges and ignored by servers and workstations because they are not related to the current process.

Whatever your approach, modeling should answer this set of basic network/server performance questions [4]:

1. What are the most important applications?
2. Where is the logic located in relation to the users?
3. What are the peak use rates and when do they occur?
4. How will the processors (client, server, and mainframe) divide up the instructions?
5. What are the estimated data transfer rates (LAN and WAN)?

6. When do variations in data transfer rates occur?

7. How fast are the processors, disks, and networks?

7.4 A PROACTIVE NETWORK TESTING APPROACH

Network managers have traditionally taken a reactive, firefighting approach to network testing. Buchanan [1] and Cornetti [2], however, argue that network administrators should embrace a proactive stance towards network management and testing. Buchanan believes that most networks are not constructed from homogeneous products, and he says, "integrating multiple, heterogeneous products from many vendors into a complex network system often produces less-than-desired reliability and performance."

Cornetti says that, as reliance on networks increases, the more performance and reliability will be at a premium. He describes the key elements of proactive network management as:

1. Detecting faults when they occur

2. Ensuring the most efficient use of bandwidth

3. Continuously tracking network usage

4. Managing the proliferation of LAN connections

5. Taking steps to ensure levels of performance and throughput

Buchanan views network systems as having a five-phase life cycle: design, development and integration, production, and evolution. He believes that network reliability, availability, and response objectives must be specified during the design phase and measured during all of the phases. This is a proactive approach to network management and testing because it tests the network before it goes into production and while it remains in production.

The traditional approach is to measure network reliability and performance statistics only after it is in production. Cornetti's approach is somewhat traditional because he stresses proactive behavior—primarily during the production and evolution phases of Buchanan's life cycle.

Buchanan sees the driving factor for a proactive approach as the demand for user satisfaction. He holds that mission-critical client-server applications require "much higher network quality than current systems provide." Furthermore, he believes that long-term cost savings can be associated with client-server systems, and that testing is the critical success factor. Finally, he argues that C-S systems development groups have a legitimate need to test new network systems.

Buchanan argues that testing should be performed at the application layer and at the presentation layer. He says the objective of testing these layers is to measure the response, availability, and reliability of the network. He describes the tests as consisting of scripts that execute an application program and manipulate the desktop as a typical user would do. He further remarks that this kind of testing requires tools that can script application commands and control test execution across multiple nodes. The traditional network testing tools do not provide the ability to monitor the application and presentation layers.

Finally, Buchanan asserts it is necessary to measure the elementary transport machinery of the network. This includes measuring router throughput, WAN efficiency, and server and workstation input and output capacity. To test the routers, switches, and WAN links it is necessary to use traditional network analyzers. To test disk drives, adapters, and buses it is necessary to execute programs designed to test file input and output.

7.5 ELEMENTS OF NETWORK TESTING

According to Buchanan, network testing should involve many elements:

1. Network product comparison and selection
2. Application response time measures
3. Application functionality
4. Throughput and performance measurement
5. Configuration and sizing
6. Acceptance
7. Reliability
8. Regression

Network product comparison and selection should be completed during the design phase of the network system life cycle. Buchanan says that the evaluator should consider the products with respect to application response, throughput and performance, and reliability. In *How to Test Software Packages*, William Perry, the director of the Quality Assurance Institute, presents a general approach to evaluating purchased software packages that can be applied to software, including network software [8]. I have used his approach to evaluate CASE tools and automated software testing tools and I strongly urge you to consider using his approach when evaluating network products.

Buchanan says that it is necessary to measure application response time while the application is completing a series of tasks. He says this measure reflects the user's perception of the network. This type of testing is applicable through all the entire network life cycle phases.

Testing application functionality involves testing shared functionality across workstations, shared data, and shared processes. Buchanan says this type of network testing is applicable during the development and evolution phases.

One way of testing functionality, negative testing [3] examines the behavior of a networked box when it receives bad inputs from other networked boxes. Networked machines either crash or tolerate the corrupt inputs. Test cases are aimed at classes of inputs that must be tolerated (e.g., out-of-sequence packets, unexpected packets, corrupted field values in packets, or bad packet lengths).

Configuration and sizing tests measure the response of specific system configurations. The tests are conducted, the configuration is changed, and the tests are rerun. This is done for different network configurations until the desired performance level is reached.

In addition to configuration and sizing tests, it is also important to do conformance tests for such standard industry protocols as x.25 and ISDN [3]. Conformance tests should be executed under normal conditions and should be based on the information in the specification document. According to Desnoyers, each statement in the specification is a potential conformance test.

On the other hand, stress tests look at the network under "adverse conditions." [3] The point of the stress test is to overload the network device resources such as routers or hubs. Desnoyers says the key to designed network stress tests is to make them simple because simple tests are easier to design, execute, and interpret.

Concerned with response times and with latency, network performance tests determine how much work network devices can do in a set period (for example, how many clients can the network support at one time) [3]. Performance testing can help determine how many network devices will be required to meet the network's performance requirements. Desnoyers's [3] idea for designing and implementing network performance tests is to test one aspect at a time. Run the test multiple times and chart the results. Performance over multiple tests will reveal more than a single test would.

Acceptance testing of the network is, according to Buchanan, a "shakedown" of the system just before putting it into production.

Reliability testing involves running the network for 24 to 72 hours under a medium-to-heavy load. Buchanan suggests that this can be conducted as part of the network acceptance test. From a reliability point of view, it is important that the network remain functional in the event of a node failure. Thus testing the network by causing nodes to fail selectively is a critical component in the network testing arsenal.

Noted automated tools expert Jerry Durrant recommends testing the network by purposely plugging in defective hardware components that have known failure patterns [4]. Regression testing of network systems should include performance, reliability, and function testing because it must verify that revisions will not impact the production network. Durrant suggests that using previously created test scripts is the best way to conduct regression tests of network software.

7.6 The Client-Server LAN Recovery Test Plan

When all of your precautions fail and a LAN disaster occurs, you must have a disaster recovery plan in place. With the advent of networked client-server systems, the character of the disaster recovery plan has changed. It must address distributed networks, LANs, and enterprise networks, but the plan by itself is not enough. It must be tested.

Kirvan [6] says that the success of your client/server recovery plan is tied to the success of the plan's test. He describes a planned approach for testing the client-server/LAN recovery plan involving specific testing objectives, activities, and procedures. He suggests implementing it once a year.

The LAN recovery test plan objectives include:

1. Verifying the correct LAN operation
2. Verifying the correct operation of LAN backup systems
3. Verifying the proper activation and operation of on-site and/or off-site data recovery arrangements
4. Assuring that the procedures are usable
5. Assuring that the recovery priorities are realistic
6. Identifying improperly backed-up systems and network services
7. Verifying that applications, databases, and network services can be recovered
8. Analyzing the performance of the recovery team members

The testing activities are:

1. Forming the test team
2. Identifying test goals/objectives
3. Defining the test procedures
4. Reviewing the test procedures
5. Defining realistic disaster scenarios
6. Conducting the test

The test procedures include:

Test Execution

   1. Conducting test of plans to bring critical components and subsystems back on-line
   2. Conducting test of plans to bring back critical network services

Results Analysis

   3. Assessing the recovery procedures
   4. Assessing the recovery team performance
   5. Assessing interactions among recovery team members
   6. Assessing vendor responses
   7. Adjusting the recovery plan procedures

Retesting

   8. Testing the adjusted procedures

7.7 NETWORK MANAGEMENT AND TESTING TOOLS

Cornetti [2] divides network management tools into reactive and proactive categories. He defines reactive tools as those that assist the network manager when a failure occurs, and proactive tools as those that continuously monitor network performance and utilization. He sees the proactive tools as a mechanism for identifying network events that could eventually create problems.

On the other hand, Buchanan would classify a tool as reactive if it is designed to be and is used during the production and/or the evolution phase of the network life cycle [1]. From his perspective, tools that could begin to be used during the network design phase and used in all phases would be considered proactive. According to Buchanan, proactive network testing tools are scarce.

From his perspective, Cornetti classifies network management and testing tools into five categories:

1. Network monitors
2. Network analyzers
3. Network management stations
4. Network operating system software tools
5. Auto-diagnostic tools

Network monitors track network traffic for LANs and WANs. Network analyzers provide detailed views of network bottlenecks and problems by decoding traffic patterns. Network management stations allow managers global and local views of the network. Network Operating System software tools present information on CPU usage, server conditions, etc. Auto-diagnostic tools establish baselines for network variables, notify management of deviations from the baseline. For proactive network management a suite of these tools is necessary, but not sufficient.

For modeling the enterprise network and for testing and monitoring the application and presentation layers, an additional set of tools is required [5]. The tools the network load emulators mentioned above use test scripts of captured network tasks. Load tests are usually conducted after hours using one workstation as the master console that controls the playback of test scripts running on a group of networked workstations. Capturing activity at the level of each client's GUI collects the test results.

The benefit of this approach is that the network load is generated from multiple points. This avoids Nemzow's [7] criticism that a network emulation model that simulates multiple users from a single source in the network is not a true test of the network because they do not compete for bandwidth and do not experience collisions or realistic latencies.

As I discussed in chapter 6, several varieties of load-testing (AKA stress testing or multiuser testing) tools are commercially available. Three of the most notable products are Mercury Interactive's LoadRunner, Promark's Win-Robot, and SQA's LoadTest. All three products use multiple-point load testing.

LoadRunner/UX and LoadRunner PC are used for multiple-point simu-lated load testing in Unix and Windows environments, respectively. LoadRun-ner tests client-server application/database performance for multiple users on TCP/IP networks.

SQA's LoadTest and Promark's WinRobot are similar in nature. WinRo-bot uses test scripts generated with SQA's Robot product to emulate network loads. SQA's LoadTest and WinRobot function very much the same.

7.8 CONCLUSION

Network testing is a necessary but difficult series of tasks. Its difficulty is compounded by the fact that client-server development may be targeted for an existing network or for one that is yet to be installed. It is further complicated because client-server applications usually share network resources with other applications and with networked services such as printers, etc. Proactive net-work management and proper capacity planning can save developers and testers from a lot of headaches during and after system installation. In addi-tion, performance and stress testing tools such as those described above can ease the network testing burden.

7.9 REFERENCES

1. Buchanan, Robert. "Weird Science (Proactive Testing for Network Systems)." *LAN Magazine*, Vol. 9, No. 7, July 1994, pp. 115–9.

2. Cornetti, Richard. "Special Report: The Case for Proactive Network Management." *The LocalNetter*, Vol. 14, No. 3, March 1994, pp. 84–91.

3. Desnoyers, Peter. "A Guide to Network Product Testing." *INTERNETWORK*, Vol. 6, No. 12, December 1995, p. 3(3).

4. Durrant to Mosley, conversation at STAR Conference, 1996.

5. Hamilton, Dennis. "Don't Let Client/Server Performance Gotchas Getcha." *Data-mation*, Vol. 40; No. 21; November 1, 1994; p. 39.

6. Kirvan, Paul. "LAN Recovery Plan Testing as Critical as the Plan." *Communica-tions News*, Vol. 31, No. 11, November 1994, p. 42. Reprinted with permission of the American Society of Association Executives, 1575 I St., N.W., Washington, DC 20005-1168, © 1996–97, ASAE, (202) 626-2723; www.asaenet.org.

7. Nemzow, Marty. "Keeping a Lid on Network Capacity." *LAN Magazine*, Vol. 9, No. 13, December 1994, pp. 61–4.

8. Perry, William E. *How to Test Software Packages: A Step-by-Step Guide to Assuring They Do What You Want.* John Wiley & Sons, New York, 1986.

9. Rossheim, John. "Sometimes You Can Just Use Your Wits (How to Estimate and Manage Network Traffic)." *PCWEEK*, Vol. 11; No. 33; August 22, 1994; p. 21.

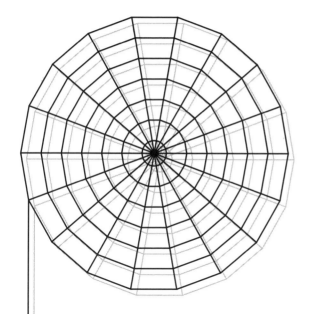

Cross-Level Functional Testing: A Data-Driven Framework-Based Approach to Automated Testing

8.1 DEVELOPING AUTOMATED TEST SCRIPTS

Automated test scripts can be either recorded or programmed using a test tools test-scripting language, or if an automated test tool is not available, they can be recorded using the Windows macro recorder function. Regardless of which method you choose, following a few simple test case design rules will result in more robust and easier-to-maintain test cases. Adhikari [1] cites four test case design principles that are in use at Charles Schwab:

1. Design independent test cases
2. Design self-contained tests
3. Design home-based test cases
4. Design nonoverlapping test cases

Test case independence assures that one test case does not depend on the successful completion of another test case in order to run. It also assures that automated test suites will run to conclusion when left unattended.

The Scientific Method was founded on testing. As scientists conduct experiments, they test only one condition for each repetition. This ensures that the results of each experimental trial are a direct function of the condition that was varied. If two or more variables are changed simultaneously, it is very difficult to pinpoint the one that is responsible for the observed outcome of the experiment. Of course, in science, as in applied endeavors, it is sometimes not possible to create ideal experimental conditions.

In testing software, if two test cases are not independent, two things may happen. First, the subsequent test case may fail to execute, and second, isolating the cause of any failures becomes extremely difficult. It is possible to design independent test cases, but constructing independent test cases is sometimes very difficult.

The purpose of software testing is to identify new errors while the purpose of debugging is to locate and remove known errors [25,27]. "Fat" test cases (those that cover many test conditions) are used to identify new errors. "Lean" test cases (those that cover only a single test condition) are used to locate and remove known errors. So, test cases that are not independent are better and more economical for finding errors because fewer are required, but additional independent test cases are frequently required to find and remove the errors.

It becomes a trade-off. If your purpose is to have automated test cases that are executed in batch mode via shell procedures, you want independent test cases. The major drawback is that more test cases may be required to find the same number of errors than fewer and fatter manual test cases would discover. Another drawback is that more test cases require more maintenance of the test suite. In short, the more test cases, the more testing costs.

Self-contained tests use test cases that have testing requirements implemented in baseline databases. Maggio [21] describes the need for base states in test scripts. Base states eliminate linear dependence among test cases. He argues that because an initial precondition surrounds the verification process within each test script and ends with a postcondition, it is isolated from other test scripts. Furthermore, it will pass or fail regardless of previous or future application conditions. Setting up base states requires using home-based test cases.

All home-based test cases start from the same point in the application. According to Maggio, the application must be in a specific state such as its initial state when it is first executed (the precondition). This means that the application should be open, with no child windows or dialog boxes open, and all menus should be enabled. The corollary to this is that when the test cases finish they must return the application to home base (the postcondition). When I use SQA TeamTest, I start from the standard desktop and use SQA to open and close the AUT.

Constructing home-based test cases is very important because there is less chance of test case execution failures when each test case begins from a known point and cleans up after itself. In an automated suite of test scripts, this assures that each script begins under the same set of conditions as its predecessors, helping assure that the test scripts are independent.

No gap and no overlap means that test cases should cover all aspects of the system functions and that test case redundancy should be eliminated. Testers sometimes have a tendency to test everything; they will even test for conditions that can never occur. Comprehensive testing is not possible [26,28]. So, the tester is charged with testing *as much as is possible*, given the available time and resources.

Testing economics dictate the use of fat test cases to identify new software errors. These test cases are not just randomly selected. They are designed and constructed according to guidelines that ensure adequate testing coverage with a limited number of test cases. Techniques such as those discussed below (cause-effect graphing, equivalence partitioning, boundary analysis, error guessing, decision logic tables, and basis testing), when used in combination, result in a test database that covers all system functions and minimizes test case redundancy.

Automated test cases should test:

1. That the application does what it is intended to do (known as either constructive or positive testing)

2. That the application does not do anything that it is not supposed to do (this is known as either destructive or negative testing)

3. That the application is robust (i.e., can handle spurious data without crashing); when possible, specific positive and negative results should be identified as expected outputs of specific test scripts

Fuchs [13], who prefers writing automated test scripts as opposed to recording them, offers a three-step approach for creating automated test scripts. The first step is to design the test case. He says each test script should contain from one to ten closely related scenarios. Test scripts with more than ten scenarios should be separated into multiple test scripts. Each scenario should be associated with a unique expected result.

The second step is to run the tests manually. He argues that automated tests are best for finding errors during regression tests and that manual testing is better for the first test cycle. The first set of tests should be the most productive at finding new errors whereas the regression tests should find more errors related to the evolution of the software. Regression tests do, however, find errors that were missed originally. I have seen regression testing identify errors that were in software systems since their inception (in one case, this amounted to more than 20 years of use with the error present in the system until regression testing led to its discovery).

The third step is to automate the test cases. For each test scenario, the test script should contain sections that

Perform setup

Perform the test

Verify the result

Log the results

Handle unpredictable situations

Decide to stop or continue the test case

Perform cleanup

The setup activities the test script must perform include defining common variables, constants, functions, and procedures the test will use; starting the application under test; creating any required directories and data files; and updating reference tables.

The testing activities should simulate how a user would use the application under test. An important point to make here is that scenarios must execute in the order in which they are written because this represents how the user will perform the work. The functional requirements document can be a place to start when identifying typical business scenarios. A better way, however, is to observe someone actually using the system or doing the tasks manually, but in many cases this will not be possible until the system is already under test.

Verifying results involves checking the initial and final states for the controls involved in each user action and checking the database for expected and unexpected changes. The only way to verify application functionality with respect to business rules and business rule interactions is to confirm that changes have actually occurred to associated data values.

Logging results means keeping a record of the pass/fail status of each test case. The results can be viewed after the tests are finished, and test logs from different test executions can be compared.

Handling unpredictable situations involves trapping unexpected events and recovering from them. Unexpected events can include unexpected keystrokes, unexpected windows, expected windows that are not present, and system-level interrupts and automated test script runtime errors.

Deciding to stop or continue should happen at the end of each scenario, and depends on the pass/fail status of the scenario just executed. In some instances, the subsequent scenario can still run even if the preceding one failed. In other situations, a later scenario would provide invalid test results if an earlier one or more have failed.

Performing the cleanup involves closing the application under test, deleting any no-longer-needed directories and data files, resetting reference data and usually returning the test case to home base.

Fuchs also suggests organizing the test scripts into test suites that are executed from shell scripts. The MS Visual Test on-line documentation suggests designing a functional area test suite, a regression test suite, a benchmark test suite, a stress test suite, and an acceptance test suite.

One functional area test suite should be developed for each functional area you can identify in the application under test.

The regression suite should test previously tested system features to determine if they continue to function correctly as corrections, tuning, and enhancements are added to the system during its maintenance phase.

The benchmark suite tests system performance under varying conditions such as different hardware and software platforms, and contrasting system loads.

The stress suite tests the system under such extreme conditions as heavy system loads during peak usage times.

The acceptance suite tests the software to determine if it meets the minimum standards for user acceptance of the system. The purpose is to determine if the system is ready to withstand the rigors of beta testing and/or production use.

8.2 RECORDING VS. PROGRAMMING TEST SCRIPTS

Recorded test scripts have their limitations and frequently must be edited before they work properly. Additionally, many test conditions represent functional variations of one test case. Therefore, many variations of the same test script must be constructed, and one way to do this is to record the first script and edit it to produce the variant scripts or to write a test script template and modify it for each variation. In either method, to do any meaningful testing you must become proficient in the test scripting language.

Many testers prefer to write test scripts rather than record them [13]. In fact, Segue's QA Partner tool did not have test script recording capabilities until release 2.01. Don Felgar, a frontline tester, who has experience with several automated testing tools, says in a USENET comp.software.testing article:

> I don't see any good reason to record tests. If you can record it then it works, right? What are we supposed to do, guess what will be broken in the next release. Hummm, I have a feeling that the developers will gray out this menu item erroneously during the next release. I better record a test.... I believe that automated software testing is complex enough that it must at some level involve coding, so folks may as well admit that and bite the bullet.

Fuchs [13] suggests creating a test case script template. The template file could contain common header information, setup routines, and include files. The tester would use the template as a starting point to write test cases, keeping the portions of the template that are relevant and deleting the portions not required for a particular testing circumstance.

Of course, not everyone is a programmer and many testers are individuals who have business domain experience but not technical expertise. Often, people who know the business make much better testers than people who have technical expertise because they have a different perspective, an extended perspective and more knowledge of the business processes. Software developers have an internal view of the system under development while users have an external view.

Thus, a typical scenario for automated testing tool use should include all of the above: developing some test scripts via the recording facility, creating functional variations of template test scripts through the tool's editor, and, possibly, writing test scripts from scratch via the tool's script editor.

The crux of this situation is that test scripts that have been recorded using the test tool's recording facility are somewhat appropriate for testing the GUI but not for testing an application's functionality.

If you intend to test business objects, database objects, and their associated rules with your test tool, then simply recording test scripts and editing them will not suffice. In client-server systems rule-based validations can occur at many levels, but they commonly involve GUI-level validations and business rule–level validations. The business-rule validations occur at the level of the server through application logic or through stored procedures and triggers in the database. The GUI validation occurs in the interface code that executes on the desktop. To test at either of these levels you must develop test data that exercises the application's ability to enforce the validation rules.

The problem is that if you were to record *all* of the specific data input scenarios (functional variations of the recorded test scripts) that might be required to test the application's functionality, you would be sitting at the computer and inputting data for years. The solution is to develop test data files and create specialized test scripts to read in the data they contain. This type of test script contains some recorded portions, but most of it has to be written by a tester who is competent in the tool's test scripting language.

This approach has been generically dubbed "data-driven" [18] and is extremely effective for testing 2- and 3-tier client-server applications. The data drives what is tested and how it is tested. This is the only manner in which you can effectively test application functionality with an automated test tool.

A modular test script design technique known as framework-based testing [18] has evolved as a complement to data-driven testing. Framework-based testing is really structured scripting [20] for test script design and construction as we once had structured programming for program design and construction [5, 19, 25, 34, 35]. Structured scripting follows different rules from those of structured programming, however, and is not nearly as rigorous.

An excellent review of the evolution of software testing automation was published in the February 1999 issue of *Software Development* [20]. In it, Kit discusses the path from the first uses of capture/playback tools to the third generation and on to future generations of automated software testing.

The most important point that Kit discusses is that naive test tool users believe the hype that recording and playing back user interactions with the application under test is sufficient to test the application. This is a continuing problem. Based on the e-mails I receive and the questions and comments that are posted to tool user news groups, I estimate that 70% of the current crop of automated test tool users are inexperienced.

Individuals who attend the data-driven scripting seminar that Bruce Posey, the Archer Group, and I give develop a complete suite of recorded test scripts during the seminar. Many then abandon the recorded scripts when they return to work, and they develop a completely new set of data-driven scripts that are modular and function-driven.

Kit very clearly describes the key lesson we have learned. Treat test case design as separate from test script design. This idea must be extended further to separate test data construction from the test script construction. Do not embed test data in the test script.

8.3 MANAGING MANUAL AND AUTOMATED TEST SCRIPTS

Because test scripts are fairly complicated and many may be required during the test, it is best to organize them in *test case folios*. The test cases in the folio can be grouped according to the design objectives or requirements of the system they test. Based on Hetzel's [15] earlier work, scripted test case folios should include at least five objectives:

1. Detail the objects to be tested
2. Describe restrictions and limitations on script use
3. Give an overall description of the test scenario
4. Organize groups of scripts according to purpose
5. Describe the expected behaviors for each script

The test case folios can be constructed and maintained with many different desktop tools. At a minimum a word processor and/or a spreadsheet is required. Of course, it is much better if the test case folio can be created with the testing management components of automated software testing tools. For example, SQA's Manager component does not embed items such as the test plan or test case folio, but it allows the user to set internal document locators to these items.

In addition, GUI testing tools should include test management components that can organize test scripts and link them to test requirements. Two products that already have these capabilities are Rational's TeamTest (SQA Manager component) and Mercury Interactive's WinRunner (TestDirector component).

8.4 Test Suite Maintenance

A suite of automated tests is itself a software system, containing the same problems that the system it is designed to test contains. It is prone to errors and extremely sensitive to changes. So, when you test a C-S system with automated test scripts you are dealing with two systems that have to be maintained. This doubles the maintenance problem.

Steve Fuchs [13], program manager for Microsoft's MS Test product (a component in Rational Software's arsenal of software development and testing products), believes the macro recording capabilities of the major test tools cause several maintenance problems because:

1. The software product will change during its life cycle
2. If it is successful it will be reproduced in other languages
3. The next version of the product will have a better user interface
4. There will be less time to test subsequent versions of the product

He argues that because the product will change scripts will contain invalid events. The effort needed to isolate and rerecord those portions of the script will be substantial. He says that the scripts will contain very little context information about the events, which makes maintenance harder. The scripts will also contain hard-coded function calls, which will require extensive updating for even minor user-interface changes. He concludes that even simple changes can affect 50–90% of the test scripts.

Fuchs's arguments are valid because new system releases do impact automated test suites. Recorded test procedures will most likely require some updating when new versions of the system include changes to any of the system layers (interface layer, data layer, or function layer). Consider that when we change a software module, we must determine which other modules are affected by this change. Now when we change a software module we must also determine which test scripts will be affected by the change.

Automated test suites add a new constraint on the system itself. James Bach of Software Testing Laboratories (in the USENET news group comp.software.testing article) says, "automation systems constructed from scripts are very complex and hard to maintain. The more complex a system is, the more likely it is to fail." The implication here is that the test scripts themselves can be error prone. So do we write test scripts to test the test scripts?

Another concern is the impact of software and/or hardware platform changes: As Bach says, "Any change in such a platform will cause widespread failure of test automation, unless the change was specifically anticipated." Bach has experienced problems with test automation stemming from DOS updates and the change to a Novell network. He was forced to add platform-related processes to the test automation. He found that only subtle configuration differences could cause automated test suites to fail.

To be fair to the automated test tool vendors, I must add that the test suites are much more robust than they used to be. Many of the conditions that caused earlier test suites to fail are now trapped and logged, and the testing process continues.

Test suite maintenance begins far in advance of the actual testing. It is always advisable to start designing and constructing test scripts and test data as soon as you have enough information to begin. The problem that you will encounter is that the test scripts and test data must be revised each time the developers change the software. If you have little or no control over how developers insert changes during the analysis and design processes, it will drive you crazy trying to keep the automated test scripts and test data up to date.

A compromise solution is to begin designing, but not constructing, test scripts and test cases, as soon as possible. This eliminates 50% of the maintenance burden; you only have to update the design and not rerecord or reprogram the test scripts. At some point, as the actual test date nears, you have to begin construction, but the longer you can put it off, the less pretest maintenance you will have to do. This approach can be enhanced by also constructing paper-and-pencil test scripts that can be easily modified.

Ultimately, data-driven testing can reduce the level of test script and test data maintenance by 70–80% and is a better approach than all of the others.

8.5 Data-Driven Testing

Data-driven testing uses archived test data, usually in the form of simple comma separated values (CSV) text files, to drive the automated testing process. It can be expanded to include control data, as well as test data. Both GUI- and server-level data validation rules, representing an application's functionality, are tested. The control data drives the test script by directing it to the appropriate location in the application to execute the test and by indicating what type of test to execute.

Data-driven test scripts use simple text files, are highly maintainable, can be used by nonprogrammers, document what tests are being executed, allow dynamic data input via "placeholders." The input data controls test execution.

The content of data-driven tests can include [18,26]:

1. Control parameters that you can input to the program
2. Sequences of operations or commands that you use to make the program execute
3. Sequences of test data that you drive through the program
4. Placeholders that cause the test script to create a dynamic data value at runtime
5. Documents that you have the program read and process

The test data should be designed using the techniques described in the sections, "Black Box" and "White Box" approaches. The test conditions and actual test data values are entered into spreadsheets that are used to develop the CSV files the scripts use.

Kit [20] has proposed designing test cases at a higher level of abstraction. He suggests that a test case preprocessor be developed that interprets the test case design in the spreadsheet and creates the data executed by the scripts. To do this, he suggests the need for a high-level test case design language. He has developed an "interpreter script," which contains functions that read and interpret commands contained in the spreadsheet. The commands include instructions that control the test scripts' navigation of the application under test, as well as commands that direct the input of data into GUI fields.

What Kit is suggesting we have already accomplished but in a slightly different manner. By embedding control codes in the data the script reads, we direct and control the test script's behavior with respect to the application under test (AUT). Furthermore, when the application changes, we only have to change a control code in the test data. We do not have to maintain the code in an interpreter script. Our approach is more economical in terms of test script maintenance. However, our approach is somewhat more laborious in that we export the spreadsheet data to the CSV files before the test script is executed (we use SQA TeamTest Suite). However, Andrew Tinkham, who regularly posts to the SQA users' group (http://www.dundee.net/sqa.htm), has developed a set of SQA TeamTest script functions that read the MS Excel spreadsheets and directly pull the data into the AUT. This users' group is an excellent resource for tips and tricks to use when developing automated tests. Even if you use a product other than SQA TeamTest, you will find useful information in this forum.

The advantages of data-driven test scripts are

1. It is not necessary to modify the test script when the test data require changes.
2. It is not necessary to modify the test script when it is necessary to add additional test data as the test data is appended to the existing text file.
3. It is not necessary to modify the test script when the application under test is modified because you merely reset the control data values by changing or adding new ones.
4. It is easy to modify the data records with a text editor.
5. Multiple input data files can be created and used when required.

8.6 STRUCTURED TEST SCRIPTING

The major advantage of structured test scripting is that it isolates the application under test from the test scripts. It also provides a set of functions in a shared function library. The functions are treated as if they were basic commands of the test tool's programming language. Structured test scripts can be programmed independent of the user interface.

Structured scripting can occur at multiple levels [18]: the menu/command level, executing simple commands; the object level, performing actions on specific things; and the task level, taking care of specific, commonly repeated tasks.

8.6.1 Developing Framework-Driven Structured Test Scripts

The following hints [26] will help you develop structured test scripts. Write

1. Functions for all features of the application under test
2. Functions for custom controls
3. Functions around language-specific commands
4. Functions for tasks that are used repeatedly
5. Functions for large complex tasks that are used across test scripts

8.7 WRITING EFFECTIVE TEST SCRIPTS AND TEST DATA

The following list of do's for writing effective automated test scripts is taken from the workbook [26] of the advanced SQA TeamTest script-writing seminar offered by CSST Technologies and the Archer group.

DO

Use structured test script design

Implement data-driven controls

Develop and use script-writing guidelines

Limit script sizes

Break scripts down by functionality

Document scripts well

Organize test scripts into related groups

Use shell scripts

Include test parameters in data files, such as .ini files, settings files, and configuration files, rather than as constants embedded into the test script

Prompt users for input specifics with preset defaults

Create error traps and provide the user with feedback

The following are do's and don'ts for creating effective test data.

DO

Use the test data design techniques discussed in the section "Functional Test Case Design"

Place the data in simple text files

Document what tests are being executed

Allow dynamic data input via "placeholders"

Use input data to control test execution

DON'T

Use capture/playback as the principal means of creating test scripts

Use test scripts that individuals code on their own, without following common standards and without building shared libraries

Use poorly designed scripting frameworks

Here are some additional tips and tricks taken from our advanced scripting class.

1. Construct separate test scripts for adding, deleting, and updating data records and for verifying the edits.
2. Create a single test script for general menu properties, system menu properties, keyboard shortcuts, and tool bars.
3. Create an additional script for object properties tests for all major GUI screens.

4. Develop and use test script templates for adding, editing, and deleting test data records.

5. Avoid hard coding items such as data paths, file names, and constants. Instead, use global include files as header files (for example, in SQA use .sbh—SQABasic Header) for constants and definitions.

6. Use Source (for example, in SQA use .sbl—SQABasic library) for executable code such as functions.

Avoid letting the main script become too complex. Break complex testing activities/tasks into small pieces. Use subroutines, functions, and additional procedures when necessary. Convert subroutines that require input variables to functions. Functions are better than subroutines because they return a pass/fail code that indicates whether the procedure executed correctly. Back up scripts before making major modifications. Use a configuration management process/tool for test script version control.

8.7.1 Improving Test Script Maintainability

Use plenty of comments. Insert a comment heading at the beginning of the script for complex test procedures. Use a product such as Cyrano for documenting test suites.

8.8 FUNCTIONAL TEST DATA DESIGN

There are three basic approaches to design: requirements based, code based, and a hybrid of the two.

8.8.1 Black Box (Requirements-Based) Approaches

8.8.1.1 Cause-Effect Graphing   This approach involves identifying specific causes and effects that are outlined in the requirements document. *Causes* are conditions that exist in the system and account for specific system behaviors known as effects. *Effects* can be either states that exist temporarily during the processing or system outputs that are the result of the processing. The causes and effects are entered into a cause-effect diagram that can be used to create test cases.

8.8.1.2 Equivalence Partitioning   This approach uses the system requirements to identify different types of system inputs. Each input type is defined as an equivalence class and rules are devised to govern each class. The rules become a basis for creating test cases.

8.8.1.3 Boundary Analysis   This approach strives to identify boundary conditions for each equivalence class. The conditions are used to create test cases containing input values that are on, above, and below the edges of each equivalence class.

8.8.1.4 Error Guessing This approach uses the tester's experience and intuition to plug gaps in the test data developed with the other approaches.

8.8.2 Gray Box or Hybrid (Requirements-Based but Can Also Be Code-Based) Approaches

8.8.2.1 Decision Logic Tables This approach looks at combinations of equivalence classes and can be used to develop test cases from any portion of the requirements that contain complex decision logic structures that would result in If/Then/Else logic in the system processing or from source code listings.

8.8.3 White Box (Code-Based) Approaches

8.8.3.1 Basis Testing In this approach test cases are designed to exercise all control flow paths through each program module. It addresses control flow as it occurs due to branching within the module. In Visual Basic, branching is the result of If/Then/Else/Endif statements, GoTo statements, For/Next loops, While/Wend loops, and Select Case statements. Source code listings or program flow charts are used to identify the branch points in each module, and this information is used to construct Control Flow Diagrams that are used to design the test cases.

The objective is to identify and test the basis set of logic paths. The basis set consists of a set of control paths that have path elements common to all of the paths through the module. The total set of module paths can be constructed by disassembling the basis paths and reassembling them in different combinations. Each different combination accounts for one of the module's logic paths.

Each module has a finite number of unique logic paths although the number may be quite high. The philosophy in testing only the basis paths is that if the building blocks that are common to all paths are tested, it is not necessary to test all of the module's logic paths. This results in a significant saving in the number of test cases needed for each module.

8.9 REQUIREMENTS-BASED APPROACHES

8.9.1 Requirements-Driven Cause-Effect Testing

Elmendorf [8,9] describes the cause-effect graphing method as "disciplined specification-based testing." Based on Elmendorf's work, Myers [27] defines a cause-effect graph as "a formal language into which a natural-language specification is translated." The graph is a "combinatorial logic network" using notation similar to, but simpler than, standard electronics notation. More precisely, it is a Boolean graph describing the semantic content of a written functional specification as logical relationships between causes (inputs) and effects (outputs).

As a Black Box technique, cause-effect graphing can be used early in the development process in conjunction with review procedures such as desk checking and walkthroughs. It is a versatile approach because the test cases generated can be used during all subsequent levels of testing.

8.9.1.1 The Cause-Effect Graph

Cause-effect graphs are models of complex narrative software descriptions as digital logic circuits that can easily be used to develop functional test cases [8]. Each circuit is a pictorial representation of the semantics portrayed in the written specifications. The semantic information in the cause-effect graphs is translated into Limited-Entry Decision Tables (LEDT) that are used to construct the actual test cases. An LEDT is a binary truth table in which each rule represents a logical path through a program segment.

The only requirement for using and understanding cause-effect graphs is knowledge of Boolean logical operators. **AND**, **OR**, and **NOT** are the most commonly encountered operators, but **NAND** and **NOR** may be required in some instances. Tables 8.1, 8.2, and 8.3 are truth tables for the **AND, OR,** and **NOT** operators, respectively. Tables 8.4 and 8.5 represent the **NAND** and **NOR** operators, respectively.

Table 8.1 Truth Table for Logical AND

A	B	
	1	0
1	1	0
0	0	0

Note: The ANDed variables are "A" and "B."

Table 8.2 Truth Table for Logical OR

A	B	
	1	0
1	1	1
0	1	0

Note: The ORed variables are "A" and "B."

Table 8.3 Truth Table for Logical NOT

	B	
	1	0
A	0	1

Note: The NOTed variables are "A" and "B."

Table 8.4 Truth Table for Logical NAND

A	B	
	1	0
1	0	1
0	1	1

Note: The NANDed variables are "A" and "B."

Table 8.5 Truth Table for Logical NOR

A	B	
	1	0
1	0	0
0	0	1

Note: The NORed variables are "A" and "B."

The basic cause-effect graph notation is illustrated in Figure 8.1. There are four fundamental configurations and two infrequently used negative forms.

☞ **Identity** defines a situation in which node Y is true if node X is true. In Boolean terms, if X = 1, Y = 1, else Y = 0.

☞ **AND** defines a circumstance where X and Y must be true for Z to be true. Again, in Boolean logic, Z = 1 only if X = 1 and Y = 1, else Z = 0.

☞ **OR** defines a condition in which either X or Y must be true if Z is to be true. In Boolean format, Z = 1 if X = 1 or Y = 1, else Z = 0.

☞ **NOT** defines the instance where Y is true only if X is false. In Boolean logic, Y = 1, if X = 0, else Y = 1.

☞ **NAND** defines the situation where, if both X and Y are false, Z is true. In Boolean, Z = 1, if X = 0 and Y = 0, else Z = 0.

☞ **NOR** defines the condition where, if neither X nor Y is true, Z is true. In Boolean notation, if neither X = 1 nor Y = 1, Z = 1, else Z = 0.

Here is a word of caution about the use of negative logic: It can lead to unnecessarily complex logical combinations and should be purposely avoided when possible. If the situation is a **NAND** or **NOR**, try to restate the logic in the positive before developing the cause-effect graph.

From a cause-effect perspective, some combinations of causes may be impossible because of semantic or syntactic constraints. In addition, certain effects may mask other effects and when this occurs it must be indicated on the graph. Consequently, the notation for constraints (shown in Figure 8.2) must be used in conjunction with the basic cause-effect notation.

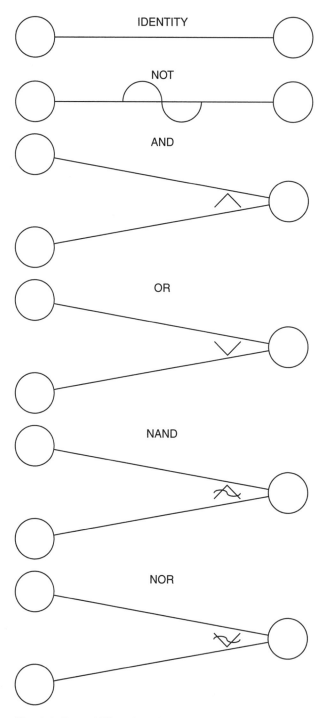

Fig. 8.1 Cause-Effect Graphing—Basic Notation

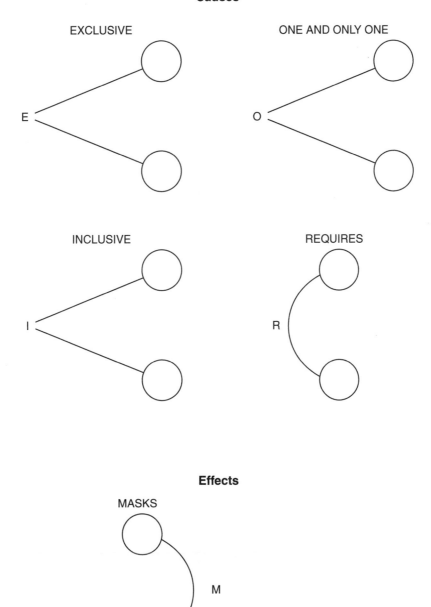

Fig. 8.2 Cause-Effect Graphing—Constraint Notation

Constraints on Causes

☞ ***Exclusive*** constraints define the situation where cause X and cause Y cannot simultaneously be true. If X = 1, Y = 0; if Y = 1, X = 0, however, both causes X and Y can simultaneously be equal to 0.

☞ ***Inclusive*** constraints define the situation in which either X or Y must always be true. If X = 0, Y = 1; if Y = 0, X = 1. Causes X and Y may simultaneously be equal to 1, but the state where X = 0 and Y = 0 is not a possibility.

☞ ***Requires*** constraint defines the circumstance where Y must be true if X is to be true. If X = 1, Y = 1. The states where X = 0 and Y = 0 simultaneously and where Y = 1 but X = 0 are also possible.

☞ ***Only*** defines the instance where one and only one of X and Y must be true. If X = 1, Y = 0; if Y = 1, X = 0. Causes X and Y cannot both be simultaneously equal to 1 or simultaneously equal to 0.

The **Inclusive**, **Only**, and **Requires** constraints are used with the logical *and* operator. The **Exclusive** constraint is used with the logical *or* operator.

Constraints on Effects

☞ ***Masks*** define the circumstance where, if effect V is true, effect Z is forced to be false. If V = 1, Z = 0.

8.9.1.2 Developing Test Cases   The following procedure for deriving test cases using the cause-effect method is adapted from Myers's work [27].

1. Divide the specification into "workable" pieces. Do not attempt to create a single graph for the entire specification. Large specifications are too complex and must be taken in smaller (less complex) segments that are more understandable.

2. Identify the causes and effects in each specification segment. A cause is a unique input condition or class of input conditions (an equivalence class). An effect is an output condition or a system transformation (an alteration of the system database).

3. Translate the semantic relationships in each segment into Boolean relationships linking the causes and effects in a cause-effect graph.

4. Annotate each graph with the constraints affecting the causes and effects.

5. Trace the binary condition states (which can be perceived as *true-false* or *1 – 0* at each node in the graph) and identify each unique combination of binary states that link a cause to an effect.

6. Draw an LEDT summarizing all of the possible condition-state (rule) combinations (see Figure 8.3).

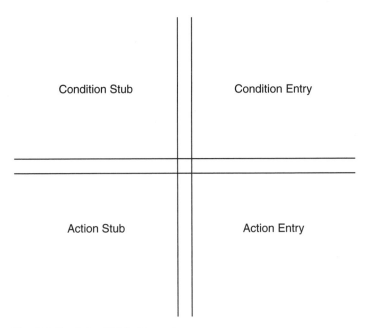

Fig. 8.3 Decision Table Format

7. List the causes in the Condition Stub of the table and the effects in the
   Action Stub. Describe each combination of condition states (causes) in
   the condition-entry quadrant of the table. Divide the entry side of the
   table into *Rules*, one for each unique combination of condition states in
   the cause-effect graph. Finally, indicate which state combinations are
   associated with specific effects by placing an X in the column that represents the condition-state combination (rule) next to the invoked effect.

8. Convert each column (rule) in the decision table into a test case.

Identifying the unique combinations of condition states in the cause-
effect graph (see step 7 above) is a reasonably difficult task. Furthermore,
there is no check for completeness as in the DLT procedure described below.
However, tracing backward from an effect through each of the possible combinations of intermediate input values using the primary input values will yield
a set of distinct condition states. As before, the following procedure is adapted
from Myers [27].

1. Work with a single effect (output) at a time.

2. Set that effect to the *true* (1) state.

3. Work backward through the graph and identify all the combinations of
   causes (inputs) that will force this effect to the *true* state. The number of
   possible combinations may be reduced because of the constraints on the
   causes.

4. As stated in the guidelines above, create a column in the decision table for each combination.

5. Determine the *true* or *false* (1 or 0) states for all other effects for each combination.

8.9.2 Equivalence Partitioning, Boundary Analysis, and Error Guessing

Equivalence partitioning and boundary analysis are complementary Black Box test case design strategies that are very useful early in the development life cycle. They are techniques that translate written specifications into function-based test data. Restrictions upon input that are described in the functional specification document are used to define *classes* of input and output. Equivalence partitioning describes categories of input only, while boundary analysis can define both classes of input and classes of output.

Both techniques result in two basic kinds of input classes: valid and invalid input classes. A single class will describe the valid input and one or more classes will describe invalid types of input. Test cases representative of each class are created and added to the test data set.

Myers [27] has established a set of guidelines for identifying equivalence classes and a set of rules for constructing test cases that cover each class. An additional set of rules governs the creation of test cases for the boundaries of the equivalence classes.

8.9.2.1 Defining Equivalence Classes   Defining equivalence classes is to some extent a trial-and-error process. It is based largely upon intuition and experience and it may be something you have been or are currently doing as part of your testing activities. There are, however, general guidelines that can expedite the process. As adapted from Myers, they are:

1. For input descriptions that specify a range of possible values (continuous input), identify one valid equivalence class which is representative of the values included in the range, and identify two invalid equivalence classes: one for values that lie above and one for those below the range.

2. For input descriptions that define a set of values, each of which is processed differently (discrete input), identify one valid equivalence class for each value and one additional equivalence class that represents a value not included in the set.

3. For data typed input (e.g., the data types numeric and alphabetic), create one valid equivalence class representing the correct data type and at least one equivalence class representing a data type that would be considered incorrect.

4. For mixed data types (e.g., the data type alphanumeric), with specific mandatory conditions (e.g., as in part-number where the first position in part-number must always be an alphabetic character), identify one

equivalence class in which the conditions are met and one equivalence class in which the conditions are not met.

5. Review the equivalence classes looking for instances where the classes may be further subdivided. The classes are subdivided only if values discovered in a class are not all processed in the same manner.

Myers says it is helpful to create a table with three columns—a left column where each external input restriction is separately listed, a center column where the valid equivalence classes are described, and a right column where the invalid equivalence classes are placed. Arbitrarily number all equivalence classes in the table. Organizing and numbering the equivalence classes in this manner simplifies the test case construction. Figure 8.4 illustrates the tabled information from equivalence partitioning and boundary analysis as it was applied to a control table used by a C language program from an application I helped to test.

Equivalence Partitioning/Boundary Analysis Table 1 GLOBAL_TBL Test Conditions		
Input Conditions	**Valid Equivalence Classes**	**InValid Equivalence Classes**
Connect_Type	Character "P," "I," "F," "D"	Not "P," "I," "F," or "D" Empty
Start_Time	HHMM Value 24 Hour Clock	Empty Not HHMM value
End_Time	HHMM Value 24 Hour Clock	Empty Not HHMM value
Pause_All	"N," "Y," or Space	Not "N," or "Y," or Space
Stop_All	"N," "Y," or Space	Not "N," "Y," or Space
Poll_Increment	Integer Value in Seconds	Non-Integer Value
Redial_Increment	Integer Value Set to 900 Seconds	Value Less than 900 Seconds Value Greater than 900 Seconds Negative Value Non-Integer Value
Site_Loop_Time	Integer Value Set to 60 Seconds	Value Greater than 60 Seconds Value Less than 60 Seconds Negative Value Non-Integer Value
Connection_Loop_Time	Integer Value Set to 60 Seconds	Value Greater than 60 Seconds Value Less than 60 Seconds Negative Value Non-Integer Value
Connection_Wait_Time	Integer Value Set to 600 Seconds	Value Greater than 600 Seconds Value Less than 600 Seconds Negative Value Non-Integer Value

Fig. 8.4 An Example Black Box Test Case Design Diagram

8.9.2.2 Constructing Test Cases from the Tabled Equivalence Classes The rules that follow for building test data are predicated on testing economy. They allow for the least number of test cases that can be created and executed with a reasonable level of confidence that we are testing effectively. It is possible to create fewer test cases, but these collapsed test cases will be less effective because of the error-masking phenomenon.

Error masking can occur when a test case contains more than one invalid value. The system will evaluate each value separately and the evaluation process may terminate when the first invalid value is discovered. If this happens, the remaining invalid values are not processed, which means we don't know what would have happened had they been processed. In some computing languages, the ANDing operation (a Boolean operation) found in conditional actions exemplifies this. If the first condition is in the *false* or *off* state, the state of the second condition is not checked. We cannot know what the system's behavior regarding the second condition will be unless its condition state is evaluated.

An abbreviated version of the test case construction guidelines Myers proposed is:

1. All of the valid equivalence classes can be incorporated into a single test case.
2. Each invalid equivalence class must be represented by a separate test case.

8.9.2.3 Defining Boundary Conditions for Equivalence Classes Myers defines boundary conditions as values that fall on, above, or below the edges of equivalence classes. We can conclude that those values above and below the edges will have already been identified if the rules defined above have been used to develop the equivalence classes. So, the only new test cases we will create are the ones representing the values on each of the bounds. Consequently, boundary analysis is secondary to equivalence partitioning in implementation order. In addition, there is one major difference between the two techniques: Boundary analysis can also be applied to the output domain.

The guidelines presented below are once again adapted from Myers's work.

Input Domain

1. For continuous input, write test cases that represent the lowest and highest valid values within the range.
2. For discrete ordered sets of input, construct test cases that represent the first and last elements in the set (e.g., a sequential input file).

Output Domain

1. For continuous output, construct input test cases that will cause output values to be generated for the highest and lowest value in the output range.

2. For discrete ordered sets of output, write input test cases that ensure that the first and last output elements will be processed (e.g., ensure that the first and last detail lines in an output report are printed).

8.9.3 Error Guessing

Error guessing is the process of using intuition and past experience to fill in gaps in the test data set. There are no rules to follow. The tester must review the test records with an eye to recognizing missing conditions. Two familiar examples of error-prone situations are dividing by zero and calculating the square root of a negative number. Either of these will result in system errors and garbled output.

Other cases where experience has demonstrated errors may occur are the processing of variable-length tables, the calculation of median values for odd- and even-numbered populations, cyclic master file/database updates (improper handling of duplicate keys, unmatched keys, etc.), overlapping storage areas, overwriting of buffers, forgetting to initialize buffer areas, and so forth. I am sure you can think of plenty of circumstances unique to your hardware/software environments and use of specific programming languages.

Error guessing is as important as equivalence partitioning and boundary analysis because it is intended to compensate for their inherent weaknesses. As equivalence partitioning and boundary analysis complement one another, error guessing complements both of these techniques.

8.10 HYBRID APPROACHES

8.10.1 Decision Logic Tables

Decision logic tables (DLTs) are unique in the fact that they can be constructed from segments of the system's functional specification, or may be based on program flow charts or source code listings. From a testing perspective, this approach could be classed as either White Box or Black Box—hence the Gray Box classification.

If you are already familiar with DLTs you may wish to skip this section.

But the DLT is a design tool, so why should it be included in a discussion of test case design strategies? Because the DLT can be viewed as a path coverage approach that offers an advantage basis testing does not: The DLT format allows a test for completeness that ensures no path in any module is omitted. In addition, DLT looks at combinations of equivalence classes (testing their interaction).

The structural complexity of the module is computed as the product of the number of possible states for each condition for each decision. This produces a much larger complexity value than the value of C that would be obtained if McCabe's metric (explained in the "Basis Testing" section) were used. The value that is produced represents the total possible logical combinations of condition states, not the number of independent combinations. Thus the value of the total table complexity will differ from the Cyclomatic complexity. The advantage in knowing the total table complexity is that logical completeness can be verified. Thus, the DLT approach addresses the major criticism of White Box strategies that they cannot account for missing paths.

Developing one test case for each rule in the embedded DLT can create a complete set of test cases for a specific program module. One DLT diagram is constructed for each program module. Test cases from each DLT are subsequently merged to form a test data set that may in turn be merged with other test data sets created using other White Box and/or Black Box methods.

From a testing perspective, the DLT is an important tool for software reliability [2,26]. The DLT is a tabular diagram that is used to clarify complex logic that has previously been specified in a design narrative [14]. DLTs deal only with conditional logic, allowing the designer to easily understand a situation that contains many decision steps. Such decisions will ultimately end up in If/Then/Else form in the final program. A distinct advantage is that the decision-making logic of DLTs is void of the If/Else nesting, which often occurs in the narrative description and is perpetuated in the program code. Even structured English descriptions may contain If/Else nesting.

The problem with If/Else nesting is that of increasing structural complexity. Our ability to deal with complexity falls off rapidly after a certain level has been reached [24,32]. When this happens, we begin to introduce errors into our work. The goal of a decision table is to reduce a narrative to a set of conditions and actions that can be easily implemented in If/Then/Else form.

Conditions and the actions dependent on those conditions represent everything except simple sequence. In the selection construct the actions are dependent upon the state of the condition being evaluated. Most selections are limited to two mutually exclusive alternatives; however, some decisions involve evaluating conditions with more than two mutually exclusive alternatives. The DLT format does not distinguish between limited-entry and extended-entry conditions. It merely organizes the conditions and actions so the proper actions are associated with the right condition-state combinations.

The iteration construct, as well, can be modeled using conditions and actions. A loop is a repeated set of actions. In some instances, the set is repeated if a condition that represents the exit criterion is true (the While or pretest loop) and in others the set is repeated until the condition that represents the exit criterion is false (the Until or posttest loop). Any loop can be specified if two things are known: what actions are going to be repeated (conditional on the exit criterion) and the condition state required in order to exit the loop (exit criterion). Consequently, iteration can be portrayed with a DLT.

8.10.1.1 DLT Format   A DLT is drawn with four quadrants, Condition Stub, Condition Entry, Action Stub, and Action Entry (refer to Figure 8.3). Conditions are listed in top-down fashion in the Condition Stub in order of their impact on the processing logic. More comprehensive conditions are listed first.

For instance, end-of-file is the most comprehensive condition of all because processing stops when it is reached. Consequently, it would be listed first. In Control Break processing, the innermost processing level would be represented in a DLT as the last condition listed in the Condition Stub and the condition representing the outermost level would be listed first.

Condition state names are placed in the Condition Entry quadrant at a level corresponding to the condition they define. The number of condition states for a specific condition defines the *condition complexity* of that condition.

Actions are entered in the Action Stub, listed in the order in which they will execute from top to bottom. Which actions are dependent on which condition state combinations is specified in the Action Entry quadrant, which is divided into rules.

A rule is a vertical column through the entry side (both condition and action) of the table. It represents a unique combination of condition states and the actions that are executed when that combination occurs. The number of rules in a DLT is a function of the product of the condition complexities for all of the conditions in the Condition Stub. A DLT containing 3 conditions with each condition having 2 possible states would contain 8 rules ($2 \times 2 \times 2 = 8$). The value 8 also represents the *table complexity*, which is a measure of the total number of logic paths through the table.

8.10.1.2 Enumerating the Rules

Step 1. The rules in a DLT are determined by dividing the entry side of the table into the same number of rules as there are condition states for the first (most comprehensive) condition in the Condition Stub (see Table 8.6).

Step 2. Divide each of the previously created subdivisions into the same number of rules as there are condition states in the second (next most comprehensive) condition (see Table 8.7).

Table 8.6 Enumerating the Rules

End of File?	No	Yes
Process Transaction Exit		

Table 8.7 Enumerating the Rules

End of File?	No				Yes			
Transaction Type?	A	C	D	O	A	C	D	O
Process Transaction Exit								

Step 3. Repeat Step 2 for each of the remaining conditions in the condition
stub.

Developing the table in this manner ensures that all possible condition-
state combinations are present.

8.10.1.3 Specifying Actions   When all of the rules have been enumerated,
the actions dependent on each rule may be specified. More than one action can
occur as a consequence of a particular rule. If several actions are dependent on
a single rule, they should be listed in top-down sequence in the Action Stub.
Placing an X in the column that represents the rule across from the action
indicates which actions are executed (see Table 8.8).

8.10.1.4 Condition-State Indifference   Certain condition states, when they
occur, overrule other condition states. When this happens the dominant condition state is indifferent to the values of subsequent condition states that may
finish out the logical combination of states defining the rule.

Indifference is important because when it occurs the table can be collapsed. A *collapsed* table is one that is stated more precisely: Rules that have
different logical significance, but which result in the same set of actions, are
combined into a single rule. From a software-testing standpoint, one test case
must be generated for each rule in the table, and when rules can be collapsed
because of condition-state indifference, fewer test cases have to be constructed
(see Table 8.9).

Table 8.8 Indicating the Actions

End of File?	No				Yes			
Transaction Type	**A**	**C**	**D**	**O**	**A**	**C**	**D**	**O**
Process Transaction	X	X	X					
Exit				X	X	X	X	X
Rule Complexity =	1	1	1	1	1	1	1	1

Note: X in colum specifies action taken

Table 8.9 Rule Complexity in Collapsed Table

End of File?	No				Yes
Transaction Type	**A**	**C**	**D**	**O**	—
Process Transaction	X	X	X		
Exit				X	X
Rule Complexity =	1	1	1	1	4

Note: X in colum specifies action taken

Collapsing the table in no way changes the total table complexity. Collapsed rules account for more than one logic path. *Rule complexity* is defined as the number of logical combinations of condition states (paths) for which the rule accounts.

Gane and Sarson [14] have defined a set of guidelines for collapsing DLTs.

1. Find a pair of rules for which the action(s) is (are) the same and the condition-state values are the same, except for one condition in which they differ.

2. Replace that pair of rules with a single rule using the indifference symbol (~) for the condition that was different.

3. Repeat guidelines 1 and 2 for any other pair of rules meeting the indifference criteria.

8.10.1.5 Proof of Completeness   Proof of completeness for a given DLT lies in the fact that the total table complexity can be computed as the product of the condition complexities, or as the sum of the rule complexities. If the product of the condition complexities equals the sum of the rule complexities, the table is proved complete: No logical combinations of condition states are missing.

The reason completeness can be proven is because of the fundamental premise of DLTs that "given a finite number of conditions with a finite number of condition states, a known number of combinations exist" [14].

8.10.1.6 The DLT as a Software Testing Tool   DLTs are an excellent tool for developing test cases based on path coverage criteria because the number of paths is dependent on the number of decisions in a module (see the discussion of basis testing below). They are also excellent because the tables incorporate all the decisions in a module in one format, with every possible combination of condition states (each combination is logic path) covered [11,12,26]. Moreover, the completeness check discussed previously ensures that no paths are forgotten.

Thus, each table results in a finite number of test cases being added to the test data set. Because a test case is generated for each of the rules in the table, the tester can be confident of completely testing the module's logic from a path coverage perspective. Furthermore, if the embedded DLT can be collapsed, complete coverage can be attained with even fewer test cases. From the standpoint of testing economics, the smaller the number of test cases required for adequate coverage, the better.

Using the conventions set forth by Myers [27] concerning the development of test data records using equivalence classes, we can generate heuristics that we can use to fill in the test data set.

1. For all DLTs, assign an arbitrary number to each rule in the embedded DLT, continuing until all of the rules across tableaux are uniquely identified.

2. Until each rule representing a valid input value is covered, write a single test record covering as many of the valid rules as possible.

3. Until each rule representing invalid input value is covered, write a single test record covering one and only one of the rules.

Because the rules set forth by Myers [27] for creating test cases for equivalence classes are also applicable to the tabular format of the DLT diagram, a set of test data that are similar and in some instances redundant with the test data from equivalence classes is produced. The advantage of the DLT method over the equivalence class method is primarily the ability to prove completeness. In equivalence, partitioning has no inherent way to determine that a set of all possible classes has been identified. From a Black Box perspective, each equivalence class identifies a unique type of input to the module and each unique kind of input will invoke a distinct pathway through the module. A rule in a DLT identifies a unique set of circumstances (which, in turn, defines a unique kind of input). In this sense, the two test case design methods are equivalent, with the difference residing in the guidelines for establishing equivalence classes vs. the guidelines for enumerating the rules in the DLT.

For a complete discussion of DLTs as a tool for generating test data that includes comprehensive examples, refer to Mosley [26]. You might also want to investigate an extension of the DLT term structured tableau methodology [1,6,11,12] as well.

8.10.1.7 An Automated DLT Design Tool Logic Technologies offers LogiCASE, an automated reengineering and design tool based on DLTs. The Designer module allows a user to construct DLTs from requirements and design specifications. The Designer is fully functional, including a completeness check that will add missing rules to the table, and a **Reduce** command that will collapse the table to its most concise form. The Designer can translate the finished decision tables into C, Basic, FORTRAN, xBASE, COBOL, and English language statements.

The Reengineering module allows DLTs to be developed from selected C source code segments. It does not support reengineering for any other languages. The reengineering component automatically removes contradictions and redundancies from the source code and the table, using a process called "disambiguation."

There is a limit of 20 conditions, 20 actions, and 10,240 rules per table. However, LogiCASE supports a nested table structure, which allows users to decompose larger tables into a set of smaller, less complex tables. It accomplishes this by allowing include files that contain other tables to replace actions and conditions.

The LogiCASE product can be obtained from Logic Technologies, 56925 Yucca Trail, Suite 254-A, Yucca Valley, CA 92284, Phone: 800-776-3818, Fax: 619-228-9653.

8.11 CODE-BASED APPROACHES

8.11.1 Basis Testing Overview

Basis testing is a White Box test case technique employing control flow graph representations of program module logic. Control flow graphs are network diagrams graphically depicting the logical pathways through a module. Test cases are created based on a set of independent paths enumerated from the graph. Thomas J. McCabe developed this method, formally known as "structured testing," and informally as basis testing. I will discuss McCabe's approach as a White Box test case development strategy and not as a testing methodology. For a comprehensive discussion of McCabe's methodology, see his original work [22,23].

The major advantage of McCabe's approach is that it incorporates the Cyclomatic number as a measure of program/module complexity. The disadvantage is that the control flow charts are generated from either a flow chart before a module is coded or from the source listing after construction is completed. There are two problems with this approach. First, control flow graphs are logical in nature and flow charts and source listings are inherently physical or implementation dependent. Second, there is not a set of explicit guidelines for systematically converting the physical information contained in flow charts and source listings into the logical detail depicted in control flow graphs.

The second approach has several advantages. Control flow graph construction occurs earlier in the design process, and test case design happens before physical design (via flow charts) and coding. This facilitates design reviews, walkthroughs, and inspections, but more important, program and module testing are placed within the framework of a formal structured systems design methodology.

8.11.1.1 The Basis Testing Technique
Basis testing, as described by McCabe [23], uses source code or flow charts to generate control flow graphs of program modules. The flow graphs enumerate the independent control paths and calculate the Cyclomatic number $V(G)$, a measure of procedural complexity (see Myers's extension to the Cyclomatic complexity measure [28]). A basis set of test cases, covering the independent paths, is then created.

A control flow graph is a network diagram in which nodes represent program segments and edges are connectors from given segments to other program segments. Edges depict a transfer of control from one node to another and can represent any form of conditional or unconditional transfer. A node represents a decision with multiple emanating edges. A loop is a node with an emanating edge that returns to the node. A region is an area within a graph that is completely bounded by nodes and edges. Each graph has an entry and exit node. A path is a route through a graph that traverses edges from node to node, beginning with the entry node and ending with the exit node.

A node is a block of sequentially executed (imperative) actions and an edge is a transfer of control from one block to another. The If/Then/Else/Endif and nested If/Then/Else/Endif are also examples of statements that conditionally transfer control to specific groups of actions.

Structured programming doctrine advocates that program logic be designed using only the logical constructs of sequence, selection, and iteration (e.g., see Boehm and Jacopini [5], King [19], and Orr [29,30]).

Internal structural complexity in program modules is a consequence of the number of functions the module implements, the number of inputs to the module and outputs from the module, and the number of decisions in the module. Structured programming doctrine dictates that a module should implement *one and only one function* [34,35]. If this basic rule of thumb is followed, complexity due to the number of functions is minimized. Structured programming dogma also stands on the premise that each module has but a single entry point and a single exit point. If such is the case, complexity due to the number of inputs and outputs can be controlled because the module interface is simplified. This leaves complexity because of the number of decisions as the major structural dimension contributing to module complexity.

McCabe's complexity measure is an indication of a module's decision structure. It measures procedural complexity as a function of the number of decisions in the graph. Cyclomatic complexity is a useful metric because it is also representative perceived complexity. Miller [24] found that the maximum amount of information the human mind can simultaneously process is three "bits." He defined a bit as the amount of information required in order to discriminate between two equally likely alternatives. The total number of alternatives is two raised to a power equal to the number of discriminations that are involved in a complex decision.

Based on his findings, Miller formulated the *7±2* rule which is why your telephone number is 7 digits long. A 7-number string is optimal for memorization of phone numbers as each digit is a discrimination alternative. Miller determined that the maximum number of alternatives humans can handle simultaneously is 9. If this principle is applied to the decision structure of program modules, the number of bits a programmer must process to understand a complex decision is a function of 2 raised to a power that represents the number of conditions contained in the decision. An If/Else nest three levels deep has 2^3 (8) alternatives to comprehend—below the limit established by Miller. But adding another nested decision raises the number of alternatives to 16—well beyond the inherent limit. Consequently, a module with a Cyclomatic complexity greater than 10 is too complex for the human short-term memory to comprehend at one time and must be decomposed into several less complex modules. If it is not made less complex it will be error prone and difficult if not impossible to test.

If the Cyclomatic number (C) is greater than 10, a module should be reconstructed or it may be untestable. King [19] suggests such modules can be rendered less complex through decomposition into two or more subordinate modules. Decomposition necessitates redesign and/or recoding depending on whether the control flow graphs were constructed from program listings or flow charts. The earlier structural complexity can be better measured from the standpoint of module design.

The Cyclomatic number can be calculated using any of three simple equations. The first equation representing the Cyclomatic number is:

$$C = E - N + 2$$

where

C is the Cyclomatic number (C has been substituted for $V[G]$

2 is used instead of $2P$ [P is usually 0] to simplify and make the notation more meaningful)

E is the number of edges

N is the number of nodes

The Cyclomatic complexity is computed as a function of the relationship of edges to nodes.

Complexity can also be computed as a function the regions in the control flow graph. Edges cannot cross one another, and regions formed by violations of this rule are not "legitimate" regions. Only legitimate regions can be included in the calculation of complexity.

The equation based on the number of regions is:

$$C = R + 1$$

where

C is again the Cyclomatic number

R is the number of legitimate regions

The Cyclomatic number can also be computed based upon the number of primitive decisions in the graph. A primitive decision is one evaluating the condition states associated with a single condition. Nested conditions and conditions connected by logical operators should be treated as though they were completely separate decisions.

The equation is:

$$C = D + 1$$

where

D is the number of primitive decisions

The advantage of the latter two equations is that they are easier to understand and use. In fact, the control flow graph does not have to be constructed to use the third equation. The number of decisions in the program flow chart or source listing can be counted and substituted for D in the equation.

These equations are applied to individual program modules. A measure of the total program complexity can be derived from the sum of the individual module complexities with a factor subtracted out for redundant nodes. A redundant node is a node in a high-level module, such as the mainline module, that would be replaced by a subdiagram if the called module were called in-line as part of the superordinate module.

The equation is:

$$C_t = C_i + 2 - (N - 1)$$

where

C_t represents the total program complexity

C_i represents the individual module complexities

N is the number of modules in the program

The value of C in each module represents the upper boundary for the maximum number of independent paths through a given program unit. If a set of control paths is constructed equal to C, test cases that exercise those paths will adequately test the module and constitute the basis set of test cases. The basis set does not necessarily execute all possible paths through a segment, but rather a subset from which all other paths can be fabricated.

Once the Cyclomatic number is known, the independent paths can be enumerated. To enumerate the basis set of paths:

1. Identify all nodes with either a unique letter or number.
2. Begin at the entry node and travel the network using the left-most path to exit node. List the nodes contained in the path and indicate on the diagram the edges traversed.
3. Follow the previous path backward until a node is encountered that has one or more unmarked emanating edges. Begin at the entry node and follow the preceding path to the node with an unmarked edge. Continue from that point to the exit node using the left-most unmarked edge.
4. If the new path at any time intersects a previous path follow the latter path to the exit node.

When no unmarked edges remain, the basis set of paths is complete. The total number of paths must equal C. If a set of paths that equals C cannot be created, then the module is poorly designed and overly complex. It is best to redesign such modules.

It is extremely helpful when constructing the test cases to annotate the decision nodes with the condition being tested and to label the *true* and *false* branching edges (see figure 8.5). A test case is considered to be created when it will execute each independent path at least once. The basis set of test cases must also exercise each conditional branch at least once. A test case is an input data record containing either a valid or an invalid value for each data field.

Figure 8.5 is a control flow graph for the C program logic that processed the Global Table illustrated in Figure 8.4.

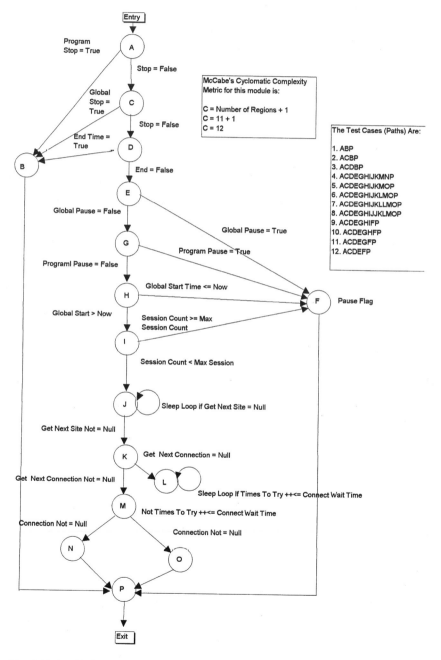

Fig. 8.5 Arc Polling Software Main Module Control Flow Graph

8.11.2 Testing Object-Oriented Applications

Although this is not a book about object-oriented (OO) testing, many client-server software development efforts follow that development approach. They employ OO design and programming during the development process, and developers use automated object-oriented development tools. Thus, it is important to include these methods among the weapons in your testing armory.

Siegel [33] says the major issue in testing object-oriented systems is how to assure the integrity of a system that is designed to allow the user bounded but relatively unlimited flexibility.

Isn't this a question that applies to client-server systems in general? In fact, this is the goal of any C-S system. Thus, we can benefit by approaching the functional testing of C-S systems as the testing of highly flexible complex systems. Siegel states that OO systems are exactly of this complex and flexible character. So, the testing of client-server and object-oriented systems offers a common basis for comparison.

In fact, the PD/CTS approach discussed in chapter 3 was developed for use with OO programming environments such as C++ and Smalltalk. It is structured so that OO systems can be developed and tested very rapidly (Siegel speaks of two weeks for each OO component).

Object-oriented systems are designed in a layered, hierarchical set of abstractions (object classes). Object-oriented design (OOD) is a formal method that is iterative and incremental. The argument for OOD is that it approximates the way people work, allowing developers to analyze and design a little, code a little, test a little, and then do it all again, in iterative cycles.

Siegel suggests that object classes must be tested for complete code coverage within each class and should also include comprehensive testing of the methods or processes for all classes; the usage relationships within and between classes; any new and modified methods for derived or instantiated classes; and, finally, combinations of usage relationships between methods defined for the class, including inherited methods using a method redefined by the class.

8.11.2.1 Object-Oriented Testing Strategies   OOD requires early testing as part of a parallel design and development approach. Siegel suggests that the major impact of OOD is not on the types of testing needed, but on the amount of testing required. He argues that traditional White Box and Black Box testing strategies are still useful in an OO environment. He believes that the analysis of class structure in well-designed OO systems, with respect to usage and visibility, yields all testable combinations of object classes.

In fact, he suggests that testers must test the traditional minimum and maximum values, values above and below range, zero values, null values, and other special cases for each object class. This is exactly what the equivalence-partitioning, boundary-analysis, and error-guessing testing approaches have always accomplished. Siegel's work suggests that these three test case design techniques should be employed to design test cases for each object class.

Furthermore, DLTs that can model the relations among equivalence classes can be used to design test cases for relationships among object classes. Using DLTs to test class relationships addresses the object visibility issue. DLTs can be used to model interobject relationships and the indifference criterion can be used to determine an object's visibility to other objects. When indifference occurs, one object determines the system's behavior, and the other objects' effects are not expressed by the system. When indifference occurs, the number of test cases is reduced. Thus, when one object dominates the system response, that object is the only one that must be tested.

8.11.2.2 White Box OO Tests   At a minimum, White Box test strategy for OO software should include: provision for designing and managing a library of testing history; allocation of resources to perform, document, and review class and method analysis; development of a test apparatus comprising stubs, drivers, and object libraries; use of standard procedures, naming conventions, and libraries; maintenance of regression test suites and procedures; and production or purchase of tools to automate capture/replay/comparison, execution of the test suite, and verification and documentation of results [34].

8.11.2.3 Black Box OO Tests   Black Box test strategy for OO software should include: purchase of tools and training early in the development period; provision for analyzing application-domain relationships (using control flow graphs is helpful); preparation and review of test scenarios during requirements analysis and system design; use of prototyping and reviews with users; use of automated regression testing; consideration of the extent of flexibility and abstraction that should be built into the system (the more there is, the more the techniques above may be needed) [34].

8.11.3 OO Testing Resources

There are many good books and articles on OO testing [4,7,10,17,31,33]. Two excellent OO testing bibliographies are available on the World Wide Web. Robert Binder Systems Consulting (RSBC), Inc., maintains a comprehensive bibliography at http://www.rsbc.com/pages/ootbib.html/ and Edward Bernard maintains an equally useful bibliography at http://www.toa.com/pub/html/testbib.html/.

8.12 CODE-LEVEL ERROR CHECKING

In addition to the test case design approaches discussed above, testing MS Windows client-server applications requires the tester to deal with several new areas. Dynamic Link Libraries (DLLs), Application Programming Interface (API) calls, and memory leaks require consideration. Areas of concern at the programming-language level include read and write checks, DLL checks, API checks, dynamic memory checks, stack memory checks, static memory checks, type mismatches, locked and freed file handles, null and out-of-range pointers, invalid arguments, and conflicting flags. These types of errors are typically found in programs written in the most popular client-server development languages: Visual Basic (VB) and C/C++.

A point of concern with VB is that it is both a compiled and an interpreted language. The reason for this concern is the way developers use VB when writing their code. Frequently they do not compile the source code until just before it is given to the test team. They do all of the development and any testing (which is not usually very much) in interpreted VB. This has caused many problems, particularly in cross-Windows environments.

In one instance a developer was developing VB in Windows 95 and testing interpreted code in Windows 95. The system, however, was targeted to run on Windows NT, Windows 95, and Windows for Workgroups 3.11. The testers frequently reported problems in the other Windows environments that could not be reproduced in the development environment.

I puzzled over this until I realized the developer was using the interpreter and not compiling his code until it was time to create the executable file that was included in the build.

8.12.1 Test Drivers to Test Hidden Objects

Is structured capture/playback just for GUI testing? The GUI is a shell and structured capture/playback approaches are excellent for assuring that the user interface works, but can you test application functionality with a client-based GUI approach? Eric Schurr of Rational Software, Inc., says that any function that returns a value to the interface can be tested. He is essentially correct, but in many instances the test of the function is at best indirect. An input value may undergo many transformations before it is used by the function that is under test. If testers understand all of the transformations, they probably can devise and input values that will test the application function in question. Many times, though, testers don't have access to such in-depth knowledge of the application's internal specifications or the specifications are incomplete or incorrect with respect to the requirements.

What about testing *hidden* objects—objects that do not appear on the GUI screen? Certain application functions such as operating system behaviors, server functions, stored procedures, and data transfers do not return any output via the GUI. These functions result in the setting of internal states when the application runs and, in many instances, the setting, variable values, flags, etc. disappear when the application stops running. These activities occur in the application layer and in the data layer, not in the user interface layer. So, how can testers test these functions?

Front-line client-server testers are finding that software modules known as "drivers" are an effective way to test hidden objects. The testers use the drivers to feed contrived data directly to the object that implements the function under test. This makes the design and construction of test data simple and straightforward. The driver accepts the input and displays the result outside of the GUI.

The advantage of this approach is that it bypasses other intermediate levels of processing and is particularly productive when testing functions that are normally invoked by remote procedure calls. In some instances, it is the only way to test a hidden object.

The scripts that run the driver are written using the scripting language or recorded via capture-playback tools such as SQA TeamTest, Mercury Interactive's WinRunner, Segue's QA Partner or manually typed into the GUI text boxes, etc. In this manner, the tester performs a direct test of the hidden objects' functionality.

As an alternative to constructing a separate GUI for each driver, testers can choose to call the drivers from test scripts and return a pass/fail code that the test tool recognizes. This method eliminates the need to create the GUI for the driver because the test scripts that call the driver can run against the application GUI. The two approaches are identical in the level of testing that can be achieved.

SQA TeamTest allows the tester to create user-defined test cases that can run executables or make calls directly to DLLs to test remote procedure calls. The latest version of SQA TeamTest supports calling most DLL functions and has rich support for logging events. This approach eliminates the need for specially written test DLLs. Figure 8.6 illustrates a user-defined call from an SQA TeamTest test script to an executable file. Figure 8.7 illustrates a user-defined call to a DLL from an SQA TeamTest test script.

Fig. 8.6 User-Defined EXE Call Example from SQA TeamTest

```
#include <windows.h>

#include "rbudf.h"

int PASCAL WinMain (hInstance, hPrevInstance, lpCmdLine, nCmdLine, nCmdShow)

HANDLE hInstance;          /* current instance*/
HANDLE hPrevInstance;      /* previous instance*/
LPSTR lpCmdLine;           /*command line*/
int nCmdShow    ;          /*Show-window type (open/icon)*/

{
    //Define Local Variable
    int iStatus;

    /* Assume RunTest returns 1 if SUCCESSFUL and 0 if an error occurs*/

    iStatus=RunTest ();
    if (iStatus==1)
        UDFSetResult ((HANDLE)NULL, RBUDF_PASS);
    else
        UDFSetResult ((HANDLE)NULL, RBUDF_FAIL);
}
```

Fig. 8.7 User-Defined DLL Call Example from SQA TeamTest (Adapted from SQA TeamTest User Documentation)

```
C Source File USR_DEF.c

#include <windows.h>.
#include "rbudf.h

WORD FAR PASCAL UserDefFunc (VOID)
{
int iStatus;

/* perform your test */
/* if test passes…*/
return (RBUDF_PASS);

/* if test fails.. */
return (RBUDF_FAIL);
}
```

Segue Software has developed an extension kit (EK) for QA Partner, a component of the Quality Works tool suite, that allows testers to develop drivers (in C code) and test nondisplayable application logic through DLL calls from its 4Test scripting language. The EK is also the mechanism Segue has chosen to address testing in cross-platform environments. The EK provides the physical (environment-specific) hooks to logical objects in test scripts written in 4Test.

Coding and/or recording the test procedures that feed the driver is tedious and time consuming. So expect a lot of work up front. Some testers see this as a disadvantage of capture-playback tools, however, the payoff once the test procedures are recorded and stored in the test repository makes it worthwhile. Stored test procedures can be supplemented and replayed to regression test the software each time a correction or enhancement is made. This can save up to 50% over the testing resources for manual testing.

There are many newer test tools (Rational PerformanceStudio, etc.) that capture http protocols, SQL calls, etc., and then use the recorded call to test an application using a proxy server. This is a common approach used by the major performance/load test products. Although designed as performance testing tools, they could also be used to test single-user functionality outside of the GUI for a more direct test of a specific function or group of functions.

In addition, products such as SQA Suite are able to detect and examine objects such as hidden PowerBuilder DataWindows. SQA is extremely adept at handling PowerBuilder code and recognizes PowerBuilder Objects by their internal names. It is also very good at doing this with VB code, but the SQA OCX must be loaded in order for SQA to recognize the VB internal object names.

8.12.2 Memory Leaks

Memory leaks have received a lot of press lately. What is a memory leak? Memory leaks occur because many Windows programs use memory inefficiently. Frequently, they do not release memory when terminated and continue to accumulate and hold even more memory when they are opened and closed more than once during a Windows session (as you can see, "memory leak" is a bit of a misnomer). Eventually you run out of memory.

You have probably experienced a Windows message stating that there is not enough memory to run the program you are trying to start. So, you close all the other applications and try to start it again, but you still receive the same error message. Finally you exit Windows and restart Windows, which frees up all of the trapped memory. Now your program runs.

8.12.3 Testing APIs

Commercially available operating systems and software and hardware products have defined software interfaces known as APIs. Any software that interacts with one of these products must conform to the API rules. APIs can define rules for passing information to be contained in external function calls, external variables, and symbolic names that represent numeric values or collections of variables [16]. API requirements include specification of Parameters, Function Return Values, Feature Test Macros, Variable Types, and Headers.

According to Jones, API function calls are susceptible to errors in the values they accept as arguments and in the values they return. Type-mismatch errors in function calls will be flagged at compile time, but errors in the logic that makes the function calls and the logic that checks the return values will not. Frequently, parameters and return values that have specific value limits need to be checked by logic with multiple relational operators. This complicates the logic and makes this an error-prone area.

DLTs can be invaluable in clarifying the complex logic that checks the return codes of API calls. As with functions, objects that are defined within an API have specified limits that indicate the values they can contain. Both objects and functions can be tested using the equivalence partitioning and boundary analysis approaches.

Another area where API problems can occur is in headers used to identify function calls. The headers sometimes do not reflect the API requirements. Common problems include incorrectly specified arithmetic types, syntax violations, and incorrect number values for macros (symbolic names) [16].

Jones describes two things API tests must do: scan the application source code to identify all uses of external identifiers and be able to verify identifiers in the application against a database that describes the APIs and the identifiers they define.

Jones also summarizes the information API tests should produce. They should uncover violations of the defined interface (number and type) and identifiers referenced that are not known in the API, including headers, functions, external identifiers, and macros.

With the capacities of the current generation of automated testing tools, it should be relatively easy to create API test drivers that can be called from the test scripts and return a pass/fail value to the test scripts. This method has been used to test DLLs via SQA TeamTest test scripts in previous product versions. Segue's EK could also be used to create API-checking test scripts.

8.12.4 Automated Testing Tools for Code-Level Testing

Nu-Mega Technologies, Inc. (currently part of Compuware, Inc.), developed two powerful tools for error-checking and debugging MS Windows applications. The first, BoundsChecker, is an automatic error detection and analysis tool for C/C++ development. It inserts code into the programs using a compile-time instrumentation (CTI) technology. CTI detects errors that can remain unnoticed by regular compilers and symbolic debuggers. BoundsChecker detects 12 different types of errors:

☞ Invalid Windows API parameters

☞ Invalid Windows API return codes

☞ Invalid ANSI C parameters

☞ Invalid ANSI C return codes

☞ Memory leaks

☞ Resource leaks

☞ Dynamic memory overruns

☞ Stack memory overruns

☞ Data and heap corruption

☞ Memory-locking problems

☞ Null-pointer manipulations

☞ Processor faults

BoundsChecker is available in both 16- and 32-bit environments for MS-DOS, Windows 3.x, Windows 95, and Windows NT. Figure 8.8 specifically details the kinds of errors BoundsChecker can identify.

Fig. 8.8 BoundsChecker C++ Error Categories (adapted from a table found at the NuMega website, http://www.numega.com)

Error-Checking Technology	Error
Write Checking	Dynamic Memory Overrun
	Stack Memory Overrun
	Static Memory Overrun
	Writing Array Out Of Range
	Writing Dangling Pointer

Fig. 8.8 BoundsChecker C++ Error Categories (adapted from a table found at the NuMega website, http://www.numega.com) (Continued)

Error-Checking Technology	Error
	Writing Null Pointer
	Writing Uninitialized Pointer
	Writing Overflows Memory
API Checking	API Failure: Windows Function Failed
	API Failure: Windows Function Not Implemented
	Format String Is Inconsistent
	Freed Handle Is Still Locked
	Handle Is Already Locked
	Invalid Argument: Illegal Format Specifier
	Invalid Argument: Bad Source Pointer
	Invalid Argument: Conflicting Combination Of Flags
	Invalid Argument: Format String Is Not Followed By Valid Arguments
	Invalid Argument: General
	Invalid Argument: Invalid Pointer To Format String
	Invalid Argument: Not Enough Arguments For Format String
	Invalid Argument: Out Of Range
	Invalid Argument: Not Enough Arguments For Format String
	Invalid Argument: Illegal Flags
C++ Checking	Inconsistent Use Of Delete Operator
	Memory Allocation Conflict
	Virtual Function Table Is Invalid
Compile Checking	Cast Of Pointer Loses Precision
Compile Checking (continued)	Function Has Inconsistent Return Type
	Global Declarations Are Inconsistent
	Mismatch In Argument Type
	Reading Array Out Of Range
	Returning A Pointer To A Local Variable
	Writing Array Out Of range
	Writing Overflows Memory

Soft-ICE is a powerful tool for debugging Windows system crashes. (Since I have had several major problems with virtual device drivers in Windows 95 that resulted in system crashes, I see the value of such a tool.) Soft-ICE provides source- and machine-level debugging, and it can debug the following system crashes.

☞ Virtual device drivers (VxDs) and dynamically loadable VxDs
☞ DLLs
☞ Windows device drivers
☞ Interrupt-service routines
☞ 16- and 32-bit Windows applications
☞ DOS device drivers
☞ DOS applications running under Windows

8.13 DATA-DRIVEN TESTING AND FRAMEWORK-BASED TEST SCRIPT EXAMPLES

SQA's version of the BASIC programming language is almost as powerful as the real thing yet is designed to enhance testing capabilities. It can be used to read test data from input files and to write the results to output files. It can launch sophisticated SQL queries allowing testers to capture before and after snapshots of database tables.

An example of a real-world tax exemption application will be used to illustrate the data-driven approach to automated testing. Figure 8.9 describes an operational set of test objectives that were used to develop the test conditions that Figure 8.10 illustrates. This figure is excerpted from an MS Excel worksheet that defines test conditions for the sample application. The test conditions are Black Box and include equivalence partitions, boundary conditions, and error-guessing conditions.

Fig. 8.9 Operational Testing Objectives for Creating Test Conditions in Excel Spreadsheet

---

For Each GUI Screen Include Data Input Records That Cover the Following Conditions.

1. At least one GOOD record where all fields contain valid data (Passes all GUI and Server-level edits)
2. Include at least one GOOD Duplicate record
3. Include one INVALID record for GUI edit defined in the test requirements
4. Include one INVALID record for each server edit (Business Rule) defined in the test requirements
5. Include one or more records for each type of special processing described in the test requirements
6. Include one or more records for each type of Y2K date processing described in the test requirements

Fig. 8.9 Operational Testing Objectives for Creating Test Conditions in Excel
Spreadsheet (Continued)

For Each Alpha Field
> Character Strings longer than stated field size
> Spaces
> Nulls
> Special Characters
> Numeric

For Each Numeric Field
> + and – Values
> Leading Sign Values
> Trailing Sign Values
> Zeroes
> Nulls
> Spaces
> Special Characters
> Alpha

For Ranges
> Value less than lower bound
> In range value
> Value greater than upper bound

For Range Boundaries
> Value equal to lower bound
> Value equal to upper bound

For Each Date Field
> Months 00 and 13
> Days 00 and 32
> Feb. 28, 29, 30
> Dates equal to the current date
> Dates greater than the current date
> Dates less than the current date

US Format
> M/D/Y
> MM/DD/YYYY
> MM-DD-YY
> MM-DD-YYYY

Invalid Format
> YYYY/MM/DD
> MM/YYYY/DD
> DD/YYYY/MM

Fig. 8.9 Operational Testing Objectives for Creating Test Conditions in Excel
Spreadsheet (Continued)

Y2K Dates
 Formats
  MM/DD/YY (Implicit Century)
  MM/DD/YYYY (Explicit Century)
 Dates and Date Ranges
  01/01/1900 to 12/31/2050
 Two-digit user input
  12/31/1999
  01/01/2000
  01/03/2000
  01/02/2000 to 01/07/2000
 Two-digit system date input
  12/31/1999
  01/01/2000
  01/03/2000
  01/02/2000 to 01/07/2000
 Two-digit date input from files
  12/31/1999
  01/01/2000
  01/03/2000
  01/02/2000 to 01/07/2000
 Leap Year Dates
  02/28/2000
  02/29/2000
  02/28/2004
  02/29/2004
  02/28/2008
  02/29/2008

For the following situations test general date integrity
 Date Arithmetic
 Date Conversion

 Sort Dates
 Search Dates
 Dates in Variables
 Dates in Assignment Statements
 Date Values as Constants
 Dates Used in Indexing
 Dates Used in Linked Lists
 Dates Used in Internal Tables

Fig. 8.10 Excerpted Test Conditions for Sample Application

Item/Event	Valid Conditions	Invalid Conditions	Expected Behavior	Comments
Customer Detail/ License List Screen				
GUI Fields				
FEIN	Numeric— can be edited	Not Numeric	Will accept only numeric characters	May be controlled via key press
		Zeroes		May be controlled via key press
		Special characters		May be controlled via key press
		Cannot be edited		May be controlled via key press
Customer Name	Alpha—can be edited	Non-alpha	Will accept only alpha characters	May be controlled via key press
		Blank spaces		May be controlled via key press
				May be controlled via key press
		Special characters		May be controlled via key press
		Cannot be edited		May be controlled via key press
Address1	Alpha—can be edited	Blank spaces	Will accept only alpha characters	May be controlled via key press
				May be controlled via key press
		Special characters		May be controlled via key press
		Cannot be edited		May be controlled via key press
Address2	Alpha—can be edited	Blank spaces	Will accept only alpha characters	May be controlled via key press
				May be controlled via key press
		Special characters		May be controlled via key press
		Cannot be edited		

Fig. 8.10 Excerpted Test Conditions for Sample Application (Continued)

Item/Event	Valid Conditions	Invalid Conditions	Expected Behavior	Comments
City	Alpha—can be edited	Non-alpha	Will accept only alpha characters	
		Blank spaces		
		Special characters		
		Cannot be edited		
State	Alpha—can be edited	Non-alpha	Will accept only alpha characters	
		Blank spaces		
		Special characters		
		Cannot be edited		
Zip	Alpha—can be edited	Blank spaces	Will accept only alpha characters	
		Special characters		
		Cannot be edited		
Phone	Numeric—can be edited	Non-numeric	Will accept only numeric characters	
		Zeroes		
		Blank spaces		
		Special characters		
		Cannot be edited		
Contact	Alpha—can be edited	Blank spaces	Will accept only alpha characters	
		Special characters		
		Cannot be edited		
Comments	Alpha—can be edited, 255 characters max	Blank spaces	Will accept only alpha characters	

Fig. 8.10 Excerpted Test Conditions for Sample Application (Continued)

Item/Event	Valid Conditions	Invalid Conditions	Expected Behavior	Comments
		Special characters		
		Cannot be edited		
		Does not hold 255 characters		
CustID	Alpha— noneditable	Can be edited	Display Only	
Branded	Alpha— noneditable	Can be edited	Display Only	
License ID Number	Alpha— noneditable	Can be edited	Display Only	
Federal Type	Alpha— noneditable	Can be edited	Display Only	
Country Code	Alpha— noneditable	Can be edited	Display Only	
State Code	Alpha— noneditable	Can be edited	Display Only	
County Code	Alpha— noneditable	Can be edited	Display Only	
City Code	Alpha— noneditable	Can be edited	Display Only	
Tax type	Alpha— noneditable	Can be edited	Display Only	
Product Code	Alpha— noneditable	Can be edited	Display Only	
Tran Type	Alpha— noneditable	Can be edited	Display Only	
Exempt Pct	Alpha— noneditable	Can be edited	Display Only	
Effective Date	Alpha— noneditable	Can be edited	Display Only	
Expiration Date	Alpha— noneditable	Can be edited	Display Only	
Comments	Alpha— noneditable	Can be edited	Display Only	
License Detail Screen GUI Fields				

Fig. 8.10 Excerpted Test Conditions for Sample Application (Continued)

Item/Event	Valid Conditions	Invalid Conditions	Expected Behavior	Comments
Exempt License ID	Alpha—can be edited	Non-alpha	Should accept only valid alpha characters	
		Blank spaces		
		Special characters		
		Cannot be edited		
Tax Type ID	Alpha—can be edited	Non-alpha	Should accept only valid alpha characters	
		Special characters		
		Cannot be edited		
Transaction Type ID	Alpha—can be edited	Non-alpha	Should accept only valid alpha characters	
		Blank spaces		
		Special characters		
		Cannot be edited		
Exempt %	Numeric—can be edited	Non-numeric	Should accept only valid numeric characters	
		Blank spaces		
		Zeroes		
		Special characters		
Cert Effective Date	Standard Date Format, MM/DD/YYYY	Not in standard date format		
		Zeroes in month		
		Zeroes in day		
		Zeroes in year		

Fig. 8.10 Excerpted Test Conditions for Sample Application (Continued)

Item/Event	Valid Conditions	Invalid Conditions	Expected Behavior	Comments
		Accepts two-digit year		
		Does not handle Feb 28		
		Does not handle Feb 29		
		Does not handle Feb 30		
		Does not handle month 13		
		Does not handle day 32		
		Does not handle year 1999		
		Does not handle year 2000		
		Does not handle year 2001		
		Accepts wrong format e.g. DD/MM/YYYY or YYYY/MM/DD		
		Accepts blanks		
		Accepts spaces		
		Accepts special characters		
Cert Expiration Date	Standard Date Format, MM/DD/YYYY	Not in standard date format		
		Zeroes in month		
		Zeroes in day		
		Zeroes in year		

Fig. 8.10 Excerpted Test Conditions for Sample Application (Continued)

Item/Event	Valid Conditions	Invalid Conditions	Expected Behavior	Comments
		Accepts two-digit year		
		Does not handle Feb 28		
		Does not handle Feb 29		
		Does not handle Feb 30		
		Does not handle month 13		
		Does not handle day 32		
		Does not handle year 1999		
		Does not handle year 2000		
		Does not handle year 2001		
		Accepts wrong format e.g. DD/MM/YYYY or YYYY/MM/DD		
		Accepts blanks		
		Accepts spaces		
		Accepts special characters		
Comment	Alpha—can be edited, 255 characters max		Accepts anything	
Federal Type	Alpha—can be edited	Non-alpha	Accepts only valid alpha characters	
		Blank spaces		

Fig. 8.10 Excerpted Test Conditions for Sample Application (Continued)

Item/Event	Valid Conditions	Invalid Conditions	Expected Behavior	Comments
Country Code	Alpha—can be edited	Special characters		
		Cannot be edited		
		Non-alpha	Accepts only alpha characters that are valid Country codes	
		Blank spaces		
		Special characters		
		Accepts invalid country codes		
		Cannot be edited		
State Code	Alpha—can be edited	Non-alpha	Accepts only alpha characters that are valid state codes	
		Blank spaces		
		Special characters		
		Accepts invalid state codes		
		Cannot be edited		
County Codes	Alpha—can be edited	Non-alpha	Accepts only alpha characters that are valid County codes	
		Blank spaces		
		Special characters		
		Accepts invalid County codes		
		Cannot be edited		

Fig. 8.10 Excerpted Test Conditions for Sample Application (Continued)

Item/Event	Valid Conditions	Invalid Conditions	Expected Behavior	Comments
City Code	Alpha—can be edited	Non-alpha	Accepts only alpha characters that are valid City codes	
		Blank spaces		
		Special characters		
		Accepts invalid City codes		
		Cannot be edited		
FEIN	Alpha—can be edited	Non-alpha	Accepts only alpha characters that are valid FEIN values?	
		Blank spaces		
		Special characters		
		Accepts invalid FEIN values?		
		Cannot be edited		

The test conditions were used to develop the test data that SQA TeamTest test scripts executed. The test data was designed in the same Excel workbook on a different sheet. Figures 8.11 and 8.12 illuminate two portions of the total test data set that was created—test data for creating a new customer and for adding licenses for the new customer.

Fig. 8.11 Example Test Data for Adding New Customer

ID	Record Code	FEIN	Customer Name	Address 1	Address 2	City	State	Zip	Comments	Phone	Contact
1	0	00-1234567	Acme Company	123 North South St.	Suite 101	Clayton	MO	63105	Good test record	314-555-9876	Joe Smith
2	E	00-123456789	Acme Company	124 North South St.	Suite 102	Clayton	MO	63106	Too many FEIN #	314-555-9877	Joe Smith

Fig. 8.11 Example Test Data for Adding New Customer (Continued)

ID	Record Code	FEIN	Customer Name	Address 1	Address 2	City	State	Zip	Comments	Phone	Contact
3	E	00-123	Acme Company	125 North South St.	Suite 103	Clayton	MO	63107	Too few FEIN #	314-555-9878	Joe Smith
4	E	00-abcdefg	Acme Company	123 North South St.	Suite 101	Clayton	MO	63105	Non numeric	314-555-9876	Joe Smith
5	E	00-0000000	Acme Company	123 North South St.	Suite 101	Clayton	MO	63105	Zeros	314-555-9876	Joe Smith
6	E	00-!@#$%^&	Acme Company	123 North South St.	Suite 101	Clayton	MO	63105	Special Characters	314-555-9876	Joe Smith
7	E		Acme Company	123 North South St.	Suite 101	Clayton	MO	63105	Blank FEIN	314-555-9876	Joe Smith
8	E		Acme Company	124 North South St.	Suite 102	Clayton	MO	63106	Spaces for FEIN	314-555-9877	Joe Smith
9	E	00-1234567	1234456789	123 North South St.	Suite 101	Clayton	MO	63105	Numeric Customer Name	314-555-9876	Joe Smith
10	E	00-1234567		123 North South St.	Suite 101	Clayton	MO	63105	Spaces for CN	314-555-9876	Joe Smith
11	E	00-1234567		123 North South St.	Suite 101	Clayton	MO	63105	Blank CN	314-555-9876	Joe Smith
12	E	00-1234567	!@#$%^*&*()?":><	123 North South St.	Suite 101	Clayton	MO	63105	Special Characters	314-555-9876	Joe Smith
13	E	00-1234567	Acme Company		Suite 102	Clayton	MO	63105	Spaces for Address1	314-555-9877	Joe Smith
14	E	00-1234567	Acme Company		Suite 103	Clayton	MO	63105	Blank Address1	314-555-9878	Joe Smith
15	E	00-1234567	Acme Company	!@#$%^&*()	Suite 104	Clayton	MO	63105	Special Characters	314-555-9879	Joe Smith
16	E	00-1234567	Acme Company	127 North South St.		Clayton	MO	63105	Spaces for Address2	314-555-9880	Joe Smith
17	E	00-1234567	Acme Company	128 North South St.		Clayton	MO	63105	Blank Address2	314-555-9881	Joe Smith
18	E	00-1234567	Acme Company	129 North South St.	!@#$%^&*()	Clayton	MO	63105	Special Characters	314-555-9882	Joe Smith
19	E	00-1234567	Acme Company	130 North South St.	Suite 108		MO	63105	Spaces for City	314-555-9883	Joe Smith
20	E	00-1234567	Acme Company	131 North South St.	Suite 109		MO	63105	Blank city	314-555-9884	Joe Smith

Fig. 8.11 Example Test Data for Adding New Customer (Continued)

ID	Record Code	FEIN	Customer Name	Address 1	Address 2	City	State	Zip	Comments	Phone	Contact
21	E	00-1234567	Acme Company	132 North South St.	Suite 110	!@#$%^&	MO	63105	Special Characters	314-555-9885	Joe Smith
22	E	00-1234567	Acme Company	133 North South St.	Suite 111	Clayton		63105	Spaces for State	314-555-9886	Joe Smith
23	E	00-1234567	Acme Company	134 North South St.	Suite 112	Clayton		63105	Blank State	314-555-9887	Joe Smith
24	E	00-1234567	Acme Company	135 North South St.	Suite 113	Clayton	#@	63105	Special Characters	314-555-9888	Joe Smith
25	E	00-1234567	Acme Company	134 North South St.	Suite 112	Clayton	ZZ	63105	Illegal State	314-555-9887	Joe Smith
26	0	00-1234568	Acme Company	135 North South St.	Suite 113	Clayton	MO	63105-1234	Good test record	314-555-9888	Joe Smith
27	E	00-1234567	Acme Company	134 North South St.	Suite 112	Clayton	MO		Spaces for Zip	314-555-9887	Joe Smith
28	E	00-1234567	Acme Company	135 North South St.	Suite 113	Clayton	MO		Blank Zip	314-555-9888	Joe Smith
29	E	00-1234567	Acme Company	134 North South St.	Suite 112	Clayton	MO	!@#$%-^&*(	Special Characters	314-555-9887	Joe Smith
30	E	00-1234567	Acme Company	135 North South St.	Suite 113	Clayton	MO	63105	Special Characters	314-555-9888	Joe Smith
31	E	00-1234567	Acme Company	134 North South St.	Suite 112	Clayton	MO	63105	Spaces for phone number	- -	Joe Smith
32	E	00-1234567	Acme Company	135 North South St.	Suite 113	Clayton	MO	63105	Blank phone number		Joe Smith
33	E	00-1234567	Acme Company	134 North South St.	Suite 112	Clayton	MO	63105	Special Characters	!@#-$%^-&*()	Joe Smith
34	E	00-1234567	Acme Company	135 North South St.	Suite 113	Clayton	MO	63105	numeric contact name	314-555-9888	123 456789

Fig. 8.12 Sample Data for Adding Customer License

	Record Code	Exempt License ID	Federal Type	Trans Type ID	Product Code	Exempt %	Cert Effective Date	Cert Expiration Date	Comments
1	0	00-1234569	123	ST	9876	1.2345	1/1/97	12/31/99	Good Test Record
2	0	AA-1234569	123	ST	9876	1.2345	1/1/97	12/31/99	Good Test Record
3	0	ABCDEFG	123	ST	9876	1.2345	1/1/97	12/31/99	Good Test Record
3	E		123	ST	9876	1.2345	1/1/97	12/31/99	Spaces for ELI

Fig. 8.12 Sample Data for Adding Customer License (Continued)

	Record Code	Exempt License ID	Federal Type	Trans Type ID	Product Code	Exempt %	Cert Effective Date	Cert Expiration Date	Comments
4	E		123	ST	9876	1.2345	1/1/97	12/31/99	Blank ELI
5	E	!@#$%	123	ST	9876	1.2345	1/1/97	12/31/99	Special Characters for ELI
5	E	00-1234569		ST	9876	1.2345	1/1/97	12/31/99	Spaces for Fed Type
6	E	00-1234569		ST	9876	1.2345	1/1/97	12/31/99	Blank Fed Type
7	E	00-1234569	!@#	ST	9876	1.2345	1/1/97	12/31/99	Special Characters for Fed Type
8	E	00-1234569	ABC	ST	9876	1.2345	1/1/97	12/31/99	Alpha Characters for Fed Type
9	E	00-1234569	123		9876	1.2345	1/1/97	12/31/99	Spaces for TTI
10	E	00-1234569	123		9876	1.2345	1/1/97	12/31/99	Blank TTI
11	E	00-1234569	123	!@#	9876	1.2345	1/1/97	12/31/99	Special TTI
12	E	00-1234569	123	123	9876	1.2345	1/1/97	12/31/99	Numeric TTI
13	E	00-1234569	123	ST		1.2345	1/1/97	12/31/99	Spaces for Product Code
14	E	00-1234569	123	ST		1.2345	1/1/97	12/31/99	Blank PC
15	E	00-1234569	123	ST	ABCD	1.2345	1/1/97	12/31/99	Alpha Characters for PC
16	E	00-1234569	123	ST	!@#$	1.2345	1/1/97	12/31/99	Special Characters PC
17	E	00-1234569	123	ST	9876		1/1/97	12/31/99	Spaces for Exempt %
18	E	00-1234569	123	ST	9876		1/1/97	12/31/99	Blank Exempt %
19	E	00-1234569	123	ST	9876	a.bcde	1/1/97	12/31/99	Alpha Characters for Exempt %
20	E	00-1234569	123	ST	9876	!.?><*	1/1/97	12/31/99	Special Characters for Exempt %
21	E	00-1234569	123	ST	9876	1.2345		12/31/99	Spaces for Cert Effective
22	E	00-1234569	123	ST	9876	1.2345		12/31/99	Blank Cert Effective
23	E	00-1234569	123	ST	9876	1.2345	January 1, 1997	12/31/99	Alpha Characters for Cert Effective
24	E	00-1234569	123	ST	9876	1.2345	!@/#$/ ^&*(	12/31/99	Special Character for Cert Effective
25	E	00-1234569	123	ST	9876	1.2345	1/1/97		Spaces for Cert Expiration Date
26	E	00-1234569	123	ST	9876	1.2345	1/1/97		Blank Cert Expiration Date
27	E	00-1234569	123	ST	9876	1.2345	1/1/97	December 31, 1999	Alpha Characters for Cert Expiration Date
28	E	00-1234569	123	ST	9876	1.2345	1/1/97	!@/#$/ ^&*(	Special Characters for Cert Expiration Date
29	E	00-1234569	123	ST	9876	1.2345	1/1/97	12/31/99	Spaces for Tax Type ID
30	E	00-1234569	123	ST	9876	1.2345	1/1/97	12/31/99	Blank Tax Type ID
31	E	00-1234569	123	ST	9876	1.2345	1/1/97	12/31/99	Numeric Characters for Tax Type ID
32	E	00-1234569	123	ST	9876	1.2345	1/1/97	12/31/99	Special Characters
33	E	00-1234569	123	ST	9876	1.2345	1/1/97	12/31/99	Spaces for Country Code
34	E	00-1234569	123	ST	9876	1.2345	1/1/97	12/31/99	Blank Country Code
35	E	00-1234569	123	ST	9876	1.2345	1/1/97	12/31/99	Alpha Characters for County Code
36	E	00-1234569	123	ST	9876	1.2345	1/1/97	12/31/99	Special Characters for Country Code
37	E	00-1234569	123	ST	9876	1.2345	1/1/97	12/31/99	Spaces for State Code
38	E	00-1234569	123	ST	9876	1.2345	1/1/97	12/31/99	Blank State Code
39	E	00-1234569	123	ST	9876	1.2345	1/1/97	12/31/99	Numeric State Code

Fig. 8.12 Sample Data for Adding Customer License (Continued)

	Record Code	Exempt License ID	Federal Type	Trans Type ID	Product Code	Exempt %	Cert Effective Date	Cert Expiration Date	Comments
40	E	00-1234569	123	ST	9876	1.2345	1/1/97	12/31/99	Special Characters for State Code
41	E	00-1234569	123	ST	9876	1.2345	1/1/97	12/31/99	Spaces for County Code
42	E	00-1234569	123	ST	9876	1.2345	1/1/97	12/31/99	Blank County Code
43	E	00-1234569	123	ST	9876	1.2345	1/1/97	12/31/99	Alpha Characters for County Code
44	E	00-1234569	123	ST	9876	1.2345	1/1/97	12/31/99	Special Characters for County Code
45	E	00-1234569	123	ST	9876	1.2345	1/1/97	12/31/99	Spaces for City Code
46	E	00-1234569	123	ST	9876	1.2345	1/1/97	12/31/99	Blank City Code
47	E	00-1234569	123	ST	9876	1.2345	1/1/97	12/31/99	Alpha Characters for City Code
48	E	00-1234569	123	ST	9876	1.2345	1/1/97	12/31/99	Special Characters for City Code

The approach used to create the test data is described extensively in my previous work [25]. To reiterate briefly, it is only necessary to create one good record that will be added. All other records contain at least one bad data value that should be rejected by either the GUI validation processes or by the business rules validation processes. Remember, only one invalid value should be present in each input record. Putting more than one error value in a single test record can cause errors [27]. The test data values are exported to a sequential CSV file that an SQA test script reads as input during test execution.

Figure 8.13 is an example of an SQA test script that reads the input data from two text files and places the data values in text boxes on the GUI. The script adds new customer records and new licenses for the customers. Figures 8.14 and 8.15 illustrate the contents of the sequential CSV input files (Reccustl.txt and Reclcnse.txt, respectively).

Fig. 8.13 RECADD Test Script Listing

```
'$include "global.sbl"
Declare Sub AddLicense
'Declare global variables
Global fld(256) as string
Global lfld(256) as string
Global FirstRecord
Sub Main

'Dimension Local Variables

    Dim Result As Integer
    Dim I as Integer
    Dim Msgtext
    Dim Goodrec as Integer
    Dim Badrec as Integer
    Dim LGoodrec as Integer
    Dim LBadrec as Integer
    Dim Testtype
    Dim reccode
```

Fig. 8.13 RECADD Test Script Listing (Continued)

```
    'Initially Recorded: 06/09/98  08:18:15
    'Test Procedure Name: Data Entry Template
    'Generic add customer location records
'Initialize variables
    Goodrec=0
    Badrec=0
'Open Input files containing test data
    Open "H:\SQA\data\Reccustl.txt" for Input as #1
    Open "H:\SQA\data\Reclcnse.txt" for Input as #2
'Begin processing loop
    Do while Not EOF(1)
    'Read data
    'Must be edited to match number of fields on window
        Input #1, reccode,fld(1),fld(2),fld(3),fld(4),fld(5),fld(6),fld(7),
        fld(8),fld(9),fld(10)
    'Check error code for skip record condition
        If (Left$(reccode,1) = "H")      then
            GoTo NoProcess
        End If
    'Check error code for good and bad record count
        If (Left$(reccode,1) = "0") then
            Goodrec=goodrec + 1
        Else
            Badrec=Badrec + 1
        End If
    'Put data in GUI fields
            Window SetContext, "Name=w_wce_frame", ""
            MenuSelect "File→New"
            Delayfor 2000

            'Puts data values in GUI fields

            Window SetContext, "Name=w_wce_frame", ""
            Window SetContext, "Name=w_customer_maintenance;ChildWindow", ""
            InputKeys fld(1)
            DataWindow Click, "Name=dw_customer_record;\;Name=customername",
                        "Coords=23,9"
            InputKeys fld(2)
            DataWindow Click, "Name=dw_customer_record;\;Name=address1",
                        "Coords=19,9"
            InputKeys fld(3)
            DataWindow Click, "Name=dw_customer_record;\;Name=address2",
                        "Coords=19,10"
            InputKeys fld(4)
            DataWindow Click, "Name=dw_customer_record;\;Name=cityname",
                        "Coords=13,12"
            InputKeys fld(5)
            DataWindow Click, "Name=dw_customer_record;\;Name=stateprovince",
                        "Coords=14,8"
            InputKeys fld(6)
            DataWindow Click, "Name=dw_customer_record;\;Name=zipcode",
                        "Coords=22,13"
            InputKeys fld(7)
            DataWindow Click, "Name=dw_customer_record;\;Name=description",
                        "Coords=24,11"
```

Fig. 8.13 RECADD Test Script Listing (Continued)

```
            InputKeys fld(8)
            DataWindow Click, "Name=dw_customer_record;\;Name=contact",
                              "Coords=21,9"
            InputKeys fld(9)
            DataWindow Click, "Name=dw_customer_record;\;Name=phoneno",
                              "Coords=11,9"
            InputKeys fld(10)
        'Save the data record
            Window SetContext, "Name=w_wce_frame", ""
            MenuSelect "File→Save"
            Delayfor 2000

        'Add a license if there is one

            If (Left$(reccode,1) = "0") then
                Call AddLicense
            End If

            Window SetContext, "Class=Shell_TrayWnd", ""
            TabControl Click, "ObjectIndex=1", "Coords=378,12"
'Goto label for skipping through loop without processing anything

NoProcess:

'End of processing loop

Loop

'Close all data files

    Close #1
    Close #2

'Write the number of good and bad records process to test log

    Msgtext= "Customer Location Records Added:  Good= " & Goodrec & "  Bad= " &
        Badrec
    SQALogMessage sqaNone, Msgtext, ""
    Msgtext= "Customer License Records Added:  Good= " & lGoodrec & "  Bad= " &
        lBadrec
    SQALogMessage sqaNone, Msgtext, ""
End Sub

Sub  AddLicense

    'Dimension Local variables

    Dim Result As Integer
    Dim lreccode

    'Initialize local variables

    LGoodrec=0
    LBadrec=0

    'Initially Recorded: 06/09/98  13:29:54

'Read license data

    Input #2,
        Lreccode,lfld(1),lfld(2),lfld(3),lfld(4),lfld(5),lfld(6),lfld(7),lfld(8),lf
        ld(9),lfld(10),lfld(11),lfld(12),lfld(13)

'Begin processing loop

    Do while Not EOF(2)

    'Check error code for skip record condition

        If (Left$(lreccode,1) = "H")     then
            GoTo NoLicense
        End If
```

Fig. 8.13 RECADD Test Script Listing (Continued)

```
      'Put data in GUI fields

      Window SetContext, "Name=w_wce_frame", ""
      Window SetContext, "Name=w_customer_maintenance;ChildWindow", ""
      PushButton Click,  "Name=cb_new_license"

      Window SetContext, "Name=w_license_maintenance", ""
      InputKeys lfld(1)
      DataWindow Click, "Name=dw_1;\;Name=federaltype", "Coords=20,10"
      InputKeys lfld(2)
      DataWindow Click, "Name=dw_1;\;Name=transactiontypeid", ""

      Window SetContext, "DropDownLB", "Activate=0"
      Window Click, "", "Coords=21,3"

      Window SetContext, "Name=w_license_maintenance", ""
      DataWindow Click, "Name=dw_1;\;Name=productproductgroupid", "Coords=23,15"
      InputKeys lfld(4)
      DataWindow Click, "Name=dw_1;\;Name=exemptpercentage", "Coords=22,9"
      InputKeys lfld(5)
      DataWindow Click, "Name=dw_1;\;Name=effectivefrom", "Coords=21,10"
      InputKeys lfld(6)
      DataWindow Click, "Name=dw_1;\;Name=effectiveto", "Coords=22,5"
      InputKeys lfld(7)
      DataWindow Click, "Name=dw_1;\;Name=tax_type_id", "Coords=6,12"
      InputKeys lfld(8)
      DataWindow Click, "Name=dw_1;\;Name=countryid", "Coords=10,10"
      InputKeys lfld(9)
      DataWindow Click, "Name=dw_1;\;Name=stateprovince", "Coords=38,10"
      InputKeys lfld(10)
      DataWindow Click, "Name=dw_1;\;Name=countyid", "Coords=27,18"
      InputKeys lfld(11)
      DataWindow Click, "Name=dw_1;\;Name=cityid", "Coords=24,14"
      InputKeys lfld(12)
      DataWindow Click, "Name=dw_1;\;Name=description", "Coords=35,11"
      InputKeys lfld(13)
'     DataWindow Click, "Name=dw_1;\;Name=countryid", "Coords=10,10"
'     Window SetContext, "Name=w_license_maintenance", ""
'     InputKeys lfld(10)
'     DataWindow Click, "Name=dw_1;\;Name=stateprovince", "Coords=38,10"
'     Window SetContext, "Name=w_license_maintenance", ""
'     InputKeys lfld(11)
'     DataWindow Click, "Name=dw_1;\;Name=countyid", "Coords=27,18"
'     Window SetContext, "Name=w_license_maintenance", ""
'     InputKeys lfld(12)
'     DataWindow Click, "Name=dw_1;\;Name=cityid", "Coords=24,14"
'     InputKeys lfld(13)

      'Save License Record

      Window SetContext, "Name=w_license_maintenance", ""
      PushButton Click, "Name=cb_save"

      'Check License error code to determine which command button to click
'     AN ATTEMPT TO CLOSE THE CHILD WINDOW
'      PushButton Click, "Name=cb_close"
'      Window SetContext, "Caption=Close", ""
'      InputKeys "y"
'      PushButton Click, "Name=cb_close"

      If Lreccode=0 then
'         PushButton Click, "Name=cb_new_license"

          PushButton Click, "Name=cb_new"
      else
```

Fig. 8.13 RECADD Test Script Listing (Continued)

```
        PushButton Click, "Name=cb_close"
    End If

    'Read Next License record

    Input #1,
        lreccode,lfld(1),lfld(2),lfld(3),lfld(4),lfld(5),lfld(6),lfld(7),lfld(8),lf
        ld(9),lfld(10),lfld(11),lfld(12),lfld(13)
'Goto label used when no record is to be processed

NoLicense:

'End of processing loop

loop
End Sub
```

Fig. 8.14 Reccustl.txt Input File Listing

```
"0","00-1234567","Acme Company","123 North South St.","Suite
        101","Clayton","MO","63105","Good test record","John Smith","3145559876"
"E","00-123456789","Acme Company","124 North South St.","Suite
        102","Clayton","MO","63106","Too many FEIN #","John Smith","3145559876"
"E","00-123","Acme Company","125 North South St.","Suite
        103","Clayton","MO","63107","Too few FEIN #","John Smith","3145559876"
"E","00-abcdefg","Acme Company","123 North South St.","Suite
        101","Clayton","MO","63105","Non numeric","John Smith","3145559876"
"E","00-0000000","Acme Company","123 North South St.","Suite
        101","Clayton","MO","63105","Zeroes","John Smith","3145559876"
"E","00-!@#$%^&","Acme Company","123 North South St.","Suite
        101","Clayton","MO","63105","Special Characters","John Smith","3145559876"
"E","","Acme Company","123 North South St.","Suite
        101","Clayton","MO","63105","Blank FEIN","John Smith","3145559876"
"E","          ","Acme Company","124 North South St.","Suite
        102","Clayton","MO","63106","Spaces for FEIN","John Smith","3145559876"
"E","00-1234567","1234456789","123 North South St.","Suite
        101","Clayton","MO","63105","Numeric Customer Name","John
        Smith","3145559876"
"E","00-1234567","00-000000","123 North South St.","Suite
        101","Clayton","MO","63105","Zeroes for CN","John Smith","3145559876"
"E","00-1234567","          ","123 North South St.","Suite
        101","Clayton","MO","63105","Spaces for CN","John Smith","3145559876"
"E","00-1234567","","123 North South St.","Suite 101","Clayton","MO","63105","Blank
        CN","John Smith","3145559876"
"E","00-1234567","!@#$%^*&*()?:><","123 North South St.","Suite
        101","Clayton","MO","63105","Special Characters","John Smith","3145559876"
"E","00-1234567","Acme Company","                        ","Suite
        102","Clayton","MO","63105","Spaces for Address1","John Smith","3145559876"
"E","00-1234567","Acme Company","000000","Suite 102","Clayton","MO","63105","Zeroes
        Address1","John Smith","3145559876"
"E","00-1234567","Acme Company","","Suite 103","Clayton","MO","63105","Blank
        Address1","John Smith","3145559876"
"E","00-1234567","Acme Company","!@#$%^&*()","Suite
        104","Clayton","MO","63105","Special Characters","John Smith","3145559876"
"E","00-1234567","Acme Company","127 North South St.","
        ","Clayton","MO","63105","Spaces for Address2","John Smith","3145559876"
"E","00-1234567","Acme Company","000000","Suite 102","Clayton","MO","63105","Zeroes
        Address2","John Smith","3145559876"
```

Fig. 8.14 Reccustl.txt Input File Listing (Continued)

```
"E","00-1234567","Acme Company","128 North South
      St.","","Clayton","MO","63105","Blank Address2","John Smith","3145559876"
"E","00-1234567","Acme Company","129 North South
      St.","!@#$%^&*()","Clayton","MO","63105","Special Characters","John
      Smith","3145559876"
"E","00-1234567","Acme Company","130 North South St.","Suite 108","
      ","MO","63105","Spaces for City","John Smith","3145559876"
"E","00-1234567","Acme Company","130 North South St.","Suite
      108","000000","MO","63105","Zeroes for City","John Smith","3145559876"
"E","00-1234567","Acme Company","131 North South St.","Suite
      109","","MO","63105","Blank city","John Smith","3145559876"
"E","00-1234567","Acme Company","132 North South St.","Suite
      110","!@#$%^&","MO","63105","Special Characters","John Smith","3145559876"
"E","00-1234567","Acme Company","133 North South St.","Suite 111","Clayton","
      ","63105","Spaces for State","John Smith","3145559876"
"E","00-1234567","Acme Company","133 North South St.","Suite
      111","Clayton","00","63105","Zeroes for State","John Smith","3145559876"
"E","00-1234567","Acme Company","134 North South St.","Suite
      112","Clayton","","63105","Blank State","John Smith","3145559876"
"E","00-1234567","Acme Company","135 North South St.","Suite
      113","Clayton","#@","63105","Special Characters","John Smith","3145559876"
"E","00-1234567","Acme Company","134 North South St.","Suite
      112","Clayton","ZZ","63105","Illegal State","John Smith","3145559876"
"O","00-1234568","Acme Company","135 North South St.","Suite
      113","Clayton","MO","631051234","Good test record","John
      Smith","3145559876"
"E","00-1234568","Acme Company","135 North South St.","Suite
      113","Clayton","MO","63105-1234","Zip code with a dash","John
      Smith","3145559876"
"E","00-1234567","Acme Company","134 North South St.","Suite
      112","Clayton","MO","        ","Spaces for Zip","John Smith","3145559876"
"E","00-1234567","Acme Company","134 North South St.","Suite
      112","Clayton","MO","00000","Zeroes for Zip","John Smith","3145559876"
"E","00-1234567","Acme Company","135 North South St.","Suite 113","Clayton","MO","
      ","Blank Zip","John Smith","3145559876"
"E","00-1234567","Acme Company","134 North South St.","Suite
      112","Clayton","MO","!@#$%-^&*(","Special Characters","John
      Smith","3145559876"
"E","00-1234567","Acme Company","135 North South St.","Suite
      113","Clayton","MO","63105","Spaces for CName","        ","3145559876"
"E","00-1234567","Acme Company","135 North South St.","Suite
      113","Clayton","MO","63105","Blank CName","","3145559876"
"E","00-1234567","Acme Company","135 North South St.","Suite
      113","Clayton","MO","63105","Numbers in CName","12345 6789012","3145559876"
"E","00-1234567","Acme Company","135 North South St.","Suite
      113","Clayton","MO","63105","Zeroes in CName","000000 000000","3145559876"
"E","00-1234567","Acme Company","135 North South St.","Suite
      113","Clayton","MO","63105","Special Characters","$^&*()
      ?><{}","3145559876"
"E","00-1234567","Acme Company","134 North South St.","Suite
      112","Clayton","MO","63105","Spaces for phone number","John Smith","  -  -
      "
"E","00-1234567","Acme Company","134 North South St.","Suite
      112","Clayton","MO","63105","Zeroes for phone number","John
      Smith","0000000000"
"E","00-1234567","Acme Company","135 North South St.","Suite
      113","Clayton","MO","63105","Blank phone number","John Smith",""
"E","00-1234567","Acme Company","134 North South St.","Suite
      112","Clayton","MO","63105","Special Characters","John Smith","!@#-$%^-
      &*()"
```

Fig. 8.15 Reclcnse.txt Input File Listing

```
"0","00-1234569","123","ST","9876","12345","01011997","12311997",
      "SLT","1","MO","250","1125","Good Test Record"
"0","AA-1234569","123","ST","9876","12345","01011997","12311997",
      "SLT","1","MO","250","1125","Good Test Record"
"0","ABCDEFG","123","ST","9876","12345","01011997","12311997",
      "SLT","1","MO","250","1125","Good Test Record"
"E","         ","123","ST","9876","12345","01011997","12311997",
      "SLT","1","MO","250","1125","Spaces for ELI"
"E","123","ST","9876","12345","01011997","12311997","Blank
      ELI","1","MO","250","1125",,"SLT"
"E","!@#$%","123","ST","9876","12345","01011997","12311997",
      "SLT","1","MO","250","1125","Special Characters for ELI"
"E","00-1234569","   ","ST","9876","12345","01011997","12311997",
      "SLT","1","MO","250","1125","Spaces for Fed Type"
"E","00-1234569","","ST","9876","12345","01011997","12311997",
      "SLT","1","MO","250","1125","Blank FedType"
"E","00-1234569","!@#","ST","9876","12345","01011997","12311997",
      "SLT","1","MO","250","1125","Special Characters for Fed Type"
"E","00-1234569","ABC","ST","9876","12345","01011997","12311997",
      "SLT","1","MO","250","1125","Alpha Characters for Fed Type"
"E","00-1234569","123","       ","9876","12345","01011997","12311997",
      "SLT","1","MO","250","1125","Spaces for TTI"
"E","00-1234569","123","","9876","12345","01011997","12311997",
      "SLT","1","MO","250","1125","Blank TTI"
"E","00-1234569","123","!@#","9876","12345","01011997","12311997",
      "SLT","1","MO","250","1125","Special TTI"
"E","00-1234569","123","123","9876","12345","01011997","12311997",
      "SLT","1","MO","250","1125","Numeric TTI"
"E","00-1234569","123","ST","    ","12345","01011997","12311997",
      "SLT","1","MO","250","1125","Spaces for Product Code"
"E","00-1234569","123","ST","","12345","01011997","12311997",
      "SLT","1","MO","250","1125","Blank PC"
"E","00-1234569","123","ST","ABCD","12345","01011997","12311997",
      "SLT","1","MO","250","1125","Alpha Characters for PC"
"E","00-1234569","123","ST","!@#$","12345","01011997","12311997",
      "SLT","1","MO","250","1125","Special Characters PC"
"E","00-1234569","123","ST","9876","        ","01011997","12311997",
      "SLT","1","MO","250","1125","Spaces for Exempt %"
"E","00-1234569","123","ST","9876","","01011997","12311997",
      "SLT","1","MO","250","1125","Blank Exempt %"
"E","00-1234569","123","ST","9876","abcde","01011997","12311997",
      "SLT","1","MO","250","1125","Alpha Characters for Exempt %"
"E","00-1234569","123","ST","9876","!?><*","01011997","12311997",
      "SLT","1","MO","250","1125","Special Characters for Exempt %"
"E","00-1234569","123","ST","9876","12345","        ","12311997",
      "SLT","1","MO","250","1125","Spaces for Cert Effective"
"E","00-1234569","123","ST","9876","12345","","12311997",
      "SLT","1","MO","250","1125","Blank Cert Effective"
"E","00-1234569","123","ST","9876","12345","January 1","1997","Alpha Characters for
      Cert Effective","SLT","1","MO","250","12311997"
"E","00-1234569","123","ST","9876","12345","!@/#$/^&*(","12311997",
      "SLT","1","MO","250","1125","Special Character for Cert Effective"
"E","00-1234569","123","ST","9876","12345","01011997","           ",
      "SLT","1","MO","250","1125","Spaces for Cert Expiration Date"
"E","00-1234569","123","ST","9876","12345","01011997",",
      "SLT","1","MO","250","1125","Blank Cert Expiration Date"
"E","00-1234569","123","ST","9876","12345","01011997","December 31","Alpha
      Characters for Cert Expiration date","SLT","1","MO","250","1999"
"E","00-1234569","123","ST","9876","12345","01011997","!@/#$/^&*(",
      "SLT","1","MO","250","1125","Special Characters for Cert Expiration date"
```

Fig. 8.15 Reclcnse.txt Input File Listing (Continued)

```
"E","00-1234569","123","ST","9876","12345","01011997","12311997",
      "    ","1","MO","250","1125","Spaces for Tax Type Id"
"E","00-1234569","123","ST","9876","12345","01011997","12311997",
      "","1","MO","250","1125","Blank Tax Type Id"
"E","00-1234569","123","ST","9876","12345","01011997","12311997",
      "123","1","MO","250","1125","Numeric Characters for Tax Type Id"
"E","00-1234569","123","ST","9876","12345","01011997","12311997",
      "!@#","1","MO","250","1125","Special Characters"
"E","00-1234569","123","ST","9876","12345","01011997","12311997",
      "SLT","   ","MO","250","1125","Spaces for Country Code"
"E","00-1234569","123","ST","9876","12345","01011997","12311997",
      "SLT","","MO","250","1125","Blank Country Code"
"E","00-1234569","123","ST","9876","12345","01011997","12311997",
      "SLT","A","MO","250","1125","Alpha Characters for County Code"
"E","00-1234569","123","ST","9876","12345","01011997","12311997",
      "SLT","$","MO","250","1125","Special Characters for Country Code"
"E","00-1234569","123","ST","9876","12345","01011997","12311997",
      "SLT","1","   ","250","1125","Spaces for State Code"
"E","00-1234569","123","ST","9876","12345","01011997","12311997",
      "SLT","1","","250","1125","Blank State Code"
"E","00-1234569","123","ST","9876","12345","01011997","12311997",
      "SLT","1","98","250","1125","Numeric State Code"
"E","00-1234569","123","ST","9876","12345","01011997","12311997",
      "SLT","1","()","250","1125","Special Characters for State Code"
"E","00-1234569","123","ST","9876","12345","01011997","12311997",
      "SLT","1","MO","   ","1125","Spaces for County Code"
"E","00-1234569","123","ST","9876","12345","01011997","12311997",
      "SLT","1","MO","","1125","Blank County Code"
"E","00-1234569","123","ST","9876","12345","01011997","12311997",
      "SLT","1","MO","ABC","1125","Alpha Characters for County Code"
"E","00-1234569","123","ST","9876","12345","01011997","12311997",
      "SLT","1","MO","$%^","1125","Special Characters for County Code"
"E","00-1234569","123","ST","9876","12345","01011997","12311997",
      "SLT","1","MO","250","   ","Spaces for City Code"
"E","00-1234569","123","ST","9876","12345","01011997","12311997",
      "SLT","1","MO","250","","Blank City Code"
"E","00-1234569","123","ST","9876","12345","01011997","12311997",
      "SLT","1","MO","250","ZYXW","Alpha Characters for City Code"
"E","00-1234569","123","ST","9876","12345","01011997","12311997",
      "SLT","1","MO","250","%&$*","Special Characters for City Code"
```

Figure 8.16 is an example of a script that retrieves the records from a database table, runs a script that adds new records, and retrieves the records from the table a second time. It is used to verify that the records were added to the table. The verification here is that n... new records were added.

Fig. 8.16 Add Record Verification Procedure

```
'$include "GLOBAL.SBH"
'$CStrings
    'Initially Recorded: 10/01/97  12:40:55
    'Test Procedure Name: Get Txxxx table
Sub Main
    Dim Result As Integer
    Dim Fileparms As String*128
    Dim Length_1 As Long
```

Fig. 8.16 Add Record Verification Procedure (Continued)

```
      Dim Length_2 As Long
      Dim wrstr As String
'tnum is a global variable in GLOBAL.SBH that must be set to the table number in
      test

' if tnum = '00' error

    If tnum = "00" then

        'Error

        SQALogMessage sqaFail, "Calling procedure Error", _
        "The calling procedure did not set the Table number in 'tnum'"
        Exit Sub
    End If

'Build the isql input file
    Open "w:\\sqa97\\inhouse\\sqlscrpt\\sqlin.txt" for Binary Access Write as #1
        Len=2
    wrstr= "select * from T"+tcnum+"\r\n"
    Put #1, 1, wrstr
    wrstr= "go\r\n"
    Put #1,, wrstr
    Close #1
    DelayFor (2000)

'Build the parm string for SQAShellExecute
    Kill "w:\\sqa97\\inhouse\\outdata\\t"+tnum+".txt"
    Fileparms = "w:\\sqa97\\inhouse\\sqlscrpt\\sqlin.txt
        w:\\sqa97\\inhouse\\outdata\\t"+tcnum+".txt"
    SQAShellExecute "gett.bat","w:\\sqa97\\inhouse\\sqlscrpt\\",Fileparms
    DelayFor (5000)
    Result = FileT (Exists, "Name=w:\\sqa97\\inhouse\\outdata\\t"+tnum+".txt",
        "CaseID=GETTCF1")

    length_b = 0
    length_a = 0

'Get the file length before the add record procedure is called
    length_b = FileLen("w:\\sqa97\\inhouse\\outdata\\t"+tnum+".txt")
    Kill "w:\\sqa97\\inhouse\\outdata\\t"+tnum+".txt" 'get rid of the first version
        of the file
    DelayFor (1000)

'Call the add record procedure
    CallProcedure RECADD
    DelayFor (5000)

'Re-acquire the txxxx table
    SQAShellExecute "gettc.bat","w:\\sqa97\\inhouse\\sqlscrpt\\",Fileparms
    DelayFor (5000)
    Result = FileT (Exists, "Name=w:\\sqa97\\inhouse\\outdata\\tc"+tnum+".txt",
        "CaseID=GETTCF1")

'Get the file length after the add record procedure is called
    length_a = FileLen("w:\\sqa97\\inhouse\\outdata\\t"+tnum+".txt")

'Test it
    If length_b = length_a Then
        'Error
        SQALogMessage sqaFail, RECADDadd record failure", _
        "The T"+tnum+" table does not indicate new (additional) records."
    Else
        SQALogMessage sqaNone, "The Txxxx table shows new records", ""
    End If

'set tnum to "00" to insure calling procedure sets in a legal table number

    tnum = "00"
End Sub
```

If further, perhaps visual, inspection of the stored data is required to determine if the values in each record were written correctly, utilities such as WISQL, MS Query, and VISDATA can be used. With testing tools that support ODBC protocols directly, you do not have to use an external utility program to access the database. SQA TeamTest is ODBC-compliant and this utility script was rewritten to directly access any database we need to verify.

The test script illustrated in Figure 8.13 is data driven but it was not designed from the framework-based perspective. It could be retrofitted in or made more structured. For example, the file open could be broken out into a separate procedure. In addition, the DOS path names could be entered as variables that could be specified at runtime. Figure 8.17 depicts a procedure for the open input file function. As another example, the read input record function could be implemented as a separate procedure, as in Figure 8.18. The portion of the test script that places the data in the GUI fields could also be put into its own procedure (see Figure 8.19).

Fig. 8.17 Open Input File Procedure

```
'$include "Global.sbh"
Sub Main
    Dim Result As Integer

    'Initially Recorded: 06/09/98  08:40:10
    'Test Procedure Name: Reads Input for #1
    Open "H:\SQA\data\Recwce01.txt" for Input as #1
End Sub
```

Fig. 8.18 Read Input Record Procedure

```
'$include "Global.sbh"
Sub Main
    Dim Result As Integer

    'Initially Recorded: 06/09/98  08:40:10
    'Must be edited to match number of fields on window
    Input #1,
        reccode,fld(1),fld(2),fld(3),fld(4),fld(5),fld(6),fld(7),fld(8),fld(9),fld(
        10)
End Sub
```

Fig. 8.19 Populate GUI Fields Procedure

```
'$include "Global.sbl"
Sub Main

    'Initially Recorded: 06/09/98  08:44:53
    'Test Procedure Name: Puts data values in GUI fields

    Window SetContext, "Name=w_wce_frame", ""

    Window SetContext, "Name=w_customer_maintenance;ChildWindow", ""

    InputKeys fld(1)
    DataWindow Click, "Name=dw_customer_record;\;Name=customername", "Coords=23,9"
    InputKeys fld(2)
    DataWindow Click, "Name=dw_customer_record;\;Name=address1", "Coords=19,9"
```

Fig. 8.19 Populate GUI Fields Procedure (Continued)

```
      InputKeys fld(3)
      DataWindow Click, "Name=dw_customer_record;\;Name=address2", "Coords=19,10"
      InputKeys fld(4)
      DataWindow Click, "Name=dw_customer_record;\;Name=cityname", "Coords=13,12"
      InputKeys fld(5)
      DataWindow Click, "Name=dw_customer_record;\;Name=stateprovince", "Coords=14,8"
      InputKeys fld(6)
      DataWindow Click, "Name=dw_customer_record;\;Name=zipcode", "Coords=22,13"
      InputKeys fld(7)
      DataWindow Click, "Name=dw_customer_record;\;Name=description", "Coords=24,11"
      InputKeys fld(8)
      DataWindow Click, "Name=dw_customer_record;\;Name=contact", "Coords=21,9"
      InputKeys fld(9)
      DataWindow Click, "Name=dw_customer_record;\;Name=phoneno", "Coords=11,9"
      InputKeys fld(10)
End Sub
```

All of the procedures would be called then from the main test script. The main test script would be invoked in turn from a shell test procedure that starts the application, runs the main test procedure, and closes the application when the test is complete.

8.14 ADDING CONTROLS TO THE TEST DATA

The examples above demonstrate the basic ideas and implementation of the data-driven approach. To make this approach more rigorous, my associate, and scripting guru, Bruce Posey of the Archer Group has evolved the test scripts by placing control data in each data record. The control values determine how the script interacts with the application under test. As discussed above, this is an alternative approach to the one advocated by Kit [20].

In order to determine where to go and what to do in the application, the test script uses several values. For example, the test data and test scripts for an application in which several of the screens have multiple tabs could be easily developed. As illustrated in the example test record below (test data record is in boldface), the first six positions in each test data record are used as control values and the remainder as test data. The example contains only one actual data field, but the number of data fields can be very large because they are read into an array by the test script.

"G","MT1J","DELETE","","1","Delete a record","FEDERAL"

☞ Error Code (Field 1): The "G" indicates this should be a good record with no errors expected.

☞ Control Code 1 (Field 2): The "MT1J" code represents a particular menu item selection, a tab number, and a radio button selection.

☞ Control Code 2 (Field 3): "DELETE" indicates the action is to delete a record that has been previously selected with the data of "FEDERAL."

☞ Field 4 is not used in this example, but this field is secondary to Field 3 and is used as an additional control, if needed.

☞ Data Length Control (Field 5): The "1" indicates the number of data fields after the comment field.

☞ Comment Field (Field 6): "Delete a record" is the comment.

☞ Data Field 1: "FEDERAL" is value in the single data field.

8.15 CONCLUSION

Cross-level functional testing involves a mixed bag of methods and techniques. There are the ones that were developed for testing mainframe system and can now be used to design and construct test cases for execution on distributed client-server systems. There are also methods and techniques developed for testing object-oriented systems that are applicable to testing client-server systems. There are new methods and techniques that are geared to the unique aspects of testing client-server systems.

Traditional Black and White Box techniques are our legacy from the mainframe world. Techniques such as Binder's FREE methodology evolved from the object-oriented arena [4]. Techniques for testing GUIs, DLLs, and APIs are a function of the unique aspects of programming languages such as VB and Visual C++ that have come to dominate in the client-server development community.

8.16 REFERENCES

1. Adhikari, Richard. "Planning, Testing, Teamwork: A Recipe for Quality Apps." *Software Magazine*, Vol. 14, No. 3, March 1994, pp. 41–7.

2. Bartusiak, Marcia. "Designing Drugs with Computers." *DISCOVER*, August 1981.

3. Beizer, Boris. *Software Testing Techniques*, 2d ed., Van Nostrand Reinhold, New York, 1988.

4. Binder, Robert V. "Design for Testability in Object-Oriented Systems," *Communications of the ACM*, Vol. 37, No. 9, September 1994, pp. 87–101.

5. Boehm, C., and Jacopini, G. "Flow Diagrams, Turing Machines and Languages with Only Two Formation Rules." *Communications of the ACM*, Vol. 9, No. 5, May 1966.

6. Couger, Daniel. "The Structured Tableau Design Methodology (STDM)." *Computer Newsletter*, University of Colorado, Colorado Springs, 1983.

7. Doong, R. K., and Frankl, P. Case Studies in Testing Object-Oriented Software. Paper read at Testing, Analysis, and Verification Symposium, Association for Computing Machinery, New York, 1991, pp. 165–77.

8. Elmendorf, William. *Cause-Effect Graphs in Functional Testing*. TR-DD.2487, IBM System Development Division, Poughkeepsie, NY, 1973.

9. Elmendorf, William. "Functional Analysis Using Cause-Effect Graphs." *Proceedings of Share XLIII*, IBM, New York, 1974, pp. 577–87.

10. Fiedler, S. P. "Object-Oriented Unit Testing." *Hewlett-Packard Journal*, Vol. 36, No. 4, April 1989, pp. 69–74.

11. Franz, Don. *Information Systems File Structure and Program Design Workbook and Problems.*

12. Franz, Don, and Gamble, D. *Structured Tableau Design Methodology.* Specialized On-Line Systems, Inc., 1981.

13. Fuchs, Steve. *Building Smart Testware.* Microsoft Technet CD-ROM, Test Technical Notes, Vol. 4, Issue 2, February 1996.

14. Gane, Chris, and Sarson, Trish. *Structured Systems Analysis: Tools and Techniques.* Prentice Hall, Englewood Cliffs, NJ, 1979.

15. Hetzel, William. *The Complete Guide to Software Testing*, 2d ed., Prentice Hall, Englewood Cliffs, NJ, 1988.

16. Jones, Derek. Deducing an Application's Use of APIs. Knowledge Software Ltd., Farnborough, Hants, United Kingdom.

17. Jorgensen, P. C., and Eckerson, C. "Object-Oriented Integration Testing," *Communications of the ACM*, Vol. 37, No. 9, September 1994, pp. 30–8.

18. Kaner, Cem. Improving the Maintainability of Automated Test Suites, Paper Presented at Quality Week '97, http://www.kaner.com/lawst1.htm.

19. King, David. *Current Practices in Software Development: A Guide to Successful Systems.* Prentice Hall, Englewood Cliffs, NJ, 1984.

20. Kit, Edward. "Integrated, Effective Test Design and Automation." *Software Development*, February 1999.

21. Maggio, Michael D. "Automated Software-Testing Scripts." *Unix Review*, Vol. 13, No. 13, December 1995, p. 43(7).

22. McCabe, Thomas J. "A Complexity Measure." *IEEE Transactions on Software Engineering*, Vol. SE-2, No. 4, 1976.

23. McCabe, Thomas J. *Structured Testing: A Testing Methodology Using the McCabe Complexity Metric*, NBS Special Publication, Contract NB82NAAR5518, 1982.

24. Miller, George. "The Magical Number Seven, Plus or Minus Two: Some Limits on Our Capacity for Processing Information." *The Psychological Review*, Vol. 63, No. 2, March 1956, pp. 81–97.

25. Mosley, Daniel J. *The Handbook of MIS Application Software Testing: Methods, Techniques, and Tools for Assuring Quality Through Testing.* Prentice Hall Yourdon Press, Englewood Cliffs, NJ, 1993.

26. Mosley, Daniel J., and Posey, Bruce. Building Effective Real-World Test Scripts Using SQA TeamTest. Workbook from seminar offered by CSST-Technologies and the Archer Group, 1999.

27. Myers, Glenford. *The Art of Software Testing.* Wiley-Interscience, New York, 1979.

28. Myers, Glenford. "An Extension to the Cyclomatic Measure of Program Complexity." *ACM SIGPLAN Notices*, October 1977, pp. 61–4.

29. Orr, Kenneth. *Structured Systems Development*, Prentice Hall Yourdon Press, Englewood Cliffs, NJ, 1977.

30. Orr, Kenneth. *Structured Requirements Definition*. Ken Orr and Associates, Topeka, KS, 1982.

31. Perry, D. E., and Kaiser, G. E. "Adequate Testing and Object-Oriented Programming," *Journal of Object-Oriented Programming*, Vol. 2, No. 5, January/February 1990, pp. 13–19.

32. Poole, Bernard, and Prokop, Noreen. "Miller's Magical Number: A Heuristic Applied to Software Engineering." *Information Executive*, 1989.

33. Siegel, Shel M. *Strategies for Testing Object-Oriented Software*. CompuServe CASE Forum Library, September 1992.

34. Stevens, Wayne, Myers, Glenford, and Constantine, Larry. "Structured Design." *IBM Systems Journal*, Vol. 13, No. 2, 1974.

35. Yourdon, Edward, and Constantine, Larry. *Structured Design: Fundamentals of a Discipline of Computer Program and Systems Design*. Prentice Hall, Englewood Cliffs, NJ, 1979.

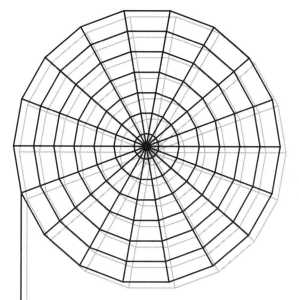

Client-Server Software Testing Metrics: Cross-Level Technical Quality Assessment

9.1 INTRODUCTION

Beware of the productivity sinkhole. Productivity and quality are two very different concepts. Many software development organizations mistakenly expect to increase quality as an orthogonal effect of increased productivity. This expectation may not be realized. In fact, the opposite can be true. Dr. Howard Rubin and Ed Yourdon conducted an international study of software development productivity and quality for the Federal Department of Industry Canada [1]. The study involved 227 companies in Canada, the United States, South America, Europe, South Africa, the Far East, and India.

The study found that Canadian software developers were much more productive than the worldwide average. They accounted for 111 function points per developer compared to the worldwide average of 92.5 function points per developer. The results also indicated that Canada had the highest defect rate: 5.12 defects per thousand lines of code. The worldwide average is 3.79 defects per thousand lines of code. The United States had the lowest overall defect rate: 2.3 defects per thousand lines of code.

The study supports the hypothesis that the faster you write software the more defects you make. The United States creates software at an average (88 function points per developer) slightly slower than the worldwide average.

Based on the rapid application development (RAD) nature of client-server development, and given the observation above, client-server systems should contain more defects than traditional mainframe systems. This makes defect management even more important. I discuss defect tracking and reporting techniques in chapter 4.

9.2 ASSESSING DEFECT TRENDS

Defect reporting should provide defect-counting metrics, in addition to the items cited in that chapter. Organizations must have available information such as the number of defects in project deliverables, the types of defects in project deliverables, the time it takes to remove defects, and which processes/products are defect prone.

For client-server, the defect distribution analysis should also look at the C-S layer in which the problems were found: the presentation layer, process layer, database layer, or communications layer.

9.2.1 Saile's Defect Metrics

Saile [10] suggests plotting these defect-related metrics. First, he tracks developer defect rates for the project. Individual developers work at constant rates of productivity and, as a side effect, also produce errors at consistent rates.

Second, he argues that you should plot the number of errors found in a week against the number of errors waiting for a developer to attend to them, and the number of errors that have been fixed and awaiting retest. This approach illustrates the number of new defects found per week, the developer-rework backlog, and the tester-rework backlog.

9.2.2 SQA TeamTest's Defect Metrics

SQA Manager also offers powerful reports and charts for analyzing defect trends. In fact, all of the data required for Saile's defect metrics is available from the SQA test repository via the reporting commands. SQA offers cumulative and noncumulative defect trend charts and tables (refer to Figures 9.1 through 9.6). I have found the Weekly Opened/Closed chart (Figure 9.4) extremely useful for determining whether the developers and testers are keeping pace with one another and for acquiring an overall feel for testing progress. These defect trend charts can also be plotted against severity and/or priority, defect owner, defect age, symptoms, test cycles, etc.

9.2.3 ANSI/IEEE Defect Metrics

ANSI/IEEE Std 982.2—1988—defines several valuable defect metrics. The first is called "Fault Density." I disagree with the name because this metric measures defect density when calculated during software development and testing. A defect is a discrepancy, whereas a fault is a discrepancy that causes the software to fail. Defects do not always result in failures. I prefer to use the term "Defect Density" in this metric.

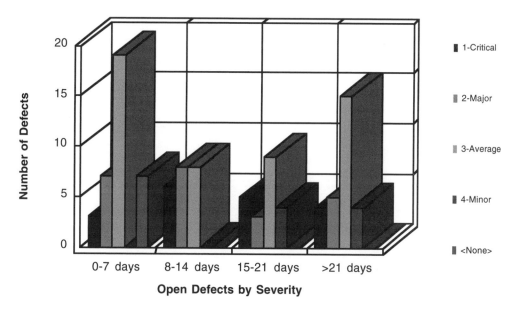

Fig. 9.1 Defect Age Report

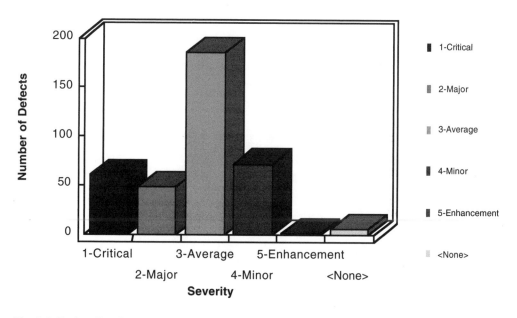

Fig. 9.2 Defect Totals Report

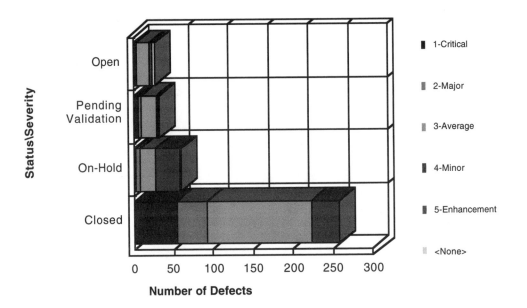

Fig. 9.3 Defect Distribution Report

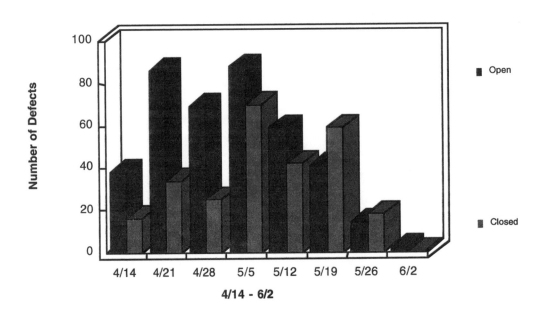

Fig. 9.4 Weekly Opened/Closed Report

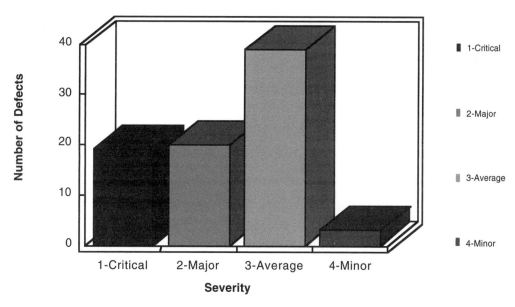

Fig. 9.5 Defects Closed This Week Report

Fig. 9.6 Table of Defect Frequencies from SQA TeamTest

Symptom	Frequency	Percent
Slow Performance	1	0.26%
Export Problem	1	0.26%
Operating System Problem	1	0.26%
Security Problem	1	0.26%
Memory Leak	1	0.26%
ArcNET Log Problem	1	0.26%
Admin/Connections Problem	1	0.26%
Logon Failure	1	0.26%
Suggestion	1	0.26%
Ini File Problem	1	0.26%
Data Errors Report Problem	1	0.26%
Poller Problem	1	0.26%
Mainframe Reports Problem	1	0.26%
GUI Nonconformance	2	0.52%

Fig. 9.6 Table of Defect Frequencies from SQA TeamTest (Continued)

Symptom	Frequency	Percent
ArcNET Services Failure	2	0.52%
Transmit File Created	2	0.52%
Program Group Icon Problem	2	0.52%
Client Will Not Run	2	0.52%
DropDown List Box Missing	2	0.52%
Archive Problem	2	0.52%
Request for Enhancement	3	0.77%
Suspicious Messages in the Log	3	0.77%
Other Features Problem	3	0.77%
Routing Table Problem	3	0.77%
Problem Reporting Problem	3	0.77%
ArcNET Installation	3	0.77%
AB-PC Will Not Dial Up	3	0.77%
Cosmetic Flaw	4	1.03%
Transmit File Not Created	4	1.03%
Import Problem	4	1.03%
EDI Problem	4	1.03%
Database Update Problem	4	1.03%
Downloads	4	1.03%
Documentation Issue	5	1.29%
Password Problem	5	1.29%
Infrastructure Not Working	5	1.29%
Invalid Data Can Be Entered	5	1.29%
Hot Key Sequence Problem	5	1.29%
Data Corruption	6	1.55%
Help Problem	6	1.55%
Data Loss	7	1.80%
Missing Feature	7	1.80%
Command Button Problem	8	2.06%
System Crash	9	2.32%
Installation Problem	9	2.32%

Fig. 9.6 Table of Defect Frequencies from SQA TeamTest (Continued)

Symptom	Frequency	Percent
Mail Failure	9	2.32%
Function Key Problem	9	2.32%
Description Codes Problem	9	2.32%
Confusing Behavior	10	2.58%
Transmit File Not Correct	11	2.84%
Question	11	2.84%
Unfriendly Behavior	17	4.38%
Unexpected Behavior	17	4.38%
Reporting Problem	17	4.38%
Display Problem	23	5.93%
Printing Problem	34	8.76%
Incorrect Operation	45	11.60%
Data Entry Problem	78	20.10%

Defect Density can be used to:

1. Predict the remaining defects when compared to the expected defect density
2. Determine if the amount of testing is sufficient
3. Establish a database of standard defect densities

Defect Density is calculated per thousand source lines of code (KSLOC) as follows:

$$Dd = D / KSLOC$$

where

Dd is the calculated Defect Density

$KSLOC$ is the number of noncomment lines of source code

Another important IEEE defect metric is "Manhours Per Major Defect." Although this measure was developed to assess defect discovery during design and code inspections, it easily can be implemented to reflect the manhours spent during testing. It is calculated as follows:

$$M = \mathrm{Sum}(T1 + T2)I/\mathrm{Sum}\ Si$$

$I = 1, \quad i = 1$

where

M is manhours

$T1$ is the time spent by the test team in preparation for test execution

$T2$ is the time spent by the test team during test execution

Si is the number of major defects uncovered during the ith test execution

I is the total number of test executions to date

9.2.4 Other Defect Metrics

One metric that I calculate is the ratio of open problem reports to total problem reports (refer to Figure 9.7). I use MS Excel to collect the data and calculate the ratios. The ratio becomes smaller and smaller as testing progresses. It eventually stabilizes (oscillates slightly above and below some value—in Figure 9.7 the value is around 0.1). When the values become stable, it signifies that you are at a point where you are not making any more progress and, if the risk permits, can stop testing. You are not making progress because you have hit the point where the developer fixes are creating as many problems as testing is finding. At this point, further testing can be self-defeating, and the whole process of test-fix-retest becomes a vicious circle.

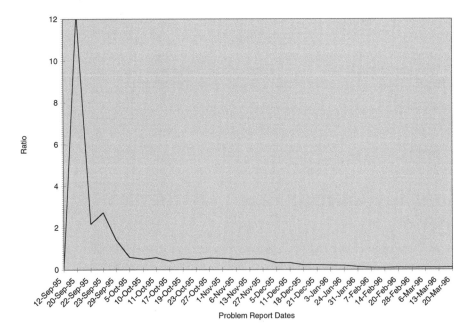

Problem Report Dates

Fig. 9.7 Defects Closed This Week

This is the time when management must make some hard decisions about what to repair and what to ignore. One rule-of-thumb is that you ignore severity 4 and 5 errors and continue to fix and test severity 1, 2, and 3 errors. A time comes when you must decide to ship the system knowing that there are probably still some 1-, 2-, and 3-level errors that have not been fixed. That is usually when the roll-out date cannot be moved back anymore.

The way to assure the lowest possible stabilized ratio is to implement a controlled coding environment via Software Configuration Management (SCM) and a regime of code reviews. A good automated SCM process will reduce the number of errors developers create when they fix previously found problems. I have observed the difference when developers are allowed to fix problems in haphazard fashion and when the fixes are controlled through an SCM tool.

Code reviews, even informal ones, will find logic errors that are not readily apparent. However their real value is in the interdeveloper communication channels that develop. Most of the new errors in problem fixes occur because one developer does not understand what another is doing. This results in the first developer changing something in his or her code that breaks something that was previously working in the other's code. Code reviews can prevent this because the developers become familiar with each other's code.

9.3 TEST COVERAGE METRICS

In an Internet communication in the UseNET news group comp.software.testing (March 16, 1996), Beizer distinguished the difference between "test completeness" and "test effectiveness." His point was that coverage measures are not measures of effectiveness, but are rather measures of completeness. Test effectiveness must be a function of a test's ability to uncover new errors in the software. Beizer went on to say that "test effectiveness depends crucially on the application, the source language, the design, the user's operational profile, the state of development, the product's past history, ...etc. We have no universal measure of test effectiveness."

The caveat here is that achieving high code coverage and branch coverage (decision coverage, condition coverage, decision-condition coverage) is necessary but not sufficient for testing effectiveness. Thus, code in which these levels of test coverage have been achieved has been tested completely from a coverage viewpoint but may not has been tested effectively.

So, test coverage metrics are at best indicators of how much you have tested not how well you have tested. This does not mean that they are not useful. It is still important to have one or more measure of how completely you have tested because every line of code should be executed and every path of control flow should be followed during unit testing as minimum test coverage requirements [6,7].

Saile suggests tracking code complexity as a method for finding errors. He says that only 50% of all the errors in a project have surfaced when all of the functionality has been coded and is ready for testing. He terms this as being "code complete." He suggests using a code coverage tool (most compilers have some sort of code coverage analyzer utility). Set your goals to test 85–90% of the code. He has found that the first 65–75% of code coverage is easy to attain, but the remaining lines of code become increasingly difficult to test. This is because certain conditions that are required to exercise the code are either impossible or very difficult to create, and probably not worth the investment to construct them.

9.3.1 McCabe's Metrics

Complex code is error prone. You can use a complexity metric such as McCabe's Cyclomatic complexity (C) as an indicator of error-prone software modules. (The calculation of C is discussed in chapter 8.) Modules with high C values should be tested rigorously.

A program's C value is the maximum number of linearly independent paths through a module of code. But knowing the number of paths to be tested is not enough. C measures the amount of testing necessary to reasonably guard against errors. You must also be able to quantify the number of paths actually tested. McCabe's Actual Complexity Metric (V[G]) represents the actual number of independent paths tested—the number of distinct independent paths traversed during the test phase.

McCabe has also devised metrics for integration testing. His Design Complexity Metric (S0) measures the amount of interaction between modules in a system. His Integration Complexity Metric (S1) measures the amount of integration testing necessary to guard against errors.

For unit testing, the McCabe Visual Test Tool (VTT) supports modified condition/decision coverage (MC/DC) testing. MC/DC is a structural coverage criterion that requires each condition (term) within a decision (expression) be demonstrated by execution to independently and correctly affect the outcome of the decision (called "Boolean instrumentation"). VTT reports both static and instrumentation Boolean metrics and truth tables.

VTT generates the following metrics:

☞ The decision (dec) metric is the number of decision outcomes in a module.

☞ The decision coverage (dec-cov) metric reports the number of tested decision outcomes in the module.

☞ The condition/decision (cd) metric is the number of condition outcomes for each decision in a module.

☞ The condition/decision coverage (cdc) metric reports the number of tested condition outcomes for each decision in a module.

☞ The modified condition/decision (mcd) metric equals the number of conditions in each decision in the module.

☞ The modified condition/decision coverage (mcdc) metric reports the number of conditions within each decision in the module that have been shown to independently and correctly affect the outcome of the decision.

☞ The multiple condition (mc) metric is the sum of the number of possible condition outcomes for all decisions in a module.

☞ The multiple condition coverage (mcc) metric reports the number of possible combinations of condition outcomes that have been evaluated for every decision in the module.

For regression testing, VTT will quantify the complexity of the design, measure the number of integration tests to qualify the design, produce the integration tests, and measure the number of integration tests that have not been executed.

Information on McCabe's automated tools can be obtained at http://www.mccabe.com/. Definitions of his metrics are at http://www.mccabe.com/features/complex.html/.

9.3.2 IEEE Coverage Metrics

IEEE Std 982.2—1988 defines a functional or test coverage metric. It can be used to measure test coverage prior to software delivery. It provides a measure of the percentage of the software tested at any point during testing. It is calculated as follows:

Function Test Coverage $= FE/FT$

where

FE is the number of test requirements that are covered by test cases that were executed against the software

FT is the total number of test requirements

9.3.3 Miscellaneous Coverage Metrics

Another measure of complexity can be obtained when decision logic tables are used to develop test cases. In DLTs, the value is the total complexity of the table that is equal to the sum of the rules in the table or to the product of the condition states for each condition in the table (see chapter 8). An added benefit of this complexity measure is that it is inherently a measure of completeness because it accounts for combinations of equivalence classes (see chapter 8) whereas McCabe's complexity metric is a measure of complexity associated with a single specific input class.

An important advantage of DLTs is that the table is a logical model of the pathways through the code. This allows them to be constructed much earlier in the development process when remedies for the problems they may uncover are not so limited.

A coverage metric that makes good sense is a test requirements coverage metric. It is based on the data available in the more powerful automated test tools. For example, SQA TeamTest's Manager allows testers to enter test requirements and to link the requirements to automated tests that are created using the robot product. The test requirements can also be linked to code modules.

These linkages allow such metrics as the percentage of requirements covered by test cases along with the percentage of "passes" and "fails" for each test requirement. In addition, the percentage of requirements metric also offers an indirect estimate of module coverage and of the number of passes and fails for each module.

9.4 CONTROLLING THE TESTING PROCESS

9.4.1 Estimating Testing Cycles

Estimating the time testing will require is a tough task. Philip Haynes wrote in *comp.software.testing* that testing time depends on several factors. They include the system size, the number of defects to be found, the required level of reliability, and the defect detection rate across testing phases.

Frequently, this prognostication involves an estimate of the total number of errors in the software. This estimate can be plugged into a formula that is used to extrapolate the total testing cycle time [2,3]. One such approach uses a weighted defect finding rate that is plotted over time. The result is a decelerating curve that follows the form of:

$$r(t) = ab^{e-bt}$$

where

a = total expected defects

b = defect finding rate divided by the total expected defects

t = cumulative hours of testing

This is similar to the approach to deciding when to stop testing I illustrated in an earlier testing book [6]. The idea was to plot cumulative test error rates over time. When the curve decelerates to an acceptable level, testing can be halted. My approach is less rigorous mathematically, but it possesses the same kind of quantitative and qualitative information.

In either case, a good estimate of the total testing time cannot be made until testing is well under way. So, any gross initial estimate can be refined using these techniques.

More ideas have been expressed in *comp.software.testing*. Bob Binder has proposed a microestimating approach using the following equation and variables.

$$TE = TD + TR + F(TB + TR)$$

where

TE is the estimate of average effort per test case

TD is the average time to design and prepare one test case

TR is the average time to run one test case

F is the average percentage of test cases finding an error

TB is the average time to repair an error

Fellow tester Kerry Kimbrough was kind enough to point out in a follow-up article in *comp.software.testing* that this model does not take into account that a test case will most likely be run more than once, and that the same test case may report more new failures in subsequent test runs.

Another, more heuristic approach is one that was used at Hewlett-Packard [4]. It too is based on a projected total number of defects. The following rules are used to determine the total test-cycle time.

1. 25% of the defects can be found and fixed at a rate of 2 hours per defect
2. 50% of the defects can be found and fixed at a rate of 5 hours per defect
3. 20% of the defects can be found and fixed at a rate of 10 hours per defect
4. 4% of the defects can be found and fixed at a rate of 20 hours per defect
5. 1% of the defects can be found and fixed at a rate of 50 hours per defect

For a system with 1000 estimated errors, the total time would be 6300 hours or 787.5 days. The breakdown would be as follows:

$(.25 * 1000) * 2 \quad = 500 \text{ hrs}$

$(.50 * 1000) * 5 \quad = 2500 \text{ hrs}$

$(.20 * 1000) * 10 = 2000 \text{ hrs}$

$(.04 * 1000) * 20 = 800 \text{ hrs}$

$(.01 * 1000) * 50 = 500 \text{ hrs}$

Total hours $\quad = 6300$

Saile [10] argues that in real-world projects you should never commit testing cycles to hard dates. He makes two important observations: Development teams typically miss their completion dates, and development managers try to hold testing to the scheduled dates. What this means is that the development schedule becomes stretched out and the testing schedule becomes squeezed.

All that you need to specify is the testing activity to be performed and the number of days required to complete the activity. If you do this for all of the activity you have identified as part of the test cycle, Saile argues that this will automatically extend the testing cycle when the development dates are missed.

9.5 ASSESSING SOFTWARE RELEASE READINESS

One question that has always plagued software developers is when will the software be ready for release. This is a very difficult question to answer—it is difficult to determine for mainframe software and it is even more difficult for distributed software.

Foody [2] offers an approach that estimates the number of errors the user will encounter after the software is released. He does, however, offer a warning that using the metric will be meaningless unless the software has been tested according to its breadth and depth. He argues that two quantities we can measure together can be used to estimate the number of defects users will experience. The quantities are *known defects* and *the defect-finding rate*. He suggests measuring the known defects in terms of open defects per 1000 lines of noncomment source code (KNCSS) and the defect finding rate as new weighted defects per 1000 hours of testing.

Foody suggests that the software is ready for release when there are no open 1 or 2 severity defects and the total for all other severity levels is less than 0.5 defect per KNCSS. He also says that the defect-finding rate should be fewer than 40 per 1000 hours of testing.

Foody also suggests continuous hours of operation (CHO) as a reliability metric that he has found useful. For on-line systems, he suggests 100 hours of continuous use as a release criterion. The software must be kept constantly active running test suites.

Other release metrics he uses are a test coverage metric. He looks at functional coverage, conditional ("branch-flow") coverage, and procedural coverage. He realizes the incompleteness of requirements and functional specifications documents, but still advocates 100% coverage of the defined functions, 80% coverage of the conditional branches, and 100% procedural coverage during testing.

The following summarizes Foody's metrics. The software is ready for release when:

1. It has been tested with a test suite that provides 100% functional coverage, 80% branch coverage, and 100% procedure coverage

2. There are no level-1 or -2 severity defects, and the absolute level of defects is lower than 0.5 defect per KNCSS

3. The defect-finding rate is less than 40 new defects per 1000 hours of testing

4. The software reaches 1000 hours of operation

5. Stress, configuration, installation, naïve user, usability, and sanity testing have been completed (chapter 10 covers these tests in more detail)

9.6 IEEE SOFTWARE MATURITY METRIC

IEEE Std 982.2—1988 defines a software maturity index that can be used to determine the readiness for release of a software system. This index is especially useful for assessing release readiness when changes, additions, or deletions are made to extant software systems. It also provides a historical index of the impact of changes. It is calculated as follows:

$$SMI = Mt - (Fa + Fc + Fd)/Mt$$

where

SMI is the software maturity index value

Mt is the number of software functions/modules in the current release

Fc is the number of functions/modules that contain changes from the previous release

Fa is the number of functions/modules that contain additions to the previous release

Fd is the number of functions/modules that are deleted from the previous release

9.7 ASSESSING SOFTWARE RELIABILITY

Perry [9] classifies software reliability metrics as "use" metrics. In order to assess reliability, a quantitative threshold must first be established for each metric. He says that reliability thresholds can be in accordance with expected reliability levels, organizational standards, comparisons to other systems, vendor specifications, or the system requirements.

Reliability should be measured throughout the entire development cycle. Reliability measurements can be taken even in analysis and design because they can be based on predicted performance as well as on performance history.

Perry [9] offers the following equation for calculating reliability.

Reliability = 1 – Number of errors (actual or predicted)/Total number of lines of executable code

This reliability value is calculated for the number of errors during a specified time interval.

Three other metrics can be calculated during extended testing or after the system is in production. These are:

MTTFF (Mean Time To First Failure)

$MTTFF$ = number of time intervals the system is operable until its first failure

MTBF (Mean Time Between Failures)

$$MTBF = \frac{\text{sum of the time intervals the system is operable}}{\text{number of failures for time period}}$$

MTTR (Mean Time To Repair)

$$MTTR = \frac{\text{sum of time intervals required to repair the system}}{\text{number of repairs during time period}}$$

For client-server systems, a lot of performance and reliability information can be gleaned from the benchmarking process. One commercially available client-server benchmarking metric, RPMark, is discussed next.

9.8 BENCHMARKING CLIENT-SERVER SYSTEM PERFORMANCE

Benchmarking client-server system performance is—to say the least—a difficult task. Of course, server and network capacity planning can go a long way toward preventing poor overall performance, but a performance benchmark seems to be the best method.

Client/Server Labs of Atlanta, GA, has acquired RPMark (Reference Performance Mark) from IBM. RPMark [1] is an indicator of performance for enterprise-level client-server systems. It can help you determine your system's optimal configuration for throughput and load balancing. RPMark is a composite metric that is taken while three concurrent workloads are running on the system: decision support queries, on-line transaction processing, and file-serving applications. RPMark gives a weighted average of performance for the three workload conditions. The higher the average, the better the performance.

The decision-support portion involves remote queries from a Visual Basic front end accessing a relation database via ODBC. Query response time varies from 3 to 10 minutes. This part of RPMark is based on the TPC-D decision-support benchmark .

The on-line transaction processing component consists of an order entry application placing new orders. Each transaction involves a customer ordering 10 new items, which triggers a series of events causing 20–40 data records to be accessed in each new transaction. This portion of the test is based on the TPC-C "new order" transaction benchmark modified to run on a PC workstation.

The applications involve, respectively, query-intensive ODBC calls from PC-based clients, on-line client-server transaction-oriented applications, and file-intensive personal productivity applications running on the client.

The PC-based client loads applications from a server and executes them in a simulation of real office automation tasks. Networked resources, data, and applications are shared by a number of clients. The applications used include Lotus 123 for Windows, Microsoft Excel for Windows, Microsoft Word for Windows, Lotus cc. Mail for Windows, Harvard Graphics for DOS, Word Perfect for DOS, and Freelance for Windows. This portion of the benchmark is based on the Business Application Performance Corporation (BAPCO) Network benchmark.

RPMark is run against standard platforms that are held constant for one year. The platforms include Compaq Proliant with twin Intel Pentium processors, which can run Windows NT, OS/2, Netware, and SCO Unix; Motorola Power PC for Windows NT and AIX; and AS/400. The platforms must be able to serve clients over Ethernet or TokenRing using SQL or ODBC.

The RPMark results for these platforms (excluding the Power PC) as published by IBM are as follows:

Configuration	OLTP	DSS	FS	RPMark
AS/400 30S	57	109	47	213
Compaq Proliant	35	45	43	123

9.9 SOME MISCELLANEOUS TEST METRICS

There is no right or wrong answer to the question of when to stop testing. Complex models to determine this have been suggested [6], but I prefer some simple ratios that are plotted in statistical quality control charts. I use the ratio of total open problem reports to total closed problem reports or the ratio of total open reports to total reports (see Figure 9.7) as an indicator of testing progress. When the ratio of total open reports to total closed reports stabilizes over time, the testing process has lost its effectiveness. At this point, the testing should be terminated because further testing is a waste of money. What is happening is that about equal numbers of errors are being detected as are being repaired and the repairs the developers are making cause the new errors.

You must realize there are still defects left in the software. The decision that must be made is can the users live with them. This decision depends on a number of things such as the associated business risk, the resources available to continue testing, the time left to continue testing, the costs associated with continued testing, etc. The best criterion to use is that all severity 1, 2, and 3 problems should be resolved prior to stopping the testing process. The user might gripe about, but can probably tolerate, the severity 4 and 5 errors that should be fixed in the next release.

SQA TeamTest also offers defect trends charts that can be used to assess testing progress. As described above, when the trends have decelerated beyond a determined point, it costs too much to continue to test because you are not returning enough errors to justify the costs of constructing and executing the test cases. The Weekly New and Open Defects (Figure 9.8) and Weekly Opened and Closed Defects (Figure 9.9) charts are particularly useful.

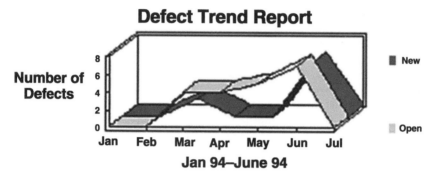

Fig. 9.8 New and Open Defects Trend Chart from SQA TeamTest

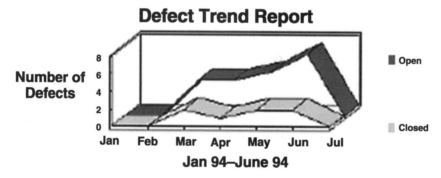

Fig. 9.9 Open and Closed Defects Trend Chart from SQA TeamTest

9.10 CONCLUSION

In order to manage, control, and improve the testing process, we must measure it. Estimates of anticipated defects along with actual defect counts, measures of structural complexity, measures of test coverage, measures of release readiness, etc., are essential to the testing process. Collecting testing metrics is not always easy, but is a necessary aspect of software testing. Unfortunately, it is also the most frequently omitted testing practice.

As automated testing tools mature, many of the essential metrics will be collected unobtrusively while testing is conducted. In addition, the tools with custom analysis and reporting capabilities will make analysis of the measures easier. Until then, we will continue to use spreadsheet packages and word processors to glean what information from metrics we can collect manually. Software testers must count test process parameters and they must interpolate those counts into meaningful statistics for management.

9.11 REFERENCES

1. APT Data Group Plc. *Capacity Planning: Hardware Benchmarking: Client Server Tools Bulletin, Part Three, Server Environments*, June 1995, pp. 3450–3.

2. Foody, Michael A. "When Is Software Ready for Release?" *Unix Review*, Vol. 13, No. 3, March 1995, p. 35(5).

3. Goel, A., and Okumoto, K. "A Time Dependent Error Detection Rate Model for Software Reliability and Other Performance Measures." *IEEE*.

4. Kohoutek, H. "A Practical Approach To Software Reliability Measurement." *Proceedings of the 29th EOQC Conference on Quality and Development*, Vol. 2, June 1995, pp. 211–20.

5. McCabe, Thomas. "A Complexity Measure." *IEEE Transactions on Software Engineering*, Vol. SE-2, No. 4, 1976.

6. Mosley, Daniel J. *The Handbook of MIS Application Software Testing: Methods, Techniques, and Tools for Assuring Quality Through Testing*. Prentice Hall, Englewood Cliffs, NJ, 1993.

7. Myers, Glenford. *The Art of Software Testing*. Prentice Hall, Englewood Cliffs, NJ, 1979.

8. Newsbytes. "Canadian Software Productivity High, Quality Low—Study." *Newsbytes*, November 22, 1995.

9. Perry, William E. *A Standard for Testing Application Software 1992*. Auerbach Publishers, Boston, 1992.

10. Saile, Bob. *Introduction to MS Test*. Microsoft Technet CD, Test Technical Notes, Vol. 4, Issue 2, February 1996.

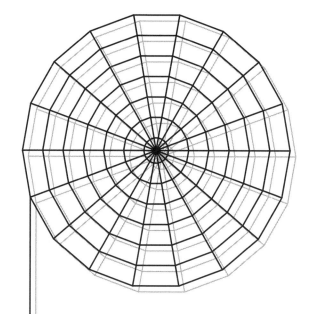

Integration and System Testing on the Desktop

10.1 CLASSICAL INTEGRATION TESTING

Integration testing, system testing, and user acceptance testing have been dubbed by Myers "testing in the large." [12] These tests are very important because they occur during the later stages of systems development and, thus, are the last tests to be executed before the system is placed in production.

The type of errors found through higher-order tests are the result of improper analysis and design of the system. These errors are the most expensive errors to correct because they are made during the early phases of development and are usually found just before, during, or after installation. Once identified, each error must be traced backwards through the development process until the cause is determined. Finally, after the cause has been discovered, all of the subsequent development tasks must be redone, resulting in a "rework cycle."

One way to prevent rework cycles is to concentrate on the development process itself. Ask why the error was made in the first place, and the answer should tell you how you should modify the development process so that type of error will be unlikely to occur again. This means that the first step to "quality" through testing is to constantly monitor and adjust analysis and design activities so that they are more effective.

10.1.1 Incremental vs. Nonincremental Testing

Integration testing is the testing of modules, programs, subsystems, and even systems to prove that they interact properly. The common link among modules, programs, subsystems, etc. is that they can both share data globally and locally defined data through specially designed and constructed interfaces.

Myers summarizes the advantages and disadvantages of nonincremental and incremental approaches to integration testing.

1. Nonincremental requires more initial effort and more work overall because drivers and stubs must be coded.

2. Nonincremental will not detect interface errors as early as incremental because the modules do not interact until late in their development.

3. Debugging is easier if incremental integration is used because errors can be associated with the "last" module that was integrated.

4. Incremental testing is more thorough because the modules are tested under many more conditions.

5. Nonincremental testing allows more parallel development work to be done than does incremental testing.

Myers also says it has been argued that nonincremental testing requires less machine time, but he feels that the machine time devoted to the initial work developing the test harness makes nonincremental and incremental testing about even in terms of machine resources they use. Myers also classified integration strategies into one type of nonincremental testing and five types of incremental testing, as delineated in Table 10.1.

10.1.1.1 Nonincremental Testing

Big Bang Testing   The Big Bang approach is most often used. It requires unit testing all of the segments in isolation, followed by integrating all of the unit-tested modules at once. If an error occurs, it will be much more difficult to isolate it because it could be in any of the units that have been integrated. Granted, there will be times when the software unit that contains the error is obvious, but you can't always count on that.

10.1.1.2 Incremental Testing   The two basic integration strategies in incremental testing are top-down and bottom-up. Everything else is either a modification of or a combination of these approaches.

Table 10.1 Incremental vs. Nonincremental Testing

Nonincremental	Incremental
Big Bang	Top-Down
	Bottom-Up
	Modified Top-Down
	Sandwich
	Modified Sandwich

Myers's incremental testing approach differs from Hetzel's [7] in that Myers does not require independent unit testing prior to module integration while Hetzel says that modules should be unit tested separately before being combined. Even though it is more work to use Hetzel's advice, I agree with him. Modules should be tested independently before integration. The success of integration testing depends on the initial quality of the modules being integrated. They should be as error-free as possible when integrated.

A very important heuristic common to all incremental testing approaches is that each module being integrated should be thoroughly tested before moving on to the next one. It is possible, particularly in top-down testing, to defer the testing of some modules. This is bad practice because the program might be completed without testers ever returning to test those modules.

10.2 INTEGRATION TESTING IN CLIENT-SERVER DEVELOPMENT ENVIRONMENTS

According to Hayes [6] software testers must rethink their test strategies, especially those associated with integration testing, because software objects have become the bottom rung in the software development chain. Objects are combined into systems and subsystems to provide end-user application software. Thus, Hayes sees integration testing today as "expanding not only in scope and complexity, but also across departments and company lines."

In general, integration during client-server development includes business objects, database objects, middleware, and application objects. These are integrated across proprietary networks and across multiple application and database servers. Integration occurs at the level of the enterprise, not at the level of the application system as in the past. In the very near future, integration will occur both at the level of the desktop and at the level of the Webtop.

To further complicate matters, the majority of software components that will require integration will come from third-party vendors. They will be integrated across both proprietary LANs and across nonproprietary WANs or some combination of the two.

Hayes sees a key element of integration testing as "creative partnerships between development and test team members and between vendors [vendors of software objects and applets] and customers.

Client-server applications incorporating objects, as their software units, require an interobject communications protocol such as Corba or DCOM. (See the discussion of these protocols in chapter 11.) What this means to the developers and to the testers is that middleware such as Microsoft's Transaction Server (MTS) must be running in order for the objects to communicate. Calls made to objects from other objects and responses to the calls are passed through this layer. The net result of this is that MTS is the layer that integrates or binds objects. This tends to blur the boundaries of the objects and of the application itself.

From the tester's perspective, integration is frequently the combination of the Visual Basic or C language executable file(s) with their respective components at the presentation, processing, and database layers of the C-S application rather than the combination of compiled software units. It is the combination of some units at the level of each layer and across layers.

The point of this discussion is that software integration and integration testing in the C-S environment is a prominent bottleneck. In my personal experience of testing client-server systems, this is where the development grinds to a halt and tedious cycles of test-repair-retest begin and the software remains 90% complete forever.

There are several reasons why this happens. The most prominent one is that the software is not integrated properly on the development side. If several C-S software developers are coding components in isolation and they do not have the opportunity to integrate the components prior to turning them over for integration testing, integration testing will fall flat on its face. I know because I have experienced this on all the C-S projects I have tested.

Software integration and integration testing are different. Integrating the software components is the responsibility of the development team. If the first time the components are used together is at the integration testing stage, you are headed for disaster. The development team must prove that the components will work together before they hand it off to testing. The test team will verify that the developers were correct and that the software components work together and they will also verify that the integrated components do not do anything they are not supposed to do or do not have any side effects.

Most defects are discovered by test cases that were meant to break the system. During integration testing, the test team should spend 95% of its effort testing the system destructively. They cannot do this when the development team has not performed any constructive testing.

I recommend that an integration server be set up on the development side that mirrors the production environment and that at least one individual be assigned the task of integrating and testing (a smoke test) the software as each build is completed. If any installation or server problems are uncovered the software is not turned over for integration testing. Many times I have experienced C-S software builds that I could not install in order to start testing; I was forced to return the build and delay the integration testing cycle.

Integration testing should occur in an environment as close to the intended production environment as possible. The software and hardware needed before integration testing can begin must be specified in the test plan.

A major problem in the way integration testing is done in C-S development is that a true system test may not ever be performed. The reason is that all of the allocated testing time ends up being used to test and retest integration builds. The result is that the system test is aborted or is replaced by a user-acceptance system test.

What I have described differs from the traditional philosophy toward integration testing discussed in the beginning of this chapter. It evolved when software components were procedures in Fortran or PL/1 programs or paragraphs in COBOL programs. To some extent, concepts such as incremental testing and nonincremental testing can still be applied in the C-S world, but they must be applied to much higher layers of the system under test.

According to Hayes [6] in today's development environment we must reevaluate integration testing with respect to who does it, when it is done, and how it is done. It cannot be done the same way anymore. Both developers and testers must do it, it must be done earlier in the development process, and automated testing tools must support it. Such a tool is NuMega Technologies' BoundsChecker for C++, which instruments the C code with runtime error checking that intercepts and monitors events between objects. The BoundsChecker family also includes API Gen, which generates an API test framework for component calls. For further discussion of BoundsChecker refer to chapter 8.

10.3 CLASSICAL SYSTEM TESTING

For mainframe projects, system testing is carried out during the formal testing phase of the SDLC. This stage consumes the largest chunk of testing resources: approximately 12.5% of allocated reserves [11]. Discussions of system testing normally refer to the activities of this stage of development.

System testing activities are intended to prove that the system meets its objectives. Some experts argue that the purpose of system testing is to prove that the system meets its requirements. This is not entirely true unless you consider acceptance testing as a type of system testing because the purpose of acceptance testing is to demonstrate that the system meets the user's requirements. Acceptance testing is a *validation* process whereas system testing, in the strictest sense, is a *verification* process. Regardless of whether it represents verification or validation, system testing represents an "external" view of the system.

This is true because requirements represent the eventual system user's view of the system (an external viewpoint). Users do not understand nor do they care about how the system works as long as it is useable. Their opinions of the system are formulated strictly from what their senses tell them when they use the system. They interact with the system via a user interface with a set of manual procedures designed to invoke specific responses from the system. If the interface is difficult to master or the system's responses are inappropriate, the system is not useable. System testing should be approached from this perspective.

If you are thinking "but objectives are specified internally by the design team," you are correct. However, objectives are direct technical translations of requirements into design goals that must be achieved. Therefore, objectives are formulated from external considerations. If this basic translation process results in objectives that do not reflect the requirements, a discrepancy exists which must not be allowed to exist beyond system testing.

For clarity in our discourse on system testing, we will define and discuss three types of system testing, one of which incorporates what is known as acceptance testing [11]. They are system verification testing, customer verification testing, and customer validation testing. The first two kinds are designed to verify that the system does meet its design objectives. They are destructive in nature and are intended to pinpoint for correction those areas where the system does not accomplish its objectives. The third type is designed to validate the system and is intended to be a positive (confidence-building) experience demonstrating how the system fulfills the requirements.

The key words here are "verify" and "validate." System verification testing occurs in a test environment using test data. This is exactly what happens with system testing. The test team consists of members of the development group and system operations staff plus quality analysts, auditors, and end-user representatives. The project team leader directs the test, which is actually conducted by the IS staff with input from the test team.

Another instance of testing as a verification procedure involves users who repeat the previous test. The test is again executed in a simulated non-production environment. The same typical processing day is used together with the previously used scripts. In this case, the IS staff acts in an advisory capacity.

The purpose of customer validation testing is to demonstrate that the system works as it was intended to. The only way to prove that a product functions correctly is to use it in the real world on real data. Sounds a lot like acceptance testing doesn't it? The things we have said about acceptance testing apply to this type of system test as well.

The common thread among the three kinds of system tests is that they are implemented formally—according to a written plan. A major criticism of system testing in general is that it is frequently done in an informal manner. This results in some portions of the system being tested more thoroughly than others or in some portions not being tested at all. Scripts impose the formality of a specific scenario on the testing process, making the testers actors in the play who are compelled to learn and execute their lines. Of course, some improvisation is acceptable, but only within strictly specified limits.

10.4 DEVELOPING SYSTEM TEST CASES

Test cases for system testing consist of scripts that enact a specific scenario. If we think of system testing as a "play," each script can be considered an act in the play. Most often a script represents a typical user's session in an on-line system or a typical transaction-processing event in a batch system. For both types of system the play would conclude after enough scripts were executed to represent a normal processing cycle.

As an example of the kinds of events a script might include, let's consider an on-line system that creates and services customer accounts for a cable TV company. In a normal day, customers are added to and removed from the system database; new customers must be authorized and deleted customers must be deauthorized; some customers may require reauthorization and credits for lost viewing time; and customers request pay-per-view authorization for special movie and sporting events. A system test of these activities must comprise scripts intended to thoroughly exercise each one. Furthermore, the scripts must be "destructive." They must include attempts to make the system do things it is not supposed to do or scripts that represent mistakes the user might make. System test scripts are also cross-functional in nature. As you can see by the example above, a script that would be developed exercises several system features.

10.5 ESTABLISHING AND DOCUMENTING THE EXPECTED RESULTS

System test scripts are not complete unless each includes the expected result(s). In many situations, however, the results may vary from day to day, week to week, month to month, etc. When this is the case, the result associated with a particular script will vary depending on the values stored in the database from one update cycle to the next. Hard coding the expected result would mean that the test script must be changed each time the database changes. This causes a script maintenance nightmare.

The best way to handle this problem is to have the system testers do dynamic database queries while conducting the system test. The database query returns the database record, which is the basis of the result on the screen. Thus, what is displayed becomes what is expected, based on the record in the database.

The limitation on validating a test script this way is that the tester can only say that the displayed results are correct given the current state of the database. This sheds no light on whether or not the data itself is correct. The validation of the database will have to be completed by seeding the database loads/updates with known values that should appear in the database.

10.6 SYSTEM TESTING IN THE CLIENT-SERVER DOMAIN

Client-server software development is RAD based. In the majority of C-S projects, a formal methodology is not applied and there is no formal testing stage. Furthermore, an impact of RAD is that formal system development deliverables are frequently omitted. As such, the functional requirements/functional specifications documents are usually completed after development is well under way or after system implementation.

Thus, a system test based on user requirements or a functional design objective is not possible. In client-server development environments, the system test is usually a glorified integration test. So, how can you conduct a system test in RAD environments? There are two plausible approaches.

The first method is to base the system test on the results of a business risk analysis (see chapter 4). By focusing system test cases on high-risk areas you are lowering the chances of a catastrophic system failure. You are also using the "intelligence" of the risk analysis to orient your effort. Test cases based in some level of logic are much more effective at finding errors than test cases based on a "swag" (Scientific Wild Ass Guess). C-S development system test cases are too often based on a "wag," which is even less effective than a swag. Using the results of the risk analysis is definitely a step above either a swag or a wag.

The second framework is scenario-based client-server testing [2], devised by Robert Binder. His approach is very simple but requires some level of information gathering from the eventual system users and requires some intuitive assignment of probabilities to the identified scenarios.

In general, system testing in the client-server world should include the same kinds of tests as in the mainframe environment, but it must also address the interactions of all of the different layers in a C-S software system. So, system testing for C-S must include test scripts that address the user interface layer, the application layer, and the data layer in a cross-layer fashion. Thus, there are many types of system tests that must be completed in a C-S environment.

Foody [5] suggests that configuration tests for client-server systems check areas such as the operating system version, GUI toolkit version, the display type, the CPU version, and the network card. He noted that configuration defects are more prone to happen when the development team members all have similar hardware and software environments. I have also made this observation; many times developers have said to me "it worked on my machine" when the software release refused to load on the test machines, or when I found errors in the test environment that did not show up on developer machines.

With respect to installation testing, Foody [5] recommends that testers perform "localization" testing. This assures that the software runs on all of the different targeted hardware and software platforms. This type of testing can identify problems such as hardcoded values that may be incompatible with certain hardware and software configurations. This approach can also identify labels and messages that cannot be translated into different languages when software is being used internationally.

This is an area that has recently come to the forefront. It has been termed "Cross-Windows" testing by the trade press and by testing tools vendors. Many C-S systems must operate in both 16- and 32-bit Windows environments. I was involved in testing a $125,000,000 enterprise-level C-S system that was slated to run on Windows NT, Windows 95, and Windows 3.11 for Workgroups. We encountered many problems relating to the differences between the 16-bit Windows for Workgroups and the 32-bit Win95 and Win NT environments. In addition, the software system was going to be released at over eight hundred sites in the U.S. and Canada. The hardware and software configurations ranged from 286 XTs to 586 Pentiums and from DOS through Windows 3.1, Windows 3.11, Windows 95, Windows NT, and OS/2.

Thus, the software had to operate in eight hundred completely unique environments. Localization testing was not done, because it would have involved a major expense and a time-consuming effort. We were only able to replicate the tests on Windows 95 and NT. This resulted in major problems when the system was released to the field with respect to Windows 3.11 and to an unanticipated OS/2 machine. After that experience, I appreciate how valuable it would have been to test in each of the target environments.

Foody [5] also recommends naïve-user testing with users who are completely unfamiliar with the product under test. Naïve-user testing can reveal many interface and documentation problems. For example, icons which were considered meaningful may prove completely absurd to a naïve user, and statements in on-line help and user manuals, thought to be understandable, may turn out to be clear as mud or may be misconstrued to mean something they do not.

A last item Foody recommends is "sanity check" testing. This particular test uses the install master tape (or disk) and it is executed on a "clean" machine. An additional test of sanity should be conducted on a machine that is loaded with the standard user's desktop configuration. Many companies now install a standard desktop image on new computers. This is followed by an execution of a kernel subset of the test suite much as is required for regression testing. Its purpose is to avoid mistakes such as forgetting to copy some of the install files or libraries to the install tape or disks.

Foody's sanity check testing is really installation testing. With respect to the project mentioned above, we called our sanity check "installation and checkout" (smoke) testing. This set of tests was run every time a new build was given to the test team. Frequently, the new build would not install and had to be returned to the developers. Examples of the kinds of problems we found are missing DLLs, out-of-date executable files, and corrupt databases.

One factor compounded our problems tremendously. The install program was written in-house and it was completely unreliable. There are plenty of commercially available installation programs. They are proven and reliable. The best thing you can do to simplify installation testing is to buy one of those packages. Fighting with an unreliable installation process confuses the issue. You are faced with determining whether the installation problems are due to the system being installed or to the program installing the system.

10.7 SYSTEM TESTING AND AUTOMATED TESTING TOOLS

The ultimate use of automated testing tools would be a completely automated and unattended system test. This, however, is not yet feasible. In fact, system testing requires a tremendous amount of manual labor, even if you use an automated testing tool. Automated test scripts cannot emulate the spontaneity of users. The paradoxical nature of automated test scripts is that they cannot be used for verification unless the system is working correctly when you record or write the scripts. The completed scripts are played back to verify the system functions. It is only after verification that the scripts can be replayed to regress the system. So, system test cases must be manually written and executed the first time around and then automated separately or as a byproduct of the system test proper.

The value of automation is that the test scripts are available for use during postrelease regression testing because the objective of regression testing is to repeat the entire system test as accurately as possible after each system release. Of course, this is not what happens with manual tests because the labor and overhead costs are tremendous. As I suggested in chapter 3, the majority of organizations do no regression testing whatsoever. If automated test tools offer one possibility for improving software testing, it is that they make regression testing cost effective and more companies may be able to implement it.

The approach I recommend is to define test data for each manual test script execution and minimize the number of automated test scripts. For example, a single system test scenario that has five manual test scripts may only have one automated test script for that scenario after the system test is completed. When all of the scenarios have been executed, a complete set of automated test scripts is available.

10.8 Documentation Testing

Documentation testing is an important part of the system test. Documentation, however, means something different in desktop systems. A user manual and an operations manual are traditionally written for mainframe systems. In client-server systems these manuals are considered optional.

Two developments—the general knowledge of Windows OS and usability engineering of the user interface—have reduced, but not eliminated, the need for a written user manual. Thus, user manuals are not always going to be written for these systems. This places the documentation burden squarely on on-line manuals or on the help facility. When the user has a question about the application and how it works, these may be the only alternatives. So, it is important that they work correctly.

10.8.1 On-Line Help

For client-server systems, evaluating the help screens for completeness, correctness, consistency, and usability is the most important form of document testing. These can be evaluated by using the help screens during the system test or they can be appraised as a separate component of the overall testing strategy.

For usability, the help topics must be written in unambiguous English using clear, concise, and complete sentences that are organized into paragraphs expressing single subjects. The "one function, one module" rule of structured design can be rephrased as "one subject, one paragraph" for system help topics. It is also important to include enough detail about a particular topic or provide jumps to more detail. The detail should be in the form of step-by-step instructions where possible.

Be comprehensive. There are many "little" features in Windows-based desktop systems that tend to be overlooked when the system is documented. A typical example is when the user selects an item from a list of similar items. The user can highlight the item and press the Enter key or can double-click on the item or can drag and drop the item when multiple modes of selection are available. Be careful to point this out in the documentation. Developers are fond of putting little shortcuts into their software and they generally forget to tell the document specialist. A good source for finding out about these features is to quiz the test team members. If there are subtle features, the testers will find them sooner or later.

For assessing help usability, I recommend an informal to semiformal review. It should include one or more users, developers, and a test specialist/ QA analyst. The review should last no more than two hours and it should result in an action list that the development team uses during the follow-up period. If there are many action items a re-review should be conducted [9,11].

Because help documents are set up as hypertext documents, testing the program's help screens involves more than just proofreading. An interesting tool, Microsoft HULK (Help Universal Kit), is available through the Microsoft Developer Network (issued quarterly on CD ROM). HULK is a tool for building, editing, modifying, and testing help files. HULK was developed at Microsoft WorldWide Products Group in Ireland. Even though it is available on the MS Developer Network, Microsoft does not support it.

HULK offers functionality checking and text consistency checking. The functionality testing includes a general check of the syntax, keywords, topic titles, context strings, and hotspots. The text consistency testing includes a check of jump text, page title, and topic title.

HULK's *general syntax check* can cover all help source files or just updated files. It searches for missing or incomplete footnotes and for hotspot text that is not coupled with a hotspot code. It automatically displays an error log file at the completion of the test.

The *keywords check* searches for duplicate keywords that would be listed two or more times in the help search dialog box. The results of the check are displayed on the screen.

The *topic titles check* looks for duplicate topic titles that share one or more keywords. This would display two or more identical topic titles in the help search dialog box. Once again, the results are automatically displayed on the screen.

The *context strings check* hunts for two or more help topics that have identical context strings. The help engine uses context strings as unique identifiers for choosing which topic to display when a jump or pop-up is executed. If duplicates are present, help displays the first topic it finds with the requisite context string. The results of the check are automatically displayed.

The *hotspots check* looks for mouse-initiated jumps and pop-ups that might fail to work in the compiled help file. Again, the results are automatically displayed on the screen.

The *jump text check* looks for identical or similar hotspots that are used in more than one topic. The check produces an alphabetical listing of similar and identical hotspots. A quick scan of the list allows the tester to find identical hotspots that are not phrased in a consistent manner.

The *jump text and page title check* find jumps whose text does not match the target page title. This is important because the target page title and the jump text should be identical.

10.9 COMMERCIALLY AVAILABLE HELP AUTHORING TOOLS

There are several help authoring tools on the market [1,3,4,8]. The two that have the most powerful features, including the ability to test the help file, are RoboHELP and ForeHelp.

RoboHELP is a help file generator that uses the Windows help compiler [1,8]. This is its major drawback because help file authors are forced to learn the commands associated with the help generator. RoboHELP is an interface that runs in conjunction with MS Word, which is how the text files are created prior to being compiled into help files. RoboHELP includes some testing capabilities.

For more information on RoboHELP WinHELP Office, contact Blue Sky Software Corp., 7777 Fay Ave., Suite 201, La Jolla, CA 92037, 619-459-6365 or 800-677-4WIN, http://www.blue-sky.com.

Another commercially available product, *ForeHelp*, allows you to see how your help project works before you compile it. By pressing a function key (F10) you can view the help topics just as the user will see them [10]. ForeHelp opens an abbreviated version of the standard help window. This allows you to follow typical user browse paths, test jumps, search on key words, etc. But it will not allow you to use the **File**, **Edit**, and **Bookmark** menus while in test mode.

Using a product such as ForeHelp makes many of the tests described above unnecessary because this product provides a completely integrated authoring environment. So it is not necessary to start up five or six tools at the same time when working on a help project. Having to do so in the past has been one of the major factors contributing to errors in help file projects.

You can obtain more information about ForeHelp from ForeFront, Inc., 5171 Eldorado Springs Dr., Boulder, CO 80303, 303-499-9181.

10.10 CONCLUSION

All things considered, incremental testing is very different in C-S environments. It is much broader in scope. Integration testing occurs across multiple layers and components.

System testing is still an important component is the tester's arsenal. Even in client-server software development, the system test remains the "heart" of the testing process. It is metamorphosing into an automated process, reducing the labor and resource costs traditionally associated with manual system testing.

The most important thing to remember when designing and constructing system tests is to think as though you were a user. The most important things to do when you execute the system in a client-server environment are to do performance/stress testing, configuration, and localization testing. These are not the only areas you should test, but they are common problem areas with client-server systems.

10.11 REFERENCES

1. Ambler, Scott. "Windows Help File Creation Made Easy." *Computing Canada*, Vol. 21; No. 19; September 13, 1995; p. 16(1).

2. Binder, Robert. "Scenario-Based Testing for Client-Server Systems." *Software Testing Forum*. Vol. 1, No. 2, November-December, 1993, pp. 12-17.

3. Cline, Dana. "How May I Help You?" *Software Development*, Vol. 3, No. 6, June 1995, p. 67(5).

4. Cogswell, Jeff, and O'Conner, Kelly. "Help Is Here to Stay: Six Help Tools Make It Easy to Lend a Hand." *Windows Tech Journal*, Vol. 4, No. 3, March 1995, p. 69(5).

5. Foody, Michael A. "When Is Software Ready for Release?" *Unix Review*, Vol. 13, No. 3, March 1995, p. 35(5).

6. Hayes, Linda G. "Automated Testing for Everyone." *OS/2 Professional*, November 1993, p. 51.

7. Hetzel, William. *The Complete Guide to Software Testing*, 2d ed. QED Information Sciences, Inc., Wellesley, MA, 1988.

8. Isaacson, Portia. "The Sky's the Limit for Help Writes." *Computer Reseller News*, No. 622; March 20, 1995; p. 52(2).

9. King, David. *Current Practices in Software Development: A Guide to Successful Systems*. Prentice Hall, Englewood Cliffs, NJ, 1984.

10. Lewis, Mike. "Take the Work Out of Help Authoring." *Data Based Advisor*, Vol. 13, No. 8, September 1995, p. 26(2).

11. Mosley, Daniel J. *The Handbook of MIS Application Software Testing: Methods, Techniques, and Tools for Assuring Quality Through Testing*. Prentice Hall, Englewood Cliffs, NJ, 1993.

12. Myers, Glenford. *The Art of Software Testing*. Wiley-Interscience, New York, 1979.

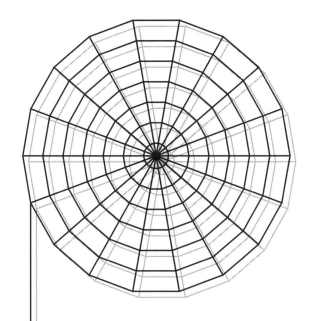

CHAPTER **11**

Testing Webtop
Client-Server
Applications

Client-server computing has moved the focus of computing from host-based applications to distributed applications. It is characterized by platform-dependent client-centric applications that run on local proprietary networks ("native" client-server). *The Forrester Report* [3] has described a new computing model of "Internet Computing." The Report states that Internet computing extends and improves the client-server model: "Remote servers and clients cooperating over the Internet to do work." Internet computing has extended and recentralized client-server applications on platform-independent nonproprietary networks via the Internet. The Internet is a virtual development environment that supports application software that runs on virtual machines (e.g., Java applets). Furthermore, Internet application development is component-based development.

The Report differentiates between what is currently happening on the World Wide Web and Internet computing. With true Internet computing, users will not go to a site and request a file, or run a Java script through their browser, but they will request a "session" and will receive client code from the remote server. With the code loaded on the client computer, the two will begin to communicate and exchange data. The Report describes this as a "conversation."

In this fashion, Internet computing will be truly interactive. It will feature computing sessions that are global and on a massive scale as opposed to client-server, which is localized and limited to a small group of users.

What this means for testing Internet computing applications is that in specific areas such as multiuser performance security and server/database the need for testing will become even more compelling. In addition, testing all aspects of the client's session software will be a priority. The same techniques that are being used to test client-server desktop application software can also be used to test the Internet computing client software.

Finkelstein [2] views the trend toward Internet and Intranet computing as a move back to "server-centric" computing. The first generation of client-server computing has resulted in fat clients and thin servers. The majority of the application logic is stored on the PC, with the exception of triggers and stored procedures. In some instances, the application logic is deployed on both the client and the server.

Finkelstein sees the trend toward fat servers as reducing the difficulty of application development, testing, and deployment. From that viewpoint, he argues that testers will not have to test for the hundreds of possible PC hardware and software configurations that can exist. His conclusion is based on the HTML browser as the front end for Internet applications.

He also sees this as simplifying application code debugging and correction because an error will only be found in one place and will have to be corrected in only one place—the server. The corrected code will automatically be downloaded to the client the next time the user starts a session.

For many applications, these assumptions may be entirely true, as they will communicate directly with an Internet application server. The Forrester group reasons that the current HTML browsers will be replaced by more complex Internet applications that can dynamically interact with the server application logic as opposed to the current static browser software.

Electronic Commerce (e-commerce) is fast becoming the most important use of Internet computing. The Newport Group, Inc., an IT research firm, has determined [4] that 10% of total IT budgets was allocated for e-commerce in 1998. This amount will increase to 13% in 1999, to 23% in the year 2000, and a whopping 30% by 2005.

The Newport group research into web-based development and testing found that the most important forms of testing for Web-based and e-commerce applications are, in order, load, functional, regression, performance, and stress testing. It is interesting that security testing was not included. Security is one of the most important aspects of e-commerce.

11.1 TESTING INTERNET/INTRANET APPLICATIONS

According to an excellent white paper [5] published by Software Quality Automation, Inc., there will be two types of client-server application development models for Internet/Intranet computing: browser-based and hybrid.

☞ Browser-based applications: This is the typical model in which users access Internet applications through web browsers such as Netscape Navigator or Microsoft Internet Explorer. The applications run on a web server. Such applications can have connections to database servers and can implement component-based content in the browser via Java or

ActiveX components. This model is different from native client-server because it follows hypertext links and loads the applications. It is a thin client/fat server approach.

☞ Hybrid applications: Many applications will be a mix of native client-server and the browser-based models. These applications will have direct access to web servers from within the C-S applications themselves. Such applications are frequently referred to as web-enabled client-server applications. On the other side of the coin, Internet applications will contain Visual Basic VBX's, ActiveX's, or PowerBuilder objects that have previously been found only in native C-S applications.

Many characteristics of an Internet application can affect how we test it. Among the characteristics compounding the difficulties testers face is the dynamically generated web page (active server pages). The page is not retrieved by following a link, but is created by the application on the fly. These pages will be much more difficult, if not impossible, to test directly. So we will have to rely on test cases that are designed to invoke the dynamic pages and capture the results via the browser GUI.

Another characteristic to consider is dynamic database connections. An Internet application may connect to many different databases and database servers during a conversation. The web servers use APIs (Netscape's NSAPI or Microsoft's ISAPI) to establish the connections. Obviously, it is going to be difficult to test all of the possible API calls that result from dynamic database connections.

A third characteristic is Java/ActiveX content. Many Internet applications will be featured components that can be downloaded and executed on the client. These *applets* are designed to run on the virtual machine. This does not mean that they will execute correctly in every client environment. Thus, some cross-platform testing is still necessary. Applets can also run on the server or client and server simultaneously.

Security testing presents an important problem. Applets can be used to breach the security of corporate Intranets even when adequate firewalls have been implemented. This means that security testing will be an important component in any plan to test Internet applications. Both Microsoft and Netscape have taken steps to increase the security of their browser products, but two factors will defeat their efforts. Not all Internet applications will be implemented via a browser, and there are extremely intelligent hackers out there who will find a way to crack the current security measures.

Another characteristic is the remote application server. A large portion of the processing logic of an Internet application will run on a remote application server that sits between the web server and the database servers. This is the epitome of the thin client/fat server model. The problem is that many of the application features will combine NSAPI or ISAPI and Java, VB, or CGI scripts.

The fifth characteristic troubling to testers is that many applications will bypass the web server altogether. These applications will feature direct connections enabling users to download objects via TCP/IP using Microsoft's Distributed Common Object Model (DCOM) or Object Management Group's Common Object Request Broker Architecture-Internet InterOperability Protocol (CORBA-IIOP).

Testing Internet applications includes the challenges of testing native C-S applications as well as others. Like native client-server, the GUIs are easy to use and hard to test; the development environment is multivendor, the target environment is highly dynamic, and performance is an issue.

Testing Internet apps is important because it ensures the performance, scalability, security, functionality, and interoperability of Internet-based client-server applications.

11.1.1 Testing Challenges

Testing Internet-based applications presents several challenges. First, the GUI exhibits radically different behaviors. The current interface to the Internet is via web-page browser software packages such as Netscape Navigator or MS Internet Explorer. C-S applications that use the Internet make calls to invoke a browser as their interface. So, what are you testing when you test the GUI for an Internet application? You are testing the look and feel, behavior, performance, and security of the HTML-based web pages that the application generates.

The current situation is that the GUI (browser-displayed web page) is easy to use but hard to test. It is difficult to test because the web-page objects are foreign to many of the software testing tools currently on the market, which were designed to test client-server desktop application GUIs. Many test tool vendors have rushed to market specialized test tools that recognize web-page GUI objects, including URL's and Java applets, which have been problem areas. Rational's Test Suite 7.1 includes support for testing browser objects and applets. Other vendors, including Mercury Interactive and Segue, have opted to market separate Internet testing products.

Another challenge is the multivendor environment. This impacts testing because many Internet applications are constructed from third-party components—and will be even more so in the future. The problem is to assure that different vendors' components work together properly in the completed application.

The changing deployment environment also presents problems for testers. The application must be tested in all target deployment environments. This does not mean all possible target environments, but the subset that your organization plans to support. It also means that different browser configurations (that are required in the different environments) must be tested because they will affect the display and behavior of your application's web pages.

The Internet is an environment that adds multiple layers to any application that is implemented there. These layers are parceled on top of the traditional layers that client-server applications have. The existence of the web server is a new layer that affects performance and security. Security itself is a much more complicated problem that, in essence, represents a new layer. ISAPI will place a new interface layer on top of other C-S software interface layers. The new objects that are embedded in web pages put an additional layer in place.

Performance and scalability are very important to Internet applications. Both vertical and horizontal scalability are required with respect to performance.

11.1.2 Testing Aspects

Testing Internet applications involves testing the functionality and content of web pages and applets. It also involves testing third-party components for functionality and compatibility. Browser compatibility also needs to be tested.

An especially important area is performance testing. Client stress, client load, Web server load, application server load, and DBMS server load are all types of performance test that must be executed to determine usability and scability of Internet applications. Performance testing is discussed at length in section 11.4.2.

11.2 Classes of Tests—The Internet GUI

11.2.1 Developing and Testing Internet GUIs

There is a wave of World Wide Web home-page construction that involves documents and programs that run on web servers and are structurally different from the applications that run on the desktop. Web pages are interactive documents that address a highly sophisticated and mobile audience [4]. Web surfers move through the convoluted space of the WWW at a rapid pace. It is important that web pages be designed so that their information can be retrieved rapidly. It is also important to avoid long page-load times, which can happen if designers add too many, or too large, graphics files to the page.

In addition, web pages are located on many different types of servers with different configurations. Web site should be "browsable" by as many different web browsers as possible, designed for compatibility as opposed to specificity. Web browsers allow users to customize their browsing environment. This can lead to an effect that is a lot different from what the designer had in mind. Colorful and highly textured backgrounds make text hard to read, and using red and green make the page almost impossible to perceive by red/green colorblind users.

11.2.2 Usability and the Web Page Interface

To assess web-page design quality, it is important to understand the nature of
Hypertext Markup Language (HTML) documents. There are products that
enable users with only a little understanding of HTML to develop web pages,
but their use is a risky process. Even though web-page editors such as HOt-
Metal check the HTML for syntax errors (much as a compiler checks program
source code for errors) syntactically correct HTML does not assure a successful web page.

  According to Callaway [1] web-page developers must consider the compo-
sition of the expected base of users, the kinds of hardware and software they
will be using, and how they are connected to the net. The designer must also
remember that the majority of web browses support customization. The users
can change the font, the font size, the background, the background colors, and
so forth. These settings can affect how the web page loads.

  The design of the web page will determine what a user will see and how
fast the page is loaded, and this is ultimately controlled by the web server–,
web browser–software and by the power of the user's computer. For example,
if the designer does not create a title for the page, it affects how some web
browsers will see your page and whether they will even find it. Not all browsers have the graphics capabilities of Netscape's Navigator product; some are
text based. I learned this the hard way as I omitted the title from my company's web page and immediately received an e-mail from a user, whose
browser was text-based, suggesting that I had better include a title.

  Callaway has created a list of "Home Page Horrors" that should be exam-
ined when testing a web page:

1. Overuse of graphic symbols (e.g., of under construction signs): Many
   pages have too many of these signs and they blitz the viewer. A similar
   problem is the use of "New" and "Updated" signs. How long should an
   addition be considered new and when is it time to take down the updated
   sign? Some of the graphics symbols appear to be permanent fixtures on
   some web pages.

2. Flashing hypertext: Flashing or blinking is very difficult to bring into
   focus. This problem is compounded on pages with busy backgrounds.

3. Brazen backgrounds: Flashy backgrounds make the text very difficult to
   read, and they take longer to load.

4. Unorganized hyperlinks: Hyperlinks should be grouped into related sets
   of links. Designers should avoid the tendency to link to any and everything from anywhere on the page.

5. Overly complex frame structures: Frame structures should have a purpose. The page should be broken into viewing frames only when it will
   help the viewer better understand the content.

6. Big graphics and/or lots of graphics: This is my particular pet peeve. I
   hate to wait for pages that are loaded down with graphics. My company

web page has very few graphics and I have received a lot of praise from viewers for keeping it that way.

7. Too many hyperlink layers: Viewers should not have to go through several hyperlink layers to finally find the information they want.

8. Designing for a specific browser: This can be avoided by determining which features are browser specific and removing them.

9. The use of red and green: Many viewers are red/green color blind. The page should not be a maze of colors either. Avoid highlighting text in red.

10. The "wow" factor: Avoid glitz. Web pages with good content are more valuable to viewers than snazzy ones.

11.3 TESTING WORLD WIDE WEB PAGES

As software testers it is our responsibility to critique web page design via a formal review process much like the GUI review discussed in chapter 3. Thus, a web-page design review should be the first step in the testing process. Either manual or automated dynamic testing should follow the review.

For purposes of dynamic web-page testing, I view testing the page as being very similar to testing a page in an on-line help file (refer to the section on "Documentation Testing" in chapter 10). Both documents are hypertext and both have active links. They differ in that the help links are to local documents while the web-page links are to documents on local and global web servers. In either case, what must be tested is the jump, linked text, and hotspots.

11.3.1 Navigation and the Web Page Interface

The navigation links in the web page must be thoroughly tested. Even when there is a *Back* button in the browser itself, it is important to assure that the navigation does not result in a dead end or in a "404 Object Not Found" error.

Navigation is especially important when dynamic HTML pages are created and displayed as report pages that have dynamic content. The *Back* button cannot be used to return to a previous page because it will reload the cache, not recreate the page content as the user wants and the developer intended. Navigation through dynamic web pages must be tested to assure that the user can go to and return from all nested pages that compose a report.

I tested an application that displayed sales information to local branch offices as dynamic HTML pages. The *Back* button on the browser was disabled and other buttons were provided to go from one report to another, from report page to report page, and to go to more detailed levels within the same report. What I determined through testing was that several of the intended navigation buttons were missing; consequently, several navigation paths were not available. Luckily I had access to a navigation diagram which alerted me to the problems.

11.4 TYPES OF TESTS FOR INTERNET APPLICATIONS

11.4.1 Browser Tests

Browser tests are not designed to test the browser software, but rather to test the browser's behavior against the application in its target environment. The primary questions are which browsers will be supported, what client configurations will be supported, who is to install the browser (application development or tech support), is an installation procedure/checklist available, and are all necessary add-ins provided.

Browsers installed by different developers can react differently to the same application if a common installation procedure was not followed. I have also found that browsers launched standalone can behave differently from those launched from the application GUI. Browser testing must assure that the supported browsers are installed and configured so that they will behave as expected.

11.4.2 Performance Tests

Internet-based client-server applications service a much larger audience than conventional C-S applications (millions of users as opposed to hundreds). In addition, the inclusion of graphics, audio, and video files embedded in web pages severely affects performance. Popularity of a web site will impact performance during times of peak usage. Try browsing sites such as www.cnn.com during major news events and www.weather.com during major storms—it is virtually impossible to make a connection.

Another factor that affects performance is the nature of the web page being loaded and whether or not the page was loaded previously. Static pages load much faster than dynamic pages, provided they are not too heavily laden with graphics. Dynamic web pages such Microsoft's active server pages generally require more time to load because they are constructed at the time they are viewed. As discussed above, active server pages are used for applications that require dynamic data updates such as report-based applications in which the report pages must always include the most recent information.

Encryption also affects performance. Several types of encryption exist for implementing secure transactions across the Internet. The type of encryption chosen determines the level of performance depending on the baggage it carries.

Both single-user and multiuser performance testing should be completed for Internet applications. All supported hardware/software configurations should be tested.

Performance measurements should be taken during light, normal, and heavy (both peak and long-term) usage periods. Performance measures that can be garnered include:

☞ CPU usage

☞ Response time for static pages and dynamic pages

☞ Memory usage

☞ Disk space/caching

These metrics can be collected manually or through test scripts that automatically grab starting and ending times and also access system statistics.

11.4.3 Functionality Tests

Specialized applets and scripts that control what happens when web pages are loaded must be tested to assure that they function as expected. Common Gateway Interface (CGI) scripts and Java applets are used for many purposes in web pages. Testing must assure that they do what they were intended to do and that they do not do anything they were not intended to do. The second assurance also has security implications as Java applets sometimes have been used for less-than-respectable and illegal tasks.

Applets should be tested two ways. First they should be tested standalone using the virtual machine interface that will execute them when they are embedded in a downloaded web page. Second, they should be tested within the completed web page.

Objects and components (OCX, VBX, Active-X, and application specific) should be tested to assure that component-server, component-client, and component-component interactions/dependencies operate correctly.

Internet application transactions must be tested to assure their accuracy and that the results are complete and correct. They must also be tested to assure that their performance is adequate and acceptable. They have to be tested for their ability to recover from inactivity timeouts and from external events.

Reports that are generated and displayed via Internet applications must be tested to assure their correctness, completeness, accuracy, and consistency. In addition, they must be tested for data security so that users only see the information to which they have security privileges. For example, one branch office may not be allowed to see another branch office's reports and it would be a security breach if they were able to view this information.

Databases that are accessed by web-enabled applications must be tested to assure that their data is correctly formatted and displayed, inserted, updated, and deleted. In addition, the database security must be tested to assure that only those with the required privilege levels can view and manipulate the data. Database tests can be complicated by the methods that create database connections. There are direct connections and dynamic connections to databases, and the latter will be more difficult to test because the right set of circumstances must occur before the connection is made.

Regression testing of web pages is a must. The dynamic nature of the WWW requires that a link be retested at least once a month. Links change and links disappear. Automated test tools for Internet applications make the regression testing effort trivial.

11.4.4 Security Tests

Testing the security of your web-enabled applications starts at the level of the web server. The web server is your LAN's window to the world and, conversely, is the world's window to your LAN. It is your responsibility as a tester to assure that only passive, restricted viewing of your window occurs. The primary culprit in violating this restriction is buggy server software. The following excerpt was taken from the WWW Security FAQ [6].

> It's a maxim in system security circles that buggy software opens up security holes. It's a maxim in software development circles that large, complex programs contain bugs. Unfortunately, Web servers are large, complex programs that can (and in some cases have been proven to) contain security holes. Furthermore, the open architecture of Web servers allows arbitrary CGI scripts to be executed on the server's side of the connection in response to remote requests. Any CGI script installed at your site may contain bugs, and every such bug is a potential security hole.

On the other side of the coin, web surfing by your company's employees also presents a security hazard. Active content (ActiveX, Java applets, etc.) can allow malicious software to invade your system. Downloading files is a common user activity that is a tremendous security risk. Browsers are a pathway for viruses, etc., to bypass your firewall.

In addition, browsing the Internet leaves an electronic record of the user's surfing activities. This audit trail allows anyone to construct an accurate profile of the surfer's tastes and predictable behaviors. If you check the cookies on your computer, you will probably have one from DoubleClick, a company that profiles your use of the Internet and sells that information.

Three types of security risks have been identified. The primary risk is errors in the misconfiguration of the web server that would allow remote users to

1. Steal confidential information
2. Execute commands on the server host, thus allowing the users to modify the system
3. Gain information about the server host that would allow them to break into the system
4. Launch attacks that will bring the system down (e.g., an e-mail bomb that floods the server with bogus e-mails)

Browser-side risks are secondary:

1. Active content that crashes the browser, damages your system, breaches your company's privacy, or creates an annoyance
2. The misuse of personal information provided by the end user

Interception of sent data is tertiary:

1. Browser to server
2. Server to browser
3. Introduction of viruses via software downloads

The interception of data can occur on

☞ The network on your company's side (browser and server connections)
☞ The Internet Service Provider's (ISP) connection
☞ The ISP's regional connection

In general, the more complex the operating system the more susceptible it is to attack. Unix is more open to security attacks than Windows 95/NT. Some server software programs are more security conscious than others. An axiom is that the more features the server supplies, the more security problems it will have.

Some security features of the server to test are the extent that it

1. Restricts access to directories based on the browser's ISP address
2. Restricts access to users who provide a password
3. Restricts document transfer
4. Allows dynamic directory listings

Another area to investigate is server-side include files. Includes can direct the system to execute a variety of system commands and CGI scripts. A web-page hit counter is an example of a server-side include file that can be embedded in an HTML document.

11.5 WEBTOP TESTING TOOLS

Mercury Interactive's WebTest is an automated testing tool that automates web-page testing. WebTest, used in conjunction with either WinRunner or Xrunner, can be used to record user interaction with the web page and to replay the recorded test scripts for verification purposes. Rerunning the test scripts can reveal missing links and missing content.

In addition, WebTest can be used with LoadRunner to test performance. The web site is load tested with virtual web users. Each virtual user transmits and receives HTML messages to and from the web server. This approach can simulate thousands of hits while measuring and graphing response times.

11.6 CONCLUSION

Internet-based client-server applications are much more complex than proprietary LAN-based C-S systems. Thus they are more difficult to test. In addition, automated tools for testing Internet applications are just beginning to mature. As more and more tools become available that recognize browser objects, Java applets, URLs, etc., the task will become considerably easier. Some automated testing tool vendors have already marketed products that are aimed at e-commerce applications.

11.7 REFERENCES

1. Callaway, Erin. "The Web Is a Different World for GUI Design: Interactive Internet Interfaces Demand a Different Set of GUI Programming Skills." Reprinted from *PCWeek*, Vol. 12; No. 45; November 13, 1995; p. 26(1). Copyright © 1995, ZD, Inc.

2. Finkelstein, Richard. "How Internet Applications Overcome Client/Server obstacles." *Internet Development Trends*, a supplement to *Application Development Trends* (http:www.spg.com), June 1996, pp. 15–16, 18.

3. Forrester Research, Inc. *The Forrester Report*. Forrester Research, Inc., 1033 Massachusetts Ave., Cambridge, MA 02138.

4. Newport Group, Inc. *The Challenges of the E-Commerce Enterprise*. Newport Group, Inc., 1995.

5. SQA, Inc. *Automated Software Quality for Internet / Intranet Applications: The SQA Solution*. A white paper, SQA, Inc., 1996.

6. WWW Security FAQ. Copyright © *World Wide Web Consortium (Massachusetts Institute of Technology, Institut National de Recherche en Informatique et en Automatique, Keio University)*. All Rights Reserved. http://www.w3.org/consortium/legal/.

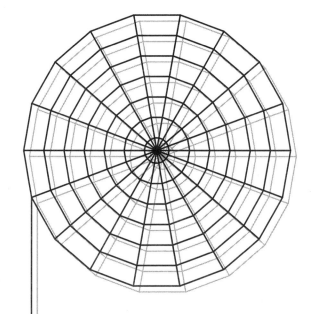

C H A P T E R **12**

Year 2000 Testing

12.1 INTRODUCTION

The year 2000 problem (Y2K) is one of date-related errors. According to Shoup [10], it is the result of outmoded programming assumptions. In the early decades of MIS two factors affected the storage of dates in business application systems. The first was cost. In the 1960s and 1970s computer resources, storage, in particular, were expensive. Second, COBOL was the dominant programming language of the day. COBOL programmers were taught to store dates as two-digit fields. The common date formats in use included:

YY	instead of	YYYY
MM/DD/YY	instead of	MM/DD/YYYY
YYDD	instead of	YYYYDD

When the two-digit year reaches 99 + 1 many business applications will fail. Shoup points out that the ones that do not fail may produce erroneous results such as setting the date to 01/01/00 or 0001, which will be processed as January 1, 1900.

The effects are far-reaching. Dates of birth, payment schedules, and credit card expiration dates will be affected. These effects have already begun to appear. Simpson [11] presents a simple but dramatic example of how date arithmetic will be affected: Anyone born in 1940 will be 00 – 40—which equals -40 years old.

An associate recently received a credit card with an expiration date of 00. He returned it to the issuer because he knew that he would have problems when using it. For example, one major travel company has already had some of its systems reject credit cards with expiration dates of 00. These systems think the credit cards expired one hundred years ago because they are programmed to prefix the year with the century: 19.

The ramifications are tremendous. Goldberg [3] sees year 2000 consequences as including:

☞ Potential cancellation of customer accounts, orders, and shipments

☞ Inability to create invoices and trace accounts receivable and payable

☞ Premature expiration of licenses, credit cards, and medical prescriptions

☞ Miscalculation of employee fringe benefits

I see other problems as well. In particular, an inability to produce payrolls will result in severe consequences. As just one example, having worked in the construction industry, I can tell you that construction workers refuse to begin work if their checks did not arrive on time.

Gartner Group [4] estimates Y2K testing will account for more than 50% of the effort and expenses around Y2K conversion projects. Testing Focus 2000 [8], an on-line newsletter devoted to Y2K testing issues, estimates the figure to be greater than 60%.

The problem is more complex than simply changing the date field size. Software systems are elaborate interdependencies that only work when all of the relationships among the components are as expected. Change just some of them and the others will not work.

12.2 Y2K ISSUES

The Year 2000 archive, located on the Internet at www.year2000.com/archive/, contains an issues list document file, issues.html [1]. This file is a checklist of specific issues that must be addressed. The checklist contains sections on organization and society, hardware and operating systems, data structures, application software, interfaces, analysis, modification, and validation.

All of the sections have potential interest for software testers, but the sections on data structures and application software are of particular importance.

12.2.1 Data Structures

From a verification perspective, it is necessary to test for overflow problems caused by date fields. It will be necessary to test for date values that are out of range and for date validation rules that are ambiguous. Ambiguous rules could result in all dates above a certain cut being set in the twenty-first century. Microsoft has already published its intent to do this in its product line. This approach can result in date-related problems because we may be moving into the next century, but we still have to process data with dates that occur well before the year 2000.

Furthermore, it will be necessary to test all situations where date arithmetic is done. This will mean testing computations involving time spans, due dates, etc. It will also be necessary to test all sorts that are date-based and to test database record selections based on both essential and nonessential fields that include dates as part of the index key. It will also be necessary to test database record validation expiration dates. Finally, we must test all external date fields that are not internal to the file system or database.

12.2.2 Application Software

Application software must be tested from many perspectives. First, testers must consider the programming languages used. Each language and its compile/runtime libraries will have specific date processing formats and constraints. Traditional date validations have included testing

☞ The months 00 and 13

☞ The days 00 and 32

☞ The days February 28, 29, and 30

☞ U.S. and international date formats

☞ Out-of-cycle dates

For century 2000 changes, the date validations must be expanded. In the applications themselves specific characteristics to test are:

☞ Leap year processing

☞ The change to daylight saving time (the date may be stored as a "time-date" field)

☞ The use of 99 to indicate last record

☞ The use of 00 to indicate a null record

☞ 99 and 00 as default values

☞ Special interpretations of 00

☞ Hard-coded 19 in 4-digit date fields

☞ Use of the less-than sign to find the century

☞ The years 1999, 2000, and 2001

☞ The use of hard-coded error trapping

☞ Ineffective error trapping when invalid dates are entered

☞ The use of dates as parts of names in database entities

☞ The downloading of short YY date fields from the mainframe

☞ The proper inputting of dates via user interface screens/windows/dialog boxes, etc.

12.3 LEVELS OF Y2K TESTS

Rettich [8] lists several types of Y2K tests and their objectives. He described application tests and vendor tests.

The same types of application tests that have always been executed must be run for Y2K testing:

☞ Unit testing: Fundamental to all testing projects. The code-based approaches I discussed in chapter 8 can easily be used to verify Y2K conversion at that level.

☞ Component testing: Assures that the conversions do not disrupt individual component functioning and that interactions among system components work properly. This is Y2K integration testing.

☞ System testing: Assures that the system conversions work properly from an external cross-functional point of view.

☞ Regression testing: Assures that the conversions do not cause failures in seemingly unrelated systems or subsystems.

☞ Preproduction testing: Verifies that the system works with a sample set of production data.

☞ Production testing: This is Y2K user-acceptance testing in which the system is run with live production data.

☞ ISV application integration testing: Verifies that any software developed prior to, or as a part of, the Y2K conversion by independent software vendors functions as expected.

In addition to these tests, I suggest that you also do parallel testing, when resources are available, either during system or preproduction testing and alpha testing as an intermediate step in the conversion process.

12.4 Y2K TEST PLANNING

Cooke [2] stresses that Y2K testing must be planned if the strategic results of the Y2K effort are to be achieved. Many year 2000 experts emphasize the need to carefully plan Y2K projects. Many of them, however, have forgotten the importance of testing the project frameworks they have offered. On the other hand, Shoup has included testing as a tactical component of Sections II and III of his approach [10].

Rettich [8] suggests some Y2K testing do's and don'ts.

DO

1. A complete inventory of what must be tested
2. Check libraries, macro and subroutine libraries' dialogs, and sort parameters
3. Test data feeds that are from outside of the company

4. Reserve resources for evaluating test tools and train staff in their use

5. Pilot test your Y2K test tools

6. Allocate resources to develop the tests

7. Regression test your application against Y2K-compliant operating system, compilers, and utilities

8. Collect performance measurements during testing

DON'T

1. Assume that Y2K testing can be done as part of normal maintenance

2. Underestimate the resources Y2K testing will require

3. Assume that production will shut down for testing

4. Assume that production runs are an effective way to test Y2K conversions

5. Overlook data files and databases

6. Overlook the testing of public domain/shareware libraries

Simpson [11] describes what is probably the biggest DON'T of all. Do not think you can test year 2000 compliance by simply setting the system date to 23:59 P.M. on December 31st 1999. The result can be dangerous. Advancing the date on a network or a PC may result in expired software licenses that could block reentry and some programs are written to respond to resetting the clock as fraud. Despite what the industry pundits say, carefully weigh the consequences of tinkering with the date on networked systems.

12.5 CLIENT-SERVER APPLICATIONS AND YEAR 2000 COMPLIANCE

The Y2K problem is not isolated to mainframe applications and their associated programming languages. There are already legacy client-server applications in production in business organizations around the world. Many of these software systems are not Y2K compliant. There are several reasons why this situation exists.

First, there are numerous international and U.S. date formats in use. In addition, there are many different forms of dates in use: the Gregorian date, the Julian date, etc. Any processing logic that handles date conversions, format conversions, or type conversions is subject to the Y2K problem if the conversion logic is not coded correctly.

Second, many client-server applications rely on either a date pulled from the server or from the client machines. In many instances, the time and date settings in the system control panel will ultimately affect the final form of the date the application uses. The date processing logic in the application must be coded to process the year portion of the date as a four-position field, and if it is not, the results are unpredictable.

In other instances, the C-S application may pull the date from the system BIOS or from the real-time clock. If the application is running on a server or a client that is not Y2K compliant with respect to these entities, it will most likely fail when processing Y2K related dates. It is not considered legitimate to pull the date from these areas since the advent of the 32-bit OSs, but some applications may still be doing so. The results will again be unpredictable unless the C-S application is coded to handle and override dates received from the control panel, BIOS, and real-time clock.

Third, user input via the GUI can be an extremely error-prone process. This is especially true in that we are converting users from mainframe systems where they were accustomed to entering dates with a two-digit year to client-server systems where they will have to enter a four-digit year. One school of thought is that, when converting mainframe systems to client-server, you need to preserve the mainframe-user interface. This is because it is considered an easier transition for the user if the C-S interface looks, feels, and acts like the old mainframe interface. Although this is a gigantic mistake, I have seen it done in several major conversion efforts. Even in this case, the users should be forced to enter a four-digit year in all date-related input fields.

Fourth, many client-server applications interact with older legacy systems that pass dates with two-digit years and many client-server systems must in turn pass dates with two-digit years back to these systems. The conversion process may—or may not—be implemented correctly when it comes to dates beyond 12/31/1999. These systems are written in languages such as Visual Basic, Delphi, and PowerBuilder. Thus, systems written in these languages, although considered Y2K-friendly languages, are not necessarily Y2K compliant.

12.6 YEAR 2000 TESTING APPROACH FOR EXISTING CLIENT-SERVER SOFTWARE SYSTEMS

Given the many complexities of client-server software, and given the multitude of development environments in which C-S systems can be built, it is very important to follow a standard testing process when regression testing Y2K remediated software. The following procedure should be followed.

1. Define date standards and date usage rules for all of the C-S development platforms (e.g., Visual Basic, PowerBuilder, Delphi, Visual FoxPro) that are in use in your organization. You cannot test for Y2K compliance unless you have these standards in place. You need them to baseline the expected behavior of the C-S applications you need to test.

2. Plan to spend 40–80% of allocated Y2K resources for testing. A lot of this time may be spent in the repair-retest effort if the date-related problems turn out to be difficult to identify or to repair. Use a good defect tracking system that implements workflow control over test-repair-retest cycles.

Testing Y2K fixes is the same type of build-level regression testing that should be performed in any C-S development project. With this in mind, remember that a major problem that occurs in normal build-related regression testing is related to the number of repaired errors that suddenly return in subsequent builds. A good version control process and tool will substantially reduce the number of recurring errors. Requiring the programmers who remediated the software to sign off on the unit testing they performed will also reduce the number of recurring problems. If possible, obtain the test cases/data they used for unit testing to verify the level of unit testing that was completed.

3. Derive a Y2K date checklist. Use the checklist to determine which dates will be tested and include those dates in the test plan developed in the next step of this process.

4. Develop a Y2K test plan for each C-S application that has been remediated using the Y2K test plan template shown in Figure 12.1. Prior to test execution, obtain all of the required signatures on the test plan signoff page.

   Use the date information from the Y2K checklist to determine which dates to test. In addition, use the platform-specific date processing rules described in the sections below that pertain to how Visual Basic and PowerBuilder handle dates to add platform-related test cases.

5. Establish baseline behaviors for remediated applications using dates prior to 12/31/1999. These baselines will be used to compare to expected behaviors based on the standards discussed in number 1 above and to compare against when testing dates beyond 12/31/1999.

6. Test the application using the Y2K dates indicated in the Y2K checklist and in the Y2K test plan.

7. Write up the results as illustrated in Figure 12.2.

8. Obtain all required signatures on the test results sign-off page. Place all of the test-related documents in a package that can be given to your organization's Year 2000 audit committee for final approval. An audit committee should approve and archive complete Y2K test results for each application under test.

Fig. 12.1 A Y2K Test Plan Template

Y2K Test Plan Template

1. Overview

    Scope

        This document covers the scope of Y2K test for all projects

           [application name goes here]

        Each individual application will be tested according to the objectives described under System Verification Testing below

---

Fig. 12.1 A Y2K Test Plan Template (Continued)

---

2. Test Management and Procedure Controls

Test Team

[team members' names]

Testing Deliverables

This test plan will suffice for all xxx applications listed in the Scope section above. The test objectives are described in the System Verification Testing section.

Test Analysis, Reporting, and Tracking Mechanisms

The results will be stored in SQA's test repository database under the Y2K project. The results will also be presented to all interested parties via test log Quick reports. Copies of the reports will be forwarded to appropriate managers, as well as printed and stored in a Y2K folder that can be viewed by the interest concerns. The folder will be held in the QA group by _____.

Testing Management Tools

SQA Suite 6.1 will serve as the primary test management tool. A Y2K project will be created in Manager and all Y2K-related defects will be entered under that project. The Y2K-related test scripts will also be managed via SQA Manager.

Y2K test data will be designed in Excel spreadsheets, one for each application, and the data will be constructed as CSV files that will be executed using SQA Robot.

Test execution results will be stored as SQA test logs. One test log will be generated for each set of test data.

System Verification Testing

Y2K Compliance of System

For Each Date Field

Y2K Dates

        Months 00 and 13

        Days 00 and 32

        Feb. 28, 29, 30

US format

        M/D/Y

        MM/DD/YYYY

        MM-DD-YY

        MM-DD-YYYY

Invalid formats

        YYYY/MM/DD

        MM/YYYY/DD

Fig. 12.1 A Y2K Test Plan Template (Continued)

DD/YYYY/MM

Formats

MM/DD/YY (Implicit Century)

MM/DD/YYYY (Explicit Century)

Dates and Date Ranges

01/01/1900 to 12/31/2050

Two-digit user input

12/31/1999

01/01/2000

01/03/2000

01/02/2000 to 01/07/2000

Two-digit system date input

12/31/1999

01/01/2000

01/03/2000

01/02/2000 to 01/07/2000

Two-digit date input from files

12/31/1999

01/01/2000

01/03/2000

01/02/2000 to 01/07/2000

Leap Year Dates

02/28/2000

02/29/2000

02/28/2004

02/29/2004

02/28/2008

02/29/2008

For the following situations test general date integrity

Date Arithmetic

Date Conversion

Sort Dates

Search Dates

Dates in Variables

Dates in Assignment Statements

Fig. 12.1 A Y2K Test Plan Template (Continued)

Date Values as Constants

Dates Used in Indexing

Dates Used in Linked Lists

Dates Used in Internal Tables

Signature:_____   Date: _____
Y2K Project Manager

Signature:_____   Date: _____
Project Manager

Signature:_____   Date: _____
Quality Assurance Manager

Signature:_____   Date: _____
Tester

Fig. 12.2 Real-World Example Y2K Test Results

The Mainframe Legacy Project

Generic Tax Application Y2K Test Results

System Verification Testing

Y2K Compliance of System

Y2K compliance testing was completed for effective dates and end dates in the following Generic Tax screens/tabs:

Tax Rate→Area→Area Option Set

Tax Rate→Region→Region Option Set

Tax Rate→Tax→Main Screen

Tax Rate→Tax→Detail Screen→Collections

Tax Rate→Tax→Detail Screen→Product

Tax Rate→Tax→Detail Screen→Base Inclusion

Tax Rate→Tax→Detail Screen→Transaction Type

Tax Rate→Tax→Detail Screen→Discounts

Tax Rate→Rate→Main Screen

Tax Rate→Rate→Detail Screen→Base Inclusion

Tax Rate→Rate→Detail Screen→Transaction Type

Tax Rate→Rate→Detail Screen→Discounts

Tax Rate→Rate→Detail Screen→Region's Exemptions

Tax Rate→Rate→Detail Screen→Exemptions

Region Maintenance→Region List

Fig. 12.2 Real-World Example Y2K Test Results (Continued)

Region Maintenance→By Region→Header

Region Maintenance→By Region→Detail

Region Maintenance→By Region→Header

Region Maintenance→Retailers By Region→Detail

Account Maintenance

Miscellaneous Maintenance→Product Cross Reference

PBSG→Sales Option

PBSG→Deliveries Option

Product Code Override

Retailer Inquiry screens were not tested because they are display-only screens. The Report Selection screen was not tested because there was no data available that could be displayed.

Y2K Dates - For Each Date Field

Months 00 and 13

Days 00 and 32

Feb. 28, 29, 30

These dates were tried for each effective date and end date field. Months 00 and 13, days 00 and 32, and Feb. 30 were found to be keypress inhibited and could not be entered. Feb. 29 was found to be keypress inhibited in non-leap years.

Invalid formats

YYYY/MM/DD

MM/YYYY/DD

DD/YYYY/MM

All invalid date formats were found to be keypress inhibited or disallowed with further validation.

Formats

MM/DD/YY (Implicit Century)

MM/DD/YYYY (Explicit Century)

Explicit Century is the only format accepted by the application.

Dates and Date Ranges

01/01/1900 to 12/31/2050

Dates well after 01/01/2000 were not a problem. The dates 01/01/2010 and 01/01/2049 were tested and treated correctly.

Two-digit user input

12/31/1999

01/01/2000

Fig. 12.2 Real-World Example Y2K Test Results (Continued)

01/03/2000

01/02/2000 to 01/07/2000

Two-digit user input was found to be keypress inhibited.

Two-digit system date input

12/31/1999

01/01/2000

01/03/2000

01/02/2000 to 01/07/2000

System date input was not tested because the application does not use the system date. This is per the development team's input.

Two-digit date input from files

12/31/1999

01/01/2000

01/03/2000

01/02/2000 to 01/07/2000

Input is via GUI only with the exception of the RAC processes. So all input was tested through the GUI input fields.

Leap Year Dates

02/28/2000

02/29/2000

02/28/2004

02/29/2004

02/28/2008

02/29/2008

The application was found to accept and correctly process all of the leap year dates above.

For the following situations test general date integrity

Date Arithmetic

Date Conversion

Sort Dates

Search Dates

Dates in Variables

Dates in Assignment Statements

Date Values as Constants

Dates Used in Indexing

Dates Used in Linked Lists

Fig. 12.2 Real-World Example Y2K Test Results (Continued)

Dates Used in Internal Tables

The only general date integrity processing that was tested is the last processed date that is in the PROCESSSTATUS table which determines the cutoff for Generic history records. The last processed date was tested for 12/31/1999, 01/01/2000, and 01/03/2000. It worked correctly in each instance.

The sort and filter functions that are implemented via PowerBuilder PFC's were found to work correctly for effective dates and end dates that included Y2K dates (12/31/1999, 01/01/2000, and 01/03/2000).

Signature: _____   Date: _____
Y2K Project Manager

Signature: _____   Date: _____
Project Manager / MLP

Signature: _____   Date: _____
Quality Assurance Manager

Signature: _____   Date: _____
Tester

It is important to repeat this procedure over and over for each application under test. Doing so will guarantee consistent Y2K testing across all of your existing client-server software.

This approach can also be used for department-level PC systems that began as spreadsheet applications and have evolved into isolated database applications. These types of systems are particularly nasty to assess, remediate, and test because they were usually klugged together on the spur of the moment. They are also difficult because they have no rhyme or reason due to their lack of design. They usually are built with whatever tools the department had available at the time or with whatever tool was favored by the individual building the system.

12.7 CLIENT-SERVER DEVELOPMENT PLATFORMS AND Y2K COMPLIANCE

12.7.1 Visual Basic and Y2K Compliance

Visual Basic is a "Y2K-friendly" language but this does not mean that client-server applications written in Visual Basic will be Y2K compliant. Ultimately VB can be said to be Y2K compliant only when the programmer completely understands the techniques used in date processing.

Various versions of VB process short dates differently. The world would be a better place if all VB applications were written in VB 5 and above, but they are not, and VB 3 and 4 react differently to short dates than VB 5 does. To confuse the issue further, VB 3 and 4 act differently depending on which date-related function you are using.

Date "windowing" is not even present in VB 3 and 4, but it is part of the functionality of VB 5 and above. Accordingly, VB assumes that a date with a two-digit year that is greater than 29 is in the 1900s and a date with a two-digit year less than 30 is in the 2000s. Thus, VB has a fixed date window. This is a solution for handling short dates, but not a perfect one. If you analyze VB's date window, you'll soon realize that it will not provide the correct date in every instance. Even after the year 2000, there will be dates—e.g., birthdates—that will be used in some time of processing and that will extend beyond the limits of the VB fixed date window.

The following strategy can be used to assess VB applications with respect to Y2K compliance. First, identify Y2K noncompliant areas of the code. It is best to use an automated code scanner to parse the source code and related libraries looking for date-type code. Date-type code includes any piece of code that could be involved in date processing such as variables that are acted upon by date functions and other variables that assume the value of the suspect variables through assignment statements, etc. In VB, the following date-related functions should be checked: CDate, CVDate, DateAdd, DateDiff, DatePart, Date-Value, ISDate, and Format.

Second, identify Y2K noncompliant data input fields. In many older VB applications the user may not be required to enter a four-digit year. Develop a list of all input fields that accept a date from the user. If any of the date input is accomplished via a calendar utility, identify all areas in the application that use the utility to accept dates from the user.

Third, identify possible Y2K noncompliant data file records/formats. Examine all files that input to and output from the VB application for date fields that are not Y2K compliant. This is especially important for files that are downloaded to the VB application from the mainframe and for files that are created for uploading to the mainframe. It is also important for files that are exported to other client-server applications or to common desktop applications such as the MS office suite of applications.

Fourth, identify possible Y2K noncompliant database columns in databases that internally store or externally display dates with only two-digit years. Of course, the newer version of these products are Y2K compliant, but older versions of MS Access, FoxPro, etc. are not, and Y2K problems can arise.

Fifth, scan all library (DLL) version stamps to assure that the runtime libraries are the latest Y2K-compliant versions. For example, it is known that older versions of the automation library that is used by MS office applications are not Y2K compliant. This is very important as these libraries are system files and when they change, the behavior of a number of applications will change.

For example, VB 4 does not have any date windowing functionality and neither does version 2.1 of OLEAUT32.DLL. Version 2.20.4049 of OLEAUT32.DLL and above does have and will add to your VB application date windowing functionality. So, applications that are developed with the earlier version of this library will behave differently when distributed and executed on machines that have the newer version. This can cause date-related logic to function differently than expected.

Once the assessment steps described above have been completed, the VB developer should:

☞ Convert all code that uses a two-digit year for date type/format conversions

☞ Convert all code that uses a two-digit year in date-related calculations/logical comparisons, etc.

☞ Convert all input fields that use a two-digit year

☞ Convert all output files that use a two-digit year (note that in some instances the two-digit year may have to remain because the other system has not been converted to a four-digit year)

☞ Convert all database columns that use a two-digit year

☞ Convert all reports and display fields that use a two-digit year

After the remediation has been completed, all of these areas must be tested to assure that the conversions were correctly implemented. Additionally, the applications must be regression tested to assure that the conversion process did not result in some areas of the application not working as they previously worked.

12.7.2 PowerBuilder and Y2K Compliance

Although Sybase has certified PowerBuilder (PB) versions 5.0.04 and 6.0.00 as being Y2K compliant, this does not guarantee that client-server applications developed on these platforms will be Y2K compliant. PB applications are not isolated from the operating systems on the PCs where they execute. PB format masks and edit masks interact with control-panel date settings. In addition, edit masks and format masks interact with one another and edit masks can override format masks. These masks are used in string functions, date comparisons, date calculations, etc.

PowerBuilder is Y2K compliant in that the DATE and DATETIME variables always store date values with a four-digit year. PB also has built-in date windowing. The rules that PB date-related functions implement when converting two-digit years are:

00–49 assumed to be year 2000 and above

50–99 assumed to be year 1900 through year 1950

So where's the rub? One problem comes when edit masks are incorrectly specified as [shortdate]. When the edit mask is used in date comparisons, date calculations, to store the system date, etc., the results can be unpredictable.

How can a PB developer identify all of the possible Y2K date-related failure points in an application? There are two possible alternative approaches. First, the developer could use the Object Searcher in the Advanced Developer's Toolkit to locate date-related edit masks in datawindows. Second, an assessment and remediation tool such as PB2000 from ServerLogic can be used to identify and remediate possible Y2K date-related issues in PB code.

12.7.2.1 PB Y2K Assessment and Testing   The following approach should be used to verify that your PB applications are Y2K compliant.

1. Verify that date comparisons work correctly for these combinations because they are often used in PB date calculations:

    19xx and 19xx

    19xx and 20xx

    20xx and 20xx

2. Verify that valid non–leap year dates and valid leap year dates compare as valid when used alone or in calculations.

3. Verify that four-digit edit masks correctly handle the date when the control panel is set to YY

4. Verify that all date conversions to and from strings work correctly

5. Verify that all conversions executed in SQL statements to derive a date are correct

12.7.2.2 Enforcing a Four-Digit Year on Application Startup   Sybase recommends checking the operating system registry date formats on startup of your application. It is best to force the application to execute with the control panel set to short date style: YYYY. This assures that no date has an implied century, which can result in date confusion.

12.8 PC and Unix Server Testing for Y2K Compliance

12.8.1 Compliance Dimensions

Verifying Y2K compliance of PC and Unix servers involves four dimensions [7]:

1. Correctness of the time and date
2. Compliance timespan
3. Phases of time and date
4. Operating system API layer

12.8.2 Remediation and Testing Approach

Any client-server application that relies on a time and date obtained from the server is subject to possible Y2K-connected problems stemming from one or more of these areas. To identify, remediate, and test Y2K issues for applications that retrieve and use dates from a server use the following approach.

☞ Identify specific time and date items that are passed between the application under test and the server

☞ Identify the format and content of the data items

☞ Identify how the date items are passed (hardware/software mechanisms)

☞ Identify all potential points of failure

☞ Execute baseline tests with non-Y2K dates

☞ Remediate the application(s)

☞ Reexecute baseline test to assure that the application has not been regressed by the remediation process

☞ Develop and execute tests that address each specific Y2K-related remediation

What time and date elements are passed between the application and server layers? A number of different values can be passed [7]. They include unadjusted values, values adjusted for time zones, and values adjusted for daylight saving time.

Accordingly, in 16-bit OSs these time and date values can be accessed by the application through the operating system APIs; by generating an interrupt that the operating system, the BIOS, or the RTC must handle; via direct access to device drivers; or by direct physical addressing of the BIOS or RTC I/O port. In 32-bit OSs the operating system traps and services all requests for the time and date.

In 32-bit OSs the points of failure do not include the BIOS and RTC, but do include APIs, DLLs, and device drivers. Thus in 32-bit OSs Y2K date failures are going to be related to issues at these levels. According to Nickles [7], there are statistically more time- and date-related failures here than in the BIOS and RTC levels. The failures are frequently related to having the wrong versions of the layers installed on the server.

For Y2K compliance of 16-bit server platforms, test:

☞ OS APIs

☞ The BIOS

☞ The RTC

For Y2K compliance of 32-bit server platforms:

☞ Test and validate OS APIs.

☞ Verify that the correct versions of DLLs and device drivers are loaded.

☞ Upon continued failure that cannot be isolated to APIs, DLLs, or device
drivers, test the BIOS and the RTC.

The problem of testing time- and date-related APIs can be complex
because OSs such as the NT have as many as 20 or more time- and date-
related APIs. In addition, network logon scripts may be used to configure the
network time and date, based on the server time and date.

Client-server applications can pull time and date information from the
server using any of these interfaces and are thus subject to Y2K date-related
failures from many directions. To assure Y2K compliance, all paths that an
application uses to obtain the time and date must be identified. When the
application is tested for Y2K compliance, the process must include tests that
exercise these application/server time and date interfaces for all Y2K date values that are possible failure junctures. All applications that use time and date
information from the server should be tested in this manner.

12.8.3 Server Time and Date Standard

All servers should support a time and date standard with to-the-second accuracy [9]. They should perform time and date correctly for the time span from
01/01/1970 00:00:00 through 01/18/2038 22:14:09 (2147483647) coordinated
universal time.

They should correctly handle time and date information in the following
forms: coordinated universal time, local time, leap year, time zones, and daylight savings time.

They should support both 16-bit and 32-bit time and date APIs, including
those that are OS proprietary and those defined by ANSI, POSIX, and
SPEC1170.

12.9 Y2K AND PC DESKTOP SOFTWARE

12.9.1 Desktop Application Compliance

The Y2K problem may appear to be predominantly a mainframe problem, but
many PC applications have also been written using the two-digit date format.
Furthermore, many of the applications that receive a two-digit date are programmed to assume that the century is 19. This is what happens when the
application receives the date from user input or as part of data downloaded
from a mainframe. Microsoft [6] has stated that its 32-bit operating environments, Windows95 and Windows NT, store dates as 16-bit fields and can store
dates up to the year 2099. However, the Win32 environment is not able to tell
the difference when short dates are entered. For example, the year 20 will be
assumed to be 1920 not 2020. Microsoft is in the process of updating its software products to assume the year 2000. This will not solve the problem completely, as many organizations may not move to the newer software until well

after the beginning of the next century. Thus, Microsoft [5] advocates training developers to program for safe dates. The safe date recommendations are:

1. Use the operating system runtime library date format as much as possible.
2. Use long dates when short dates may be misrepresented as outside of the current century.
3. Use the formal date format of the development environment or database.
4. When implementing a custom date format use more than a two-digit year.

From the tester's perspective, it is our obligation to assure that these recommendations have been used in the PC applications software and client-server systems we test. This can be done by formal inspection of the code and by simulated date test cases. In addition, we must assure that third-party runtime libraries do not cause failures, that mainframe-accessed dates do not cause failures, and that custom-built software does not cause date-related failures.

Access 95 (YY dates) has a date-format life expectancy only until the year 1999; Excel 95 (YY dates), until the year 2019; Access 97 (YY dates) and Excel 97 (YY dates), until the year 2029; Visual C++ (4.x) runtime library (32 bits), until the year 2036; Project 95 and earlier (32 bits), until the year 2049; and Excel 95 (long dates YYYY), until the year 2078.

The following products are believed to have date-format life expectancies until the year 2099: MS-DOS file system—FAT16 (16 bits), Windows 3.x file system—FAT16 (16 bits), Windows 95 file system—FAT16 (16 bits), Windows 95 runtime library—WIN32 (16 bits), Windows for Workgroups—FAT16 (16 bits), Windows NT file system—FAT16 (16 bits), and Windows NT runtime library—WIN32 (16 bits).

Windows 95 file system—FAT32 (32 bits) is expected to have a safe date-format life until the year 2108. Access 95, Excel 97, and Visual FoxPro, all with long dates YYYY, and SQL Server with datetime, should have date-format life expectancies until the year 9999. And Windows NT file system—NTFS (64 bits) is expected to operate safely into future centuries.

A word of caution for anyone developing or testing applications developed for Windows NT 3.51, Service pack 4 or below: Do not use the file system date-time stamp as a means to recognize executables or data files for installation purposes. During installation testing on a major client-server application, we discovered that when NT adjusts for daylight savings time it rolls back the time stamp on every single file on the hard drive. This resulted in the complete failure of our installation process.

12.9.2 The Microsoft Automation Libraries

The automation libraries are present in Windows 95 and NT 3.51 and later. The files are

☞ Oleaut32.dll

☞ Olepro32.dll

☞ Asycfilt.dll

☞ Stdole2.tbl

These files are either installed when the operating system is or may be installed when an application that requires them is installed. Applications that use them include Microsoft Office 95 and later, Visual C++, Visual Basic, Visual Interdev, Windows 95, Windows 98, Windows NT Workstation, and Windows NT Server.

The libraries contain routines that interpret two-digit years when creating serial dates. Consequently, many applications use them for date handling. The libraries have been revised several times. The danger is in having various versions of these files distributed among the desktop computers throughout your company. If this situation exists, you will not be able to predict, much less certify, the behavior of client-server software that is distributed on those machines. As an example, if you enter the date 01/01/05 on an NT 3.51 machine and it does not have the service packs installed, the date will be interpreted as 01/01/1905. On NT 3.51—with the service packs—and on NT 4.0 the date will be interpreted as 01/01/2005.

According to Microsoft, the libraries handle dates as follows: Before version 2.20.00.4054, the two-digit date cutoff point is 1999. For versions 2.20.00.4054 up to 2.29.xx.xxxx, the two-digit date cutoff point is 2029. For versions 2.30.00.xxxx and later, the two-digit date cutoff point is a user-determined value.

The remedy for this Y2K problem is to survey all of the client and server machines in your organization and bring all of them up to par by installing the latest, or at least a consistent, version of the automation library files.

12.10 YEAR 2000 DESKTOP REMEDIATION PROCESS

This section summarizes the Year 2000 issues that must be addressed on every desktop, identifies a remedy for each concern, and defines a procedure for administering the fix. Figure 12.3 shows a convenient checklist you can use in remediation.

A work plan should be developed in MS project for scheduling the remediation resources and activities.

12.10.1 Desktop Remediation Issues

12.10.1.1 Desktop Date Settings   The desktop short date settings can affect how Office's various applications format the date. If the short date setting is M/D/YY it will cause Office to override templates in which the date style is MM/DD/YYYY.

Fig. 12.3 Y2K Desktop Remediation Checklist

Desktop Feature Tested/Audited	Version Number	Compliant (Y/N)	Partially Compliant (Reason)	Not Compliant (Reason)	Remediation Applied (Y/N)
BIOS					
Automation Library					
Operating System					
DOS					
Windows 3.1					
Windows 3.11					
Windows 95					
Windows 98					
Office Applications					
Excel					
Access					
Power Point					
Word					
Outlook 97					
Internet Explorer					

12.10.1.2 BIOS The hardware manufacturer may certify the BIOS, but it depends on the model in question. For example, both Dell and Compaq have certified a number of their hardware BIOSs to be compliant, based on the national Software Testing Laboratory's YMARK2000 BIOS test software program. Machines that are not listed as compliant by their manufacturers must be tested and, if necessary, a Flash BIOS patch must be applied.

12.10.2 Operating Systems

12.10.2.1 DOS

DOS 5.0a, 6.0, 6.2, and 6.21 All of these versions of DOS assume a twentieth-century date if the date is entered with a two-digit year, and they will not accept a two-digit date (e.g., 00) for year 2000. The correct date can be entered if the user enters a four-digit via the DOS DATE command. Failure to enter the correct four-digit date will result in an "Invalid Date" error. External commands that require a date must be entered with a four-digit year for Y2K-related dates. In addition, the DOS command MSBACKUP does not recognize dates greater than 1999.

12.10.2.2 Windows 3.1; Windows for Workgroups 3.11, 16-Bit Win; and Windows for Workgroups 3.11, DOS   Windows 3.1, 16-bit, and Windows 3.1, DOS present a leap-year problem. The date cannot be set to 02-29-2000 in the control panel via the mouse; however, the keyboard can be used to set an 02-29-2000 date. The system date does roll correctly when left alone.

12.10.2.3 Windows 95, 32-bit Retail; Windows 95 (OSR) 4.00.950a, 32-Bit Win; and Windows 95 (OSR) 4.00.950b, 32-Bit Win   If you still use Windows file manager (WINFILE.EXE) you should be aware that it will not correctly display dates of 2000 and beyond. In addition, COMMAND.COM will not display four-digit dates. The system DATE command cannot handle two-digit dates from 00–79 appropriately. Finally, the date is displayed incorrectly in the Find File or Folders Date tab.

12.10.2.4 Windows 98   Surprisingly, Microsoft's most recent version of Windows is not yet Y2K compliant. Windows 98 has several Year 2000 issues that include Java applications that make use of the java.txt. The SimpleDateFormat class library can interpret dates incorrectly; the Phone Dialer applet does not display the date correctly; the COMCTL32.DLL - Date/Time Picker function might not return the correct date when Regional Settings from the Control Panel is set to the short date style; the Time and Date control applet displays the 29th day of February on years other than leap years when the date is adjusted using the spinner controls; the year 2000 will not be accepted as a valid entry when entered as 00 when setting custom date information while viewing the properties of Microsoft Wordpad or Word documents; booting the system at the exact moment the real time clock rolls over to the next century will cause the system to display incorrect date/time values; there are problems with DHCP where IP designations set after 3/01/2000 are recounted as having been set a day previous on the client; xcopy does not accept dates with two-digit years for the span 80–99.

12.10.3 MS Office Automation Libraries

In many organizations, various versions of the Office automation libraries exist due to repeated installs/updates of MS Office suite products. Thus, different users might have different versions of the automation libraries. The problems arise in how the different versions interpret dates with two-digit years. Microsoft has indicated that versions before 2.20.00.4054 cannot handle year

2000 and beyond (the cutoff is 1999), versions 2.20.00.4054 to 2.29.xx.xxxx can correctly process two-digit year dates up to 2029, and versions 2.30.00.xxxx and further, the date limit is determined by the user.

12.10.3.1 Access 2.0, 16-Bit Microsoft Access 2.0 interprets dates with a two-digit year format to be in the twentieth century. The range is as follows. Dates 1/1/00 through 12/31/99 are construed as 1/1/1900 through 12/31/1999. If you enter four-digits for the year, Access 2 will interpret the date as being in the twenty-first century.

12.10.3.2 Access 95 This version of Access has problem with two-digit years in imported text files. They are understood as being in the twentieth century. Access's date window is 1930–2029. The date interpretation is dependent on the version of the automation libraries that are installed. In addition, the interpretation is dependent on the current century as follows. The Windows 95 version of OLEAUT32.DLL interprets the dates 1/1/00 through 12/31/99 as 1/1/1900 through 12/31/1999 if the current century is the twentieth, and interprets the same date range as 1/1/2000 through 12/31/2099 if the current century is the twenty-first.

12.10.3.3 Access 97/7.0 32-Bit Microsoft Access 97 interprets two-digit dates to be in the twenty-first century using the window 1/1/00 through 12/31/29. Dates in the twentieth century use the window 1/1/30 through 12/31/99.

12.10.3.4 Excel 5.0, 97 Microsoft Excel uses several default date formats. The most common is the system short date style. If the system short date style is YY, then even when the user types a YYYY date, it will default to the yy format when displayed. If a user enters a date in a M/D/YY format, values below 30 are considered to be year 2000, and values equal to or above 30 are interpreted as 1900. The DATE() function cannot handle two-digit years because it accepts numeric parameters. In addition, it calculates dates less than 1900 as offsets from 1900. Finally, date formats such as Dec 99 will not behave correctly.

12.10.3.5 Outlook 97 MS Outlook 97 presents a problem when the system date is year 2000 or greater: it will assume a date of 01/01 is 01/01/2099 instead of 01/01/1999. This affects the use of Outlook functions such as the calendar in which the Go To Date feature will set the day to 01/01/2099. In addition, custom forms that use dates in calculations will be incorrect.

12.10.3.6 MS Internet Explorer Internet Explorer will view a cookie as expired when it uses a two-digit year of 00. Internet Explorer will see pages on a web site as expired and will not cache them locally if the server communicates a two-digit year of 00 in the HTTP header.

12.11 REMEDIATION ACTIONS

12.11.1 Desktop Date Settings

12.11.1.1 Windows 3.1, Windows 3.11, Windows 95, and Windows 98   The Short Date Style should be changed to MM/DD/YYYY.

12.11.2 Operating Systems

12.11.2.1 Windows 3.1, Windows 3.1 16-bit, and Windows 3.1 DOS

12.11.2.2 Windows 95 (Windows 95, 32-bit Retail; Windows 95 [OSR] 4.00.950a, 32-Bit Win; and Windows 95 [OSR] 4.00.950b, 32-Bit Win)

File Manager   The updated **WIN95Y2K.EXE** file resolves the Y2K issue for all versions of Windows 95. This file also contains the updated version of **WIN-FILE.EXE**.

Command.com   The Y2K issue is resolved by the following updated file for Windows 95 retail release and OEM Service Release 1 (4.00.950A): COM-MAND.COM dated 3/23/98 10:51am 93,034 bytes.

The following updated file resolves the issue for Windows 95 OSR2, OSR 2.1 (4.00.950B), and OSR 2.5 (4.00.950C): COMMAND.COM dated 3/23/98 11:12am 93,974 bytes.

The WIN95Y2K.EXE file contains both updated versions of COM-MAND.COM and installs the correct version.

Winfile.exe   Running the Windows 95 Winfile.exe patch [w95filup.exe] corrects the problems with file manager.

Find File   Installing Microsoft Internet Explorer 4.0 or later will resolve this issue.

12.11.2.3 Windows 98   Running the Windows 98 update corrects all of the Y2K issues discussed above.

12.11.3 MS Office Automation Library

Microsoft has recommended that developers use a common Automation Library for handling dates. All desktops should be updated with the latest version of the automation libraries.

12.11.3.1 General

☞ Upgrade all desktops to Office 97.

☞ Install Office 97 Service Release 1 on all desktops.

☞ Install Office 97 Service Release 2 on all desktops.

12.11.3.2 Access 2.0

☞ All Access 2.0 implementations should be upgraded to Access 97.

☞ All Access 2.0 queries should be reconstructed and optimized after 97 installation.

12.11.3.3 Access 95

☞ All Access 95 implementations should be upgraded to Access 97.

☞ All Access 95 queries should be reconstructed and optimized after 97 installation.

If the application is not upgraded to Access 97, then to make Access 95 Y2K compliant, OLEAUT32.DLL must be version of 2.20.4118 or greater.

12.11.3.4 Excel 5.0, 97   You will need Office *97 SR-2 Patch* as a prerequisite.

Change the system default short date format to include a four-digit year. Get in the habit of using four-digit-year formats for dates in Microsoft Excel.

Install the Excel add-ins, Date Migration Wizard, Date Fix Wizard, and Date Watch Wizard.

Note that a bug has been found in the DATE Watch Wizard that disables the undo feature in MS Excel in both the menu and the tool bar button.

12.11.3.5 Outlook 97   For complete compliance when using Outlook 97, you need to use a Year 2000 compliant mail server, such as Exchange Server 4.0 SP5 or Exchange Server 5.0 SP2 or greater.

For Outlook 97 version 8.0, 8.01, 8.02 or 8.03, obtain the 8.04 version of OUTLLIB.DLL from the Office 97 SR-2 Patch in order to handle short dates properly when scheduling events that span the century boundary.

12.11.4 MS Internet Explorer 4.0, 4.01

Service Pack 1 for Internet Explorer 4.0/4.01 resolves the Y2K issue.

12.12 REMEDIATION PROCESS

Remediated desktops should be tracked via the asset ID and its associated information collected and stored in a product such as LANDesk. Information in an enterprise's database pertaining to the version of Windows/DOS that is loaded, what applications are loaded, and what versions of the applications are present should be used to guide remediation activities. As desktops are remediated, they need to be identified and that identification stored.

As an alternative to on-site remediation activities, the process can be completed remotely across the network with Microsoft, Systems Management Server (SMS) or a package such as Install Shield.

12.12.1 Prerequisites

The following prerequisites should be met prior to desktop remediation.

Word 97	run SR-2
Word 95	run SR-1, and SR-2
Word 6.0	upgrade to Word 95, run SR-1, and SR-2
Excel 97(8.0xx)	run SR-2
Excel 95(7.0xx)	run SR-1, and SR-2
Excel 5.0	upgrade to Excel 95, run SR-1, and SR-2
Access 97(8.0xx)	run SR-2
Access 95(7.0xx)	run SR-1, and SR-2
Access 2.0	upgrade to Access 95, run SR-1, and SR-2
PowerPoint 97(7.0xx)	run SR-2
PowerPoint 95(7.0xx)	run SR-1, and SR-2
PowerPoint 4.0	upgrade to PowerPoint 95, run SR-1, and SR-2
Office 97(8.0xx)	run SR-2
Office 95(7.0xx)	run SR-1, and SR-2
Internet Explorer 4.0 (32 bit)	run Internet Explorer 4.01 Service Pack 1 (Not contained on the Year 2000 CD)

12.12.2 Remediation Toolkit

A standardized Y2K desktop remediation toolkit should be assembled. All toolkit components should be located in the network directory "Sliapp1\ data\Y2Kproj\Desktop Remediation." Each member of the remediation team should be provided with a diskette/CD containing the complete toolkit when in the field.

Note: The contents of the toolkit below assume that MS Office 97 including MS Access 97 and all of the related service packs in the prerequisites listed above have been previously installed. If not, then the Office 97 service packs [SP1 and SP2] should be added to the toolkit.

The following components should be included:

1. Desktop inventory information document (hardware and software, versions, etc.) for the location being remediated

2. List of known "gotchas" to avoid when upgrading/remediating desktop software

3. BIOS Testing software, YMARK2000

4. BIOS-compliance information from the vendor for each brand of installed desktop machine

5. BIOS patches for desktop machines known to be noncompliant

6. Windows 95 patch for Command.com and DIR command date entry problems (win95y2k.exe)

7. Win95y2k.exe readme file

8. Windows 95 Winfile.exe patch (w95filup.exe)

9. Excel add-ins for Excel 97 (Datefix.exe, Datemig1.exe, and Datewtch.exe)

10. Readme files for Excel 97 add-ins (Datefix.exe, Datemig1.exe, and Datewtch.exe)

11. Latest versions of the automation library (OLEAUT32.DLL versions 2.30.00.xxxx and forward)

12. Service Pack 1 for Internet Explorer 4.0/4.1

13. Windows 3.1 File Manager Patch (w31filup.exe)

14. Windows 3.11 File Manage Patch (wfwfilup.exe)

15. Automation Library update (msvbvm50.exe)

16. Internet Explorer service pack 1

12.12.3 Testing and Remediation Tasks

12.12.3.1 General

1. Verify the desktop ID using the information based on the Asset ID that is located on the PC cover.

2. Record the ID number on the checklist.

3. For Windows 95 and 98, verify that the information is complete and correct for the applications displayed under Programs in the Start menu.

4. For Windows 3.1 and 3.11, verify that an icon is present for each application or that the application is executed from the **Run** command in the **File** menu.

12.12.3.2 Windows 3.1, Windows 3.11

1. Open the Control Panel window.

2. Choose the international icon.

3. Select the Date Format area and click on the Change button.

4. Click on the Day Leading Zero option box.

5. Click on the Month Leading Zero option box.

6. Click on the Century (1990 vs. 90) option box.

7. Click the OK button.

8. Close the Control Panel window.

12.12.3.3 Windows 95 Desktop Date Settings

1. Click on the Start button.

2. Select Settings.

3. Select Control Panel.

4. Double-click on Regional Settings.

5. Click on the Date tab.

6. Change the Short Date Style setting to mm/dd/yyyy.

7. Click on the OK command button.

8. Close the Control Panel.

12.12.3.4 BIOS Testing and Remediation

1. Check vendor hardware-compliance list for the model under investigation.

2. If compliant, skip steps 3 through 5.

3. If the vendor lists the model as noncompliant, apply the appropriate software patch or Flash BIOS upgrade.

4. If the model cannot be found in the vendor's list, test the BIOS with Ymark2000.

5. If it is found to be noncompliant, tag system for replacement.

12.12.3.5 Automation Libraries

1. Open Windows Explorer.

2. Go to C:\Windows\System directory.

3. Select the file OLEAUT32.dll and perform a right mouse click.

4. Select the properties command.

5. Select the Version tab.

6. The version must be at least 2.20 or newer.

7. If the version is older than 2.20 you must replace it.

8. The new version can be copied from the toolkit CD/disk to the Windows System directory.

12.12.3.6 Alternative Method   If needed, this procedure will enable you to determine which version of the automation library is present.

1. Click on the Start button. Go to Find→Files or Folders.

2. Enter Oleaut in Named Section. Choose [C:] to look in.

3. Highlight OLEAUT32.dll.
4. Click on File→Properties.
5. Select the Version tab.
6. If file version is 2.20.4118 or higher, the download below is not required. If file version is less than 2.20.4118, then install OLEAUT32.DLL version 2.20.4118.
7. Download is necessary for Access to follow the two-digit date window of 1930–2029.

12.12.4 Operating Systems

12.12.4.1 Windows 3.1

1. Apply the Windows 3.1 File Manager Patch (w31filup.exe).

12.12.4.2 Windows 3.11

1. Apply the Windows 3.11 File Manage Patch (wfwfilup.exe).

12.12.4.3 Windows 95

1. Apply the Windows 95 patch for Command.com and DIR command date entry problems (win95y2k.exe).
2. Follow the directions in the Win95y2k.exe readme file.
3. Apply the Windows 95 Winfile.exe patch (w95filup.exe).
4. Follow the directions in the W95filup.exe readme file.
5. The Windows 95 upgrade file are included in the toolkit CD/Disk.

12.12.4.4 Windows 95, 98

1. The Windows Update is the online extension of the Internet Explorer install.
2. Start the Windows Update service from the link on the **Start** menu.

12.12.4.5 MS Office

General

1. Check the service pack versions that are installed.
2. Both Office 97 service packs 1 and 2 should be installed.
3. If the service packs are not installed, use the Microsoft Year 2000 TechNet CD to install them.

Excel

1. Open Excel.
2. The splash screen contains MS Office/Excel version information.
3. If you miss the version information in the splash screen, click on the **Help** menu.
4. Click on the **About** command.
5. If the version is Excel 5.0 or older, the Office software is not Office 97 and is not Y2K compliant. Contact your local help desk to institute an upgrade process.
6. If the version is Office 97 or after, the upgrade is already installed and you must install the Excel Y2K add-ins.
7. Install the Datefix.exe add-in for Excel 97. Follow the directions in the readme file for Datefix.exe.
8. Install the Datemigl.exe add-in for Excel 97. Follow the directions in the readme file for Datemigl.exe.
9. Install \ the Datewtch.exe add-in for Excel 97. Follow the directions in the readme file for Datewtch.exe.

Access

1. Open Access.
2. The splash screen contains Access version information.
3. If you miss the version information in the splash screen, click on the **Help** menu.
4. Click on the **About** command.
5. If the version is Access 2.0 or 95 (7.0), the Office software is not Y2K compliant. Contact your local help desk to institute the upgrade process to Access 97 (8.0).
6. If the version is Access 95 and it cannot be upgraded, applying the automation library update will bring it into compliance.
7. Use the Toolkit CD to install the library.

Outlook 97

1. Open Outlook.
2. The splash screen contains the Outlook version information.
3. If you miss the version information in the splash screen, click on the **Help** menu.
4. Click on the **About** command.
5. If the version is Outlook 97 For Outlook 97 version 8.0, 8.01, 8.02 or 8.03, installing the 8.04 version of OUTLLIB.DLL from the Office 97 SR-2 Patch brings Outlook into compliance.

6. Use the Toolkit CD to install the library file.

Internet Explorer 4.0, 4.01

1. Open Internet Explorer.
2. The splash screen contains the explorer version information.
3. If you miss the version information in the splash screen, click on the **Help** menu.
4. Click on the **About** command.
5. If the version is 4.0 or 4.01, check for "SP1" behind the version number. If it is not listed then Service Pack 1 must be installed.
6. Use the Toolkit CD to install the service pack.

12.13 REFERENCES

1. Bouwens, Serge. Year 2000 Issues (Version 2.0). The year 2000 archive, www.year2000.com/archive/issues.html.
2. Cooke, Larry W. Test Planning—Enterprise Wide Year 2000. Published in *Testing Focus 2000* by TESTMASTERS, testmasters@testtools.com, March 1997.
3. Goldberg, Steven H. *Year 2000 Computer Failures: Managing the Business and Legal Risks.* Cosgrove, Eisenberg, & Kiley, P.C., Boston.
4. Kearney, Dick. "Beating the Clock: How to Assess Your Year 2000 Conversion Effort." *INFORMATIONWEEK*, April 15, 1996.
5. Microsoft Corporation. *Implications of the Year 2000 on Microsoft Products.* Microsoft Corporation, Redmond, WA, 1996.
6. Microsoft Corporation. *Year 2000 Resource CD.* Microsoft Corporation, Redmond, WA, November, 1998.
7. Nickles, Alfred E. A Technical Review of PC and Unix Year 2000 Compliance. A White Paper, http://www.f2k.com/f2k_white_paper.html.
8. Rettich, Artis. News Summary Published in *Testing Focus 2000* by TESTMASTERS, testmasters@testtools.com, 888-828-2188, January 1997.
9. Server Test Standard. Http://www.f2k.com/server_test_standard.html.
10. Shoup, Larry. "A High-Level Perspective on Year-2000 Business Issues." *IT Metrics Strategies*, Vol. III, No. 7, July 1997.
11. Simpson, Alan. Year 2000 FAQ, www.ComLinks.com.

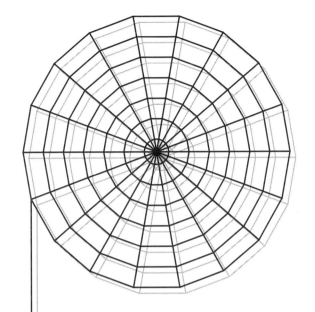

Selecting an Automated Client-Server Software Testing Tool Suite

13.1 WHY AUTOMATE?

Automating testing reduces testing errors and costs. Human beings are error prone in the things they do. This is not a bad thing, it is just a consequence of being human. Think what a boring place a perfect world would be. Thus, software testing, as with any other activity done by humans, is error prone. It is so because testing involves a complex set of tasks. As I discussed in chapters 8 and 9, the more complex a task is, the more likely we are to make errors. Automating testing reduces the number of errors because it removes the human component, and it allows the testing process to be perfected over multiple uses.

Automating testing also eliminates the effects of individual differences. Each tester is unique and each faces and carries out his or her work according to individual makeup. This can result is vastly different levels of testing effectiveness due to the tester's education, training, experience, and work habits. Automating the testing process forces testers to follow a repeatable testing process that is consistent across testers because they are following the procedures embedded in the tool.

Automating testing captures knowledge that is ordinarily kept in the tester's brain. Testers, not unlike software developers, are highly mobile and will probably work for several major companies during their careers. This means that the knowledge of how they tested your software is going to depart with them, and if it is not written down it will be gone completely. If the testing process is documented and implemented via a testing tool, the knowledge stays in the test repository, and even a new hire can step up with a bit of training on the tool and can understand how the software was tested in the past.

Automating testing removes the randomness of test cases. Manually constructed test cases tend to be randomly designed and executed even when testing has been planned ahead of time. Automated test cases that have been created according to intelligent guidelines (as discussed in chapter 8), enforced by the tool, and stored in the tool's test repository will not be randomly distributed. They will not leave testing gaps or redundantly test the same sections of the code. Thus complete test coverage is a more readily achievable goal with an automated suite of test tools.

In this sense, an automated test suite can be thought of as replacing Beta testing [13] because Beta testing is a random process that misses a lot of the errors in the final system. An automated test suite can achieve results in situations where a quick response is necessary while Beta testing can take weeks to months to achieve the same results.

Testing automation reduces the costs of testing in one major area: labor costs. As is the case with software development, the most intense costs associated with software testing are the cost of the humans who do the testing. Automation can significantly reduce the number of person hours the testers spend executing test cases and analyzing test results. Designing and constructing test cases with an automated testing tool does require an initial investment of person hours up front, but the overall human effort has been shown to be reduced by 50% (see Figure 13.1).

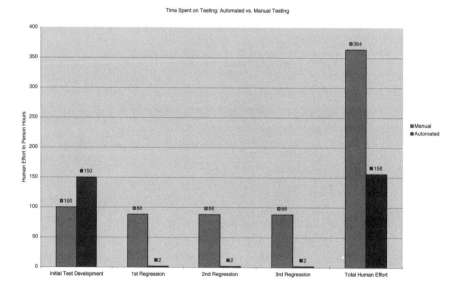

Fig. 13.1 Manual Testing Effort vs. Automated Testing Effort
This figure was adapted from the chart in the Rational Visual Test 4.0 Visual Test Tour online document provided with Visual Test 4.0 software package.

Testing is a major bottleneck in many development projects. Automating testing reduces the bottleneck because it allows testing to occur as the code is written [14]. It reduces the developers' tendency to sacrifice quality for productivity.

13.2 AUTOMATED TEST TOOLS

Test tools are not easy to define because testers use many different software packages to ease the work they have to do. They use file comparators to do before and after comparisons. They use symbolic debuggers to step through code when trying to isolate an error or they embed print commands at program break points. They use bounds checkers to test for out-of-range conditions and memory leaks. They use driver and stub code modules to emulate unfinished software components during integration testing. They use word processors to develop test plans and spreadsheets to design test case folios. All in all, software testers are extremely creative when looking for and implementing tools to support testing.

In my previous text [15] I covered three classification perspectives for software testing tools: David Gelperin's classification scheme [9], Software Quality Engineering Classification framework [3], and Poston's test tools framework [18]. I suggest you refer to these sources for an overview of formal test tool classification schemes.

Informally, testing tools can be anything from compilers to special capture/playback systems designed specifically to test GUI-based applications. According to Roger Sherman, Director of Testing at Microsoft, Inc., C and C++ are used to generate test cases to test API layers in commercial software packages [20]. MS Test (now known as Visual Test) is used for testing through interfaces and for managing the testing process. MS Basic is used for interapplication testing and is the language in which Visual Test 4.0 test scripts are written. Verification testing of Microsoft's commercial products is accomplished using Smart file comparisons, directly querying the application under test, directly querying the operating system, and with screen dumps and comparisons.

Bob Saile, Quality Assurance Development Manager at Microsoft, reminds us about the Software Development Kit (SDK) debug version of the operating system. He says, "If you do not make a test run under the debug operating system you are shipping with BUGS!" He says that the debug version will catch bad API calls, memory leaks, and failures to release system resources [19].

According to Sherman [20], Microsoft has several types of test case execution manager tools that are home grown. For instance, the Teacher/Pupil test manager runs tests unattended at night. The client machine with the application under test is the Pupil and the Server is the Teacher. The teacher downloads the automated test suite and the pupil executes it. The teacher controls the test and can even reboot the Pupil machine if a test case causes a catastrophic failure. A second test manager application is the use of "Monkeys," which drive an application in random fashion. They send keystrokes, etc. that were probably not intended by the designer/developer. Monkeys can determine how robust an application is. Sherman says that they are working on "intelligent" Monkeys that can send the interface input that simulates specific user type profiles. Sherman says that, in this manner, he can determine true Mean Time To Failure values and can trace the keystrokes that led to the failure.

13.3 AUTOMATED TESTING TOOL SELECTION

The first step in selection is to define your organization's client-server testing requirements. There are many definitions of what a C-S system is, and there are many diverse hardware and software implementations that are being dubbed client-server. For instance, client-server in its broadest sense does not require a specialized GUI platform nor does it require a network. A C-S system without a GUI or a network is a real possibility for systems that fit Hurwitz's Front-Ending C-S system model [11]. The truly distributed systems will be the ones that require specialized C-S platforms and development tools.

Eckerson [6] defines a set of Client-Server test tool requirements. In his estimation, the tool must

1. Support object-level record and playback
2. Provide integrated test management
3. Have a robust high-level scripting language
4. Support variable methods of comparing test results
5. Run on all of the platforms you support
6. Work in both 16- and 32-bit Windows environments
7. Support foreign languages
8. Support a range of test methods
9. Support custom controls
10. Support synchronized and unattended playback
11. Be reliable

The Windows operating system environment (including MS Windows and X Window Systems) is particularly challenging when it comes to test automation. As discussed in chapter 5 on GUI testing the Windows environment is completely unique. Thus, it requires automated testing tools which can simulate keyboard strokes and mouse actions; compare actual and expected results for application windows that can move around, change size, have focus, and not have focus; develop test scripts that can deal with unexpected events such as General Protection Faults (GPFs) [6].

13.3.1 "Wish List" for Automated C-S Testing Tools

The tools should meet these general requirements: First, they should have clear descriptive documentation, an online tutorial, and an extensive on-line help facility. Second, they should have good vendor technical support. Third, they should provide good performance at a reasonable price. Fourth, they should be hardware/software platform independent (no tool fills this last requirement yet).

The better tools should have document testing management capabilities (as noted by Eckerson [6]) on specification, test case folios, a test execution log, test results analysis and reporting facilities, defect logging and tracking facilities, and should cover all seven areas of C-S testing as outlined in Figure 4.6.

Fortunately, a plethora of tools is available to automate test management functions. Many of the new testing tools include good testing management facilities, but if you have already selected one that has not, there are other options available. Many of the older testing tools are specifically designed to implement test planning functions. It is not necessary, however, to have a special tool for this purpose as any spreadsheet or word processing package can be acceptable for use in planning and controlling software testing.

With respect to the GUI, a tool should have a test scripting language—proprietary or otherwise. The language should not be too complicated or cryptic because not every tester will have the necessary programming background that some of the more complex scripting languages require. The tool should have both object- and event-level test script recording capabilities with automatic level switching when necessary. It should have unattended (batch-mode) playback. Tools with scripting languages, such as Visual Basic (which requires that test scripts be compiled prior to playback), should reduce the compiles to background processes so that the tester can continue using the tool to create or edit other scripts in the foreground.

The tool should provide true object-oriented recording, which invokes capturing the object itself and is not just mapping the object's location on the screen or within a window. True object-oriented recording can distinguish among such actions as a mouse click, an Enter keypress, and a menu command. Location-mapped object recording causes problems when new Windows controls are added to list boxes or menus and previous controls are deleted or moved to a lower or higher position in the list.

The tool should be able to capture and compare windows/screens, Windows controls, text fields in Windows, and list items in Windows list boxes and menus.

With respect to server and network testing, the tool should have the capacity to do both volume and stress testing of the database and network servers. Volume testing refers to running a large number of test cases (e.g., a large number of network users and messages) for an extended period of time (24 hours at a minimum) on the system. Stress testing requires running an enormously large number of test cases in a short time period on the system.

Stress testing is analogous to the type of activity ATM systems experience during the lunch hour when a very large number of people are trying to extract money to buy lunch. In addition to design, construction, and execution of test cases, these tools should capture parameters such as network load conditions, etc.

Functional testing tools should provide code-level and logic-level test data coverage. Functional testing tools should be complementary with the use of data-driven testing and framework-based testing as the primary approaches for test data design and test script design, respectively.

The tools should be able to implement testing methods such as fundamental requirements testing (cause-effect graphing) [1,2,7,8,10,15,16] and scenario-based testing [7]. They should work in conjunction with equivalence partitioning, boundary analysis, DLTs, and error guessing [1,15,16] and address logic coverage from a functional perspective. To provide code-level functional testing, they should encompass methods such as statement, condition, decision, condition/decision, and multiple decision/condition coverage and basis testing.

System testing is still best when done manually but I hope better tools soon will be available to assess user satisfaction and system usability. The criteria for these two types of assessments should be distinguished as measures of attitude (satisfaction) and of behavior (usability). Any measure of user satisfaction is in effect a measure of the user's attitudes toward the system, and measures of usability ideally are based on observations of user behaviors while using the system.

All of the tools available for the previous sections can be reused to implement build-level regression testing as well as postimplementation regression testing.

In addition, technical quality requires tools that can measure client and server application code complexity. The tools should provide a complexity metric such as McCabe's Cyclomatic complexity [12], and they should provide logical code maps that can identify potential problem modules. Furthermore, the better tools will provide the capacity to restructure the code to reduce its structural complexity and its error proneness.

Such tools should also provide requirements-level measurement and reengineering. For example, tools that automate the development of DLT representations of the requirements provide a requirements-level complexity metric and also provide a check for requirements completeness.

13.4 TEST TOOL SELECTION PROCESS RECOMMENDATIONS

Automating the software testing process is an important step that takes time and resources. It requires training in the testing process itself and in the testing tool. There are substantial learning curves associated with some testing tools while others are very intuitive. The audience is also an important consideration as many different individuals with differing backgrounds can become involved in software testing at various points. It is for these reasons that I have devoted an entire section to recommendations.

For many companies, the situation is one of living with two different development environments that have different testing tool requirements and with a diverse tool users' audience that includes mainframe and client-server developers, quality assurance and technical support personnel, and users.

The mainframe environment is very important to the continued support of the computing effort. In most organizations, it is still the dominant environment. At the same time, these organizations are gradually moving into the client-server computing environment with its graphical user interface. The client-server development environment consists of both proprietary LANs and WANs as well as the nonproprietary Internet. These environmental considerations are extremely important in the selection of automated testing tools.

13.4.1 Preselection Recommendations

There are critical steps to be taken prior to selecting an automated testing tool suite. Jerry Durrant suggests that you begin by cataloging your company's existing software tools and then grouping them by the hardware and software platforms they service. Next, name all the activities your company expects the tools to support and construct a matrix showing activities vs. tools coverage. Analyze and prioritize any activities the tools aren't presently supporting; include time, difficulty, precision, and repetition of the activities in your analysis [4].

Once you have compared these activity needs to possible tools and solutions, you'll need an understanding of what is required in your current development and test environment compared to the company's hardware and software plans for the future. Next, you need to develop a set of software testing tool objectives based on the tool's roles and goals. Finally, create a plan to implement your software testing tool objectives.

Durrant [3,4,5] suggests that software tool implementation should be avoided during any major software system implementation or restaffing periods. He further suggests that other times to avoid are when software development efforts are distressed or significant software is being released.

13.4.2 Recommended Test Tool Evaluation Process

Your company should consider the following time frames in a tool evaluation process. Approximately one week should be allotted for developing software testing tools requirements. Examining software testing tools functionality, summarizing the data, and prioritizing the characteristics should be completed in the following two weeks. An additional week should be set aside for pretrial demonstrations. Lastly, one month may be allotted for a trial period [4].

Simultaneously, your company should be developing a long-term vision for software tool support. This vision should incorporate your company's overall software development methodology and testing process; the future computing environment at your company; the automated support necessary for the software testing process and its supporting mechanisms (as described in the Test-Rx model), and any software testing automation as part of an effort to automate the entire development process.

13.4.3 Recommended Tool Suite Characteristics

Your company should look for a software testing tool suite that:

1. Supports both the Mainframe and Client-Server environments when required
2. Supports testing of desktop and webtop C-S applications
3. Can be purchased from a single vendor
4. Is purchased from a large vendor that has the potential to stay in business
5. Is expandable as future testing needs change
6. Provides automated test management
7. Provides automated test execution and results logging
8. Provides automated defect tracking and problem reporting
9. Provides automated test results reporting
10. Supports interface testing needs in mainframe and client-server environments
11. Supports functional testing needs in mainframe and client-server environments
12. Supports system and user acceptance testing needs in mainframe and client-server environments when required
13. Supports regression testing in mainframe and client-server environments when required
14. Allows all of the tests to be designed and constructed on PC workstations but run in mainframe and client-server environments when required

13.5 POSTSELECTION RECOMMENDATIONS

13.5.1 Internal Marketing

Once a tool has been acquired, your company should establish an internal marketing effort [5]. Internal promotion should provide high visibility for the value and applicability of the tool(s).

The strategic elements of an internal promotion program should include regular written and verbal communications to users and nonusers and individual and group-related activities and promotion efforts. Your approach might include a tool-specific newsletter or public e-mail folder, informal verbal dialogs, round table discussions, and scheduled users' conferences where tool-use do's and don'ts can be discussed.

Use the above forums to publicize the successful use of the tools. Always share analysis of tool failures that might eliminate incorrect implementation, incorrect usage, and negative attitudes of users as causes.

13.5.2 Test Tool Administrator

As a consultant in software testing tools automation I have learned that a tool administrator is a necessity. It is extremely important that tool users have a central point of contact when problems arise. The tool administrator should act as the tool-use coach, problem solver, and as the liaison between the tool vendor and the users.

The administrator should develop and document a set of standards and guidelines for tool use. The administrator should also be responsible for setting up global and project-related default values in the test tool database (test repository) and for any customization requested by tool users.

Test tool administrators should devote at least half of their time to administration and use the rest of their time for testing software using the tool. A perfect scenario would be to have a full-time person in this role.

13.5.3 Testing Tools Reference Guides and Other Resources

13.5.3.1 *SQE Testing Tools Reference Guide* The best reference on the market today is the *Testing Tools Reference Guide* [3] authored by Jerry Durrant and published by Software Quality Engineering of Orange Park, FL. The guide provides one-page summaries of the tools available and has an excellent tools cross-referencing system that enables quick reference to related tools. The guide is periodically updated and the latest issue contains summaries of the leading client-server testing tools.

Software Quality Engineering is located at 330 Corporate Way, Suite 300; Orange Park, FL 32073; voice 904-278-0707, 800-423-8378; and e-mail sqeinfo@sqe.com. The SQE web page is at http://www.sqe.com.

13.5.3.2 The Ovum Test Automation Tools Evaluation Guide/Service

Ovum, Ltd., of the United Kingdom, offers *Ovum Evaluates: Software Testing Tools*, a service that presents evaluations of over 25 of the industry-leading software tools. This guide analyzes the products from the user's perspective. Subscribers to this guide receive a new installment every two months. Each installment contains three evaluations and a feature article. In addition, subscribers are offered a free telephone inquiry service.

The Ovum package price is a bit hefty: $2775. Ovum, Ltd. is located at 1 Mortimer Street, London, WIN 7RH, and its web site is at http://www.ovum.com.

13.5.3.3 Other Resources *Software Management Technology Reference Guide* has a chapter on testing tools. It is published by Software Maintenance News, Inc., 141 St. Marks Place, Suite 5F, Staten Island, NY, 10301; voice 718-816-5522; fax 718-816-9038. The cost is $95 for the *Guide*, or $35 for the testing chapter.

Technical Solutions, Inc., 16199 NW Joscelyn St., Beaverton, OR 97006, voice 503-690-2341, offers a *Guide to Software Test Automation Tools.*

The CAST Report is sold by Cambridge Market Intelligence for £495. The phone number is +44-171-924-7117.

The Air Force Technology Support Center offers a *Software Test Technologies Report*. For more information, contact Greg Daich, OO-ALC/TISE, STSC, Hill AFB, UT 54056, voice 801-777-8057.

For Unix environments, an informative text is *Unix Test Tools and Benchmarks* by Rodney C. Wilson, Prentice Hall, Upper Saddle River, NJ, 1995 (ISBN 0-13-125634-3).

The *Automated Testing Handbook* can be ordered from The Software Testing Institute, 2639 Elm, No. 304, Dallas, TX 75226; voice 214-741-3046; fax 214-741-3319; $29.95, plus $3 S&H. It can also be ordered directly on the World Wide Web at http://www.ondaweb.com/sti/stiorder.htm.

13.5.3.4 Brian Marick's Software Testing Tools FAQs As a public service, Brian Marick has created and periodically updates several Frequently Asked Questions (FAQs) lists in conjunction with the USENET news group comp.software.testing. It is derived from supplier e-mail and hardcopy brochures and references on the Internet. Marick can be contacted at Testing Foundations, marick@testing.com. His first list, the FAQ of Testing Tools Suppliers, can be viewed at http://www.stlabs.com/marick/faqs/tools.htm.

Marick also maintains an FAQ of Test Evaluation tools. It includes descriptions of such tools as adapath, Branch validator, C-Cover, CodeTEST, CoverTest, CTC++, GCT, Hindsight/TCA, Hindsight/TPA, Insight / Insure++, LDRA toolset, Logiscope MCcov, MCasm, and Mcobj. This FAQ can be viewed at http://www.stlabs.com/marick/faqs/t-eval.htm.

He also maintains an FAQ of Non-GUI Drivers and Test Suite Managers at http://www.stlabs.com/marick/faqs/t-driver.htm. This list includes descriptions of AdaTEST, ANVL, ARTT, Automator, BenchWorks, Cantata, CTB, DejaGnu, and many more.

13.6 CONCLUSION

Automating software testing is an important task. It is even more important in light of the complexity client-server brings to the application development process. Test automation arms the tester with an arsenal of utilities that have the potential to substantially reduce the effort associated with testing C-S systems.

Testing economics dictate the automation of the testing process. As indicated in Figure 13.1, an automated testing process can save up to 50% of the person hours normally required for testing. One major reason for this saving is that automated test scripts allow much of the testing to occur unattended. Also indicated in Figure 13.1 is an increased level of effort up front due to the work related to recording and editing test scripts. There are now intelligent scripting products such as Segue's GO product, which reduce the effort of recording test scripts. These products will result in even more savings.

As Bill Gates of Microsoft has indicated, software testing takes at least 50% of development resources and accounts for at least 50% of the cost of software development. As other software development organizations begin to realize the value of testing and devote more and more resources to it, the importance of test automation will be realized.

13.7 REFERENCES

1. Beizer, Boris. *Software Testing Techniques*. Van Nostrand Reinhold Electrical/Computer Science and Engineering Series, New York, 1983.

2. Bender, Richard. *Requirements-Based Testing*. Richard Bender & Associates., Inc., Larkspur, CA.

3. Durrant, Jerry E. *Testing Tools Reference Guide: A Catalog of Software Quality Support Tools*. Version 5, SQE, Orange Park, FL, 1994.

4. Durrant, Jerry E. "Tools of the Trade." First published in *Partners Progress Magazine*, this article is available at www.avnet.co.uk/SQM/QiC/articles/durrant/21.html.

5. Durrant, Jerry E. "What Is Internal Marketing?" First published in *Partners Progress Magazine*, this article is available at www.avnet.co.uk/SQM/QiC/articles/durrant/22.html.

6. Eckerson, Wayne W. "Client-Server Test Tools: Client-Server Computing Has Created a Need for Robust New Test Tools and Test Methodologies." *Open Information Systems*, Vol. 9, No. 11, November 1994, pp. 3–21. The Patricia Seybold Group, Boston, MA.

7. Elmendorf, William. *Cause-Effect Graphs in Functional Testing*. IBM System Development Division, TR-DD.2487, Poughkeepsie, NY, 1973.

8. Elmendorf, William. *Functional Analysis Using Cause-Effect Graphs*. Proceedings of Share XLIII, New York, pp. 577–87, 1974.

9. Gelperin, David. "Devining Five Types of Testing Tools." *Software News*, August 1987.

10. Hetzel, William. *The Compete Guide to Software Testing*, 2d ed., QED Information Sciences, Wellesley, MA, 1988.

11. Hurwitz, Judith. *Understanding Client Server Models*. Technology Assessment Report, Hurwitz Consulting Group, Inc., Watertown, MA, 1994.

12. McCabe, Thomas J. *Structured Testing: A Testing Methodology Using the McCabe Complexity Metric*. NBS Special Publication. Contract B82NAAR5518, 1983.

13. Microsoft Corporation. *Ms Test 3.0: Automated Testing for Windows*. Microsoft Technet CD, Test Technical Notes, Vol. 4, Issue 2, February 1996.

14. Microsoft Corporation. *Ms Visual Test Automated Testing for Rapid Development*. Microsoft Technet CD, Test Technical Notes, Vol. 4, Issue 2, February 1996.

15. Mosley, Daniel J. *The Handbook of MIS Application Software Testing: Methods, Techniques, and Tools for Assuring Quality Through Testing*. Prentice Hall Yourdon Press, Englewood Cliffs, NJ, 1993.

16. Myers, Glenford. *The Art of Software Testing*. Wiley-Interscience, New York, 1979.

17. Perry, William E. *How to Test Software Packages: A Step-by-Step Guide to Assuring They Do What You Want*. John Wiley & Sons, New York, 1986.

18. Poston, Robert. "A Complete Toolkit for the Software Tester." *American Programmer*, Vol. 4, No. 4, April 1991, pp. 28–37.

19. Saile, Bob. *Introduction to MS Test*. Microsoft Technet CD, Test Technical Notes, Vol. 4, Issue 2, February 1996.

20. Sherman, Roger W. *Building in Quality from the Start*. Microsoft Technet CD, Test Technical Notes, Vol. 4, Issue 2, February 1996.

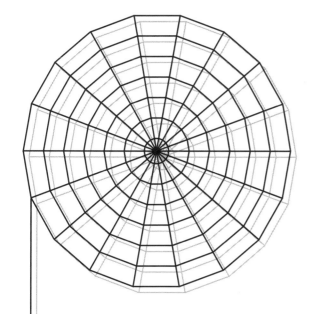

CHAPTER 14

Software Testing Process Improvement: A Framework

14.1 INTRODUCTION

The software testing process is an extremely important part of software development. Yet, in most organizations, it falls far short of the accepted ideal practice. During Software Engineering Institute (SEI) self-assessments and process characterizations within one major U.S. corporation, Koltun [4] uncovered less than ideal conditions for software testing. He characterized the state of software testing practice as "lacking." He found that, even when planned, software testing usually lacks focus; preparation is usually inadequate; resources are always inadequate; the testing function is improperly staffed; test execution is not followed by adequate analysis of test results; testing activities in general do not follow standard industry practice. Although these findings vary from organization to organization, they are generally applicable to the software testing functions in the majority of U.S. companies.

Consequently, software testing process improvement has become a major issue in recent years. It was ranked as one of the top three improvements organizations planned to implement in 1995–96 according to the results of the 1995 QAI survey on Software Testing [7]. It was also listed as one of the areas most in need of improvement in that survey. In the 1996 survey [8] 92% of the respondents indicated their organizations plan to enhance the software testing processes in 1996–97. Informal conversations with the attendees at recent QAI testing conferences revealed that their primary reason for attending is to gather information they can use to improve the software testing process. As of late, the majority of inquiries concerning software testing consulting services are requests for help in software test process improvement.

In response to those requests, CSST Technologies, Inc., and SQM Solutions, divisions of Toro Technologies, Inc., have developed a framework for improving the software testing process that they use to assess the software evaluation and testing processes. The approach entails the following:

☞ Using a proprietary survey instrument to capture the current evaluation and testing processes including supporting elements and automated testing tool set(s)

☞ Using data reduction and statistical analysis techniques to analyze the data

☞ Documenting a set of recommendations for evaluating and testing process improvement in a formal written action plan

The software evaluation and test process improvement paradigm is based on the fusion of a conceptual and an operational model of these processes. The theoretical model is the proposed Software Evaluation and Key Practice Area (KPA) [1]. It was intended for inclusion in release 2.0 of the Software Engineering Institute's (SEI) Capability Maturity Model (CMM); however, it was not incorporated in that version, but is currently still under consideration for inclusion. The operational model is CSST Technologies TEST-Rx ("Test Prescription") methodology.

14.1.1 The CMM

The CMM is a conceptual model that has come into wide use to assess the effectiveness of an organization's ability to develop quality software systems. The model has five stages of maturity spanning from Initial (chaotic) to Optimized (under statistical process control). Each stage is associated with a set of KPAs that map out the goals an organization must achieve in order to move to that level of development capability. A KPA defines the process goals, commitment levels, abilities to perform, activities performed, and the measures and verification of those activities. The concept of KPAs is generically illustrated in Table 14.1.

14.1.1.1 The Evaluation and Test KPA   Within the framework of the proposed KPA, evaluation is defined as "the activity of verifying the numerous system specifications and models produced during the software development process," and testing is defined as "the machine-based activity of executing and validating tests against the requirements and code."

The Software Evaluation and Test KPA requires:

1. Identifying the development products to be evaluated/tested
2. Determining the specific kinds of evaluations/tests to be implemented
3. Defining the criteria for success for evaluation/test activities
4. Designing the evaluations/tests
5. Performing the evaluations

    6. Verifying evaluation results

    7. Constructing the tests

    8. Executing the tests

    9. Verifying test results

  10. Verifying test criteria coverage

  11. Logging, tracking, and reporting identified defects

  12. Keeping a set of meaningful evaluation and test metrics

  13. Analyzing and reporting evaluation/test results to management and users

Table 14.1 The SEI Software Capability Maturity Model with Key Practice Area Examples

Key Practice Area 1	Initial	Repeatable	Defined	Managed	Optimized
Goals					
Commitment					
Abilities					
Activities					
Measures					
Verification					
Key Practice Area 2					
Goals					
Commitment					
Abilities					
Activities					
Measures					
Verification					
.					
.					
.					
.					
Key Practice Area n					
Goals					
Commitment					
Abilities					
Activities					
Measures					
Verification					

If all of the various KPA goals are met for levels 2 and 3 in the CMM, an organization's software development process is a repeatable and defined process. As an integral part of the development process, evaluation and testing should also be repeatable defined processes. An evaluation and testing process that meets the Evaluation and Test KPA goals is a repeatable defined process.

14.1.1.2 Evaluation and Test KPA Goals   The proposed Software Evaluation and Test KPA contains four broad goals that must be met in order to have a clearly defined, documented, and successful software evaluation and testing process that encompasses the areas described above. The four goals are:

1. To have established Quantitative and Qualitative evaluation/test criteria for each software project deliverable
2. To execute evaluation/tests in a timely manner to verify that the success criteria have been met
3. To assure that evaluation/testing are effective enough to minimize the impact of defects during development and to minimize operational disruptions after implementation
4. To identify, log, and track defects and other variances to their successful closure

CSST Technologies and SQM Solutions have extended the CMM Evaluation and Test KPA by adding a fifth and sixth goals.

5. To analyze evaluation/test results and formally report them to project management and other interested parties
6. To implement regression testing as a standard practice

14.1.2 TEST-Rx

An important point to keep in mind is that software evaluation and testing is not an isolated function. It occurs in conjunction with other software development activities and within the context of the software development life cycle. Achieving the Evaluation and Test KPA goals, commitment levels, abilities, and activities involves improving not only those activities that are specifically evaluation or testing but also those tasks that support the evaluation and testing process. A method for operationalizing specific steps of the evaluation and testing process and its supporting elements is required. TEST-Rx (see chapter 4) outlines a set of process steps and supporting elements that, when implemented, will achieve the Test KPA goals, establishing the proper commitment levels, providing the required abilities, and defining the necessary evaluation and test activities.

TEST-Rx is a standardized software testing process for use with any software development testing project. The process provides a baseline for software testing activities pertaining to the project. A standard testing process is required because it improves the effectiveness and efficiency of testing for the project.

Although evaluation is treated as a supporting element in TEST-Rx, its importance in the overall framework is not overlooked.

TEST-Rx consists of a series of steps that are described in Table 14.1. Each step consists of a set of "tasks." Completion of a step results in a set of "deliverables." In some instances, deliverables, or partial deliverables, can be ascertained from individual tasks, or series of tasks within a particular step.

The steps apply within the context of a generic SDLC. The life cycle deliverables that are required as inputs to several of the process steps can be produced within any commercial methodological framework such as Summit-D. Previous steps in the testing process produce all other inputs. In addition, all testing process deliverables are produced by specific tasks with specific steps.

TEST-Rx represents a conglomeration of techniques from several sources. It is based on the work of Mosley [5], Perry [6], and IEEE Standards 829 [2] and 1008 [3].

14.1.2.1 Methodology

Survey Design. The survey questionnaire consists of more than 100 questions. It is divided into two sections. The first section addresses the proposed Evaluation and Test KPA. The second section addresses TEST-Rx considerations. The questions in each section are divided into subgroups.

The Evaluation/Test KPA is designed such that the first six questions cover the six Evaluation and Test KPA goals described above. Within each goal, subsequent questions assess the commitment to perform, the ability to perform, the activities currently performed, and measures of the process. For clarity, evaluation and test processes are assessed in separate sections of the questionnaire.

The remaining section is divided into 10 subgroups based on the CSST Technologies Software Testing Process and Supporting Elements. The first subgroup is organized around standards, methods, techniques, and tools for evaluation. The second subgroup is structured around standards, methods, techniques, and tools for testing. The third subgroup is centered on resources for performing evaluation. The fourth subgroup is on resources for testing. The fifth subgroup covers test support mechanics. The sixth subgroup includes eight inquiries about software configuration management. The seventh subgroup assesses software testing deliverables configuration management. The eighth subgroup is related to defect tracking. The ninth subgroup looks at test workflow control. The tenth subgroup asks about automated tools for test and test support mechanisms.

Survey Process Survey information is captured during two-hour sessions in which the questions are asked by one or more interviewers of one to four employees per session. The interviewees include such representative groups as IS Managers, IS Developers, Quality Assurance, Technical Support, and IS customers. Individuals from other areas may be included, but they should be somehow involved in the software development projects. The interviewers record the survey responses and note important comments that clarify the information.

Survey Analysis   The survey results are presented graphically as Kiviat charts with weighted percentages graphed on the axes. Figure 14.1 illustrates this technique using fictional data. It shows the status quo for each goal on a separate axis. The weight score for each goal gives a dramatic view of how far the organization is from achieving the goal. These depictions were chosen because it is very easy to spot the deficient areas visually, and because they can be striking when used to emphasize the differences between the ideal and the status quo.

Evaluation/Test Key Process Area Goals   Questions for goals, commitment, and abilities are scored by calculating weighted percentage values. The weighted values are calculated in the following manner. For questions with Yes/No answers, the values are simple counts, with one answer per group of interviews unless the interviewees could not agree to a single answer. The results are calculated as the percentage of "yes" answers over the total answers. For questions with graded answers, grades 0 through 5 are applied as a weight to the counts and the percentages used for evaluation become weighted percentages.

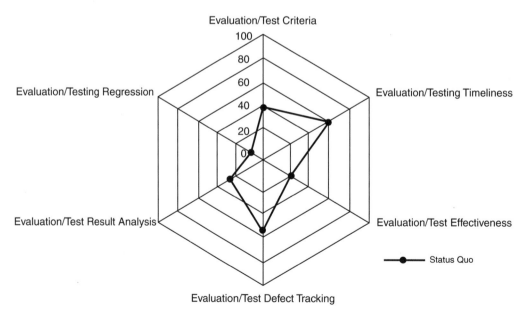

Fig. 14.1 Example Evaluation Test KPA Goals—Status Quo Plotted as Weighted Percentages

Related Results The results in this section are not scored with weighted percentages, but are based on "yes," "no," or "N/A" answers and on verbal comments from the respondents.

The Evaluation and Testing Action Plan The results are used as the basis for a process improvement action plan that an organization can use to improve its evaluation and testing process. The plan addresses all of the areas of deficiency that were discovered during the survey data analysis phase. The recommendations in the plan are formally presented to the organization and followed with a written version. The organization goes over the results and recommendations during a follow-up period. At the end of that period, another formal meeting is required to answer questions and, if necessary, clarify specific recommendations.

14.2 CONCLUSION

Software evaluation and testing process improvement is very much in the mainstream of the IS community's conscience. CSST Technologies and SQM Solutions are addressing the issues identified by the Test KPA Evaluation. They provide their customers with an evaluation tool and a custom action plan to respond to the diagnostics. The cornerstone of their approach is that software product quality is best when the development process itself is quality based.

14.3 REFERENCES

1. Bender, Richard. *SEI/CMM Proposed Software Evaluation and Test KPA,* Revision 4, Bender and Associates, Larkspur, CA, April 1996.

2. Institute of Electrical and Electronics Engineers. ANSI/IEEE Std 829-1983 Software Test Documentation.

3. Institute of Electrical and Electronics Engineers. ANSI/IEEE Std 1008-1987 Software Unit Testing.

4. Koltun, Phil. "Capability Maturity Model: Testing... Testing...." *Software Process Improvement Forum*, September/October 1994.

5. Mosley, Daniel J. *The Handbook of MIS Application Software Testing: Methods, Techniques, and Tools for Assuring Quality Through Testing.* Prentice Hall, Englewood Cliffs, NJ, 1993.

6. Perry, William. *A Standard for Testing Application Software 1992.* Auerbach Publishers, 1992.

7. Quality Assurance Institute. *1995 Survey Results on Software Testing.* Quality Assurance Institute, Orlando, FL, 1995.

8. Quality Assurance Institute. *1996 Survey Results on Software Testing.* Quality Assurance Institute, Orlando, FL, 1996.

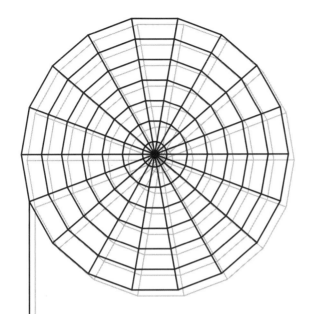

Index

A

Acceptance suite, 166
Acceptance tests, 159, 257
   executing, 100
   incident reports, 101
   log, 101
   summary report, 101
Acid test, 149
Actual Complexity Metric (McCabe), 242
Add, Change, and Delete (ACD) privileges, 148
Air Force Technology Support Center, *Software Test Technologies Report,* 320
Analog testing, 113–14
Andersen Consulting, 1
ANSI/IEEE defect metrics, 234, 239–40
Application Programming Interfaces (APIs), 14
   calls, 197–98
   testing, 201–2
Application response time measures, 158

Applications
   distributed, 4
   functionality of, 158
   software as Y2K issues, 281
Architectural model, 20
Automated defect tracking tools, 60
Automated server testing tools, 149–51
Automated testing. *See* Cross-level functional testing
Automated Testing Handbook, 320
Automated test scripts, 262
   developing, 163–66
Automated test tools, 313–14
   for code-level testing, 202–4
   selection, 314–16
      postselection recommendations in, 318–20
      recommendations for, 316–20
   and system testing, 261–64
Automating testing, reasons for, 311–13
Automation libraries
   and Y2K compliance, 300–1
   and Y2K remediation process, 302–3, 306
Autotester, 27

B

C